NUMBER TWO HUNDRED AND TWENTY-ONE

The Old Farmer's Almanac

CALCULATED ON A NEW AND IMPROVED PLAN FOR THE YEAR OF OUR LORD

2013

BEING 1ST AFTER LEAP YEAR AND (UNTIL JULY 4) 237TH YEAR OF AMERICAN INDEPENDENCE

Fitted for Boston and the New England states, with special corrections and calculations to answer for all the United States.

Containing, besides the large number of Astronomical Calculations and the Farmer's Calendar for every month in the year, a variety of

NEW, USEFUL, & ENTERTAINING MATTER.

Established in 1792 by Robert B. Thomas (1766–1846)

A cloudy day is no match for a sunny disposition.
–William Arthur Ward, American writer (1921–94)

Cover T.M. registered in U.S. Patent Office   Copyright © 2012 by Yankee Publishing Incorporated
ISSN 0078-4516   Library of Congress Card No. 56-29681

Original wood engraving by Randy Miller

THE OLD FARMER'S ALMANAC • DUBLIN, NH 03444 • 603-563-8111 • ALMANAC.COM

It Could Be The Best Cracked Skin Cream You've Never Heard Of...

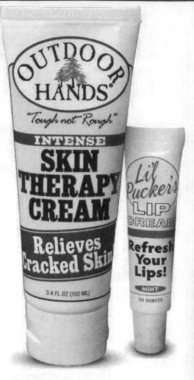

Outdoor Hands co-founder, pharmacist Austin Gore, was so disappointed by crack creams that didn't work, he made one himself. He called it Outdoor Hands Skin Therapy Cream... he figured if it worked on hands, it would work on elbows, knees, feet, lips and just about everywhere else. He was right.

Finally! A cream that cracked the code for treating cracked skin!
- Made from an uncommon blend of botanicals and oils
- Non-greasy, fully absorbed
- Deeply penetrates and hydrates to help heal from the inside out
- Works on elbows, knees, feet, heels, lips – anywhere you have cracked skin

Outdoor Hands Skin Therapy Cream Relieves Cracked Skin. Anywhere You Have It.

Also Try Outdoor Hands Poison Ivy Scrub

Ask for Outdoor Hands Skin Therapy Cream at your local farm, hardware or garden store. Or visit **www.outdoorhands.com** to find a retailer near you.

Find us on Facebook

MADE IN THE USA

11/5/12

Contents

The Old Farmer's Almanac • 2013

(continued on page 6)

Contents

(continued from page 4)

To Patrons

As the custodians of this Almanac, now in its 221st year, we are often asked how this little book, published but once each year and, by design, appearing more quaint than current, "fits" into the 21st century, when virtually any information can be delivered anywhere in seconds merely through the flick of a fingertip.

Simply put, this Almanac is about time and timeliness.

To date, no technology devised by man has been capable of altering the duration of the minutes, hours, days, weeks, months, and years that are for many people life's most precious commodity. Time can be managed, filled, passed, planned, saved, spent, lost, occasionally found, and, tragically, wasted, but it can not be stretched, slowed, sped up, or stopped.

At best, time can be used wisely and, we hasten to add, "with a pleasant degree of humor"—a phrase first used by our founder, Robert B. Thomas. As the provider of useful information 24 hours a day, 7 days a week, all year long, every year since 1792, this Almanac is as fitting (and "fitted") for the 21st century as it was for the 18th, 19th, and 20th.

Indeed, *The Old Farmer's Almanac,* which in its purest form is "a calendar of the heavens," will never fall out of fashion as long as the heavens endure. As Robb Sagendorph, our 11th editor, once observed, "The content is ahead of its time. The Almanac is a book about next year."

Like its 220 predecessors, today's Almanac delivers "all of nature's precision, rhythm, and glory" in timely and useful formats, however unrecognizable some might be to our forebears . . .

■ **on paper:** Traditional bound pages invite notations, contemplation, and collection.

■ **via our Web site:** Almanac.com facilitates easy access to hundreds of pages of weather, astronomical, planting, and other data that are updated daily.

■ **through mobile "apps":** Phones, e-readers, and tablets put the Almanac almost anywhere instantly.

■ **in social networks:** We're in constant contact with our Almanac "family" through Facebook, Twitter, and Pinterest. (Are you one of our 125,000+ Facebook fans?)

As important as time is, though, we nonetheless note an observation in one of our 18th-century editions: "We live in deeds, not years; in thoughts, not breaths; in feelings, not figures on a dial."

With this in mind, we hope that you *take your time* as you peruse and ponder this edition of the Almanac.

–J. S., June 2012

However, it is by our works and not our words that we would be judged. These, we hope, will sustain us in the humble though proud station we have so long held in the name of

Your obedient servant,

8

Visit Almanac.com

Always "useful, with a pleasant degree of humor"!

➡ **ALMANAC.COM/WEATHER**
Get daily forecasts, folklore, blogs,
history, and detailed reference.

➡ **ALMANAC.COM/GARDENING**
Grow more, better, right now!

➡ **ALMANAC.COM/ASTRONOMY**
Everything
under the Sun,
including
the Moon,
every day
(and night)

➡ **ALMANAC.COM/COOKING**
Make meals easy and delicious
with thousands of free recipes.

➡ **ALMANAC.COM/NEWSLETTERS**
• **Almanac Companion:**
Subscribe
(it's free!)
for timely new
ideas and
special offers.

• **Recipe Box:**
Subscribe
(it's free!)
for seasonal
recipes,
contests,
blogs, and
more.

➡ **ALMANAC.COM/BLOGS**
Experts share weather, gardening,
cooking, and health ideas, and
readers talk back.

➡ **ALMANAC.COM/CONTESTS**
Win fabulous prizes!
Share photos or recipes, test
your trivia knowledge, enter
our drawings—have fun!

ALMANAC.COM/VIDEOS

Learn how-to or get a giggle with us in the garden and kitchen, on full Moon days, and more.

ALMANAC.COM/MOBILE

Now optimized for your smartphone browser, with companion apps, including Full Moon Finder and more.

ALMANAC.COM/STORE

Discover unique collections of made-in-the-USA weather, gardening, and cooking products, plus a whole lot more!

ALMANAC.COM/FEEDBACK

Got a question? A comment? We love to hear from you!

 Like us on Facebook.

 Follow us on Twitter.

𝒫interest

Pin us on Pinterest.

11

2013 AT A GLANCE

MONEY MATTERS

Optimism abounds:
"Consumers are starting to become confident. Spending on autos, travel, luxury—and even a little in housing—should be strong."

—Jonathan Dahl, editor in chief, SmartMoney

➡ BY THE NUMBERS

$1,276: average spent by Americans on travel annually

$36: average "extra" money a household has to spend every day

83 percent of people want to see more companies support worthy causes

75 percent of people use a shopping list

More and more . . .
- retail stores are offering only American-made goods.
- engaged couples are registering with charities.

WORDS FOR THE WISE

Cash mob: a group of people who arrive at a designated small business at the same time to spend cash to help increase sales

We're making ends meet by . . .
- renting out our cars by the hour
- extreme grocery couponing

To get us to save . . .
- Banks are holding raffles, giving customers a chance to win each time they make a deposit.

To get us to spend . . .
- Supermarkets are installing tiles that cause grocery carts to make a "clickety-clack" sound near certain items, so that shoppers will slow down and, managers hope, buy the items.
- Retailers are removing dollar signs from posted prices.
- Restaurants are serving certain foods at certain times only, to make those dishes seem more desirable.

AROUND THE HOUSE AND GARDEN

We're recycling . . .
"We are all working with what we have these days . . . finding less expensive ways to transform spaces."

—Meg Caswell Holliday, HGTV host

. . . and appreciating the cycle of life

"As people get into growing their own food . . . they realize that it involves all of nature."
—Chip Tynan, horticulturist, Missouri Botanical Garden

Outside: We're growing kitchen herbs on west-facing walls.

Inside: We're creating vertical "green walls" with houseplants.

➡ BY THE NUMBERS

$10,000: the value a mature shade tree adds to a home

58 percent of people regularly sort their trash

WORDS FOR THE WISE

agriburbia: housing built near a farm, where residents can pick fruit and produce for personal use

zone denial: the attempt to introduce plants of marginal hardiness into a garden

What decorators are doing

- painting glossy colors on interior walls
- using dark colors or hand-painted artwork on ceilings

- rejuvenating old furniture with white or black lacquer
- setting sea glass or pebbles in concrete countertops
- installing roomy shower stalls, with music or steam delivered by push-button
- using patio furniture indoors

Ideas that make ¢ents

- nurseries grafting vegetable plants for home growers
- home gardeners hand-pollinating squash, cucumbers, and pumpkins
- **vegetable gardens on flat roofs of houses,** especially "if you don't have room in the backyard for both a garden and a space for kids to play."
  —Amy Albert, senior design editor, Builder
- **multiple master bedrooms and large kitchens,** as more multigenerational families live under one roof

Ranches are the rage

"There is a return to the midcentury modern style of the mid-1950s and early '60s."
—James Martin, The Color People, Denver, Colorado

(continued) ➡ ➡

13

- Fifty-year-old ranch homes are being designated as protected historic properties.
- Long, low-roof homes with large windows and open floor plans are in demand.

Classics making a comeback

- space-saving Murphy beds
- pocket and sliding doors
- cordwood masonry (short log cross sections set into a special mortar)

PEOPLE ARE TALKING ABOUT . . .

- ➡ "drop zones": foyer rooms, with lockers for coats and shoes
- ➡ repurposing more factories, warehouses, and churches as housing
- ➡ spraying windows with substances that reflect the Sun's heat and reduce the use of air-conditioning

Our favorite fresh pickings

- vegetables in hanging baskets
- nutrient-dense purple or red carrots, cabbage, and brussels sprouts, and orange cauliflower
- mini squashes, peppers, carrots, and potatoes (for stir-frying)
- blueberries, grapes, brambles, and strawberries

Pretty—and purposeful—plantings

- children's gardens with "plants that amaze"—elephant ears, strawberries, and scented geraniums—to inspire a lifelong connection to nature

  –Nick Nelson, landscape architect, U.S. Botanic Garden

- pollinator gardens, so that "bees flying overhead can go from one garden to another without interruption."

  –June Hutson, Missouri Botanical Garden

Awesome annuals

- **Ageratum Monarch series,** a butterfly magnet
- **Japanese anemone Pretty Lady series,** compact and great in shade
- **African daisy 3D series,** a double-flowering purple, pink, or silver bloom that stays open even at night

Eye-popping perennials

- **'Perpa',** a compact red yucca
- **'Echo Rojo',** a reblooming orange-red hot poker
- **hardy hibiscus with large blooms:** 'Strawberry Swirl', with pink and white flowers, and 'Little Princess', a dwarf variety, with scarlet, violet, and lavender blooms

  –Sonia Uyterhoeven, Gardener for Public Education, The New York Botanical Garden

(continued) ➡ ➡

CUES TO CULTURE CHANGE

At top of mind

"The reverence for constant productivity is on its way out. People are weighing the value of excessive productivity against the quality of life."

–*Shannon Hayes, author of* Radical Homemakers

➡ BY THE NUMBERS

2.8 percent of Americans walk to work

25.3 minutes: the average time that commuters spend in getting to work

100,000: kids "unschooled" at home, without classes, textbooks, or tests

We're becoming addicted to . . .

- prizes and discounts for recycling
- washing the dog and getting the car repaired at the same place
- waiting in virtual lines (being notified electronically when we're next)

Noise is news

- We're enjoying the hisses heard in the music on old cassette tapes.
- We're installing outdoor speakers that play recorded birdsongs to calm citizens and reduce crime.
- Watch for slatted wood floors at airports that play music when passengers roll their suitcases over them.

(continued) ➡ ➡

WORDS FOR THE WISE

hypermiling: competing to get the most miles per gallon

micro-enterprise: a small business drawing on hidden interests and quirky talents to help make ends meet

Our idea of fun

- classes in tree climbing
- vacationing at "black-hole" hotels (those with no online access or TV)
- guided tours to search for the Abominable Snowman
- art shows of "scent sculptures" in tents
- using cat hair to make crafts
- celebrating New Year's Eve at noon, not midnight, and going to bed early

We need all the help we can get

- Family or friends are making our New Year's resolutions, telling us to stop complaining, stop spending, lose weight, and so forth.
- Tutors, not parents, are teaching children basic social skills, such as how to politely answer the phone.
- Companies are selling, and sometimes writing, notes purportedly from parents to put into kids' lunch boxes.

Coming soon

- motorized shoes that speed us to work at up to 10 mph
- cars with gas pedals that push back when pressed too hard
- electric cars with tweets or hums that alert pedestrians to their presence

PEOPLE ARE TALKING ABOUT . . .

- urban backyard time-shares in vacant lots, with sod, grills, and sprinklers
- workers attending meetings standing up in order to keep discussions brief
- replacing cars with bicycles equipped with large cargo racks and speakers, as well as mini-engines

OUR PASSION FOR FASHION

We are what we wear

"People want clothing that looks like a human hand has touched it, as opposed to coming out of a machine."

–Mark-Evan Blackman, assistant professor of fashion design, Fashion Institute of Technology

Ideas that make ¢ents

- Business people are mastering sewing skills and making dress shirts.
- Designers are making trendy fashions with vintage sewing machines and irons.
- Fabrics are crossing over, from womenswear to menswear.

18

(continued) ⮕ ⮕

GALS are gabbing about . . .

- **pairing cheap necklaces or scarves** with good clothing to look "chic, rather than chintzy."

  –Sharon Haver, editor, focusonstyle.com
- **Victorian-era undergarments** in historical fashion shows
- **wearable mood-revealing gadgets** (e.g., cat ears that droop when we're relaxed)
- **brightly colored, lensless eyeglass frames**

GUYS are abuzz about . . .

- **"Casual Friday" falling out of favor:** "Men are taking dressing for the office far more seriously, in an effort to maintain a level of job security."

  –Steven Faerm, director of fashion design, Parsons the New School for Design
- **clothes with a feminine flare:** trench coats and button-down shirts in lightweight silks, polo shirts with silk ribbon collars, T-shirts with beading, and satin jackets
- **orange parkas with wooden toggles** like those worn by historic Antarctic explorers, but in high-tech fabrics

LADIES like elegance . . .

- pajamas in public, with high heels

- dresses of silky fabric made from sour milk
- stiffened jackets and capelets with pleated ruffles and short jackets in shiny satin fabrics
- paisley scarves
- brown shades, with lilac, yellow, pink, and blue
- vegetable, insect, floral, and jungle prints

MEN prefer preppy . . .

- soft, unconstructed blazers for weekend wear
- braided belts and penny loafers
- comfortable classics: ski sweaters and "grandpa" cardigans

- seasonal suits in new, soft fabrics
- "Nantucket red" cotton canvas pants or shorts that fade to salmon pink
- Buffalo plaids in unexpected colors (orange, yellow, and purple) subtly woven into the traditional patterns
- navy blue with khaki

20

(continued) ⇒ ⇒

ON THE FARM

Doing double duty

"Many of our farms [are] actually two businesses in one. There's the agriculture side, the planting, cultivating, and harvesting of crops for . . . large-scale buyers, and then there's the farm enterprise side, . . . like pick-your-owns, farm stands, educational tours, on-farms activities, value-added products, and community farmers' markets."

—Douglas H. Fisher,
Secretary of Agriculture, New Jersey

Food from tiller to table

- More farmers are offering dinners on their farms made with their own produce.
- Chefs who farm are putting their produce and meat on their menus.

PEOPLE ARE TALKING ABOUT . . .

- farmers teaching how to cook, pickle, and keep bees
- farmers who sold their acreage for housing that was never developed buying back the land at a fraction of their selling price
- young adults competing for farm apprenticeships

OUR ANIMAL FRIENDS

All in the family

"The 'humanization' of pets—if it's good for the kids or me, it is good for my pet—has led to pet owners purchasing high-quality foods and accessories to pamper their pets."

—Jessica Guzman, spokesperson for
the World Pet Association

PEOPLE ARE TALKING ABOUT . . .

- interior decor the color of a pet's fur, making stray hairs less conspicuous
- agility contests, with tiny dogs or cats racing through timed obstacle courses
- mock weddings, with dogs as bride, groom, flower girl, and minister
- wellness plans that provide pets with preventative health care

COLLECTORS' CORNER

Expect higher highs, lower lows

"The best items will continue to bring record prices, and common and middle-of-the-road items will either stay the same or decline a bit."

—Leila Dunbar, appraiser, New York City

Sell these now

- **artwork from children's books** enjoyed by baby boomers
- **posters from early horror and sci-fi movies**

22

(continued) ⇒ ⇒

■ **American clockwork toys from the late 19th century**

Buy these now

■ **classic comic books** printed in the 1930s and '40s, in like-new condition

■ **today's toys:** kids will be nostalgic for them when they reach age 40

■ **modern art, rare fungi, and homegrown liquors**

The next big things

■ **letters or diaries of people who survived a historic event, such as the Civil War:**

"The writers are often unknown folks, many times barely literate, whose reaction to tumultuous events provides us with a window on the times."

—Kathleen Guzman, appraiser, New York City

■ **tobacco-related items** such as ashtrays, advertising, and vintage matchbook covers:

"As the number of smokers continues to decline, these will rise in value."

—Rudy Franchi, appraiser, Los Angeles

■ **late–19th-century handmade, painted American wooden or metal trade signs:**

"You have a chance of making a profit. Even if not [profitable], they are a lot more attractive to look at than stock certificates or bank statements from your IRA."

—Noel Barrett, appraiser, Carversville, Pennsylvania

(continued) ➡ ➡

ATHENA PHEROM♥NES™
INCREASE AFFECTION
YOU GET FROM OTHERS

Dr. Winnifred Cutler co-discovered human pheromones in 1986
(TIME 12/1/86; NEWSWEEK 1/12/87)

Add to your fragrance. These odorless additives contain synthesized human pheromones. A vial of 1/6 oz., added to 2 to 4 ounces of fragrance, **should be a 4 to 6 months supply,** or use straight. Athena Pheromones increase your attractiveness.

unscented

♥ Maggie (NY) "When I have the Athena on, people will stop me anywhere and say 'oh my god, you smell *so* good.' The UPS man was the real clincher. For years this man would come in, nod hello and leave. **I always wore my fragrance. But once I put on the 10:13 in the first day he walked in, stopped, turned around and stared. 'Has anyone told you you are so beautiful?'"**

♥ Jed (IL) "I am a living example that the 10X does something. When I am using it there are definitely differences. I know quite a few people who happen to be female. **They are immediately more likely when we're together to be kind of -how shall I say this? -- touchy-feely, huggy.** You get greeted with a hug. I can see the difference that there is more affection. It makes life better, ok? Thanks Dr. Cutler."

Not in stores. Not guaranteed to work for everyone; will work for most. Not aphrodisiacs.

To order, call: (610) 827-2200   click: athenainstitute.com
Or mail to: **Athena Institute, Dept FA, 1211 Braefield Rd., Chester Spgs, PA 19425**

PLEASE SEND ME_____ 10:13 VIALS @ US$98.50 and/or _____ 10X Vials @ US$99.50 and___ empty blue bottle (2oz screw cap) @$5.00   for a *total price of US$_____
Enclosed is a ❑ USCheck ❑ Money Order payable to "Athena Institute"

Charge my ❑ Visa/MC/Disc# _____-_____-_____-_____ Exp_____CVV:____

Name_____ Phone: (   ) _____-_____

Address_____ City/State_____ Zip _____

email _____ Signature:_____

*PA add 6% tax. Canada add US$7.50 shipping surcharge per vial Other countries call.   FA

ATHENA PHEROM♥NES:The Gold Standard since1993™

GOOD EATS

Entertaining is easier . . .

"We will give more brunches and Sunday supper parties. These occasions are less demanding than Saturday dinners."

–Kristine Kidd, coauthor of Cooking at Home

. . . with not-so-fast food

"The notion of 'slow food' is truly taking hold. We are celebrating a way of cooking and eating from times past."

–Tanya Steel, editor in chief, Gourmet Live

Everyone's in the kitchen

"The 'cool kids' are learning to cure their own pickles, butcher their own meat, or harvest rooftop honey."

–Jodi Liano, coauthor of Cooking From the Farmer's Market

■ Adults are making butter, yogurt, ricotta, and "signature" cheese. *–Steel*

"Secret" ingredients

■ **grains** (quinoa, rice) that have been warmed before cooking so that they "sprout" in baked goods and make the nutrients easier to digest

■ **bisin,** a natural substance that kills harmful bacteria and could extend dairy and meat product shelf life for up to 3 years

■ **duck fat,** used to increase the flavor of fried chicken, french fries, and popcorn

PEOPLE ARE TALKING ABOUT . . .

➡ restaurants puréeing adult meals for tots

➡ historically accurate meals, such as Pilgrim fare (pigeon, goat cheese, hand-harvested wild rice) or recipes from ancient Romans (langoustine sausage, spelt, veal brains)

➡ warm loaves of bread sold in vending machines

Flavors that we crave

■ **vinegar** mixed with fruit juice and soda water

■ **sea vegetables:** nori, kombu, wakame

■ **hybrid fruits:** grapples, pluerrys, and peacharines

HEALTH & WELLNESS

Patient, heal thyself

"Self-care is the heart and the future of health care."

–James S. Gordon, M.D., chairman,
White House Commission on Complementary and
Alternative Medicine Policy

Your in$ide $tory

$1,000: the cost to map an entire genetic sequence

(continued) ➡ ➡

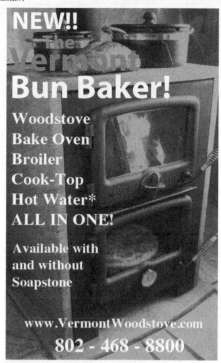

PEOPLE ARE TALKING ABOUT . . .

⇒ mirrors that show not only your reflection, but also your daily agenda, health history, and medication dosages

⇒ using "good" stress to improve performance, while avoiding harmful stress

⇒ aerobic housecleaning: doing sofa-lifts and lunges while vacuuming

Rx for the future

■ wearable gadgets to monitor the body's proteins and metabolites to prevent illness

■ antioxidants from plants and anti-inflammatory spices to combat the risk of chronic, age-related conditions

□□

Stacey Kusterbeck, a frequent contributor to *The Old Farmer's Almanac*, writes about popular culture from New York State.

BE MORE THAN A READER:

Follow *The Old Farmer's Almanac* on Facebook, Twitter, and Pinterest. Get daily advice and ideas, participate in polls, and share your thoughts and experiences.

#23

SNORING?

As recommended by Dr. Gifford-Jones M. D.

Here is proof that snoring can be corrupting your health and your marriage. Three out of 10 couples are considering divorce because of snoring says a major magazine article. You are not alone! An official survey says 48% of all people snore. 75% are affected, if you add non-snoring husbands that have snoring wives or vice versa. Snoring is caused by slack muscles in the throat. These same slack muscles can block airways and intermittently interrupt breathing all night. Many people wrote they are now sleeping like a babies. Their partners are delighted. This natural health product Sound Sleep #23 usually helps the first night. No side effects.

■ **College professor had lack of good sleeps with many interruptions** for last 8 years that made her tired during the day. Within 3 days taking Bell Sound Sleep #23 the terrible snoring stopped. I wake up feeling refreshed and energized. I can concentrate in a focused, happy manner. I feel delighted with this natural product. *Dr. Anele E. Heiges, 77, New York, NY* ■ **A life changing product.** The very first night I took the capsules and every night after I had a restful and wonderful sleep. It has been a God send and blessing. I am by nature a skeptic. The money-back guarantee convinced me to try it. *Jimmy Pay, 53, Gardendale, AC* ■ **3 Years on Bell Sound Sleep** #23. My wife and I are entirely satisfied. Snoring have completely disappeared. This has improved our lives enormously. *Leo Fortin, 60, St-Georges, QC* ■ **Basically you saved my husband's life.** For the last 5 years my husband had very bad nights. Bell #23 was nothing short of a miracle. I have my husband back. No more snoring. No more napping during the day. I am telling all our friends. *Bonnie Johnson, 64, Wichita, KS* ■ **My life changed. Sleep now 7-8 hours.** I am a retired college professor and author of books. I have no more need to nap during the day. Nothing I tried helped until I started Bell Sound Sleep. I am so delighted with this product I would like to make motivational speeches to help others. *Carmen V. Caruso, 66, Ann Arbor, MI* **On the Bell Website we list phone numbers or email addresses of actual users of this product and all other Bell products. Most are delighted to talk about their relief.**

Blood Pressure Formulation

Dr. C. Hammoud M.H., PhD, recommends this natural, effective fish peptide product to nutritionally support normal blood pressure function. A science-backed herbal phytonutrient. Promotes flexible, relaxed blood vessels. A one-of-a-kind formula that offers unprecedented nutritional support for your overall health and well-being. We have thousands of repeat customers. Blood pressure is a focal point of cardiovascular wellness. For many people it is easy to control with this natural product. Achieve your balance and maintain a healthy range.

#26

■ *"Bell Blood Pressure Combo helped me feel great."* ■ *"I have been taking Bell #26 now for one year. My mom and brother started taking it as well. Even my pastor is on it now."* ■ *"After taking Bell #26 I am happy to say I passed my pilot medical."*

CLEAR SKIN

Dr. C. Hammoud, Master Herbalist, PhD, guarantees satisfaction. Helps to maintain healthy skin from the inside simply by cleansing the blood, instead of attacking the skin from the outside with creams or washes and leaving the actual cause untreated. This makes sense. Usually you can see how it benefits your skin within days. Many people wrote they were surprised how fast it worked. Lots of testimonials from pleased users on our Bell website. There is absolutely no risk for trying Dr. Hammoud's product.

#60

■ *"Last couple of years I tried everything. Results with Bell Clear Skin #60 were unbelievable. I have beautiful skin again."* ■ *"I was skeptical. It did work quickly and better than anything else."* ■ *"I needed something that stopped the pimples from within. It worked."* ■ *"Can wear dresses that are backless again. My skin looks fantastic."* ■ *"I felt physical and emotional pain having to hide. Finally I found your Bell #60. I'm so grateful and impressed with how fast it worked with amazing results."*

Try your local health food store first. If they don't have it and don't want to order it for you, place your order on our website or call us with VISA or Mastercard S & H $9.95.

www.BellLifestyle.com
or call 1-800-333-7995

Store inquiries are welcome.

120518-Bell_Far_Almanac

Baking With

Ken Haedrich, a self-taught cook and home baker, loves to create special treats to share with family and friends.

■ KEN HAEDRICH'S LOVE OF BAKING BEGAN ON autumn Sundays when he was 9 years old. After church, his folks would pile him and his six siblings into the car and drive into the foothills of central New Jersey to buy fresh apples at farm stands. Back at home, Ken would watch his mother cut up the fruit and his father carefully mix and roll the piecrust. "The doing, the actual handwork, brought them such pleasure," he says. "But that was only half of it." Later, after the juicy pies had been sliced and served and the plates licked clean, he says, "I saw that their real joy was in sharing."

He experienced similar satisfaction in the U.S. Navy, while living with roommates off base. "We split the chores, and I just naturally gravitated to doing the cooking," he says. A friend's mother, an excellent cook and baker, introduced him to bread-baking. "I learned that baking facilitates a life-affirming cycle. We take fresh ingredients, mix and combine them just so, bake, and share the results, and then bask in the glow of having done something that makes people happy."

Following his discharge, Ken became the head cook at a group home for kids in rural New Hampshire. "I was given free rein to cook and bake nearly anything I wanted," he says. "The menu was well balanced and often baking-centric: cookies, fresh yeast bread, pies, quiche, pizza and calzones—all of this and more issued from my kitchen on a regular basis." In 5 years on the job, he says, "I got my advanced degree as a self-taught cook and baker."

It didn't stop there. In his off hours, Ken invented and perfected dishes to feed and nourish his own growing family.

All of these experiences eventually led to a successful career developing recipes and writing cookbooks (award-winning *PIE*

–photo, top left, courtesy Ken Haedrich; food photography, Becky Luigart-Staynes

You can almost smell the warm, lemony goodness of this Glazed Lemon Coconut Loaf. Find the recipe on page 32.

is one) and articles about cooking, for Almanac publications and others.

Today, Ken is "dean" of The Pie Academy (http://thepieacademy.com) and believes that baking is an activity that we crave: "Many of us are starved for a tactile distraction. Baking engages our senses, grounds us in the present, and focuses our creative energies."

Ken is also the developer and author of our newest cookbook, *The Old Farmer's Almanac Everyday Baking*. These recipes are among the 118 in that collection. Each one has been prepared with care and served with love, first to his family and friends and now to you. Try them and tell us what you think at Almanac.com/Feedback.

Glazed Lemon Coconut Loaf

BATTER:
1 cup sugar
5 tablespoons unsalted butter, melted
3 tablespoons vegetable oil
finely grated zest of 1 lemon
1 teaspoon lemon extract
1 teaspoon vanilla extract
¼ cup milk
2 large eggs, at room temperature
¾ cup buttermilk
2½ cups all-purpose flour
2½ teaspoons baking powder
¾ teaspoon salt
½ cup sweetened flaked coconut

GLAZE:
1 cup confectioners' sugar
2 tablespoons lemon juice
2 tablespoons unsalted butter, melted
¼ teaspoon lemon extract
⅓ cup sweetened flaked coconut

lemon zest (optional)

■ *For batter:* PREHEAT THE OVEN TO 350°F. BUTTER A 9x5-inch loaf pan and line it with parchment paper, if using. Combine the sugar, melted butter, oil, lemon zest, lemon extract, vanilla, and milk. Whisk well, to blend. In a separate bowl, whisk the eggs and buttermilk until evenly blended. Set aside. In another bowl, sift the flour, baking powder, and salt. Using a wooden spoon, stir a third of the dry mixture into the sugar mixture. Add half of the buttermilk mixture, stir until smooth, then add another third of the dry ingredients, the remaining buttermilk mixture, and the rest of the dry ingredients, stirring until smooth after each addition. Stir in the coconut. Scrape the batter into the prepared pan and smooth the top with a spoon. Bake on the center oven rack for about 50 minutes, until a tester inserted deep into the center of the bread comes out clean. The top will be deep golden brown.

Cool the loaf in the pan on a rack for 10 minutes. Remove the loaf from the pan and cool to room temperature.

For glaze: Combine the confectioners' sugar, lemon juice, melted butter, and lemon extract in a small bowl. Whisk well, to blend. The glaze should have the consistency of heavy cream. Adjust, as needed, with a little more sugar (to thicken) or drops of lemon juice or water (to thin). Do not use milk; it could curdle the glaze. When the bread has cooled to room temperature, spoon the glaze evenly over the top of the bread, then immediately sprinkle with the coconut. Garnish with lemon zest, if desired. **Makes 10 to 12 servings.**

(continued)

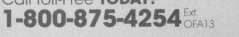

Individual Pear Cranberry Crisps

FRUIT:

3 large, ripe pears

¾ cup whole-berry cranberry sauce

3 tablespoons sugar

1 tablespoon lemon juice

1 tablespoon all-purpose flour

TOPPING:

½ cup all-purpose flour

⅓ cup old-fashioned rolled oats

⅓ cup packed light-brown sugar

¼ teaspoon cinnamon

big pinch of salt

¼ cup (½ stick) cold, unsalted butter, cut into ¼-inch pieces

■ PREHEAT THE OVEN TO 375°F. BUTTER FOUR 1-CUP individual dessert dishes or ramekins and place on a large baking sheet lined with parchment paper, if desired, for easy cleanup. Set aside.

For fruit: Peel, core, and slice the pears, cutting most of the slices in half or coarse chunks. Place in a large bowl and stir in the cranberry sauce, sugar, lemon juice, and flour. Divide the fruit evenly among the dessert dishes.

For topping: Mix the flour, oats, brown sugar, cinnamon, and salt in a large bowl. Add the butter and rub it into the dry mixture with your fingers until you have uniform, buttery crumbs. Divide the mixture evenly between the cups, patting it down lightly on top of the fruit. Place the baking sheet with the dishes on the center oven rack and bake for 30 to 35 minutes, until the topping is golden brown and the fruit is bubbling. Cool on a rack for at least 15 minutes before serving. **Makes 4 servings.** *(continued)*

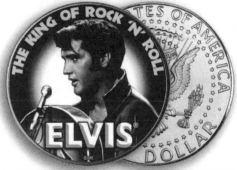

Bacon–Blue Cheese Scones

These savory scones are excellent for brunch or dinner, especially with hearty soups or stews. The dough is mixed in the food processor, and the trick is to use a light hand when pulsing the machine (do not overprocess). The scones have more "personality" if you use bigger pieces of bacon and blue cheese.

4 strips bacon, cut into 1-inch pieces

2 cups all-purpose flour

2½ teaspoons baking powder

1½ teaspoons sugar

¼ teaspoon salt

¼ cup (½ stick) cold, unsalted butter, cut into ¼-inch pieces

½ cup crumbled blue cheese

1 cup heavy cream

1 egg, lightly beaten, for glaze

■ PREHEAT THE OVEN TO 425°F. LIGHTLY BUTTER A BAKING sheet or line it with parchment paper. Set aside. Fry the bacon pieces in a nonstick skillet until crisp. Using a slotted spoon, transfer the bacon to a paper towel–lined plate. Break into small-but-not-tiny pieces when it cools. Set aside. Combine the flour, baking powder, sugar, and salt in a food processor. Pulse several times, to mix. Remove the lid, scatter the butter over the flour mixture, and pulse three or four more times, cutting the butter into small pieces. Remove the lid again and add the bacon and blue cheese. Pulse, no more than three times, to mix. Remove the lid once more and pour the cream evenly over the mixture. Pulse two or three times, just until the mixture forms large, damp crumbs; it should not ball up. Dump the crumbs onto a lightly floured surface. With lightly floured hands, gently pack the crumbs together, then pat and roll the dough into an 8-inch-diameter circle. (If the edge cracks, just pinch it together and smooth it out.) Cut the dough into eight equal wedges and place them, evenly spaced, on the baking sheet. Brush each wedge lightly with the egg. Bake on the center oven rack for 18 minutes, until golden brown. Cool on a rack. **Makes 8 scones.**   *(continued)*

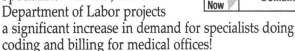

Maple Pecan Gooey Bars

CRUST:
½ cup old-fashioned
   rolled oats
⅓ cup sugar
½ teaspoon salt
1¾ cups all-purpose
   flour
¾ cup (1½ sticks)
   cold, unsalted
   butter, cut into
   ¼-inch pieces
1 tablespoon cold
   water

FILLING:
½ cup pure maple
   syrup
½ cup packed
   light-brown sugar
⅓ cup heavy cream
3 tablespoons
   unsalted butter
1 teaspoon vanilla
   extract
⅛ teaspoon salt
2 cups coarsely
   chopped pecans

■ BUTTER A 13x9-INCH BAKING PAN AND SET ASIDE.

For crust: Combine the oats, sugar, and salt in a food processor and pulse eight to ten times to chop the oats well. Add the flour and pulse several times to mix. Scatter the butter pieces over the dry mixture. Pulse until the mixture resembles a fine meal. Sprinkle the water over the mixture and pulse again, just until the ingredients start to form coarse, clumpy crumbs. (The crumbs should pack easily when pressed between your fingers.) Spread the mixture evenly in the prepared pan, pressing it with your fingertips to form a level layer on the bottom with a lip extending about ¼ inch up the sides of the pan. Refrigerate the crust for 15 minutes.

Preheat the oven to 350°F. Bake the crust on the center oven rack for 20 minutes. Cool on a rack.

(continued)

Mrs. Nelson's
CANDY HOUSE
"Your house for all occasions"

Candies! For over 51 years we have used only the finest ingredients in our candies—cream, butter, honey, and special blends of chocolates. Call for a FREE brochure. Long famous for quality candies mailed all over the world. Treat yourself or someone special today.

Come visit us today!

292 Chelmsford Street
Chelmsford, MA 01824
For Free Brochure Call:

978-256-4061

Covered Bridge Charm

elliott newman

Our medium sterling silver or 14k gold bridge charm will fit all bead-style bracelets.

For details, visit
www.elliottnewman.com

12b Central Street
Woodstock, Vermont 05091
802-457-2344 • 800-619-8757

20% Loyalty Discount with Promo Code: Almanac

100 % All natural
Hypoallergenic
Made to last

Luxurious, Natural
Alpaca Clothing
603-355-3555
www.mtcaesaralpacas.com
Visit our showroom at 441 Main St., Keene, NH
A family owned farm — *From the Rolling Slopes of Mt. Caesar in New Hampshire*

Mt. Caesar
Alpacas

For filling: While the crust cools, make the filling. Combine the maple syrup, brown sugar, cream, and butter in a medium saucepan. Bring to a full boil and boil for 30 seconds. Remove the pan from the heat and stir in the vanilla, salt, and pecans. Pour the filling over the cooled crust, spreading it evenly with a spoon. Bake on the center oven rack for 15 minutes. The filling should boil as it bakes. Transfer the pan to a rack and cool completely. Cover and refrigerate for a couple of hours, or overnight, before slicing. Slice cold, in small portions (these are sweet and rich), and serve at room temperature. **Makes 24 to 35 bars.**

OATMEAL: OLD-FASHIONED VS. QUICK

■ **Old-fashioned rolled oats are oats that have been partially cooked and flattened. Quick-cooking rolled oats are made the same way but cut into smaller pieces for faster cooking. They can be used interchangeably in baking, but I usually prefer the chewier texture of the old-fashioned variety.**

(continued)

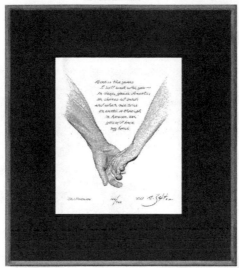

A Most Unusual Gift of Love

THE POEM READS:

"Across the years I will walk with you—
in deep, green forests; on shores of sand:
and when our time on earth is through,
in heaven, too, you will have my hand."

Dear Reader,

The drawing you see above is called *The Promise*. It is completely composed of dots of ink. After writing the poem, I worked with a quill pen and placed thousands of these dots, one at a time, to create this gift in honor of my youngest brother and his wife.

Now, I have decided to offer *The Promise* to those who share and value its sentiment. Each litho is numbered and signed by hand and precisely captures the detail of the drawing. As a wedding, anniversary or Christmas gift or simply as a standard for your own home, I believe you will find it most appropriate.

Measuring 14" by 16", it is available either fully framed in a subtle copper tone with hand-cut mats of pewter and rust at $135, or in the mats alone at $95. Please add $14.50 for insured shipping and packaging. Your satisfaction is completely guaranteed.

My best wishes are with you.

The Art of Robert Sexton, 491 Greenwich St. (at Grant), San Francisco, CA 94133

MASTERCARD and VISA orders welcome. Please send card name, card number, address and expiration date, or phone (415) 989-1630 between noon-8 P.M. EST. Checks are also accepted. *Please allow 3 weeks for delivery.*

The Promise is featured with many other recent works in my book, *Journeys of the Human Heart.* It, too, is available from the address above at $12.95 per copy postpaid. Please visit my Web site at

www.robertsexton.com

Chocolate Mud Bars

*"Mud" because
of the moist, dark
chocolate filling.
It's the best mud
you'll ever eat!*

CRUST:

1¼ cups graham
    cracker crumbs

3 tablespoons packed
    light-brown sugar

¼ teaspoon cinnamon

pinch of salt

5 tablespoons unsalted
    butter, melted

FILLING:

½ cup (1 stick)
    unsalted butter

6 ounces semisweet
    chocolate, coarsely
    chopped

¾ cup sugar

2 large eggs, at room
    temperature

½ teaspoon vanilla
    extract

¼ cup cake flour

1 cup coarsely
    chopped walnuts

**Ready, Set,
Bake!**

See page 51
for information
on purchasing
*The Old Farmer's
Almanac
Everyday Baking.*

■ Butter an 8-inch square baking pan and set aside.

For crust: Combine the graham cracker crumbs, brown sugar, cinnamon, and salt in a medium bowl. Mix well with your hands. Add the melted butter, stir well with a fork, then rub the ingredients together with your fingers until thoroughly mixed. Press the mixture evenly in the prepared pan to form a level layer on the bottom with a lip extending about ¼ inch up the sides of the pan. (Do not prebake the crust.)

For filling: Combine the butter and chocolate in the top of a double boiler over not-quite-simmering water. When melted, whisk to smooth, then remove the pan from the heat. Scrape the chocolate into a medium bowl and cool to lukewarm. Preheat the oven to 325°F. Whisk the sugar, eggs, and vanilla into the lukewarm chocolate. Stir in the cake flour, mixing until smooth. Stir in the walnuts. Scrape the batter over the crust and smooth with a spoon. Bake on the center oven rack for 35 minutes only—no longer. Cool on a rack. Refrigerate an hour or so before slicing. Serve at room temperature. **Makes 16 bars.** □□

2 Seater

Made in USA

10% Tax Credit

www.palmerind.com

Now One hand operated
Unlimited range hybrid electrics
Free Brochure 800 847 1304
Palmer Industries
PO Box 5707ARZ · Endicott NY 13763
Also Small Scooters & Motor Kits

The Davis Hill Weather Stick®

802-533-2400

davishillco@hotmail.com

PO Box 38, East Hardwick, VT 05836

Wholesale Inquiries Welcome

$5 Each plus S&H
Min. order 2

THE MOCCASIN SHOP

Men's
Women's
Children's
Call for free
catalog

mocshop.com · 1-800-936-5556

1429 Lakeshore Road · Gilford, NH 03249

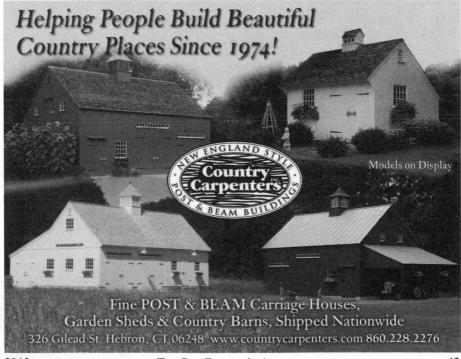

Helping People Build Beautiful Country Places Since 1974!

Models on Display

NEW ENGLAND STYLE · **Country Carpenters** INC. · POST & BEAM BUILDINGS

Fine POST & BEAM Carriage Houses,
Garden Sheds & Country Barns, Shipped Nationwide
326 Gilead St. Hebron, CT 06248 www.countrycarpenters.com 860.228.2276

56 KITCHEN TRICKS, TIPS, & TIMESAVING IDEAS

From the **THOUSANDS** sent to us by our **FANS** on **FACEBOOK**

3 Ways to Stop Beans From Causing Gas

- When slow-cooking pinto beans, add a carrot. When the beans are half-cooked, rinse and discard the carrot. Add more water and a new carrot. Finish cooking the beans.

- Add a pinch of ginger when cooking pinto beans.

➡ Add a pinch of baking soda when cooking dry beans.

Mix-Ins

-Foodcollection/Getty Images

- Mix the broken chips in the bottom of a nearly empty potato chip bag with bread crumbs and use to coat chicken or fish.

➡ Use Chex cereal instead of croutons on salads.

- Add plain, uncooked oatmeal as a filler in meat loaf instead of bread or crackers.

Fixings

- Substitute club soda for milk in pancakes to make them lighter and fluffier.

Fixings

- Add a pinch of baking powder when mashing potatoes to make them fluffier.

- **Run frozen peas under hot tap water (don't cook them). Kids love the way the peas "pop" in your mouth.**

- Keep a slice of white bread in the cookie jar to keep the cookies moist.

- **Save any amount of leftover vegetables in the freezer; in no time, you'll have enough for a chicken potpie.**

- Add a pinch of salt to bacon when frying it to prevent it from curling.

—Jon Larson/Getty Images

- **Before making piecrust, chill the bowl and utensils in the freezer. Pastry is easier to work with cold utensils.**

Savings

- Before peeling an orange or juicing a lemon or lime, grate the peel (zest) into a small container and freeze for later use.

- **Put overripe bananas into the freezer to thaw later for banana bread.**

- Juice citrus fruit by squeezing it with tongs.

- **Cut stale bread into 1-inch cubes to make croutons. Toss with seasonings and oil and bake in a 325°F oven until crisp.**

Tastings

- Dust the baking pan with cocoa or raw sugar instead of flour when making a chocolate cake.

- **Add a pinch of cinnamon to chocolate chip cookie batter.**

- Add a pinch of red pepper flakes to the water when boiling pasta.

—Smneedham/Getty Images

- **Give every baked cheese dish a squirt of mustard.**

- Add a dash of cinnamon to chili to help to smooth out the flavors and round out the heat.

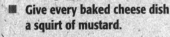

- **Sprinkle hickory-smoked salt on vegetarian dishes and sauces for a meaty taste.**

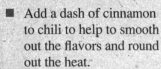

- Add a pinch of salt to ground coffee before brewing.

(continued)

Tastings *(continued)*

- Add diced apple or brown sugar to sauerkraut to eliminate some of the bitterness.

- When making a gumbo roux, use chickpea flour.

➡ **Add 1 shredded carrot to spaghetti sauce to cut acidity.**

- Jazz up burgers, chicken, soups, sauces, or breads with caraway seeds.

- **If soup or stew is salty, add one cut-up potato.**

- Cut the heat in salsa with a little sugar.

Peelings

- **Dump hot hard-boiled eggs into ice-cold water or add 1 tablespoon of vinegar or vegetable oil or 1 tablespoon of salt to the boiling water, and the shells will come off easily.**

- Rinse peeled avocados under cold water to maintain color.

➡ **Spray paper muffin cups with nonstick spray for easy peeling.**

Boiling

To keep water from boiling over . . .

- Before boiling, rub olive oil around the edge of a pan containing starchy foods.

➡ **Add 1 tablespoon of oil to a pot of boiling potatoes.**

- Lay a wooden spoon across a boiling pot.

Keeping

To increase shelf life or keep food from spoiling quickly . . .

- **Don't remove the seeds and core of cut bell peppers before storing them in the refrigerator.**

- Place cilantro and parsley sprigs in a glass of water in the fridge.

- **Dip the cut end of an unpeeled banana in sugar to prevent browning.**

- Wrap celery or rhubarb in aluminum foil and place in the refrigerator.

–Mark Weiss/Getty Images

- **When using only a portion of an onion, retain the root half, wrap, and store in the fridge.**

- Put an apple into a bag of potatoes to keep the spuds from budding.

- **Sprinkle lemon juice on sliced apples to prevent browning.**

(continued)

Keeping *(continued)*

- Put a wet paper towel into a sealed plastic bag with lettuce to keep it from turning brown.

➡ **Store yogurt, cottage cheese, and sour cream containers upside down in the fridge.**

- Freeze fresh herbs in water in ice cube trays. Pop out the frozen cubes and put them into labeled freezer bags.

- **Freeze leftover coffee in ice cube trays for use later in cold ("iced") coffee.**

Ridding

- Place a small bowl of vinegar on top of the fridge to eliminate gnats.
- **Put bay leaves into bags of flour to keep out bugs.**
- When boiling turnips, collards, or mustard greens, throw a pecan (shell on) into the pot to help eliminate odor.

Cleaning

- **Spray a spoon or measuring cup with nonstick cooking spray before measuring honey or molasses.**

- Use a Baggie on your hand when greasing baking pans.
- **Use the wax inner bags from cold cereal boxes to cover food in the microwave.**
- Gather old "net" onion bags together with a rubber band and use as a scrubby when washing dishes.

- **To remove baked-on food from a frying pan, put a dryer sheet and warm water into the pan. Soak overnight and then wash the pan.**

➡ **Spray a dirty cast iron pan generously with oven cleaner and put into a plastic bag large enough to completely contain it. Close the bag securely and set it aside for 24 hours. Remove the pan, discard the bag, and thoroughly wash and re-season the pan.**

Treat yourself or a friend to these **popular treasures** from
The Old Farmer's Almanac

2013 Engagement Calendar

A daily planner full of humor and useful advice, it's an indispensable tool for managing your life and keeping you organized. There's plenty of room for jotting down appointments and notes.

This handsome week-at-a-glance desk calendar contains pages to record important occasions, as well as 2014 and 2015 advance planners, weather proverbs, folklore, fun facts, quotes, and more!

140 page ● 7"×10" ● hardcover ● **$14.99** ● Item 03OF13CEG

The Old Farmer's Almanac 2013 Hardcover Collection

The Old Farmer's Almanac Collector's Edition

An annual tradition since 1792, the Almanac is bursting with vital information you can use to make your life better all year long. Now you can own the deluxe hardcover edition, printed on fine paper for easy readability and durability. It's the perfect gift and keepsake.

2 all-time favorites!
Save 23%!

2013 Gardening Calendar

Our all-time best-selling calendar, this is the one every gardener wants – beautiful to behold and full of humor and advice. You get green-thumb secrets ... gardening lore and timely information ... a year-round table that identifies the best days to plant ... gorgeous color illustrations and more.

Calendar: 10⅞"×16¾" (open)
Total retail value for both: ~~$25.94~~ ...
You pay just **$19.95 (23% OFF!)** ● Item 013HARDK

Everyday Baking
by Ken Haedrich

Now you can bake delicious goodies right at home, with over 100 scrumptious recipes from master baker Ken Haedrich, author of 11 coveted cookbooks and winner of the Julia Child Cookbook Award.

Learn the secrets of baking everything your heart desires, from breakfast breads to cookies & bars, pies, crisps, cobblers, and cakes for every occasion. You'll find timesaving tips, expert advice, and beautiful photos that show you just how a finished dish should look.

Every recipe has been kitchen-tested to ensure that it's easy to make and guaranteed to make your family and friends ask for more!

136 pages ● 7¼"×10½" ● Perfect-bound; heavy paper ● Glossy, stainproof cover
Color photos throughout ● **$9.99** ● Item OFEVBKNG

2013 Everyday Calendar

Get ready to smile every day! This cleverly illustrated, page-per-day calendar is filled with household, cooking, and gardening tips, plus proverbs, puzzles, and amusing facts that will surprise and delight you with every page.

Find out ...

► How to find the perfect mate
► Who was the first person to eat a corned beef sandwich in space
► What "Dog Days" really mean ... and so much more!

Calendar and plastic base can be recycled.
Gift Box ● 5¼"×5½" ● **$12.99** ● Item O3OF13CEV

The Old Farmer's Almanac
Order Form

One small fee covers S&H no matter how many items you order.

Ordered by:

Your Name _____

Address _____

City _____

State/Prov._____ Zip/Postal code _____

Item #	Description	Price	Qty.	Total
03OF13CEG	2013 Engagement Calendar	$14.99		
013HARDK	2013 Hardcover Collection	$19.95		
OFEVBKNG	Everyday Baking (brand-new!)	$9.99		
03OF13CEV	2013 Everyday Calendar	$12.99		
03OF13CGC	2013 Gardening Calendar	$9.99		
03OF13CWW	2013 Weather Watcher's Calendar	$9.99		
03OF13CFC	2013 Country Calendar	$10.99		
03OF13CERS	2013 Recipe Calendar	$9.99		

Method of Payment:

☐ **Check enclosed**
payable to: The Old Farmer's Almanac

☐ **Credit card:** (check box below)

  ☐ Visa ☐ MasterCard

  ☐ American Express

  ☐ Discover/NOVUS

1. Order subtotal		
2. Add applicable State Sales Tax		
3. Shipping & Handling*	$5.95	
4. **TOTAL AMOUNT DUE** (in U.S. dollars)		

Card #: _____ Exp. Date: _____

Signature: _____

(required for credit card orders)

OFA2013CAT

Two Easy Ways to Order

MAIL FORM TO:

The Old Farmer's Almanac
PO Box 4002828
Des Moines, IA 50340-2828

CALL TOLL-FREE:

800-ALMANAC
(800-256-2622)

*$5.95 shipping and handling applies to orders shipped in the U.S. only. For orders shipped to Canada, please add $5 (for a total of $10.95 S&H)

Cookbooks • Calendars • Gift Collections • and More!

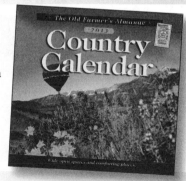

25 SE

HEFTY

Growing vegetables isn't hard if you know and practice the methods handed down by parents, grandparents, and other seasoned gardeners. Their tried-and-true tips have made edible gardening

CUCUMBE

CARROTS

PEAS

CRETS
FOR A
HARVEST

Why settle for good luck when success practically can be guaranteed?

easier and more productive for me and should give you the same results.

SOAK SEEDS

- To encourage seeds to germinate quickly, soak them in warm water with a tiny amount of hydrogen peroxide (1 teaspoon of hydrogen peroxide to 1 quart of water) for 2 hours. Then plant.

by Doreen G. Howard

–illustrated by Renée Quintal Daily

continued

GET ON A ROLL

● Lay a strip of toilet paper down the planting row, sow seeds on the paper, then cover with soil. It's easy to space dark seeds properly on a white background. The paper quickly dissolves into the soil.

GET READY FOR SECONDS

● Give legumes such as beans and peas a boost by wetting seeds and rolling them in a legume inoculant with rhizobia bacteria before planting. (Find packets in seed catalogs and at garden centers.) The bacteria convert the air's nitrogen into a form that the plant can use. When the legumes finish producing, break off the stems to leave the roots in the soil. As roots decay, they will deposit extra nitrogen in the soil for a second crop of nitrogen-loving vegetables, such as squash.

GROW FASTER WITH FUNGI

● Tomato, melon, and beet seeds (not legumes and the cabbage family) benefit from being inoculated with mycorrhizal fungi. It colonizes on plant roots, from the first, hair-like ones to the large taproots and increases the surface area of roots so that they can absorb more water and nutrients. Find mycorrhizae inoculants in seed catalogs and at garden centers.

FERTILIZE SLO-O-O-WLY

● Amend established garden beds with slow-release nutrients rather than fast-release fertilizers, which give plants a growth surge but are used up by the time plants need nutrients for vegetable development. Before planting, apply this slow-release treatment:

■ Spread an inch of compost or composted cow manure over the top of the ground.

■ Sprinkle 1 to 2 cups of slow-release fertilizer or rabbit food over every 16 square feet of planting bed. Rabbit food is compressed alfalfa meal pellets, which are nitrogen- and phosphorus-rich. Alfalfa also contains large quantities of a hormone called triacontanol, which stimulates cell division and growth in all plants. You can buy rabbit food or alfalfa pellets at pet and farm feed stores. (The pellets won't attract rabbits because they break down immediately when watered and mixed with soil.)

continued

ADVERTISEMENT
ARCTIC FRESH®
Omega 3
ULTRA PURE FISH OIL FORMULA
Proven... Pure... Potent !
#1 BRAND RECOMMENDED BY CARDIOLOGISTS
....
KEEPS PURE AND CLEAR IN FREEZER
ARCTIC FRESH HAS EPA 594, DHA 219 PER CAPSULE
IS YOURS HIGHER?
....
PHARMACEUTICAL GRADE
Thanks! Over 49,000 bottles sold!
180 GEL CAPS - $30 - Includes shipping
ARCTICFRESH.COM
941.637.7000

COUNT LEAVES

● When purchasing transplants, look for small, dark green seedlings without flowers. Cabbage and its cousins, such as broccoli and brussels sprouts, should have only two or three sets of leaves. Tomato, eggplant, and pepper transplants should have thick stems and at least four sets of leaves. Brush your hand over the tops of all transplants to see if insects fly off. If they do, buy elsewhere.

MULCH LIKE YOU MEAN IT

● After transplants have been set and plants are 2 inches high and thinned, mulch the entire bed, even between plants. Apply 2 to 4 inches of incomplete compost (this is from the pile and has broken down significantly but hasn't fully degraded), shredded leaves, or straw to keep the soil evenly moist and suppress weeds.

SEEK SHADE

● Use areas shaded by structures such as houses and fences or even other plants (but not trees) for vegetables that produce with only 3 to 6 hours of sun daily. You won't have to water these protected plants as often; salad greens will grow longer into the summer heat, and crops that are usually quick to bolt will last longer:

■ arugula, endive, leaf lettuce, spinach

■ beets, bush beans, peas, radishes, Swiss chard

■ broccoli, brussels sprouts, cauliflower

BRING FRIENDS TOGETHER

● Pair herbs and flowers with vegetables to thwart insect damage. Companion planting is centuries old, fragrant, and tasty. Try these combinations:

■ Radishes attract leaf miners away from spinach. The damage that the leaf miners do to radish leaves doesn't prevent the radishes from growing underground.

■ Nectar from dwarf zinnias lures ladybugs and other predators that help to protect cauliflower from cabbageworms.

■ Dill protects all members of the cabbage family by attracting beneficial wasps that kill cabbageworms and other pests.

■ Basil repels aphids, whiteflies, hornworms, and mosquitoes from tomatoes.

■ Garlic deters Japanese beetles.

■ Rosemary protects cabbage, beans, and carrots; it repels cabbage moths, bean beetles, and carrot flies.

continued

neseed

Good Seed, Glad Harvest™

NEW

Porcelain Doll F1
Eye-catching Pink Pumpkin

Deep ribbing with an almost square appearance. Exotic Pink exterior and deep-orange, sweet flesh.

www.**neseed**.com
Seeds for Home & Commercial Growers • (800) 825-5477

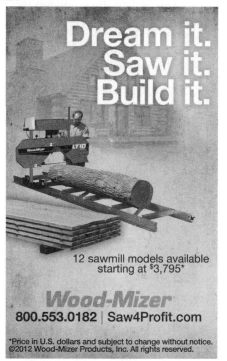

Dream it.
Saw it.
Build it.

12 sawmill models available
starting at $3,795*

Wood-Mizer

800.553.0182 | Saw4Profit.com

*Price in U.S. dollars and subject to change without notice.
©2012 Wood-Mizer Products, Inc. All rights reserved.

First Aid for your Skin
Providing Skin Care Solutions Since 1871

COLUMBIA brand products have been proudly made in the United States since 1871. They are safe, efficacious and fast-acting.

Our fast-acting ingredients instantly soothe and promote healing from:

- Sun Burn
- Poison Ivy
- Minor Cuts & Bruises
- Contact Dermatitis
- Wind & Razor Burn
- Chafing, Cracked Skin

COLUMBIA®
SKINCARE
SINCE 1871

Toll Free: (888)-871-5661
www.fcsturtevant.com/almanac
PO Box 607, Bronxville, NY 10708

THINK BIG
- Plant tiny onion bulbs for salad scallions but use transplants to produce large onions for storage. Transplants grow into bigger, denser onions.

RAISE SPUDS
- Potatoes hate continuously wet ground and will rot. Raised beds filled with fast-draining soil mix are best. To prevent scab (corky, rough skin), incorporate sulfur into the bed a week before planting seed potatoes.

GIVE SHELTER
- When sowing seeds in warm weather, cover them with boards or cardboard for 2 days to keep them moist. Carrot seeds, especially, benefit from the added moisture.

AVOID CROWDING
- Space cabbage and broccoli plants at least 18 inches apart to get huge heads. If you want small cabbage heads, plant about 6 inches apart.

SECOND THAT
- For an easy second crop of broccoli, direct-seed it between

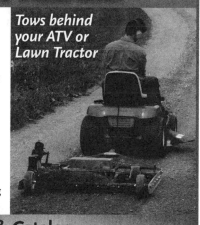

transplants in early spring. About the time when transplants mature their main heads, the seeded plants are ready to put on size. Cut off old plants at their base so that new root systems nearby are not disturbed.

SOW CLOSE

- Bush beans are more productive if you crowd them. Sow seeds 2 inches apart in all directions. Plants support each other, grow taller than normal, and produce more beans. Keep them picked for better bean production.

BE PATIENT

- If you plan to store winter squashes and pumpkins for later use, do not add extra manure (nitrogen) to the soil where they grow. Too much nitrogen in the soil reduces storability by up to 75 percent. Also, let squashes and pumpkins stay on the vines until leaves turn brown and stems wither.

BE CAGEY

- Save space and corral sprawling summer squash vines with tomato cages. Place one over each young plant and tuck developing shoots into the cage. Even bush-type squash plants stay more compact when caged.

LIGHTLY SALT

- When tomatoes, eggplants, and peppers start to flower, spray foliage with Epsom salts and warm water for more abundant and larger vegetables. Mix 2 tablespoons of salts and 1 gallon of water. The magnesium and sulfur in Epsom salts foster fruiting.

BREAK EGGS

- Keep the soil evenly moist around peppers and tomatoes and use thick mulch to prevent blossom-end rot, which happens when calcium doesn't reach plants. Most soils have plenty of it, but the mineral is transported to plant roots by water. Save crushed eggshells from the kitchen and work them into the top inch of soil around the plants to cure any calcium deficiency.

SNAG SLUGS

- Scatter coffee grounds, pine needles, or coarse sand around leafy vegetables such as salad greens and cabbage. These rough mulches rip up a slug or snail's tender underside. Earwigs suffer, too.

PRETEND THAT IT'S CHRISTMAS

- Birds peck at tomatoes. (In the U.S. South, grackles need little time to damage a tomato crop; elsewhere, blackbirds are the culprits.) To fool them, hang red Christmas ornaments on tomato plants just before fruit start to ripen.

continued

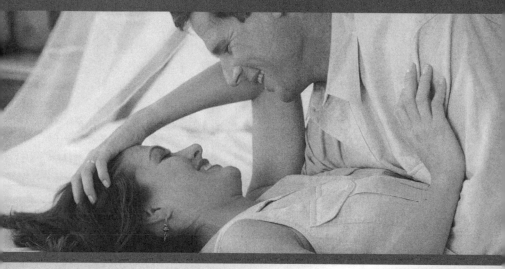

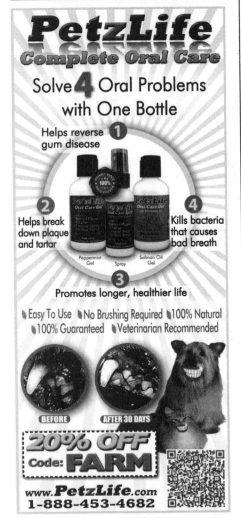
DUST!

● If you have an aphid invasion, dust plants with flour. It constipates the pests.

CHILL BEFORE SEEDING

● Fall salad crops such as lettuces and spinach can be tricky to start because garden soil is still warm when seeds need to be planted. Freeze the seeds for a week or two. This tricks an internal mechanism in the seeds so that they germinate in warm ground.

MAKE THE BED

● Spread compost over beds after harvest in late fall; top with organic mulch such as shredded fallen leaves. Compost needs time to break down and incorporate with the existing soil. Next spring, the vegetable garden will be ready to plant!

START NEXT YEAR EARLY

● Sprinkle arugula, beet, leaf lettuce, and spinach seeds over mulched beds in autumn, before the ground freezes. Even in frigid areas, seeds will sprout in early spring and start to grow before you even think about gardening!

□□

Doreen G. Howard is a frequent contributor to Almanac publications and writes a blog on **Almanac.com.** Her latest book is *Heirloom Flavor: Yesterday's Best-Tasting Vegetables, Fruits, and Herbs for Today's Cook* (Cool Springs Press, 2012).

Choose Life
Grow Young with HGH

From the landmark book Grow Young with HGH comes the most powerful, over-the-counter health supplement in the history of man. Human growth hormone was first discovered in 1920 and has long been thought by the medical community to be necessary only to stimulate the body to full adult size and therefore unnecessary past the age of 20. Recent studies, however, have overturned this notion completely, discovering instead that the natural decline of Human Growth Hormone (HGH), from ages 21 to 61 (the average age at which there is only a trace left in the body) is the main reason why the body ages and fails to regenerate itself to its 25-year-old biological age.

Like a picked flower cut from the source, we gradually wilt physically and mentally and become vulnerable to a host of degenerative diseases that we simply weren't susceptible to in our early adult years.

Modern medical science now regards aging as a disease that is treatable and preventable and that "aging", the disease, is actually a compilation of various diseases and pathologies, from everything, like a rise in blood glucose and pressure to diabetes, skin wrinkling and so on. All of these aging symptoms can be stopped and rolled back by maintaining Growth Hormone levels in the blood at the same levels HGH existed in the blood when we were 25 years old.

There is a receptor site in almost every

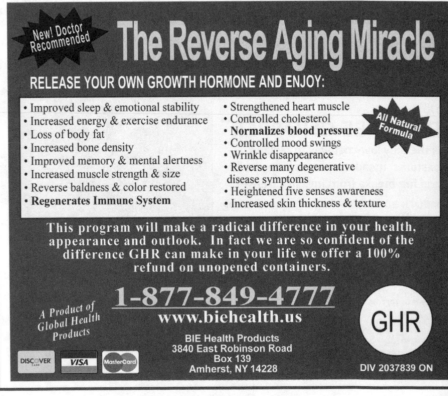

cell in the human body for HGH, so its regenerative and healing effects are very comprehensive.

Growth Hormone, first synthesized in 1985 under the Reagan Orphan drug act, to treat dwarfism, was quickly recognized to stop aging in its tracks and reverse it to a remarkable degree. Since then, only the lucky and the rich have had access to it at the cost of $10,000 US per year.

The next big breakthrough was to come in 1997 when a group of doctors and scientists, developed an all-natural source product which would cause your own natural HGH to be released again and do all the remarkable things it did for you in your 20's. Now available to every adult for about the price of a coffee and donut a day.

GHR now available in America, just in time for the aging Baby Boomers and everyone else from age 30 to 90 who doesn't want to age rapidly but would rather stay young, beautiful and healthy all of the time.

The new HGH releasers are winning converts from the synthetic HGH users as well, since GHR is just as effective, is oral instead of self-injectable and is very affordable.

GHR is a natural releaser, has no known side effects, unlike the synthetic version and has no known drug interactions. Progressive doctors admit that this is the direction medicine is seeking to go, to get the body to heal itself instead of employing drugs. GHR is truly a revolutionary paradigm shift in medicine and, like any modern leap frog advance, many others will be left in the dust holding their limited, or useless drugs and remedies.

It is now thought that HGH is so comprehensive in its healing and regenerative powers that it is today, where the computer industry was twenty years ago, that it will displace so many prescription and non-prescription drugs and health remedies that it is staggering to think of.

The president of BIE Health Products stated in a recent interview, I've been waiting for these products since the 70's. We knew they would come, if only we could stay healthy and live long enough to see them! If you want to stay on top of your game, physically and mentally as you age, this product is a boon, especially for the highly skilled professionals who have made large investments in their education, and experience. Also with the failure of Congress to honor our seniors with pharmaceutical coverage policy, it's more important than ever to take pro-active steps to safeguard your health. Continued use of GHR will make a radical difference in your health, HGH is particularly helpful to the elderly who, given a choice, would rather stay independent in their own home, strong, healthy and alert enough to manage their own affairs, exercise and stay involved in their communities. Frank, age 85, walks two miles a day, plays golf, belongs to a dance club for seniors, had a girl friend again and doesn't need Viagra, passed his drivers test and is hardly ever home when we call - GHR delivers.

HGH is known to relieve symptoms of Asthma, Angina, Chronic Fatigue, Constipation, Lower back pain and Sciatica, Cataracts and Macular Degeneration, Menopause, Fibromyalgia, Regular and Diabetic Neuropathy, Hepatitis, helps Kidney Dialysis and Heart and Stroke recovery.

For more information or to order call
877-849-4777
www.biehealth.us

These statements have not been evaluated by the FDA. Copyright © 2000. Code OFA.

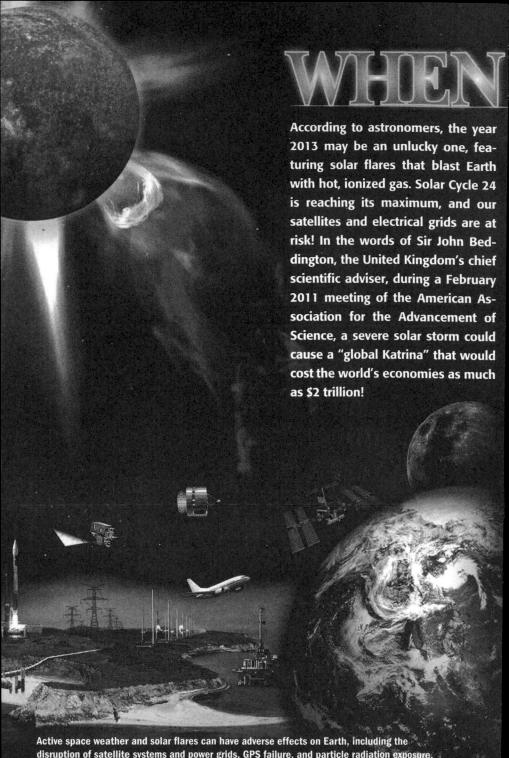

WHEN

According to astronomers, the year 2013 may be an unlucky one, featuring solar flares that blast Earth with hot, ionized gas. Solar Cycle 24 is reaching its maximum, and our satellites and electrical grids are at risk! In the words of Sir John Beddington, the United Kingdom's chief scientific adviser, during a February 2011 meeting of the American Association for the Advancement of Science, a severe solar storm could cause a "global Katrina" that would cost the world's economies as much as $2 trillion!

Active space weather and solar flares can have adverse effects on Earth, including the disruption of satellite systems and power grids, GPS failure, and particle radiation exposure.

the SUN TAKES a VACATION

by Evelyn Browning Garriss

Sound scary?

The only thing scarier than the Sun reaching a ▮▮▮ peak of an active cycle is when the Sun has a quiet cycle with almost no peak at all.

According to some solar scientists, when the Sun last had a very quiet cycle, Earth experienced the "Little Ice Age" (A.D. 1550–1850). Some of these same scientists are warning that the current cycle's "peak" of activity is the weakest in 80 years. Even more alarming, several scientists report that this is a trend and that the next cycle (number 25, projected to begin in 2020 by David Hathaway, NASA's top solar storm scientist) may exhibit lit▮▮▮ no solar activity at all.

Following the sweltering temperatures of Summer 2011 and the early spring of 2012 and decades of warning about "global warming," a cool spell may sound refreshing. Yet warnings of a possible ice age are daunting. What are the scientists talking about?

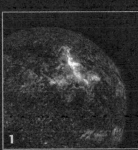

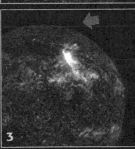

These solar flare images were observed by NASA's Solar Dynamics Observatory on January 23, 2012, and photographed 15 minutes apart. Each consecutive image displays the brightening of the solar surface as gas was superheated and magnetically charged. The eruption (seen in the third image) sent a stream of fast-moving, highly energetic protons toward Earth.

CONTINUED

–illustration opposite and photos above, NASA

WHEN the SUN TAKES a VACATION

SOLAR ENERGY
at the SOURCE

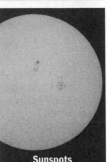

The Sun's eight layers are the core, radiative zone, tachocline, convective zone, photosphere, chromosphere, transition region, and corona.

Sunspots photographed through California haze from NASA's Dryden Flight Research Center

—Tom Tschida

This X-ray image taken by the NOAA GOES-13 satellite in 2006 depicts one of the largest solar flares ever recorded.

—NASA

The yellow ball in the sky is a busy, noisy place. The Sun is made of gas, and it rotates, generating a magnetic field—but various sections rotate differently. Its interior rotates much faster than its surface, and its equator rotates more quickly than its poles. Hot gases bubble and burst through the mix, tangling and looping the "lines" of the MAGNETIC FIELD. Sounds from

—NASA

Charged particles from the Sun's magnetic field race toward Earth's magnetosphere at thousands of miles per second.

these titanic explosions ripple through the Sun, disrupting gases and creating even more tangles. (See the effects and hear the Sun at Almanac.com/SunSounds.)

SUNSPOTS, which appear to us as dark patches, occur where these intense magnetic loops poke through the Sun's surface. Eventually, like an overstretched rubber band, each stressed magnetic field "breaks," releasing tremendous energy and spewing the magnetically charged gases into space. This explosion is called a SOLAR FLARE, and the hot spewed gases are called a CORONAL MASS EJECTION, or CME.

An increased number of sunspots indicates an increased output of solar radiation. These tangles, tears, and explosions spray Earth with increased energy, from light and heat to X rays. Satellite readings show that at the *peak* of a solar cycle (when the most sunspots occur), the Sun emits the most energy and radiation.

CONTINUED

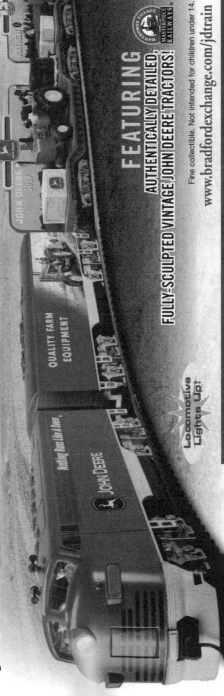

The EFFECTS of an
EXTENDED LEAVE

➡ **Scientists have been counting** sunspots and their cycles for centuries. They have also been able to reconstruct a record of solar activity for over 1,000 years by analyzing tree rings. Some of their discoveries are disturbing.

From the 9th to the 13th centuries (the Medieval Warm Period), the Sun was extremely active, with lots of sunspots and lots of radiation emitted toward Earth. Historical records show that Earth's climate was warm. Vikings grazed cattle on grasslands in Greenland and settled in Newfoundland.

Then the Sun entered a long quiet phase, during which the cycles were weak. Very few sunspots occurred (even maximum phases had minimal activity), and a lot less solar radiation reached Earth. Global temperatures dropped by 1.8°F (1°C).

This may not sound like much, but it produced effects that seem inconceivable today. In the 1600s, caravans of oxen carts laden with metal and hides departed from what is now Santa Fe, New Mexico; traveled 330 miles south; and then crossed over the frozen surface of the Rio Grande into what we know today as Mexico. From 1607 to 1814, citizens in England periodically held huge ice fairs on the frozen Thames River. In 1780, it was so cold that people walked from Manhattan to Staten Island over the frozen New York harbor.

The last drop in solar activity, which

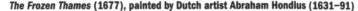

The Frozen Thames (1677), painted by Dutch artist Abraham Hondius (1631–91)

occurred from 1790 to 1830 (called the Dalton Minimum, for English meteorologist John Dalton, 1766–1844), was a time of crop failures, famines, and massive social turmoil.

It is important to note that daily, even year-to-year, variations of solar radiation have not produced noticeable changes in Earth's weather patterns. This is due, in part, to the oceans, which cover 70 percent of our planet. These bodies of water store enormous heat reserves and have a significant influence on our weather (think El Niño conditions in a warm Pacific and hurricanes in a warm Atlantic). The oceans are slow to cool; most global cooling takes place over land, especially far inland from the coast.

However, research by Danish scientists Eigil Friis-Christensen and Knud Lassen has shown that global temperatures do drop during quiet (inactive) sunspot cycles. Historically, during 11-year sunspot cycles of low activity and radiation, Earth experienced cooler temperatures and, when the quiet period was prolonged over several cycles, "little ice ages." Think of it this way: If the globe were to cool 1°F, the freeze zone would move roughly 350 miles south from its current position. (In Canada, where this would be referred to in metric measures, it sounds even more spectacular: If the globe were to cool 1°C, the freeze zone would move 1,000 kilometers south.)

CONTINUED

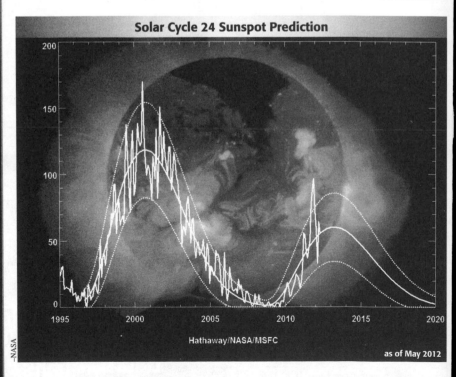

Weather

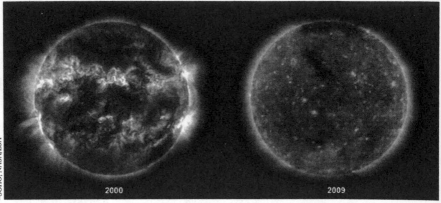

–SOHO, NASA/ESA

A comparison of the Sun's solar activity in 2000 and in 2009, illustrating the extremes of solar activity in a cycle.

2000   2009

WHEN the SUN TAKES a VACATION

TIME OFF or
RETIREMENT?

➡ **Over recent decades, the Sun** has been very active. Researchers at the Max Planck Institute for Solar System Research in Germany reported that from 1940 to 2005, solar activity was higher than it had been in the past 1,000 years. They were quick to point out that this activity could not account for all of the recent global warming (particularly that since 1980), but that it was probably a factor.

The period of heavy solar activity may be coming to a close. During 2007–09, the end phase of Solar Cycle 23, the Sun set space-age records for low sunspot counts, weak solar winds, and low solar irradiance. Current Solar Cycle 24's activity has been slow to start, and Hathaway has predicted that this cycle will be the weakest, or quietest, in a century. (This should reduce the risk of a "global Katrina"!) He has also predicted that Solar Cycle

25 will be even more feeble.

Now other scientists are agreeing with this analysis. Not only does the current sunspot cycle seem quiet, but also a number of recent reports have indicated a slowing of overall solar activity. These include studies that show . . .

▥ Sunspot magnetic fields have been steadily decreasing in strength since 1998.

▥ Streamers of the Sun's gassy outer envelope normally develop around the Sun's poles a few years before peak solar storm activity. They should have appeared as early as 2011. They did not.

▥ Jet streams that have formed inside the Sun at this time in every other cycle are not appearing.

CONTINUED

Psoriasis? Dermatitis? Dandruff? Dry, Itchy Skin?

Now you can relieve the itching and restore your skin to its clear healthy state!

Introducing Soravil™, the scientifically advanced skin therapy system whose active ingredients are clinically proven to provide immediate relief from Psoriasis, Dermatitis, Dandruff, and other bothersome skin disorders.

If you suffer from an irritating skin disorder, you must try Soravil™! Unlike anything you may have tried in the past, Soravil™ is guaranteed to provide immediate relief from the redness and irritation associated with chronic skin disorders. Our clinically tested formulas soothe, moisturize and heal dry, damaged skin...leaving it feeling smooth, supple, and healthy again! Even better, the power of Soravil™ is available in the form of Shampoo and Body Wash, so you can treat your condition as part of your daily routine. There is also easy to apply (and invisible) Body Gel and Skin Spray to take care of those stubborn flare ups. Soravil™ makes it easy for you to relieve yourself from that bothersome skin disorder.

What are you waiting for? If you want to relieve yourself from the suffering and rejuvenate your dry, itchy skin, it's time you tried Soravil™! This highly effective formula is guaranteed to work for you. So don't suffer any longer, call today for your risk-free trial, 1-800-711-0719, Offer # 909.

Success Stories:

*"Right away it cleared my arms up.
I think your product is wonderful.
Thanks so much!"*
-Judy K.

*"I am amazed at the improvement that
Soravil has made to my scalp! To say
I'm delighted would be putting it lightly."*
-David L.

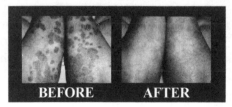

BEFORE   AFTER

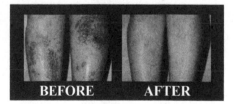

BEFORE   AFTER

Call now and get your risk-free trial!
1-800-711-0719

Mention Offer # 909 and ask how you can get a **FREE SUPPLY** of our Soravil Skin Hydration Formula.

**Active Ingredient FDA Approved • Results Guaranteed
Steroid-Free Formula • Provides Immediate Relief
Works On All Skin Types • Easy Application-No Mess**

WHEN the SUN TAKES a VACATION

Weather

In June 2011, scientists from the National Solar Observatory warned that if then-current trends continued, the Sun's magnetic fields would be too weak to generate visible sunspots by 2022. In the words of Dr. Frank Hill, associate director of the National Solar Observatory's Solar Synoptic Network, "The solar cycle is maybe going into hiatus, sort of like [a TV show in summer]."

Ah, but ice ages (even "little" ones) last longer than the summer rerun season.

Scientists have been quick to reassure the public that there is no need to worry. Historically, it took several quiet cycles in a row to produce dramatic cooling—and that was before man-made greenhouse gases entered the picture. Indeed, some scientists are claiming that a quiet Sun may slow down global warming as well as generate fewer solar storms to disrupt satellites and power systems.

The National Solar Observatory scientists won't discuss the effects of a quiet Sun on world temperatures or global warming. Too much is unknown. However, Dr. Hill made this observation: "If our predictions are true, we'll have a wonderful experiment that will determine whether the Sun has any effect on global warming."

Chilling, isn't it?   □□

Evelyn Browning Garriss, author of the *Browning Newsletter,* has been analyzing and reporting on weather for more than 30 years. Read her weekly blog at **Almanac .com/Weather.**

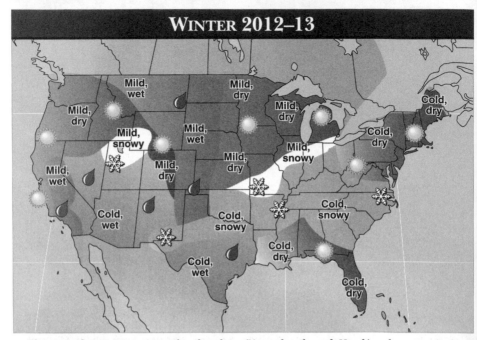

WINTER 2012–13

These weather maps correspond to the winter (November through March) and summer (June through August) predictions in the General Weather Forecast (opposite). Forecast terms here represent deviations from the normals; learn more on page 190.

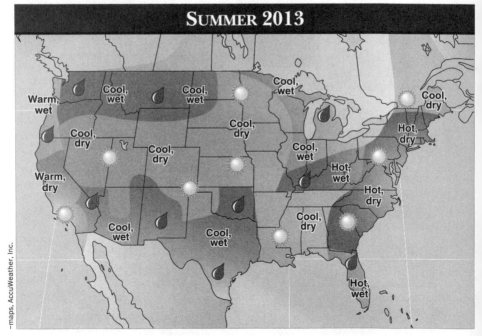

SUMMER 2013

—maps, AccuWeather, Inc.

The General Weather Forecast and Report

For regional forecasts, see pages 193–208.

With the 2013 peak of activity in Solar Cycle 24 at more than 50 percent below that of Solar Cycle 23, the La Niña diminished, and the cold phase of the PDO (Pacific Decadal Oscillation) under way, the winter of 2012–13 will be quite different than that of 2011–12. We expect that temperatures will be much colder this coming winter from the East Coast westward to a line from the Dakotas to Texas. In every place west of this line, except for portions of the Desert Southwest, temperatures will be warmer than last winter. Snowfall will be above normal near the Great Salt Lake and in the areas from El Paso to Detroit to Virginia Beach, but below normal in most other locations that typically have snow. Most of the areas suffering from drought will receive sufficient winter precipitation to bring improvement.

Spring and summer will be much rainier than normal in Florida, easing its drought, while drier-than-normal weather will continue to be the rule in much of Georgia. Summer temperatures will be hotter than normal along the Atlantic and Pacific coasts and in the Ohio Valley, but cooler than normal elsewhere. Expect fewer tornadoes than in the past couple of years, but be ready for hurricanes to threaten first the Gulf and Atlantic coasts in June and then primarily the Southeast, especially Florida, through the remainder of the hurricane season.

November through March temperatures will average below normal from New England southward through Florida and from the Carolinas westward across the southern Rockies and Desert Southwest and above normal elsewhere. Precipitation will be above normal in the High Plains, Texas, Oklahoma, the Desert Southwest, southern Rockies, and southern and central California and below normal elsewhere. Snowfall will be above normal in a swathe from the Carolinas to West Texas and within a hundred miles or so of the Great Salt Lake; it will be near or below normal elsewhere.

April and May will be warmer than normal, on average, in most of the eastern half of the country and below normal in most of the West. Rainfall will be above normal from the Carolinas southward through Florida, from the Ohio Valley southwestward through Texas, and from the Upper Midwest westward into the Dakotas; it will be near or below normal elsewhere.

June through August temperatures will average above normal in most locations within a few hundred miles of the Atlantic and Pacific Oceans and Ohio River and below normal in most other locations. Rainfall will be above normal from the Great Lakes westward to the Pacific Northwest, in the Ohio Valley and Florida, and from Texas into the Desert Southwest.

September and October will be cooler than normal in the southern Deep South and in the western third of the nation; it will be warmer than normal elsewhere. Rainfall will be above normal in Florida, the Upper Midwest, and near the Pacific Coast and near or below normal elsewhere.

To learn how we make our weather predictions and get the accuracy of our forecast for last winter, turn to page 190.

The Old Farmer's Almanac

Established in 1792 and published every year thereafter
ROBERT B. THOMAS, *founder* (1766–1846)

YANKEE PUBLISHING INC.

EDITORIAL AND PUBLISHING OFFICES

P.O. Box 520, 1121 Main Street, Dublin, NH 03444
Phone: 603-563-8111 • Fax: 603-563-8252

EDITOR *(13th since 1792):* Janice Stillman
ART DIRECTOR: Margo Letourneau
COPY EDITOR: Jack Burnett
SENIOR RESEARCH EDITOR: Mare-Anne Jarvela
SENIOR EDITOR: Heidi Stonehill
SENIOR ASSOCIATE EDITOR: Sarah Perreault
ASSOCIATE EDITOR: Amy Nieskens
INTERNS: Stephanie Brault, Heather Brown,
Montana Rogers
WEATHER GRAPHICS AND CONSULTATION:
AccuWeather, Inc.

V.P., NEW MEDIA AND PRODUCTION:
Paul Belliveau
PRODUCTION DIRECTORS:
Susan Gross, David Ziarnowski
SENIOR PRODUCTION ARTISTS:
Lucille Rines, Rachel Kipka

WEB SITE: ALMANAC.COM

NEW MEDIA EDITOR: Catherine Boeckmann
WEB DESIGNERS: Lou S. Eastman, Amy O'Brien
E-COMMERCE MANAGER: Alan Henning
PROGRAMMING: Reinvented, Inc.

CONTACT US

We welcome your questions and comments about articles in and topics for this Almanac. Mail all editorial correspondence to Editor, The Old Farmer's Almanac, P.O. Box 520, Dublin, NH 03444-0520; fax us at 603-563-8252; or contact us through Almanac.com/Feedback. *The Old Farmer's Almanac* can not accept responsibility for unsolicited manuscripts and will not acknowledge any hard-copy queries or manuscripts that do not include a stamped and addressed return envelope.

Thank you for buying this Almanac! We hope that you find it "useful, with a pleasant degree of humor." Thanks, too, to everyone who had a hand in it, including advertisers, distributors, printers, and sales and delivery people.

OUR CONTRIBUTORS

Bob Berman, our astronomy editor, is the director of Overlook Observatory in Woodstock and Storm King Observatory in Cornwall, both in New York. In 1976, he founded the Catskill Astronomical Society. Bob has led many aurora and eclipse expeditions, venturing as far as the Arctic and Antarctic.

Tim Clark, a retired high school English teacher from New Hampshire, has composed the weather doggerel on the Calendar pages since 1980.

Bethany E. Cobb, our astronomer, earned a Ph.D. in astronomy at Yale University and is an Assistant Professor of Honors and Physics at George Washington University. She also conducts research on gamma-ray bursts and follows numerous astronomy pursuits, including teaching astronomy to adults at the Osher Lifelong Learning Institute at UC Berkeley. When she is not scanning the sky, she enjoys playing the violin, figure skating, and reading science fiction.

George Lohmiller, author of the Farmer's Calendar essays, owns Our Town Landscaping in Hancock, New Hampshire. He has been writing for Almanac publications for more than 15 years, including the essays that formerly appeared in our Gardening Calendar and are now available at Almanac.com/GardeningCalEssays.

Celeste Longacre, our astrologer, often refers to astrology as "a study of timing, and timing is everything." A New Hampshire native, she has been a practicing astrologer for more than 25 years. Her book, *Love Signs* (Sweet Fern Publications, 1999), is available for sale on her Web site, www.yourlovesigns.com.

Michael Steinberg, our meteorologist, has been forecasting weather for the Almanac since 1996. In addition to college degrees in atmospheric science and meteorology, he brings a lifetime of experience to the task: He began predicting weather when he attended the only high school in the world with weather Teletypes and radar.

Doctors and Hospitals prepare for the future...

Aging Process Finally Reversed!

By Tom Wexhan, Freelance Health Writer;

FLORIDA — "Imagine your symptoms of aging GONE!" says Dr. Mitchell Matez, a well respected anti-aging specialist. "This is not just a medical discovery... this is historic!" This new nutritional breakthrough promises to change everything we "thought" we knew about growing older.

"This is going to change everything we know about Medicine..."
- *Dr. Mitchell Matez*

Let me be clear... "This is the real deal." This isn't just another cream, pill, or some anti-aging fad diet. There are no injections or painful surgeries to endure. The secret is in increasing your body's own production of HGH (human growth hormone). This procedure is extremely expensive and only available to rich, powerful people who can afford it. That is, until now...

Recently, a Florida-based company developed **TimeFIGHTERS® Advanced Anti-Aging Formula:** a new method of blending together a powerful combination of nutrients to boost your body's ability to produce more of its own HGH (Human Growth Hormone).

The Science Behind The Miracle

Scientists have traced the body's HGH production back to the pituitary gland, which controls the natural process of aging. **TimeFIGHTERS®** proprietary formulation provides nutrients and amino acids that switch on the age-reversal mechanisms in your brain. It safely returns the natural HGH production to levels you had when you were much younger. The benefits are shocking doctors across the globe.

❝Soon we'll be able to treat symptoms years before they appear. And the human lifespan may be as long as 130 years!❞
Dr. Ronald Klatz, President of the American Academy of Anti-Aging Medicine

As You Age, Your HGH Production Declines

And by age 60, you're left with a fraction of the HGH you used to have. The signs of aging become impossible to ignore... narrower shoulders and more weight around the middle... thinner skin that loses elasticity... creases and wrinkles... aching joints and brittle bones... all signs that your body is gradually breaking down.

Add to that, decreased sexual desire and ability and a loss of muscle tone that leads to a dangerous loss of agility and balance... "But none of this has to happen," says Dr. Matez.

Secret Of The Rich And Famous

Our knowledge of the age-reversing affects of HGH is nothing new. The Hollywood elite have known about it for years. That's why some older actors look like they're in their 30's. But until now an HGH boost cost $20,000 or more a year. And that's for artificial (and painful) HGH injections.

But that's all changed... **TimeFIGHTERS®** precise combination of seven amino acids and proprietary nutrients can boost your body's HGH production by a remarkable 300 to 1000%! And it costs just pennies a day for you to reap the very same benefits.

HAS THE REAL "FOUNTAIN OF YOUTH" BEEN DISCOVERED?

Doctors are astounded by reports of dramatic weight loss... sharper memory and recall... healthier cholesterol, blood pressure, vision and hearing. Others report joint pain, wrinkles and age lines have virtually vanished. And that's just the beginning. Is this a miracle or science? Some say it's both!

Results Are Obvious In The First Few Weeks

TimeFIGHTERS® is not a pill or tablet. It's a refreshing, delicious beverage mix, which makes it much more readily available so it can go to work faster. Just mix the individual packet with water and this delicious powdered drink mix rapidly absorbs into your system. It goes to work immediately. Within as little as 7 days, you'll see your energy levels rapidly increase... you'll notice you sleep more soundly, and you'll happily report a noticeable improvement in your memory and recall.

Real Science, Real Results:
"My skin is so soft now. My hair is fuller, and my nails aren't dry and brittle anymore!"
-*Brenda G. from North Carolina*

TimeFIGHTERS® benefits become stronger with continued use, leading to a surge in stamina and sexual performance, a decrease in aches and pains, smoother, more radiant skin, even clearer vision and more youthful hair and nails. But to really see what **TimeFIGHTERS®** can do for you... you have to try it for yourself.

Special Risk-Free Opportunity

For a limited time, you can order a 30-day supply of **TimeFIGHTERS®** at a super-low readers only price. "Grow young" again. Call the toll-free number below right now!

Call Now, Toll-Free! 1-888-876-2555
Priority Code: TFFA12

THE 2013 EDITION OF

The Old Farmer's Almanac
Established in 1792 and published every year thereafter
ROBERT B. THOMAS, *founder* (1766–1846)

YANKEE PUBLISHING INC.
P.O. Box 520, 1121 Main Street, Dublin, NH 03444
Phone: 603-563-8111 • Fax: 603-563-8252

PUBLISHER *(23rd since 1792)*: Sherin Pierce
EDITOR IN CHIEF: Judson D. Hale Sr.

FOR DISPLAY ADVERTISING RATES
Go to Almanac.com/Advertising-Information
or call 800-895-9265, Laura Tremblay, ext. 149

Bob Bernbach • 914-769-0051
Rod Peterson • 785-274-4479
Steve Hall • 800-736-1100, ext. 320
Susan Lyman • 646-221-4169

FOR CLASSIFIED ADVERTISING
Call Gallagher Group • 203-263-7171

AD PRODUCTION COORDINATOR: Janet Grant

PUBLIC RELATIONS
Quinn/Brein • 206-842-8922

**TO BUY OR INQUIRE ABOUT ALMANAC
PUBLICATIONS**
Call 800-ALMANAC (800-256-2622)
or go to Almanac.com/Shop

CONSUMER MARKETING MANAGER: Kate McPherson

TO SELL ALMANAC PRODUCTS
RETAIL: Cindy Schlosser, 800-895-9265, ext. 126,
or Stacey Korpi, ext. 160

FUND-RAISING WITH ALMANAC PRODUCTS
Carlene McCarty • 802-257-1440

DISTRIBUTORS
NATIONAL: Curtis Circulation Company
New Milford, NJ
BOOKSTORE: Houghton Mifflin Harcourt
Boston, MA

The Old Farmer's Almanac publications are available for sales promotions or premiums. Contact Beacon Promotions, info@beaconpromotions.com.

YANKEE PUBLISHING INCORPORATED
Jamie Trowbridge, *President;* Judson D. Hale Sr., *Senior Vice President;* Paul Belliveau, Jody Bugbee, Judson D. Hale Jr., Brook Holmberg, Sherin Pierce, *Vice Presidents.*

The Old Farmer's Almanac/Yankee Publishing Inc. assumes no responsibility for claims made by advertisers or failure by its advertisers to deliver any goods or services advertised herein. Publication of any advertisement by The Old Farmer's Almanac/ Yankee Publishing Inc. is not an endorsement of the product or service advertised therein.

PRINTED IN U.S.A.

Eclipses

■ There will be five eclipses in 2013, two of the Sun and three of the Moon. Solar eclipses are visible only in certain areas and require eye protection to be viewed safely. Lunar eclipses are technically visible from the entire night side of Earth, but during a penumbral eclipse, the dimming of the Moon's illumination is slight.

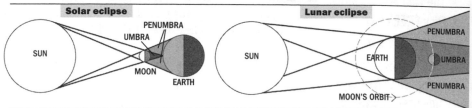

APRIL 25: Partial eclipse of the Moon. Although not visible in North America, this eclipse will be visible from Australia, Asia, Africa, Europe, and Antarctica.

MAY 9–10: Annular eclipse of the Sun. This eclipse will not be visible from North America. A partial eclipse will be visible from Hawaii on May 9 between 2:25 P.M. and 5:00 P.M. HAST. The eclipse will be visible from the central Pacific, New Zealand, Australia, and Indonesia.

MAY 24–25: Penumbral eclipse of the Moon. This eclipse will be fully visible from North America (except for Alaska) but not visible from Hawaii. The eclipse starts on May 24 at 11:43 P.M. EDT and ends on May 25 at 12:37 A.M. EDT.

Note that the penumbral magnitude of this eclipse is only 0.041! The Moon is just barely grazing Earth's shadow, making this a rather weak "eclipse."

OCTOBER 18: Penumbral eclipse of the Moon. This penumbral eclipse will be only partially visible from North America, as it will have started before the Moon has risen above the horizon. (No eclipse will be visible in western Alaska or Hawaii.) The Moon will enter the penumbra at 5:48 P.M. EDT and leave it at 9:52 P.M. EDT.

Full-Moon Dates (Eastern Time)				
	2013	**2014**	**2015**	**2016**	**2017**
Jan.	26	15	4	23	12
Feb.	25	14	3	22	10
Mar.	27	16	5	23	12
Apr.	25	15	4	22	11
May	25	14	3	21	10
June	23	13	2	20	9
July	22	12	1 & 31	19	9
Aug.	20	10	29	18	7
Sept.	19	8	27	16	6
Oct.	18	8	27	16	5
Nov.	17	6	25	14	4
Dec.	17	6	25	13	3

NOVEMBER 3: Total eclipse of the Sun. Eastern North America will see only a short partial solar eclipse during this event, at local sunrise after 6:00 A.M. EST. The eclipse will end at around 7:10 A.M. EST.

The Moon's Path

The Moon's path across the sky changes with the seasons. Full Moons are very high in the sky (at midnight) between November and February and very low in the sky between May and July.

Next Total Eclipse of the Sun

March 20, 2015: visible from northern Africa, northern Asia, and Europe.

Bright Stars

Transit Times

■ This table shows the time (EST or EDT) and altitude of a star as it transits the meridian (i.e., reaches its highest elevation while passing over the horizon's south point) at Boston on the dates shown. The transit time on any other date differs from that of the nearest date listed by approximately 4 minutes per day. To find the time of a star's transit for your location, convert its time at Boston using Key letter C **(see Time Corrections, page 234).**

			Time of Transit (EST/EDT) Bold = P.M. Light = A.M.						
Star	Constellation	Magnitude	Jan. 1	Mar. 1	May 1	July 1	Sept. 1	Nov. 1	Altitude (degrees)
Altair	Aquila	0.8	**12:49**	8:57	5:58	1:58	**9:50**	**5:50**	56.3
Deneb	Cygnus	1.3	**1:40**	9:48	6:48	2:48	**10:40**	**6:41**	92.8
Fomalhaut	Psc. Aus.	1.2	**3:56**	**12:04**	9:04	5:04	1:01	**8:57**	17.8
Algol	Perseus	2.2	**8:06**	**4:14**	**1:14**	9:14	5:11	1:11	88.5
Aldebaran	Taurus	0.9	**9:33**	**5:41**	**2:41**	10:42	6:38	2:38	64.1
Rigel	Orion	0.1	**10:12**	**6:20**	**3:20**	11:20	7:16	3:16	39.4
Capella	Auriga	0.1	**10:14**	**6:22**	**3:22**	11:23	7:19	3:19	93.6
Bellatrix	Orion	1.6	**10:22**	**6:30**	**3:30**	11:31	7:27	3:27	54.0
Betelgeuse	Orion	var. 0.4	**10:52**	**7:00**	**4:00**	**12:01**	7:57	3:57	55.0
Sirius	Can. Maj.	−1.4	**11:42**	**7:50**	**4:50**	**12:50**	8:47	4:47	31.0
Procyon	Can. Min.	0.4	12:40	**8:44**	**5:44**	**1:44**	9:41	5:41	52.9
Pollux	Gemini	1.2	12:46	**8:50**	**5:50**	**1:51**	9:47	5:47	75.7
Regulus	Leo	1.4	3:09	**11:13**	**8:13**	**4:13**	**12:09**	8:10	59.7
Spica	Virgo	var. 1.0	6:25	2:33	**11:29**	**7:29**	**3:26**	11:26	36.6
Arcturus	Boötes	−0.1	7:15	3:23	12:23	**8:20**	**4:16**	**12:16**	66.9
Antares	Scorpius	var. 0.9	9:29	5:37	2:37	**10:33**	**6:29**	**2:30**	21.3
Vega	Lyra	0	11:36	7:44	4:44	12:44	**8:36**	**4:36**	86.4

Rise and Set Times

■ To find the time of a star's rising at Boston on any date, subtract the interval shown at right from the star's transit time on that date; add the interval to find the star's setting time. To find the rising and setting times for your city, convert the Boston transit times above using the Key letter shown at right before applying the interval **(see Time Corrections, page 234).** The directions in which the stars rise and set, shown for Boston, are generally useful throughout the United States. Deneb, Algol, Capella, and Vega are circumpolar stars—they never set but appear to circle the celestial north pole.

Star	Interval (h. m.)	Rising Key	Rising Dir.*	Setting Key	Setting Dir.*
Altair	6 36	B	EbN	E	WbN
Fomalhaut	3 59	E	SE	D	SW
Aldebaran	7 06	B	ENE	D	WNW
Rigel	5 33	D	EbS	B	WbS
Bellatrix	6 27	B	EbN	D	WbN
Betelgeuse	6 31	B	EbN	D	WbN
Sirius	5 00	D	ESE	B	WSW
Procyon	6 23	B	EbN	D	WbN
Pollux	8 01	A	NE	E	NW
Regulus	6 49	B	EbN	D	WbN
Spica	5 23	D	EbS	B	WbS
Arcturus	7 19	A	ENE	E	WNW
Antares	4 17	E	SEbE	A	SWbW

*b = "by"

The Twilight Zone

Twilight is the time when the sky is partially illuminated preceding sunrise and again following sunset. The three ranges of twilight are defined according to the Sun's position below the horizon. **Civil twilight** occurs when the Sun is between the horizon and 6 degrees below the horizon (visually, the horizon is clearly defined). **Nautical twilight** occurs when the Sun is between 6 and 12 degrees below the horizon (the horizon is indistinct). **Astronomical twilight** occurs when the Sun is between 12 and 18 degrees below the horizon (sky illumination is imperceptible). When the Sun is at 18 degrees (dawn or dark) or below, there is no illumination.

Length of Astronomical Twilight (hours and minutes)

LATITUDE	Jan. 1 to Apr. 10	Apr. 11 to May 2	May 3 to May 14	May 15 to May 25	May 26 to July 22	July 23 to Aug. 3	Aug. 4 to Aug. 14	Aug. 15 to Sept. 5	Sept. 6 to Dec. 31
25°N to 30°N	1 20	1 23	1 26	1 29	1 32	1 29	1 26	1 23	1 20
31°N to 36°N	1 26	1 28	1 34	1 38	1 43	1 38	1 34	1 28	1 26
37°N to 42°N	1 33	1 39	1 47	1 52	1 59	1 52	1 47	1 39	1 33
43°N to 47°N	1 42	1 51	2 02	2 13	2 27	2 13	2 02	1 51	1 42
48°N to 49°N	1 50	2 04	2 22	2 42	—	2 42	2 22	2 04	1 50

TO DETERMINE THE LENGTH OF TWILIGHT: The length of twilight changes with latitude and the time of year. Use the **Time Corrections** table, **page 234,** to find the latitude of your city or the city nearest you. Use that figure in the chart above with the appropriate date to calculate the length of twilight in your area.

TO DETERMINE WHEN DAWN OR DARK WILL OCCUR: Calculate the sunrise/sunset times for your locality using the instructions in **How to Use This Almanac, page 100.** Subtract the length of twilight from the time of sunrise to determine when dawn breaks. Add the length of twilight to the time of sunset to determine when dark descends.

E X A M P L E :

Boston, Mass. (latitude 42°22')

Sunrise, August 1	5:36 A.M. EDT
Length of twilight	− 1 52
Dawn breaks	3:44 A.M.
Sunset, August 1	8:03 P.M. EDT
Length of twilight	+ 1 52
Dark descends	9:55 P.M.

Principal Meteor Showers

SHOWER	BEST VIEWING	POINT OF ORIGIN	DATE OF MAXIMUM*	NO. PER HOUR**	ASSOCIATED COMET
Quadrantid . . . . **Predawn**		N	**Jan. 4**	25	—
Lyrid . . . . Predawn		S	Apr. 22	10	Thatcher
Eta Aquarid . . . . Predawn		SE	May 4	10	Halley
Delta Aquarid . . . . Predawn		S	July 30	10	—
Perseid . . . . **Predawn**		NE	**Aug. 11–13**	50	**Swift-Tuttle**
Draconid . . . . .Late evening		NW	Oct. 9	6	Giacobini-Zinner
Orionid . . . . Predawn		S	Oct. 21–22	15	Halley
Taurid . . . . Late evening		S	Nov. 9	3	Encke
Leonid. . . . . Predawn		S	Nov. 17–18	10	Tempel-Tuttle
Andromedid . . . . Late evening		S	Nov. 25–27	5	Biela
Geminid . . . .**All night**		NE	**Dec. 13–14**	75	—
Ursid . . . . Predawn		N	Dec. 22	5	Tuttle

May vary by one or two days   **Moonless, rural sky*   **Bold** = *most prominent*

"For 40 Years, I was tortured by unbearable Acid Reflux"

"Now, I can even eat spicy foods again without that awful acid burn, piercing through my esophagus!"

I've Suffered With Acid Reflux for Almost 40-Years Now. Unless you experience it; you can't imagine how horrible it is. Every time I ate spicy food I would get what I called "ROT GUT". Like something was rotting in my stomach. But now I can eat anything... No matter how spicy. Even if I never could before. Let me explain...

For years I avoided a lot of foods, especially ones with even a tiny bit of seasoning. If I didn't, I'd experience a burning sensation through my esophagus— like somebody poured hot lead or battery acid down my throat. Add to that, those disgusting "mini-throw ups" and I was in "indigestion hell".

"I was beside myself. What was I gonna do? Keep taking the pills, or suffer with problems that could ultimately be my demise."

Doctors put me on all sorts of antacid remedies. But nothing worked. Or if they did, it would only be for a brief period. And then my nightmare would return.

But then my wife, who occasionally suffered with the same problem; gave me one of her prescription acid blockers. It was a miracle. I felt like I could live again. **I felt great, until about one year ago;** when I read an FDA warning that scared the heck out of me. It went something like this...

FDA WARNING! Using proton pump inhibitors (PPIs) on a long term basis, increases your risk of hip, bone and spinal fractures. That's a particular concern to me, since many acid blockers are PPI's.

I've gone through two back surgeries and bilateral hip replacements. I had to ask myself, could PPI's have been responsible for my medical woes? After all...

"THE RECOMMENDED TREATMENT FOR PRILOSEC˚, PREVACID˚ AND ALL OTHER PPI'S IS ONLY 14 DAYS— I TOOK THEM FOR 14 YEARS!"

I was "between a rock and a hard place". Stop using the PPIs and I'm a "dead man in the water". It would be unbearable. I wouldn't be able to eat anything. I'd have to go on a water diet.

But that FDA warning was scary. I knew I had to stop or else risk developing spinal stenosis. My mother had that. And I watched her die a horrible death. Her spine just fractured. It was the worst death. She didn't deserve that. And neither do I.

I had to quit. So I stopped taking PPI's for a day or so. But my indigestion was worse than ever. Then one day at dinner, a friend of mine said "why don't you try an aloe drink?" I said "aloe drink"? Jeez. That doesn't sound good at all!" The next day he brought me a case of something called *AloeCure®*. I was skeptical, but I was desperate! So instead of being an ingrate I decided to try it.

I was shocked! *AloeCure®* tasted pretty good too. It has a pleasant grape flavor that I actually enjoy drinking. I decided to experiment. I stopped taking the PPI's altogether and replaced it with a daily diet of *AloeCure®*. Then something remarkable happened... NOTHING! Not even the slightest hint of indigestion.

63-year old Ralph Burns enjoying a spicy-hot portion of Lobster Fra Diavolo. Just 15-Minutes after taking AloeCure˚

And here's the best part. The next day we had Italian food — my worst enemy. But for the first time in 40-years I didn't get indigestion without relying on prescription or OTC pills and tablets. Finally, I just didn't need them anymore!

I was so thrilled; I wrote the *AloeCure®* company to tell them how amazing their product is. They thanked me, and asked me to tell my story... the story that changed my life. I said "Sure, but only if you send me a hefty supply of *AloeCure®*. I just can't live without it. But don't believe me. You have to try this stuff for yourself.

Try It 100% Risk-Free!

The makers of *AloeCure®* have agreed to send you up to **6 FREE bottles PLUS 2 free bonus gifts** with every order— they're yours to keep no matter what. That's enough *AloeCure®* for 30-days of powerful digestive relief, absolutely free!

But hurry! This is a special introductory offer, reserved for our readers only.

Call Now, Toll-Free!
1-855-689-1061

The Visible Planets

■ Listed here for Boston are viewing suggestions for and the rise and set times (EST/ EDT) of Venus, Mars, Jupiter, and Saturn on specific days each month, as well as when it is best to view Mercury. Approximate rise and set times for other days can be found by interpolation. Use the Key letters at the right of each listing to convert the times for other localities **(see pages 100 and 234)**. *For all planet rise and set times by zip code, visit* **Almanac.com/Astronomy.**

Venus

This is a lopsided Venus year. The most brilliant of all the planets begins 2013 as a morning star too close to the Sun's glare to be readily seen and then totally vanishes during its superior conjunction behind the Sun on March 28. In early May, just after sunset, it can be glimpsed at its dimmest as an evening star low in the west. It spends the final week of May and the beginning of June floating next to Mercury and Jupiter. Venus stubbornly remains less than 10 degrees high in fading evening twilight throughout the summer and early fall. Finally, in November and especially December, Venus gains elevation while rapidly brightening to nearly magnitude –5, at which time it will be 25 degrees high.

Jan. 1	rise	5:42	E	Apr. 1	set	7:12	D	July 1	set	9:59	E	Oct. 1	set	8:06	A
Jan. 11	rise	6:00	E	Apr. 11	set	7:37	D	July 11	set	9:54	E	Oct. 11	set	7:59	A
Jan. 21	rise	6:13	E	Apr. 21	set	8:02	D	July 21	set	9:45	D	Oct. 21	set	7:55	A
Feb. 1	rise	6:21	E	May 1	set	8:28	E	Aug. 1	set	9:32	D	Nov. 1	set	7:57	A
Feb. 11	rise	6:22	E	May 11	set	8:53	E	Aug. 11	set	9:17	C	Nov. 11	set	7:00	A
Feb. 21	rise	6:17	D	May 21	set	9:16	E	Aug. 21	set	9:02	C	Nov. 21	set	7:04	A
Mar. 1	rise	6:11	D	June 1	set	9:37	E	Sept. 1	set	8:44	C	Dec. 1	set	7:03	A
Mar. 11	rise	7:01	D	June 11	set	9:51	E	Sept. 11	set	8:30	B	Dec. 11	set	6:54	A
Mar. 21	rise	6:50	C	June 21	set	9:58	E	Sept. 21	set	8:16	B	Dec. 21	set	6:31	A
												Dec. 31	set	5:49	B

Mars

The Red Planet comes close and gets bright on alternate years—and 2013 is an "off" year. It starts the year in Capricornus, too close to the Sun to be readily seen, then slides behind the Sun in conjunction on April 17. Mars re-emerges as a morning star but remains hard to see through much of the summer. It closely meets Jupiter on July 20–22. Visible before dawn in Cancer, Mars chugs in front of the Beehive star cluster on September 7 and 8, becoming a good target for viewing with binoculars. It passes close to Regulus on October 14 and 15. Mars starts to brighten by year's end, rising around midnight.

Jan. 1	set	6:15	B	Apr. 1	set	7:26	D	July 1	rise	3:52	A	Oct. 1	rise	2:38	B
Jan. 11	set	6:17	B	Apr. 11	set	7:26	D	July 11	rise	3:41	A	Oct. 11	rise	2:30	B
Jan. 21	set	6:19	B	Apr. 21	set	7:26	D	July 21	rise	3:31	A	Oct. 21	rise	2:22	B
Feb. 1	set	6:21	B	May 1	rise	5:34	B	Aug. 1	rise	3:21	A	Nov. 1	rise	2:12	B
Feb. 11	set	6:23	B	May 11	rise	5:14	B	Aug. 11	rise	3:14	A	Nov. 11	rise	1:02	B
Feb. 21	set	6:24	C	May 21	rise	4:55	B	Aug. 21	rise	3:07	A	Nov. 21	rise	12:51	C
Mar. 1	set	6:25	C	June 1	rise	4:36	A	Sept. 1	rise	2:59	A	Dec. 1	rise	12:39	C
Mar. 11	set	7:26	C	June 11	rise	4:19	A	Sept. 11	rise	2:53	A	Dec. 11	rise	12:26	C
Mar. 21	set	7:26	C	June 21	rise	4:05	A	Sept. 21	rise	2:46	B	Dec. 21	rise	12:12	C
												Dec. 31	rise	11:54	C

☞ **Bold** = P.M. ☞ Light = A.M. –illustrations, Beth Krommes

Jupiter

As 2013 opens, Jove is up in the east at nightfall. It is brilliant at magnitude –2.7 and stays in Taurus for the remainder of the winter. On January 21 and March 17, it closely meets the Moon in spectacular conjunctions. After April, the Giant Planet becomes increasingly low in the west at nightfall. It meets Venus on May 27 and 28 before it vanishes behind the Sun in mid-June. Jupiter starts to appear low in the east as a morning star by late July. It gets higher in August and starts rising before midnight in October. By November, Jupiter rapidly brightens. By the end of December, it is out all night.

Jan. 1	set	4:49	E	Apr. 1	set 12:16	E	July 1	rise	4:35	A	Oct. 1	rise	11:50	A

Jan. 1 .... set 4:49 E   Apr. 1 .... set 12:16 E   July 1 ....rise 4:35 A   Oct. 1 .... rise 11:50 A
Jan. 11 ...... set 4:06 E   Apr. 11 ...... set 11:43 E   July 11 .....rise 4:06 A   Oct. 11 ..... rise 11:15 A
Jan. 21 ...... set 3:24 E   Apr. 21 ...... set 11:12 E   July 21 .....rise 3:37 A   Oct. 21 ..... rise 10:39 A
Feb. 1 .... set 2:40 E   May 1 .... set 10:43 E   Aug. 1 .....rise 3:04 A   Nov. 1 .... rise 9:57 A
Feb. 11 ...... set 2:02 E   May 11 ...... set 10:14 E   Aug. 11 ....rise 2:34 A   Nov. 11 ..... rise 8:18 A
Feb. 21 ...... set 1:26 E   May 21 ..... set 9:45 E   Aug. 21 ....rise 2:04 A   Nov. 21 .... rise 7:37 A
Mar. 1 .... set 12:58 E   June 1 .... set 9:13 E   Sept. 1 .....rise 1:30 A   Dec. 1 ...... rise 6:54 A
Mar. 11 ..... set 1:24 E   June 11 ..... set 8:44 E   Sept. 11 ...rise 12:59 A   Dec. 11 .... rise 6:10 A
Mar. 21 ..... set 12:51 E   June 21 ....rise 5:05 A   Sept. 21 ...rise 12:26 A   Dec. 21 .... rise 5:25 A
                                                                                        Dec. 31 .... rise 4:40 A

Saturn

Saturn varies in appearance depending on the orientation of its rings. This year, in Libra, the planet is particularly beautiful, as its rings are nearly "wide open" (not edgewise to Earth). A magnification of at least 30× is needed to see the rings. Although Saturn doesn't rise until 2:00 A.M. during early January, it clears the horizon by midnight in February, by 10:00 P.M. in March, and at nightfall in April. It is out all night in April and May (attaining a very bright magnitude of 0.1 during its opposition on April 28) and remains well placed right through August. Saturn becomes low in September and goes behind the Sun in a conjunction on November 6. By December, it can be seen low in the east before dawn.

Jan. 1 ....rise 2:15 D   Apr. 1 .... rise 9:19 D   July 1 .... set 1:43 B   Oct. 1 .... set 7:50 B
Jan. 11 .....rise 1:39 D   Apr. 11 ..... rise 8:36 D   July 11 ...... set 1:04 B   Oct. 11 ...... set 7:13 B
Jan. 21 .....rise 1:02 D   Apr. 21 ..... rise 7:53 D   July 21 ...... set 12:25 B   Oct. 21 ...... set 6:37 B
Feb. 1 ....rise 12:21 D   May 1 ...... rise 7:10 D   Aug. 1 .... set 11:38 B   Nov. 1 .... set 5:57 B
Feb. 11 ..... rise 11:39 D   May 11 ..... set 5:11 B   Aug. 11 .... set 11:00 B   Nov. 11 ....rise 6:04 D
Feb. 21 ..... rise 11:00 D   May 21 ..... set 4:30 B   Aug. 21 .... set 10:22 B   Nov. 21 ....rise 5:30 D
Mar. 1 ...... rise 10:28 D   June 1 .... set 3:45 B   Sept. 1 ..... set 9:41 B   Dec. 1 ......rise 4:57 D
Mar. 11 .... rise 10:47 D   June 11 ..... set 3:04 B   Sept. 11 .... set 9:03 B   Dec. 11 ...rise 4:23 D
Mar. 21 .... rise 10:05 D   June 21 ..... set 2:23 B   Sept. 21 ... set 8:26 B   Dec. 21 ...rise 3:49 D
                                                                                        Dec. 31 ...rise 3:15 D

Mercury

Mercury alternately darts above the eastern and western skylines roughly every 2 months. A twilight phenomenon, it is nonetheless easily seen two or three times a year. This year, Mercury offers two evening star apparitions, both 40 minutes after sunset, during which its brightness is at magnitude 0 or better. The first is from February 10–20. The second is from May 27 to June 10, when it floats above brilliant Venus. Mercury offers its best morning star view from November 10–26. During the final 2 days of that apparition, it will be very close to Saturn.

DO NOT CONFUSE ■ *Mercury and Mars on February 7 and 8. Mercury is six times brighter.* ■ *Mercury, Jupiter, and Venus on May 23. Venus is the brightest, and Jupiter is highest.* ■ *Venus and Jupiter on May 27 and 28. Venus is brighter.* ■ *Mercury and Saturn in late November. Mercury is brighter.*

Astronomical Glossary

Aphelion (Aph.): The point in a planet's orbit that is farthest from the Sun.

Apogee (Apo.): The point in the Moon's orbit that is farthest from Earth.

Celestial Equator (Eq.): The imaginary circle around the celestial sphere that can be thought of as the plane of Earth's equator projected out onto the sphere.

Celestial Sphere: An imaginary sphere projected into space that represents the entire sky, with an observer on Earth at its center. All celestial bodies other than Earth are imagined as being on its inside surface.

Circumpolar: Always visible above the horizon, such as a circumpolar star.

Conjunction: The time at which two or more celestial bodies appear closest in the sky. **Inferior (Inf.):** Mercury or Venus is between the Sun and Earth. **Superior (Sup.):** The Sun is between a planet and Earth. Actual dates for conjunctions are given on the **Right-Hand Calendar Pages, 105–131;** the best times for viewing the closely aligned bodies are given in **Sky Watch** on the **Left-Hand Calendar Pages, 104–130.**

Declination: The celestial latitude of an object in the sky, measured in degrees north or south of the celestial equator; analogous to latitude on Earth. This Almanac gives the Sun's declination at noon.

Eclipse, Lunar: The full Moon enters the shadow of Earth, which cuts off all or part of the sunlight reflected off the Moon. **Total:** The Moon passes completely through the **umbra** (central dark part) of Earth's shadow. **Partial:** Only part of the Moon passes through the umbra. **Penumbral:** The Moon passes through only the **penumbra** (area of partial darkness surrounding the umbra). **See page 86** for more eclipse information.

Eclipse, Solar: Earth enters the shadow of the new Moon, which cuts off all or part of the Sun's light. **Total:** Earth passes through the umbra (central dark part) of the Moon's shadow, resulting in totality for observers within a narrow band on Earth. **Annular:** The

Moon appears silhouetted against the Sun, with a ring of sunlight showing around it. **Partial:** The Moon blocks only part of the Sun.

Ecliptic: The apparent annual path of the Sun around the celestial sphere. The plane of the ecliptic is tipped 23½° from the celestial equator.

Elongation: The difference in degrees between the celestial longitudes of a planet and the Sun. **Greatest Elongation (Gr. Elong.):** The greatest apparent distance of a planet from the Sun, as seen from Earth.

Epact: A number from 1 to 30 that indicates the Moon's age on January 1 at Greenwich, England; used in calculations for determining the date of Easter.

Equinox: When the Sun crosses the celestial equator. This event occurs two times each year: **Vernal** is around March 20 and **Autumnal** is around September 22.

Evening Star: A planet that is above the western horizon at sunset and less than 180° east of the Sun in right ascension.

Golden Number: A number in the 19-year cycle of the Moon, used in calculations for determining the date of Easter. (Approximately every 19 years, the Moon's phases occur on the same dates.) Add 1 to any given year and divide by 19; the remainder is the Golden Number. If there is no remainder, use 19.

Greatest Illuminated Extent (Gr. Illum. Ext.): When the maximum surface area of a planet is illuminated as seen from Earth.

Magnitude: A measure of a celestial object's brightness. **Apparent** magnitude measures the brightness of an object as seen from Earth. **(continued)**

Health & Wellness

Leaky bladder? Urinary urgency? Embarrassing "accidents?"

One out of two older women in the U.S. suffers from a leaky bladder and urinary urgency. But it doesn't have to happen to you. That's because there's now a doctor-approved natural remedy that can mean...

- No more leaking
- No more racing to the bathroom
- No more loss of freedom and control

...and it's guaranteed to work for you—or it's FREE! Women across the country have already put it to the test, and they love the results. Why? It's the exclusive natural formula that helps...

Banish all 6 major concerns of frequent urination at once!

Medical Science tells us a leaky bladder and frequent urination is triggered by...

1) Poor circulation
2) Sagging bladder muscles
3) Tension and spasms in urinary muscles
4) Poor urinary and bladder tissue health
5) Bacteria from the bowel that moves into the urinary tract
6) Toxins and free radicals

The result? Your bladder and urethra can shift, making it difficult for your urethra to close properly. Muscles weaken... nerves are damaged... and you leak!

This can mean wearing bulky pads and liners... always looking for the bathroom... avoiding long trips in the car... or embarrassing "accidents."

But now there's a safe, natural, pennies-a-day solution that addresses all of these triggers at once: *Pro-Advanced Formula #220™*.

You can go from "leaking" to comfort and control!

Pro-Advanced Formula #220™ includes a proprietary formula of ten scientifically researched herbs, minerals and vitamins for healthy urination that...

- Naturally strengthen your bladder muscles
- Improve your urinary health
- Lessen muscle spasms which may trigger "leaking"
- Relax muscular tension and spasms in your urinary tract
- Soothe your bladder and urinary tissues
- Work to boost bladder capacity
- Help muscles tighten—so your urge to "go" is lessened
- Help your uterus to relax and stops urgency
- Ease nighttime and daytime frequency
- Help inhibit recurrence of urinary tract concerns
- Neutralize free radicals that harm your bladder
- Keep your entire urinary tract healthy

With exclusive, proprietary natural ingredients and benefits like these, no wonder women all across America love it.

Delivers amazing results!

Have my life back! Nancy B. of Bolivia, North Carolina writes: "I've had a weak bladder for years and didn't like going out in public. Then I started taking your

formula and feel I have better control and have my life back again! Thank you."

Terrific combination of ingredients! Audrey L., of St. Louis Park, MN adds: "This formula allows me to wait two to three hours before I have to visit the rest room. It is definitely a terrific combination of ingredients that works and works well. My hat's off to you!"

Making a difference! Marilyn M. of Belle Vernon, PA writes: "I was experiencing frequency and leaking but your formula is truly making a difference!"

Can spend time away from home! Betty D., of Pueblo, Colorado adds: "I'm ok when I go grocery shopping or spend time away from home. I don't use any rest rooms. This formula is working well. Thank you!"

Dr. Karen Yale writes: "*Pro-Advanced Formula #220™* is powerful at getting to the root causes of urinary problems and nothing comes close to giving you all of these benefits. If you're tired of the stress and frustration of always having to "go", it's time you tried *Pro-Advanced Formula #220™*.

A special offer for readers of this almanac

We've made special arrangements with the distributor to give you an extra bottle of *Pro-Advanced Formula #220™* FREE! If you're suffering from any of these miserable symptoms above, we urge you to try it.

Please HURRY! Your FREE bottle is limited to available inventory, and once the supply runs out, this offer may not be repeated. Try it RISK-FREE. That's how sure we are that *Pro-Advanced Formula #220™* will work for you.

IMPORTANT: LIMITED TIME OFFER!
Call Now, Toll Free! 1-877-538-1007
Mention Priority Code: OFS12F

Objects with an apparent magnitude of 6 or less are observable to the naked eye. The lower the magnitude, the greater the brightness. An object with a magnitude of −1, for example, is brighter than an object with a magnitude of +1. **Absolute** magnitude expresses how bright objects would appear if they were all the same distance (about 33 light-years) from Earth.

Midnight: Astronomical midnight is the time when the Sun is opposite its highest point in the sky (local noon). Midnight is neither A.M. nor P.M., although 12-hour digital clocks typically display midnight as 12:00 A.M. On a 24-hour time cycle, 00:00, rather than 24:00, usually indicates midnight.

Moon on Equator: The Moon is on the celestial equator.

Moon Rides High/Runs Low: The Moon is highest above or farthest below the celestial equator.

Moonrise/Moonset: When the Moon rises above or sets below the horizon.

Moon's Phases: The changing appearance of the Moon, caused by the different angles at which it is illuminated by the Sun. **First Quarter:** Right half of the Moon is illuminated. **Full:** The Sun and the Moon are in opposition; the entire disk of the Moon is illuminated. **Last Quarter:** Left half of the Moon is illuminated. **New:** The Sun and the Moon are in conjunction; Moon is darkened because it lines up between Earth and the Sun.

Moon's Place, Astronomical: The position of the Moon within the constellations on the celestial sphere. **Astrological:** The position of the Moon within the tropical zodiac, whose twelve 30° segments (signs) along the ecliptic were named more than 2,000 years ago after constellations within each area. Because of precession and other factors, the zodiac signs no longer match actual constellation positions.

Morning Star: A planet that is above the eastern horizon at sunrise and less than 180° west of the Sun in right ascension.

Node: Either of the two points where a celestial

body's orbit intersects the ecliptic. **Ascending:** When the body is moving from south to north of the ecliptic. **Descending:** When the body is moving from north to south of the ecliptic.

Occultation (Occn.): When the Moon or a planet eclipses a star or planet.

Opposition: The Moon or a planet appears on the opposite side of the sky from the Sun (elongation 180°).

Perigee (Perig.): The point in the Moon's orbit that is closest to Earth.

Perihelion (Perih.): The point in a planet's orbit that is closest to the Sun.

Precession: The slowly changing position of the stars and equinoxes in the sky caused by a slight wobble as Earth rotates around its axis.

Right Ascension (R.A.): The celestial longitude of an object in the sky, measured eastward along the celestial equator in hours of time from the vernal equinox; analogous to longitude on Earth.

Solar Cycle: In the Julian calendar, a period of 28 years, at the end of which the days of the month return to the same days of the week.

Solstice, Summer: When the Sun reaches its greatest declination (23½°) north of the celestial equator, around June 21. **Winter:** When the Sun reaches its greatest declination (23½°) south of the celestial equator, around December 21.

Stationary (Stat.): The brief period of apparent halted movement of a planet against the background of the stars shortly before it appears to move backward/westward (retrograde motion) or forward/eastward (direct motion).

Sun Fast/Slow: When a sundial reading is ahead of (fast) or behind (slow) clock time.

Sunrise/Sunset: The visible rising and setting of the upper edge of the Sun's disk across the unobstructed horizon of an observer whose eyes are 15 feet above ground level.

Twilight: For definitions of civil, nautical, and astronomical twilight, **see page 90.** □□

CALENDAR

2012

January
S	M	T	W	T	F	S
1	2	3	4	5	6	7
8	9	10	11	12	13	14
15	16	17	18	19	20	21
22	23	24	25	26	27	28
29	30	31				

February
S	M	T	W	T	F	S
			1	2	3	4
5	6	7	8	9	10	11
12	13	14	15	16	17	18
19	20	21	22	23		
26	27	28	29			

March
S	M	T	W	T	F	S
				1	2	3
4	5	6	7	8	9	10
11	12	13	14	15	16	17
18	19	20	21	22	23	24
25	26	27	28	29	30	31

April
S	M	T	W	T	F	S
1	2	3	4	5	6	7
8	9	10	11	12	13	14
15	16	17	18	19	20	21
22	23	24	25	26	27	28
29	30					

May
S	M	T	W	T	F	S
		1	2	3	4	5
6	7	8	9	10	11	12
13	14	15	16	17	18	19
20	21	22	23	24	25	26
27	28	29	30	31		

June
S	M	T	W	T	F	S
					1	2
3	4	5	6	7	8	9
10	11	12	13	14	15	16
17	18	19	20	21	22	23
24	25	26	27	28	29	30

July
S	M	T	W	T	F	S
1	2	3	4	5	6	7
8	9	10	11	12	13	14
15	16	17	18	19	20	21
22	23	24	25	26	27	28
29	30	31				

August
S	M	T	W	T	F	S
			1	2	3	4
5	6	7	8	9	10	11
12	13	14	15	16	17	18
19	20	21	22	23	24	25
26	27	28	29	30	31	

September
S	M	T	W	T	F	S
						1
2	3	4	5	6	7	8
9	10	11	12	13	14	15
16	17	18	19	20	21	22
23	24	25	26	27	28	29
30						

October
S	M	T	W	T	F	S
	1	2	3	4	5	6
7	8	9	10	11	12	13
14	15	16	17	18	19	20
21	22	23	24	25	26	27
28	29	30	31			

November
S	M	T	W	T	F	S
				1	2	3
4	5	6	7	8	9	10
11	12	13	14	15	16	17
18	19	20	21	22	23	24
25	26	27	28	29	30	

December
S	M	T	W	T	F	S
						1
2	3	4	5	6	7	8
9	10	11	12	13	14	15
16	17	18	19	20	21	22
23	24	25	26	27	28	29
30	31					

2013

January
S	M	T	W	T	F	S
		1	2	3	4	5
6	7	8	9	10	11	12
13	14	15	16	17	18	19
20	21	22	23	24	25	26
27	28	29	30	31		

February
S	M	T	W	T	F	S
					1	2
3	4	5	6	7	8	9
10	11	12	13	14	15	16
17	18	19	20	21	22	23
24	25	26	27	28		

March
S	M	T	W	T	F	S
					1	2
3	4	5	6	7	8	9
10	11	12	13	14	15	16
17	18	19	20	21	22	23
24	25	26	27	28	29	30
31						

April
S	M	T	W	T	F	S
	1	2	3	4	5	6
7	8	9	10	11	12	13
14	15	16	17	18	19	20
21	22	23	24	25	26	27
28	29	30				

May
S	M	T	W	T	F	S
			1	2	3	4
5	6	7	8	9	10	11
12	13	14	15	16	17	18
19	20	21	22	23	24	25
26	27	28	29	30	31	

June
S	M	T	W	T	F	S
						1
2	3	4	5	6	7	8
9	10	11	12	13	14	15
16	17	18	19	20	21	22
23	24	25	26	27	28	29
30						

July
S	M	T	W	T	F	S
	1	2	3	4	5	6
7	8	9	10	11	12	13
14	15	16	17	18	19	20
21	22	23	24	25	26	27
28	29	30	31			

August
S	M	T	W	T	F	S
				1	2	3
4	5	6	7	8	9	10
11	12	13	14	15	16	17
18	19	20	21	22	23	24
25	26	27	28	29	30	31

September
S	M	T	W	T	F	S
1	2	3	4	5	6	7
8	9	10	11	12	13	14
15	16	17	18	19	20	21
22	23	24	25	26	27	28
29	30					

October
S	M	T	W	T	F	S
		1	2	3	4	5
6	7	8	9	10	11	12
13	14	15	16	17	18	19
20	21	22	23	24	25	26
27	28	29	30	31		

November
S	M	T	W	T	F	S
					1	2
3	4	5	6	7	8	9
10	11	12	13	14	15	16
17	18	19	20	21	22	23
24	25	26	27	28	29	30

December
S	M	T	W	T	F	S
1	2	3	4	5	6	7
8	9	10	11	12	13	14
15	16	17	18	19	20	21
22	23	24	25	26	27	28
29	30	31				

2014

January
S	M	T	W	T	F	S
			1	2	3	4
5	6	7	8	9	10	11
12	13	14	15	16	17	18
19	20	21	22	23	24	25
26	27	28	29	30	31	

February
S	M	T	W	T	F	S
						1
2	3	4	5	6	7	8
9	10	11	12	13	14	15
16	17	18	19	20	21	22
23	24	25	26	27	28	

March
S	M	T	W	T	F	S
						1
2	3	4	5	6	7	8
9	10	11	12	13	14	15
16	17	18	19	20	21	22
23	24	25	26	27	28	29
30	31					

April
S	M	T	W	T	F	S
		1	2	3	4	5
6	7	8	9	10	11	12
13	14	15	16	17	18	19
20	21	22	23	24	25	26
27	28	29	30			

May
S	M	T	W	T	F	S
				1	2	3
4	5	6	7	8	9	10
11	12	13	14	15	16	17
18	19	20	21	22	23	24
25	26	27	28	29	30	31

June
S	M	T	W	T	F	S
1	2	3	4	5	6	7
8	9	10	11	12	13	14
15	16	17	18	19	20	21
22	23	24	25	26	27	28
29	30					

July
S	M	T	W	T	F	S
		1	2	3	4	5
6	7	8	9	10	11	12
13	14	15	16	17	18	19
20	21	22	23	24	25	26
27	28	29	30	31		

August
S	M	T	W	T	F	S
					1	2
3	4	5	6	7	8	9
10	11	12	13	14	15	16
17	18	19	20	21	22	23
24	25	26	27	28	29	30
31						

September
S	M	T	W	T	F	S
	1	2	3	4	5	6
7	8	9	10	11	12	13
14	15	16	17	18	19	20
21	22	23	24	25	26	27
28	29	30				

October
S	M	T	W	T	F	S
			1	2	3	4
5	6	7	8	9	10	11
12	13	14	15	16	17	18
19	20	21	22	23	24	25
26	27	28	29	30	31	

November
S	M	T	W	T	F	S
						1
2	3	4	5	6	7	8
9	10	11	12	13	14	15
16	17	18	19	20	21	22
23	24	25	26	27	28	29
30						

December
S	M	T	W	T	F	S
	1	2	3	4	5	6
7	8	9	10	11	12	13
14	15	16	17	18	19	20
21	22	23	24	25	26	27
28	29	30	31			

How to Use This Almanac

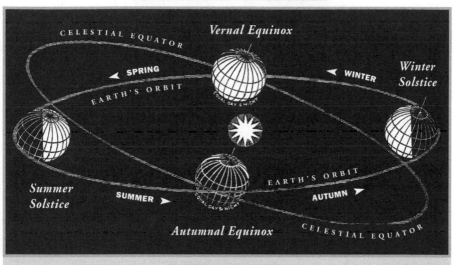

The Calendar Pages (104–131) are the heart of *The Old Farmer's Almanac.* They present sky sightings and astronomical data for the entire year and are what make this book a true almanac, a "calendar of the heavens." In essence, these pages are unchanged since 1792, when Robert B. Thomas published his first edition. The long columns of numbers and symbols reveal all of nature's precision, rhythm, and glory, providing an astronomical look at the year 2013.

Why We Have Seasons

THE SEASONS OF 2013

Vernal equinox .. March 20, 7:02 A.M. EDT   Autumnal equinox. . Sept. 22, 4:44 P.M. EDT

Summer solstice .. June 21, 1:04 A.M. EDT   Winter solstice . . . . Dec. 21, 12:11 P.M. EST

■ The seasons occur because as Earth revolves around the Sun, its axis remains tilted at 23.5 degrees from the perpendicular. This tilt causes different latitudes on Earth to receive varying amounts of sunlight throughout the year.

In the Northern Hemisphere, the summer solstice marks the beginning of summer and occurs when the North Pole is tilted toward the Sun. The winter solstice marks the beginning of winter and occurs when the North Pole is tilted away from the Sun.

The equinoxes occur when the hemispheres equally face the Sun. At this time, the Sun rises due east and sets due west. The vernal equinox marks the beginning of spring; the autumnal equinox marks the beginning of autumn.

In the Southern Hemisphere, the seasons are the reverse of those in the Northern Hemisphere. **(continued)**

CALENDAR

The Left-Hand Calendar Pages • 104–130

**C
A
L
E
N
D
A
R**

The **Left-Hand Calendar Pages** contain sky highlights, daily Sun and Moon rise and set times, the length of day, high tide times, the Moon's astronomical place and age, and more for Boston. Examples of how to calculate astronomical times for your location follow the sample month.

A SAMPLE MONTH

SKY WATCH ☆ *The box at the top of each Left-Hand Calendar Page describes the best times to view celestial highlights, including conjunctions, meteor showers, and planets. The dates on which select astronomical events occur appear on the Right-Hand Calendar Pages.*

1 2 3 4 5 6 7 8

Purchase these pages with times set to your zip code at MyLocalAlmanac.com.

Day of Year	Day of Month	Day of Week	☀ Rises h. m.	Rise Key	☀ Sets h. m.	Set Key	Length of Day h. m.	Sun Fast m.	Declination of Sun ° '	High Tide Times Boston	☾ Rises h. m.	Rise Key	☾ Sets h. m.	Set Key	☾ Place	☾ Age
1	1	Tu.	7:13	E	4:22	A	9 09	12	22 s.56	1½ 1½	8:56	D	9:19	D	LEO	19
2	2	W.	7:13	E	4:23	A	9 10	12	22 51	2 2¼	9:59	D	9:47	D	SEX	20
3	3	Th.	7:13	E	4:24	A	9 11	11	22 45	2¾ 3	11:04	E	10:15	C	LEO	21

1 To calculate the sunrise time for your locale: Note the Sun Rise Key letter on the chosen day. In the **Time Corrections** table on **page 234**, find your city or the city nearest you. Add or subtract the minutes that correspond to the Sun Rise Key letter to/from the sunrise time given for Boston.

E X A M P L E :

■ To calculate the time of sunrise in Denver, Colorado, on the first day of the month:

Sunrise, Boston, with Key letter E (above)	7:13 A.M. EST
Value of Key letter E for Denver (p. 234)	+ 7 minutes
Sunrise, Denver	7:20 A.M. MST

Use the same procedure with Boston's sunset time and the Sun Set Key letter value to calculate the time of sunset in your locale.

2 To calculate the length of day for your locale: Note the Sun Rise and Sun Set Key letters on the chosen day. In the **Time Corrections** table on **page 234**, find your city. Add or subtract the minutes that correspond to the Sun Set Key letter to/from Boston's length of day. *Reverse* the sign (minus to plus, or plus to minus) of the Sun Rise Key letter minutes. Add or subtract it to/from the first result.

E X A M P L E :

■ To calculate the length of day in Richmond, Virginia, on the first day of the month:

Length of day, Boston (above)	9h. 09m.
Sunset Key letter A for Richmond (p. 238)	+ 41m.
	9h. 50m.
Reverse sunrise Key letter E for Richmond (p. 238, +11 to −11)	− 11m.
Length of day, Richmond	9h. 39m.

3 Use the Sun Fast column to change sundial time to clock time. A sundial reads natural, or Sun, time, which is neither Standard nor Daylight time. To calculate clock time on a sundial in Boston, subtract the minutes given in this column; add the minutes when preceded by an asterisk [*]. To convert the time to your city, use Key letter C in the table on **page 234**.

ATTENTION, READERS: *All times given in this edition of the Almanac are for Boston, Massachusetts, and are in Eastern Standard Time (EST), except from 2:00 A.M., March 10, until 2:00 A.M., November 3, when Eastern Daylight Time (EDT) is given.*

E X A M P L E :

■ To change sundial time to clock time in Boston, or, for example, in Salem, Oregon:

Sundial reading (Boston or Salem)	12:00 noon
Subtract Sun Fast (p. 100)	– 12 minutes
Clock time, Boston	11:48 A.M. EST
Use Key letter C for Salem (p. 237)	+ 27 minutes
Clock time, Salem	12:15 P.M. PST

4 This column gives the degrees and minutes of the Sun from the celestial equator at noon EST or EDT.

5 This column gives the approximate times of high tides in Boston. For example, the first high tide occurs at 1:30 A.M. and the second occurs at 1:30 P.M. the same day. (A dash indicates that high tide occurs on or after midnight and is recorded on the next day.) Figures for calculating high tide times and heights for localities other than Boston are given in the **Tide Corrections** table on **page 232**.

6 To calculate the moonrise time for your locale: Note the Moon Rise Key letter on the chosen day. Find your city on **page 234**. Add or subtract the minutes that correspond to the Moon Rise Key letter to/from the moonrise time given for Boston. (A dash indicates that the moonrise occurs on or after midnight and is recorded on the next day.) Find the longitude of your city on **page 234**. Add a correction in minutes for your city's longitude (see table, above right).

–Beth Krommes

➡ Purchase the Left-Hand Calendar Pages with times set to your zip code at **MyLocalAlmanac.com**.

Longitude of city	Correction minutes
58°–76°	0
77°–89°	+1
90°–102°	+2
103°–115°	+3
116°–127°	+4
128°–141°	+5
142°–155°	+6

E X A M P L E :

■ To calculate the time of moonrise in Lansing, Michigan, on the first day of the month:

Moonrise, Boston, with Key letter D (p. 100)	8:56 P.M. EST
Value of Key letter D for Lansing (p. 236)	+ 54 minutes
Correction for Lansing longitude, 84° 33'	+ 1 minute
Moonrise, Lansing	9:51 P.M. EST

Use the same procedure with Boston's moonset time and the Moon Set Key letter value to calculate the time of moonset in your locale.

7 The Moon's Place is its *astronomical* placement in the heavens at midnight. Do not confuse this with the Moon's *astrological* place in the zodiac. All calculations in this Almanac are based on astronomy, not astrology, except for those on **pages 228–230**.

In addition to the 12 constellations of the zodiac, this column may indicate these: Auriga **(AUR)**, a northern constellation between Perseus and Gemini; Cetus **(CET)**, which lies south of the zodiac, just south of Pisces and Aries; Ophiuchus **(OPH)**, a constellation primarily north of the zodiac but with a small corner between Scorpius and Sagittarius; Orion **(ORI)**, a constellation whose northern limit first reaches the zodiac between Taurus and Gemini; and Sextans **(SEX)**, which lies south of the zodiac except for a corner that just touches it near Leo.

8 The last column gives the Moon's Age, which is the number of days since the previous new Moon. (The average length of the lunar month is 29.53 days.) **(continued)**

The Right-Hand Calendar Pages • 105–131

A SAMPLE MONTH

- Weather prediction rhyme.
- The bold letter is the Dominical Letter (from A to G), a traditional ecclesiastical designation for Sunday determined by the date on which the first Sunday falls. For 2013, the Dominical Letter is **F**.
- Sundays and special holy days generally appear in this font.
- Proverbs, poems, and adages generally appear in this font.
- Symbols for notable celestial events. (See opposite page for explanations.)
- Noteworthy historical events, folklore, and legends appear in this font.
- High tide heights, in feet, at Boston.
- Civil holidays and astronomical events appear in this font.
- Religious feasts generally appear in this font. A ᵀ indicates a major feast that the church has this year temporarily transferred to a date other than its usual one.

Day of Month	Day of Week	Dates, Feasts, Fasts, Aspects, Tide Heights	Weather
1	Tu.	New Year's Day • Holy Name • ⊕ AT PERIHELION • {9.3 / 10.0	*Flake-up*
2	W.	Georgia became 4th U.S. state, 1788 • Tides {9.4 / 9.8	*call!*
3	Th.	☾ ON EQ. • Miss Canada pageant canceled due to costs and changing times, 1992 • {9.5 / 9.6	*Sunny*
4	Fr.	St. Elizabeth Ann Seton • Circus performer General Tom Thumb born, 1838 • {9.6 / 9.4	*glows*
5	Sa.	Twelfth Night • Construction of Golden Gate Bridge began, San Francisco, 1933 • {9.8 / 9.2	*and*
6	**F**	Epiphany • ☌☿♇ • ☌♄☾ • Tides {10.1 / 9.1	*record*
7	M.	Distaff Day • Plough Monday • ☾ AT ☊ • Tides {10.4 / 9.2	*lows.*
8	Tu.	*What is new is pleasing and what is old is satisfying.*	*Whitening—*
9	W.	☾ RUNS LOW • Runner Tom Longboat died, 1949 • {11.2 / 9.8	*snow's*
10	Th.	☾ AT PERIG. • ☌♀☾ • ☌♇☾ • Tides {11.6 / 10.2	*lightening.*
11	Fr.	New ● • ☌☿☾ • Hudson Motor Car Co. unveiled first sedan-type car, 1913	*Northern*
12	Sa.	57°F, Helena, Mont., 1959 • Launch of *Deep Impact* spacecraft to study comet Tempel 1, 2005	*drifts*
13	**F**	1st S. af. Ep. • ☌♂☾ • Tides {11.9 / —	*and*
14	M.	☌♆☾ • Gideon Hawley became first state school superintendent in U.S. (for N.Y.), 1813	*southern*
15	Tu.	☾ ON EQ. • Super Bowl I played in Los Angeles, 1967	*spatters;*
16	W.	☌♀♇ • *Great spenders are bad lenders.* • {10.4 / 10.4	*latitude*
17	Th.	☌☉☾ • Ben Franklin born, 1706 • Meeting held to form Professional Golfers' Association, 1916	*is*
18	Fr.	☿ IN SUP. ☌ • First around-the-world, nonstop flight by jet concluded, 1957 • Tides {9.8 / 9.0	*all*
19	Sa.	Record-low barometer reading of 29.25" due to West Coast storm, 1988 • Tides {9.4 / 8.5	*that*
20	**F**	2nd S. af. Ep. • ☾ AT ☋ • Tides {9.2 / 8.2	*matters.*
21	M.	Martin Luther King Jr.'s Birthday (observed) • ☌♃☾ • U.S. patriot Ethan Allen born, 1738	*First*
22	Tu.	St. Vincent • ☾ AT APO. • Britain's Queen Victoria died, 1901 • Tides {9.2 / 8.1	*it*
23	W.	☾ RIDES HIGH • *Casablanca* movie copyrighted, 1943 • {9.4 / 8.3	*flurries,*
24	Th.	*Nothing shows a man's character more than what he laughs at.*	*then*
25	Fr.	Conversion of Paul • Hot drinks served on frozen Hudson River, N.J./N.Y.C., 1821	*it*
26	Sa.	Sts. Timothy & Titus • Full Wolf ○ • Tides {10.1 / 9.1	*sloshes;*

☞ **For explanations of Almanac terms, see the glossaries on pages 94, 134, and 231.**

Predicting Earthquakes

■ Note the dates in the **Right-Hand Calendar Pages** when the Moon rides high or runs low. The date of the high begins the most likely 5-day period of earthquakes in the Northern Hemisphere; the date of the low indicates a similar 5-day period in the Southern Hemisphere. Also noted are the 2 days each month when the Moon is on the celestial equator,

–Beth Krommes

indicating the most likely time for earthquakes in either hemisphere.

■ Throughout the **Right-Hand Calendar Pages** are groups of symbols that represent notable celestial events. The symbols and names of the principal planets and aspects are:

⊙	**Sun**	♆	**Neptune**
○●☾	**Moon**	♇	**Pluto**
☿	**Mercury**	☌	**Conjunction (on the same celestial longitude)**
♀	**Venus**		
⊕	**Earth**		
♂	**Mars**	☊	**Ascending node**
♃	**Jupiter**	☋	**Descending node**
♄	**Saturn**	☍	**Opposition (180 degrees from Sun)**
⛢	**Uranus**		

EXAMPLE:

☌♀☾ on the 10th day of the month (see opposite page) means that on that date a conjunction (☌) of Venus (♀) and the Moon (☾) occurs: They are aligned along the same celestial longitude and appear to be closest together in the sky.

EARTH AT PERIHELION AND APHELION

■ Perihelion: January 1, 2013. Earth will be 91,402,639 miles from the Sun. Aphelion: July 5, 2013. Earth will be 94,509,041 miles from the Sun.

2013 Calendar Highlights

MOVABLE RELIGIOUS OBSERVANCES

Septuagesima Sunday	**January 27**
Shrove Tuesday	**February 12**
Ash Wednesday	**February 13**
Palm Sunday	**March 24**
First day of Passover	**March 26**
Good Friday	**March 29**
Easter	**March 31**
Orthodox Easter	**May 5**
Rogation Sunday	**May 5**
Ascension Day	**May 9**
Whitsunday–Pentecost	**May 19**
Trinity Sunday	**May 26**
Corpus Christi	**June 2**
First day of Ramadan	**July 9**
Rosh Hashanah	**September 5**
Yom Kippur	**September 14**
First day of Chanukah	**November 28**
First Sunday of Advent	**December 1**

CHRONOLOGICAL CYCLES

Dominical Letter	**F**
Epact	**17**
Golden Number (Lunar Cycle)	**19**
Roman Indiction	**6**
Solar Cycle	**6**
Year of Julian Period	**6726**

–Beth Krommes

ERAS

Era	Year	Begins
Byzantine	**7522**	September 14
Jewish (A.M.)*	**5774**	September 5
Chinese (Lunar) [Year of the Snake]	**4711**	February 10
Roman (A.U.C.)	**2766**	January 14
Nabonassar	**2762**	April 20
Japanese	**2673**	January 1
Grecian (Seleucidae)	**2325**	September 14 (or October 14)
Indian (Saka)	**1935**	March 22
Diocletian	**1730**	September 11
Islamic (Hegira)	**1435**	November 4

**Year begins at sunset the evening before.*

THE ELEVENTH MONTH • 2012

SKY WATCH ☆ *Jupiter stands above the Moon on the 1st, rises soon after nightfall, remains out all night, and reaches its maximum brightness for the year by month's end. This year's total solar eclipse on the 13th is visible from only northern Australia and the South Pacific Ocean. The Moon hovers above low, dim Mars on the 16th and is very close to Jupiter in a beautiful conjunction on the 28th. Meanwhile, in the east before dawn, Venus rises 2½ hours before sunrise, hovers to the left of the crescent Moon on the 11th, and diminishes in brightness to its minimum by month's end. Venus and returning Saturn form a close predawn conjunction on the mornings of the 26th and 27th.*

◑	**Last Quarter**	6th day	19th hour	36th minute
●	**New Moon**	13th day	17th hour	8th minute
◐	**First Quarter**	20th day	9th hour	31st minute
○	**Full Moon**	28th day	9th hour	46th minute

After 2:00 A.M. on November 4, Eastern Standard Time is given.

Purchase these pages with times set to your zip code at MyLocalAlmanac.com.

Day of Year	Day of Month	Day of Week	☼ Rises h. m.	Rise Key	☼ Sets h. m.	Set Key	Length of Day h.	m.	Sun Fast m.	Declination of Sun °	'	High Tide Times Boston		☾ Rises h. m.	Rise Key	☾ Sets h. m.	Set Key	☾ Place	☾ Age
306	1	Th.	7:18	D	**5:36**	B	10	18	32	14 s.	42	1¼	**1½**	**7:28**	B	9:50	E	TAU	17
307	2	Fr.	7:19	D	**5:35**	B	10	16	32	15	01	2	**2**	**8:17**	B	10:40	E	TAU	18
308	3	Sa.	7:20	D	**5:34**	B	10	14	32	15	20	2¾	**2¾**	**9:10**	B	11:24	E	ORI	19
309	4	**G**	6:21	D	**4:33**	B	10	12	32	15	38	2½	**2½**	**9:07**	B	11:04	E	GEM	20
310	5	M.	6:23	E	**4:32**	B	10	09	32	15	56	3¼	**3¼**	**10:06**	C	11:40	E	GEM	21
311	6	Tu.	6:24	E	**4:30**	B	10	06	32	16	14	4	**4¼**	**11:08**	C	**12:13**	E	CAN	22
312	7	W.	6:25	E	**4:29**	B	10	04	32	16	32	4¾	**5**	—	–	**12:44**	D	CAN	23
313	8	Th.	6:26	E	**4:28**	B	10	02	32	16	49	5¾	**6**	12:12	D	**1:13**	D	LEO	24
314	9	Fr.	6:28	E	**4:27**	B	9	59	32	17	06	6½	**7**	1:18	D	**1:43**	D	LEO	25
315	10	Sa.	6:29	E	**4:26**	B	9	57	32	17	23	7½	**7¾**	2:26	E	**2:14**	C	VIR	26
316	11	**G**	6:30	E	**4:25**	B	9	55	32	17	39	8¼	**8¾**	3:38	E	**2:48**	C	VIR	27
317	12	M.	6:31	E	**4:24**	B	9	53	32	17	55	9	**9¾**	4:52	E	**3:27**	B	VIR	28
318	13	Tu.	6:33	E	**4:23**	B	9	50	31	18	11	10	**10½**	6:08	E	**4:13**	B	LIB	0
319	14	W.	6:34	E	**4:22**	B	9	48	31	18	27	10¾	**11½**	7:21	E	**5:07**	B	LIB	1
320	15	Th.	6:35	E	**4:21**	B	9	46	31	18	42	11½	—	8:30	E	**6:09**	B	OPH	2
321	16	Fr.	6:36	E	**4:20**	B	9	44	31	18	57	12¼	**12½**	9:29	E	**7:17**	B	SAG	3
322	17	Sa.	6:38	E	**4:20**	B	9	42	31	19	11	1¼	**1½**	10:20	E	**8:27**	C	SAG	4
323	18	**G**	6:39	E	**4:19**	B	9	40	30	19	25	2	**2¼**	11:02	E	**9:37**	C	SAG	5
324	19	M.	6:40	E	**4:18**	B	9	38	30	19	39	3	**3¼**	11:38	E	**10:45**	C	AQU	6
325	20	Tu.	6:41	E	**4:17**	B	9	36	30	19	53	4	**4½**	**12:09**	D	**11:50**	D	CAP	7
326	21	W.	6:42	E	**4:17**	B	9	35	30	20	06	5	**5½**	**12:38**	D	—	–	AQU	8
327	22	Th.	6:44	E	**4:16**	A	9	32	29	20	18	6	**6½**	**1:05**	C	12:54	D	PSC	9
328	23	Fr.	6:45	E	**4:15**	A	9	30	29	20	31	7	**7½**	**1:32**	C	1:55	D	PSC	10
329	24	Sa.	6:46	E	**4:15**	A	9	29	29	20	43	8	**8½**	**2:01**	C	2:56	E	PSC	11
330	25	**G**	6:47	E	**4:14**	A	9	27	29	20	54	8¾	**9¼**	**2:31**	B	3:55	E	PSC	12
331	26	M.	6:48	E	**4:14**	A	9	26	28	21	06	9½	**10**	**3:05**	B	4:54	E	ARI	13
332	27	Tu.	6:49	E	**4:13**	A	9	24	28	21	16	10	**10¾**	**3:43**	B	5:51	E	ARI	14
333	28	W.	6:50	E	**4:13**	A	9	23	28	21	27	10¾	**11¼**	**4:25**	B	6:45	E	TAU	15
334	29	Th.	6:52	E	**4:13**	A	9	21	27	21	37	11¼	12	**5:13**	B	7:36	E	TAU	16
335	30	Fr.	6:53	E	**4:12**	A	9	19	27	21 s.	46	**12**	—	**6:05**	B	8:23	E	TAU	17

 To use this page, see p. 100; for Key letters, see p. 234. ☞ **Bold = P.M.** ☞ Light = A.M.

NOVEMBER HATH 30 DAYS • 2012

E'en in these bleak November days
There's gladness for the heart that heeds. –Charles Dawson Shanly

Day of Month	Day of Week	Dates, Feasts, Fasts, Aspects, Tide Heights	Weather
1	Th.	All Saints' • ☾ AT APO. • ☌♃☾ • Tides {9.3 10.2	*Flurries*
2	Fr.	All Souls' • ☾ RIDES HIGH • Record-breaking piñata measured 60' long and 23'10.5" wide, 2008	*early,*
3	Sa.	Sadie Hawkins Day • *A good wife makes a good husband.*	*pristine*
4	G	23rd S. af. P. • Daylight Saving Time ends, 2:00 A.M. • {8.7 9.5	*and*
5	M.	Dominion Observatory time signal first broadcast by CBC Radio, 1939 • Tides {8.6 9.3	*pearly.*
6	Tu.	Election Day • ☿ STAT. • Composer Peter Ilyich Tchaikovsky died, 1893	*Winter's*
7	W.	In a cartoon by Thomas Nast, the elephant was first used to represent the Republican party, 1874 • {8.7 9.2	*come*
8	Th.	Black bears head to winter dens now. • Tides {9.0 9.3	*calling!*
9	Fr.	☾ ON EQ. • Jim Thorpe's Carlisle Indians beat Dwight Eisenhower's Army Cadets in football, 27–6, 1912	*Can*
10	Sa.	*Turkeys perched on trees and refusing to descend indicates snow.* • Tides {10.1 9.8	*we endure*
11	G	24th S. af. P. • Veterans Day • ☌♀☾ • ♆ STAT.	*so*
12	M.	Indian Summer • ☌♄☾ • Lobsters move to offshore waters. • Tides {11.4 10.5	*premature*
13	Tu.	New ● • Eclipse ☉ • ☾ AT ☊ • Tides {11.9 10.7	*a*
14	W.	☾ AT PERIG. • ☌☿☾ • Eugene Ely piloted first airplane take-off from a ship, 1910	*falling?*
15	Th.	Islamic New Year • ☾ RUNS LOW • Artist Georgia O'Keeffe born, 1887 • {12.4 —	*Some*
16	Fr.	☌♂☾ • ☌♇☾ • Crab apples are ripe now. • {10.8 12.2	*may*
17	Sa.	St. Hugh of Lincoln • ☿ IN INF. ☌ • Tides {10.6 11.9	*find*
18	G	25th S. af. P. • Physicist Niels Bohr died, 1962 • Tides {10.3 11.3	*this*
19	M.	Skunks hibernate now. • "Boss" Tweed sentenced to 12 years in prison, N.Y.C., 1873 • {10.1 10.7	*trend*
20	Tu.	☌♆☾ • 18" snow, Paradise, Mich., 1987	*distressing—*
21	W.	☾ ON EQ. • First circumnavigation of N. America in single voyage, by HMCS *Labrador,* 1954	*others*
22	Th.	Thanksgiving Day • *Feather by feather, the goose is plucked.* • Tides {9.7 9.3	*bend*
23	Fr.	St. Clement • ☌⛢☾ • Jukebox debuted, San Francisco, 1889 • {9.7 9.1	*to*
24	Sa.	Joseph Glidden granted patent for barbed wire fencing, 1874	*say a*
25	G	26th S. af. P. • René Lévesque became premier of Quebec, 1976 • {10.0 9.1	*blessing*
26	M.	☿ STAT. • Kappa Alpha Society founded, Union College, Schenectady, N.Y., 1825 • {10.1 9.1	*over*
27	Tu.	☾ AT ☋ • ☌♂♇ • ☌♀♄ • Snowstorm with lightning, eastern S.Dak., 1983	*sage*
28	W.	Full Beaver ○ • Eclipse ☾ • ☾ AT APO. • ☌♃☾ • {10.2 9.1	*and*
29	Th.	☾ RIDES HIGH • Megamouth shark caught, Catalina Island, Calif., 1984 • Tides {10.2 9.0	*onion*
30	Fr.	St. Andrew • *The earth does not shake when the flea coughs.* • Tides {10.2 —	*dressing.*

He that is of a merry heart hath a continual feast. –Proverbs 15:15

Farmer's Calendar

■ With my garden harvested and much of the crop squirreled away in the root cellar, I feel a deep sense of satisfaction knowing that I will have a safe and healthy supply of vegetables and fruit throughout most of the winter. These days, with fresh produce available year-round at the supermarket, root cellars are not usually a necessity, but in years past, they were as essential to a home as a refrigerator is today.

A typical root cellar was a room in the north corner of the basement that was vented to the outside to keep the cellar air cool and circulating. Fruit, vegetables, and other foods that needed chilly temperatures were stored inside. Shelves were often stocked with milk, butter, jars of preserves, and crocks of salt pork, while smoked meat hung from hooks in the ceiling. Barrels of homemade beer, cider, and wine were frequently kept there, too. Gardeners used the area to rest potted plants, such as geraniums, over the winter, and to force spring bulbs into early bloom.

My storage is limited to mostly root crops and a bushel or two of 'Baldwin' apples. Vines of green tomatoes hang from the ceiling to ripen over several weeks. My produce usually lasts into early spring, but if it falls a little short, I can take another route—the one to the supermarket, 15 minutes away.

DECEMBER

THE TWELFTH MONTH • 2012

SKY WATCH ☆ *Venus continues to drop ever closer to the sunrise glare; by year's end, it is very low and completes its magnificent apparition. Mercury dangles below Venus in the month's first half. Jupiter reaches its closest point to Earth on the 1st and then its opposition, in Taurus, on the 2nd, dominating the sky all night with a blazing magnitude –2.8. The Moon is absent on the 13th; it will not interfere with the intense Geminid meteor shower beginning at 8:00 P.M. that night. The Moon and Jupiter form a strikingly close holiday conjunction on the 25th, with the orange star Aldebaran dangling below them. The earliest winter since 1896 arrives with the solstice at 6:12 A.M. on the 21st.*

◑ **Last Quarter**	6th day	10th hour	31st minute
● **New Moon**	13th day	3rd hour	42nd minute
◐ **First Quarter**	20th day	0 hour	19th minute
○ **Full Moon**	28th day	5th hour	21st minute

All times are given in Eastern Standard Time.

Purchase these pages with times set to your zip code at MyLocalAlmanac.com.

Day of Year	Day of Month	Day of Week	☼ Rises h. m.	Rise Key	☼ Sets h. m.	Set Key	Length of Day h.	m.	Sun Fast m.	Declination of Sun °	'	High Tide Times Boston		☾ Rises h. m.	Rise Key	☾ Sets h. m.	Set Key	☾ Place	☾ Age
336	1	Sa.	6:54	E	**4:12**	A	9	18	26	21 s.	56	12½	**12¾**	**7:00**	B	9:04	E	GEM	18
337	2	**G**	6:55	E	**4:12**	A	9	17	26	22	04	1¼	**1¼**	**7:59**	C	9:41	E	GEM	19
338	3	M.	6:56	E	**4:12**	A	9	16	26	22	13	2	**2**	**8:59**	C	10:15	E	CAN	20
339	4	Tu.	6:57	E	**4:11**	A	9	14	25	22	20	2¾	**2¾**	**10:00**	C	10:46	D	CAN	21
340	5	W.	6:58	E	**4:11**	A	9	13	25	22	28	3½	**3½**	**11:03**	D	11:14	D	LEO	22
341	6	Th.	6:59	E	**4:11**	A	9	12	24	22	35	4¼	**4½**	—	–	11:43	D	SEX	23
342	7	Fr.	7:00	E	**4:11**	A	9	11	24	22	42	5	**5½**	12:09	D	**12:12**	C	LEO	24
343	8	Sa.	7:01	E	**4:11**	A	9	10	24	22	48	6	**6¼**	1:16	E	**12:43**	C	VIR	25
344	9	**G**	7:01	E	**4:11**	A	9	10	23	22	53	6¾	**7¼**	2:26	E	**1:18**	B	VIR	26
345	10	M.	7:02	E	**4:11**	A	9	09	23	22	59	7¾	**8¼**	3:39	E	**1:59**	B	VIR	27
346	11	Tu.	7:03	E	**4:11**	A	9	08	22	23	03	8½	**9¼**	4:53	E	**2:48**	B	LIB	28
347	12	W.	7:04	E	**4:11**	A	9	07	22	23	08	9½	**10¼**	6:04	E	**3:46**	B	SCO	29
348	13	Th.	7:05	E	**4:12**	A	9	07	21	23	12	10½	**11**	7:10	E	**4:51**	B	OPH	0
349	14	Fr.	7:05	E	**4:12**	A	9	07	21	23	15	11¼	—	8:07	E	**6:03**	C	SAG	1
350	15	Sa.	7:06	E	**4:12**	A	9	06	20	23	18	12	**12¼**	8:54	E	**7:16**	C	SAG	2
351	16	**G**	7:07	E	**4:12**	A	9	05	20	23	20	1	**1**	9:35	E	**8:27**	C	CAP	3
352	17	M.	7:08	E	**4:13**	A	9	05	19	23	22	1¾	**2**	10:09	D	**9:37**	D	AQU	4
353	18	Tu.	7:08	E	**4:13**	A	9	05	19	23	24	2¾	**3**	10:40	D	**10:43**	D	AQU	5
354	19	W.	7:09	E	**4:14**	A	9	05	18	23	25	3½	**4**	11:08	C	**11:46**	D	PSC	6
355	20	Th.	7:09	E	**4:14**	A	9	05	18	23	26	4½	**5**	11:36	C	—	–	PSC	7
356	21	Fr.	7:10	E	**4:14**	A	9	04	17	23	26	5½	**6**	**12:04**	C	12:48	E	PSC	8
357	22	Sa.	7:10	E	**4:15**	A	9	05	17	23	25	6½	**7**	**12:34**	B	1:48	E	PSC	9
358	23	**G**	7:11	E	**4:16**	A	9	05	16	23	24	7¼	**8**	**1:06**	B	2:47	E	ARI	10
359	24	M.	7:11	E	**4:16**	A	9	05	16	23	23	8¼	**8¾**	**1:42**	B	3:45	E	ARI	11
360	25	Tu.	7:11	E	**4:17**	A	9	06	15	23	21	9	**9½**	**2:23**	B	4:40	E	TAU	12
361	26	W.	7:12	E	**4:18**	A	9	06	15	23	19	9¾	**10¼**	**3:09**	B	5:32	E	TAU	13
362	27	Th.	7:12	E	**4:18**	A	9	06	14	23	16	10¼	**11**	**3:59**	B	6:20	E	TAU	14
363	28	Fr.	7:12	E	**4:19**	A	9	07	14	23	13	11	**11½**	**4:54**	B	7:04	E	GEM	15
364	29	Sa.	7:13	E	**4:20**	A	9	07	13	23	10	11¾	—	**5:52**	B	7:43	E	GEM	16
365	30	**G**	7:13	E	**4:20**	A	9	07	13	23	06	12¼	**12¼**	**6:52**	C	8:18	E	CAN	17
366	31	M.	7:13	E	**4:21**	A	9	08	13	23 s.	01	12¾	**1**	**7:53**	C	8:49	E	CAN	18

 To use this page, see p. 100; for Key letters, see p. 234. ☞ **Bold = P.M.** ☞ Light = A.M.

DECEMBER HATH 31 DAYS • 2012

Like mimic meteors the snow
In silence out of heaven sifts. –Frank Dempster Sherman

Day of Month	Day of Week	Dates, Feasts, Fasts, Aspects, Tide Heights	Weather
1	Sa.	First drive-in gasoline service station opened, Pittsburgh, Pa. 1913 • Tides {9.0 / 10.1	*Roads*
2	G	**1st S. of Advent** • ♃ at ☍ • Tides {8.9 / 9.9	*are*
3	M.	Race car driver Bobby Allison born, 1937 • Polar bear cub born, Toledo Zoo, Ohio, 2009 • {8.9 / 9.7	*icy,*
4	Tu.	☿ Gr. Elong. (21° West) • 20" snow, New Haven, Conn., 1786 • Tides {8.9 / 9.5	*driving*
5	W.	*Thunder in December presages fine weather.* • Tides {9.0 / 9.4	*dicey.*
6	Th.	**St. Nicholas** • ☾ on Eq. • Ship explosion devastated Halifax, N.S., 1917 • {9.2 / 9.2	*Mild*
7	Fr.	**St. Ambrose** • **National Pearl Harbor Remembrance Day** • "Blue Marble" Earth photo taken, 1972	*but*
8	Sa.	92°F, Ojai, Calif., 1938 • Element 111, roentgenium, first created, 1994 • {9.9 / 9.3	*sopping;*
9	G	**First day of Chanukah** • Marguerite d'Youville became first Canadian-born saint, 1990	*better*
10	M.	**St. Eulalia** • ☌♄☾ • Winterberry fruit especially showy now. • {10.9 / 9.8	*do*
11	Tu.	☾ at ☊ • ☌☿☾ • ☌♀☾ • Boll weevil monument up, Enterprise, Ala., 1919	*your*
12	W.	**Our Lady of Guadalupe** • ☾ runs low • ☾ at perig. • Tides {11.9 / 10.4	*holiday*
13	Th.	**St. Lucia** • **New** ● • ⛢ stat. • Tides {12.2 / 10.6	*shopping.*
14	Fr.	Halcyon Days begin. • ☌♇☾ • Millau Viaduct, highest bridge, officially opened, France, 2004	*Rainy,*
15	Sa.	☌♂☾ • *Put up with small annoyances to gain great results.* • Tides {10.7 / 12.2	*snowy,*
16	G	**3rd S. of Advent** • Students' satellite *STARSHINE-2* deployed, 2001	*cold*
17	M.	*The Nutcracker* ballet premiered, St. Petersburg, Russia, 1892	*and*
18	Tu.	☌♆☾ • N.J. became third state to ratify the U.S. Constitution, 1787 • Tides {10.2 / 10.5	*blowy;*
19	W.	Ember Day • ☾ on Eq. • Beware the Pogonip. • Writer Emily Brontë died, 1848	*look*
20	Th.	☌⛢☾ • 24-lb. 8-oz. horse-eye jack caught, Miami, Fla., 1982 • Tides {9.7 / 9.2	*out,*
21	Fr.	**St. Thomas** • Ember Day • **Winter Solstice** • Tides {9.6 / 8.8	*belowy!*
22	Sa.	Ember Day • First Lady Claudia "Lady Bird" Johnson born, 1912 • {9.5 / 8.5	*Yow!*
23	G	**4th S. of Advent** • *A lucky dog is rarer than a white crow.* • {9.5 / 8.4	*Santa's*
24	M.	☾ at ☋ • 63° to –21°F in 12 hours, Fairfield, Mont., 1924 • Tides {9.6 / 8.4	*driving*
25	Tu.	**Christmas** • ☾ at apo. • ☌♃☾ • Tides {9.7 / 8.6	*a plow!*
26	W.	**St. Stephen** • **Boxing Day (Canada)** • **First day of Kwanzaa** • ☾ rides high	*Feeling*
27	Th.	**St. John** • "Father of Aviation" Sir George Cayley born, 1773 • Tides {10.0 / 8.8	*yuckier?*
28	Fr.	**Holy Innocents** • **Full Cold** ○ • Snowstorm caused 1,000 traffic accidents, Mich., 1987	*Hope*
29	Sa.	Ashrita Furman stood on a Swiss exercise ball for 3 hours, 38 minutes, 30 seconds, 2003 • Tides {10.2 / —	*'13*
30	G	**1st S. af. Ch.** • ☌♇☉ • U.S. pres. Rutherford B. Hayes married Lucy Webb, 1852	*is*
31	M.	**St. Sylvester** • *All happiness is in the mind.* • {9.2 / 10.1	*luckier!*

Farmer's Calendar

■ Turning the calendar to December evokes cherished childhood memories of cutting the yearly Christmas tree from the woodlot behind our farmhouse. Sometimes, we spooked a deer on our way into the woods, adding to the excitement. I remember how proud I was on the day when my dad let me cut the tree for the first time. He pulled back hard on the branches so that the blade wouldn't bind, while I worked the bow saw back and forth with all the strength that a 6-year-old could muster.

The balsams and spruces that we harvested back then hardly resembled the well-shaped, plantation-grown trees that are commonplace today. Most of our trees had a sparse side that we hid against the wall. To fill a gap, we often had to drill a hole in the trunk and insert a branch into it. The huge spaces between the whorls of limbs were ideal for displaying the pinecones that we had gathered from the yard, the garlands of hand-strung popcorn and cranberries, and the dozens of fragile ornaments that had been passed down from one generation to the next.

My family still harvests Christmas trees from the same woodlot. It's a bit shadier now, so the trees grow with even bigger spaces between the branches. But that's okay—our collection of decorations has increased over the years as well.

SKY WATCH ☆ *The year begins with our two nearest neighbors, Venus and Mars, both vanishing into morning and evening twilight, respectively. This leaves brilliant Jupiter as the sole luminary, up in the east at nightfall at a dazzling magnitude –2.7. Having just enjoyed its opposition a month ago, Jupiter will now fade throughout the year and return to its current brilliance only in December. Saturn, in Libra, at a bright magnitude 0.6, doesn't rise until 2:00 A.M. Earth reaches perihelion on the 1st. The crescent Moon hovers to the right of Uranus, visible with binoculars, on the 16th. The month's premier conjunction is the strikingly close meeting of the Moon and Jupiter on the 21st.*

◖ Last Quarter	4th day	22nd hour	58th minute
● New Moon	11th day	14th hour	44th minute
◑ First Quarter	18th day	18th hour	45th minute
○ Full Moon	26th day	23rd hour	38th minute

All times are given in Eastern Standard Time.

Purchase these pages with times set to your zip code at MyLocalAlmanac.com.

Day of Year	Day of Month	Day of Week	Rises h. m.	Rise Key	Sets h. m.	Set Key	Length of Day h. m.	Sun Fast m.	Declination of Sun ° '	High Tide Times Boston		Rises h. m.	Rise Key	Sets h. m.	Set Key	Place	Age
1	1	Tu.	7:13	E	4:22	A	9 09	12	22 s.56	1½	1½	8:56	D	9:19	D	LEO	19
2	2	W.	7:13	E	4:23	A	9 10	12	22 51	2	2¼	9:59	D	9:47	D	SEX	20
3	3	Th.	7:13	E	4:24	A	9 11	11	22 45	2¾	3	11:04	E	10:15	C	LEO	21
4	4	Fr.	7:13	E	4:25	A	9 12	11	22 38	3½	4	—	-	10:45	C	VIR	22
5	5	Sa.	7:13	E	4:26	A	9 13	10	22 31	4½	5	12:11	E	11:17	C	VIR	23
6	6	**F**	7:13	E	4:27	A	9 14	10	22 24	5¼	6	1:20	E	11:54	B	VIR	24
7	7	M.	7:13	E	4:28	A	9 15	9	22 16	6¼	7	2:31	E	**12:37**	B	LIB	25
8	8	Tu.	7:13	E	4:29	A	9 16	9	22 08	7¼	8	3:41	E	**1:28**	B	LIB	26
9	9	W.	7:12	E	4:30	A	9 18	9	22 00	8¼	9	4:48	E	**2:27**	B	OPH	27
10	10	Th.	7:12	E	4:31	A	9 19	8	21 51	9¼	10	5:49	E	**3:35**	B	SAG	28
11	11	Fr.	7:12	E	4:32	A	9 20	8	21 41	10¼	10¾	6:41	E	**4:47**	C	SAG	0
12	12	Sa.	7:11	E	4:33	A	9 22	7	21 31	11	11¾	7:26	E	**6:01**	C	SAG	1
13	13	**F**	7:11	E	4:34	A	9 23	7	21 21	12	—	8:04	E	**7:13**	C	AQU	2
14	14	M.	7:11	E	4:36	A	9 25	7	21 10	12½	12¾	8:38	D	**8:23**	D	AQU	3
15	15	Tu.	7:10	E	4:37	A	9 27	6	20 59	1½	1¾	9:08	D	**9:30**	D	AQU	4
16	16	W.	7:10	E	4:38	A	9 28	6	20 48	2¼	2½	9:37	C	**10:34**	E	PSC	5
17	17	Th.	7:09	E	4:39	A	9 30	6	20 36	3	3½	10:06	C	**11:37**	E	PSC	6
18	18	Fr.	7:09	E	4:40	A	9 31	5	20 24	4	4¼	10:36	C	—	-	PSC	7
19	19	Sa.	7:08	E	4:42	B	9 34	5	20 11	4¾	5¼	11:07	B	**12:37**	E	ARI	8
20	20	**F**	7:07	E	4:43	B	9 36	5	19 58	5¾	6¼	11:42	B	**1:36**	E	ARI	9
21	21	M.	7:07	E	4:44	B	9 37	4	19 44	6½	7¼	**12:21**	B	**2:32**	E	TAU	10
22	22	Tu.	7:06	E	4:45	B	9 39	4	19 31	7½	8¼	**1:05**	B	**3:26**	E	TAU	11
23	23	W.	7:05	E	4:47	B	9 42	4	19 17	8½	9	**1:53**	B	**4:15**	E	TAU	12
24	24	Th.	7:04	E	4:48	B	9 44	4	19 02	9¼	9¾	**2:47**	B	**5:01**	E	ORI	13
25	25	Fr.	7:04	E	4:49	B	9 45	3	18 47	10	10½	**3:44**	B	**5:42**	E	GEM	14
26	26	Sa.	7:03	E	4:50	B	9 47	3	18 32	10½	11	**4:43**	C	**6:19**	E	GEM	15
27	27	**F**	7:02	E	4:52	B	9 50	3	18 17	11¼	11¾	**5:45**	C	**6:52**	E	CAN	16
28	28	M.	7:01	E	4:53	B	9 52	3	18 01	11¾	—	**6:48**	C	**7:23**	D	LEO	17
29	29	Tu.	7:00	E	4:54	B	9 54	3	17 44	12¼	12½	**7:52**	D	**7:52**	D	SEX	18
30	30	W.	6:59	E	4:56	B	9 57	3	17 28	1	1¼	**8:57**	D	**8:20**	C	LEO	19
31	31	Th.	6:58	E	4:57	B	9 59	2	17 s.11	1¾	2	**10:03**	E	**8:50**	C	VIR	20

To use this page, see p. 100; for Key letters, see p. 234. ☞ **Bold** = P.M. ☞ Light = A.M. **2013**

JANUARY HATH 31 DAYS • 2013

The cherished fields
Put on their winter robe of purest white. –James Thomson

Day of Month	Day of Week	Dates, Feasts, Fasts, Aspects, Tide Heights	Weather
1	Tu.	New Year's Day • **Holy Name** • ⊕ at perihelion • {9.3 / 10.0}	*Flake-up*
2	W.	Georgia became 4th U.S. state, 1788 • Tides {9.4 / 9.8}	*call!*
3	Th.	☾ on eq. • Miss Canada pageant canceled due to costs and changing times, 1992 • {9.5 / 9.6}	*Sunny*
4	Fr.	**St. Elizabeth Ann Seton** • Circus performer General Tom Thumb born, 1838 • {9.6 / 9.4}	*glows*
5	Sa.	Twelfth Night • Construction of Golden Gate Bridge began, San Francisco, 1933 • {9.8 / 9.2}	*and*
6	**F**	**Epiphany** • ☌☿♇ • ☌♄☾ • Tides {10.1 / 9.1}	*record*
7	M.	Distaff Day • Plough Monday • ☾ at ☊ • Tides {10.4 / 9.2}	*lows.*
8	Tu.	*What is new is pleasing and what is old is satisfying.*	*Whitening—*
9	W.	☾ runs low • Runner Tom Longboat died, 1949 • {11.2 / 9.8}	*snow's*
10	Th.	☾ at perig. • ☌♀☾ • ☌♇☾ • Tides {11.6 / 10.2}	*lightening.*
11	Fr.	New ● • ☌☿☾ • Hudson Motor Car Co. unveiled first sedan-type car, 1913	*Northern*
12	Sa.	57°F, Helena, Mont., 1959 • Launch of *Deep Impact* spacecraft to study comet Tempel 1, 2005	*drifts*
13	**F**	**1st S. af. Ep.** • ☌♂☾ • Tides {11.9 / —}	*and*
14	M.	☌♆☾ • Gideon Hawley became first state school superintendent in U.S. (for N.Y.), 1813	*southern*
15	Tu.	☾ on eq. • Super Bowl I played in Los Angeles, 1967	*spatters;*
16	W.	☌♀♇ • *Great spenders are bad lenders.* • {10.4 / 10.4}	*latitude*
17	Th.	☌⛢☾ • Ben Franklin born, 1706 • Meeting held to form Professional Golfers' Association, 1916	*is*
18	Fr.	☿ in sup. ☌ • First around-the-world, nonstop flight by jet concluded, 1957 • Tides {9.8 / 9.0}	*all*
19	Sa.	Record-low barometer reading of 29.25" due to West Coast storm, 1988 • Tides {9.4 / 8.5}	*that*
20	**F**	**2nd S. af. Ep.** • ☾ at ☋ • Tides {9.2 / 8.2}	*matters.*
21	M.	**Martin Luther King Jr.'s Birthday (observed)** • ☌♃☾ • U.S. patriot Ethan Allen born, 1738	*First*
22	Tu.	**St. Vincent** • ☾ at apo. • Britain's Queen Victoria died, 1901 • Tides {9.2 / 8.1}	*it*
23	W.	☾ rides high • *Casablanca* movie copyrighted, 1943 • {9.4 / 8.3}	*flurries,*
24	Th.	*Nothing shows a man's character more than what he laughs at.*	*then*
25	Fr.	**Conversion of Paul** • Hot drinks served on frozen Hudson River, N.J./N.Y.C., 1821	*it*
26	Sa.	**Sts. Timothy & Titus** • **Full Wolf** ○ • Tides {10.1 / 9.1}	*sloshes;*
27	**F**	**Septuagesima** • National Geographic Society incorporated, 1888	*trade*
28	M.	**St. Thomas Aquinas** • 8-lb. 12-oz. redeye bass caught in Apalachicola River, Fla., 1995	*your*
29	Tu.	Raccoons mate now. • Poet Robert Frost died, 1963 • {9.6 / 10.4}	*snowshoes*
30	W.	☾ on eq. • ♃ stat. • Escaped buffalo found staring into dressing-room mirror, Grand Rapids, S.Dak., 2005	*for*
31	Th.	*Stars are not seen by sunshine.* • Tides {10.0 / 10.1}	*galoshes!*

Farmer's Calendar

■ In many ways, plowing snow is hard work. The hours are unpredictable, and breakdowns or getting stuck are always possibilities. Still, I can't think of a better way to enjoy a midwinter's night. The cold is bone-chilling and the snow is mounting up at the rate of 2 inches per hour, but I'm warm and secure in the cab of my plow truck. I usually wait until the storm is over so that I have to plow my customers only once, which saves them money, but this storm is a blockbuster and I'm afraid that if I wait, my pickup won't be able to handle the heavy, wet snow.

Except for the occasional plow truck that I meet on the road, I have this wonderful world of white to myself. The night is peaceful and beautiful. I'm mesmerized by the reflection of my rotating yellow beacon on the fast-falling flakes and by the hypnotic, rhythmic slapping of the wiper blades. Snow-laden tree branches bend over the road, forming an enticing tunnel. It's almost 1:00 A.M., and I'm plowing the last driveway on my route. The snow should end by daybreak, so I'll be able to catch a few hours of sleep before starting again. The landscape will take on a new charm in the bright morning sun, but there will be cars on the road and people out shoveling and snowblowing. Then, it will be time to share my world with everyone else.

SKY WATCH ☆ *The Moon rises below Saturn, soon after midnight, on the 3rd; the pair remains well placed until dawn. Mercury, Mars, and Neptune stand very close together from the 3rd to the 7th but are extremely low as they closely follow the setting Sun. The Moon hovers to the right of Jupiter, now slightly fading to magnitude –2.4, on the 17th. On the 18th, the Moon sits to the left of Jupiter. The Moon passes very close to Virgo's bright blue star Spica on the 28th. The pair rises at around 10:00 P.M. and is nicely clear of obstructions after 11:00 P.M. By month's end, each successive day is 3 to 4 minutes longer in most of the lower United States, 4 to 5 minutes longer in most of Canada, and 6 to 7 minutes longer in Alaska.*

◑	**Last Quarter**	3rd day	8th hour	56th minute
●	**New Moon**	10th day	2nd hour	20th minute
◐	**First Quarter**	17th day	15th hour	31st minute
○	**Full Moon**	25th day	15th hour	26th minute

All times are given in Eastern Standard Time.

Purchase these pages with times set to your zip code at MyLocalAlmanac.com.

Day of Year	Day of Month	Day of Week	☀ Rises h. m.	Rise Key	☀ Sets h. m.	Set Key	Length of Day h. m.	Sun Fast m.	Declination of Sun ° ′	High Tide Times Boston		☽ Rises h. m.	Rise Key	☽ Sets h. m.	Set Key	☽ Place	☽ Age
32	1	Fr.	6:57	E	4:58	B	10 01	2	16 s.54	2¼	2¾	11:10	E	9:21	C	VIR	21
33	2	Sa.	6:56	E	4:59	B	10 03	2	16 37	3	3½	—	–	9:55	B	VIR	22
34	3	F	6:55	E	5:01	B	10 06	2	16 19	4	4½	12:19	E	10:35	B	LIB	23
35	4	M.	6:54	E	5:02	B	10 08	2	16 01	5	5½	1:27	E	11:21	B	LIB	24
36	5	Tu.	6:53	D	5:03	B	10 10	2	15 43	6	6¾	2:33	E	12:15	B	OPH	25
37	6	W.	6:51	D	5:05	B	10 14	2	15 24	7	7¾	3:34	E	1:17	B	OPH	26
38	7	Th.	6:50	D	5:06	B	10 16	2	15 05	8	8¾	4:29	E	2:25	B	SAG	27
39	8	Fr.	6:49	D	5:07	B	10 18	2	14 46	9	9¾	5:16	E	3:36	C	SAG	28
40	9	Sa.	6:48	D	5:09	B	10 21	2	14 27	10	10½	5:57	E	4:48	C	CAP	29
41	10	F	6:46	D	5:10	B	10 24	2	14 07	11	11½	6:33	D	5:59	D	CAP	0
42	11	M.	6:45	D	5:11	B	10 26	2	13 48	11¾	—	7:06	D	7:08	D	AQU	1
43	12	Tu.	6:44	D	5:13	B	10 29	2	13 28	12¼	12½	7:36	C	8:15	D	PSC	2
44	13	W.	6:43	D	5:14	B	10 31	2	13 07	1	1¼	8:06	C	9:20	E	PSC	3
45	14	Th.	6:41	D	5:15	B	10 34	2	12 47	1¾	2	8:36	C	10:23	E	PSC	4
46	15	Fr.	6:40	D	5:16	B	10 36	2	12 26	2½	2¾	9:07	B	11:23	E	PSC	5
47	16	Sa.	6:38	D	5:18	B	10 40	2	12 06	3¼	3¾	9:41	B	—	–	ARI	6
48	17	F	6:37	D	5:19	B	10 42	2	11 45	4	4½	10:19	E	12:21	E	ARI	7
49	18	M.	6:36	D	5:20	B	10 44	2	11 23	5	5½	11:01	B	1:16	E	TAU	8
50	19	Tu.	6:34	D	5:21	B	10 47	2	11 02	5¾	6½	11:47	B	2:07	E	TAU	9
51	20	W.	6:33	D	5:23	B	10 50	2	10 40	6¾	7½	12:38	B	2:55	E	ORI	10
52	21	Th.	6:31	D	5:24	B	10 53	2	10 19	7¾	8½	1:33	B	3:37	E	GEM	11
53	22	Fr.	6:30	D	5:25	B	10 55	2	9 57	8½	9¼	2:32	C	4:16	E	GEM	12
54	23	Sa.	6:28	D	5:26	B	10 58	3	9 35	9½	10	3:33	C	4:51	E	CAN	13
55	24	F	6:27	D	5:28	B	11 01	3	9 13	10	10½	4:36	C	5:23	E	CAN	14
56	25	M.	6:25	D	5:29	C	11 04	3	8 50	10¾	11¼	5:40	D	5:53	D	LEO	15
57	26	Tu.	6:23	D	5:30	C	11 07	3	8 28	11½	11¾	6:46	D	6:23	D	SEX	16
58	27	W.	6:22	D	5:31	C	11 09	3	8 05	12¼	—	7:53	E	6:53	C	VIR	17
59	28	Th.	6:20	D	5:33	C	11 13	3	7 s.42	12½	12¾	9:01	E	7:24	C	VIR	18

FEBRUARY HATH 28 DAYS • 2013

Valentine, the day when birds of kind
Their paramours with mutual chirpings find. –John Gay

Day of Month	Day of Week	Dates, Feasts, Fasts, Aspects, Tide Heights	Weather
1	Fr.	St. Brigid • Multiday storm left ice up to 4" thick, Tex. to Pa., 1951 • Tides {10.1 9.8	*A week*
2	Sa.	Candlemas • Groundhog Day • New Grand Central Terminal train station opened, N.Y.C., 1913	*of*
3	F	**Sexagesima** • ☾ at ☊ • ☌♄☾ • Tides {10.2 9.2	*snow*
4	M.	☌♂♆ • Radium E first synthetically produced radioactive substance, 1936	*keeps*
5	Tu.	St. Agatha • ☾ runs low • *There are spots even on the Sun.* • {10.4 9.0	*groundhogs*
6	W.	☌☿♆ • –10.3°F, Boston, Mass., 1855 • {10.6 9.2	*below.*
7	Th.	☾ at perig. • ☌♇☾ • Aviatrix Amelia Earhart wed George Putnam, 1931	*Diminishing,*
8	Fr.	☌☿♂ • Sandford Fleming proposed Universal Standard Time, Toronto, Ont., 1879	*but*
9	Sa.	☌♀☾ • Magnitude 6.6 earthquake struck San Fernando, Calif., 1971 • {11.5 10.4	*nowhere*
10	F	**Quinquagesima** • Chinese New Year • New ●	*near*
11	M.	☌☿☾ • ☌♂☾ • ☌♆☾ • Tides {11.5 —	*finishing.*
12	Tu.	Shrove Tuesday • ☾ on Eq. • U.S. president Abe Lincoln born, 1809	*Oh, dear,*
13	W.	**Ash Wednesday** • ☌♅☾ • Tides {10.7 10.7	*oh, dear:*
14	Th.	Sts. Cyril & Methodius • Valentine's Day • *True love never grows old.*	*Subzero*
15	Fr.	Susan B. Anthony born, 1820 • Rare sighting of yellow-billed loon, Lake Powell, Utah, 1995	*here!*
16	Sa.	☾ at ☋ • ☿ Gr. Elong. (18° East) • Winter's back breaks. • {9.7 8.9	*It's*
17	F	**1st S. in Lent** • Basketball player Michael Jordan born, 1963 • {9.4 8.4	*sunny*
18	M.	Washington's Birthday (observed) • ☌♃☾ • Elm Farm Ollie first cow to fly in plane, 1930	*and*
19	Tu.	☾ rides high • ☾ at apo. • ♄ stat. • Astronomer Nicolaus Copernicus born, 1473	*warmish,*
20	W.	Ember Day • Ralph and Carolyn Cummins had a child on this day in 1952, 1953, 1956, 1961, and 1966	*then*
21	Th.	☌♆☉ • Agriculturist Jethro Tull, inventor of the horse-drawn seed drill, died, 1741 • {9.1 8.2	*turning*
22	Fr.	Ember Day • ☿ stat. • Coolidge delivered first U.S. presidential radio broadcast, 1924	*stormish.*
23	Sa.	Ember Day • *Of a ragged colt cometh many a good horse.*	*Solar*
24	F	**2nd S. in Lent** • ☌☿♂ • Fleet Admiral Chester Nimitz born, 1885	*power,*
25	M.	St. Matthias[T] • Full Snow ○ • Tides {10.3 9.9	*followed*
26	Tu.	☾ on Eq. • Grand Teton National Park in Wyo. established, 1929 • Tides {10.5 10.2	*by*
27	W.	Actress Elizabeth Taylor born, 1932 • 103°F, Laredo, Tex., 2011 • {10.6 —	*polar*
28	Th.	St. Romanus • ☌♀♆ • *Romanus bright and clear Indicates a goodly year.* • {10.5 10.5	*hours!*

Genius unrefined resembles a flash of lightning,
but wisdom is like the Sun. –Franz Grillparzer

Farmer's Calendar

■ Although it's still winter, for some gardeners the growing season began about a month ago, when seed catalogs started filling their mailboxes. These compendiums contain much more than seductive pictures of plump, red tomatoes; crisp salad greens; and a plethora of brightly colored flowers. They provide a wealth of information perfectly suited for the lifelong learner in every gardener.

Before purchasing through mail order, compare several catalogs. Some offer only seeds, while others also include tools and gardening supplies. A few provide cooking instructions and recipes. Watch for new and improved varieties that offer increased disease resistance, more hardiness, or better flavor. It's fun to order a few novelties, such as 'All Blue' potatoes with purple skin and purple-blue flesh; limit these types to a couple per year, until you are sure that they will work for you.

It's a common mistake to order either too many seeds or not enough. Most catalogs list the number of seeds per packet and how far apart to space them. With this data and a to-scale sketch of your garden, it's easy to calculate how much to buy.

So, on a cold, blustery, February afternoon, settle down to peruse your seed catalogs. They're guaranteed to brighten even the grayest of winter days and bring you that much closer to spring.

C
A
L
E
N
D
A
R

SKY WATCH ☆ *On the 1st, the Moon hovers to the right of Saturn, which now rises at around 11:00 P.M. Jupiter, high and conspicuous in the west at nightfall, stands above and to the right of the Moon on the 17th. The Moon dangles below Saturn, which now rises at around 9:00 P.M. on the 29th. Mars, Venus, and Uranus all cluster tightly together behind the Sun on the 29th, thus becoming "invisible." This simultaneous disappearance of our two closest planetary neighbors, Mars and Venus, ensures that both will remain challenging for the next few months. Spring begins with the vernal equinox at 7:02 A.M. on the 20th, when days and nights are approximately equal everywhere and the Sun rises and sets due east and west.*

◐	**Last Quarter**	4th day	16th hour	53rd minute
●	**New Moon**	11th day	15th hour	51st minute
◑	**First Quarter**	19th day	13th hour	27th minute
○	**Full Moon**	27th day	5th hour	27th minute

After 2:00 A.M. on March 10, Eastern Daylight Time is given.

Purchase these pages with times set to your zip code at MyLocalAlmanac.com.

Day of Year	Day of Month	Day of Week	☀ Rises h. m.	Rise Key	☀ Sets h. m.	Set Key	Length of Day h. m.	Sun Fast m.	Declination of Sun ° ′	High Tide Times Boston		☾ Rises h. m.	Rise Key	☾ Sets h. m.	Set Key	☾ Place	☾ Age
60	1	Fr.	6:19	D	**5:34**	C	11 15	4	7 s. 20	1¼	1½	**10:10**	E	7:58	C	VIR	19
61	2	Sa.	6:17	D	**5:35**	C	11 18	4	6 57	2	2½	**11:19**	E	8:36	B	VIR	20
62	3	**F**	6:15	D	**5:36**	C	11 21	4	6 34	2¾	3¼	—	–	9:20	B	LIB	21
63	4	M.	6:14	D	**5:37**	C	11 23	4	6 11	3½	4¼	12:25	E	10:11	B	SCO	22
64	5	Tu.	6:12	D	**5:39**	C	11 27	5	5 47	4½	5¼	1:27	E	11:09	B	OPH	23
65	6	W.	6:10	D	**5:40**	C	11 30	5	5 24	5¾	6½	2:22	E	**12:13**	B	SAG	24
66	7	Th.	6:09	D	**5:41**	C	11 32	5	5 01	6¾	7½	3:11	E	**1:21**	C	SAG	25
67	8	Fr.	6:07	C	**5:42**	C	11 35	5	4 37	8	8½	3:53	E	**2:31**	C	CAP	26
68	9	Sa.	6:05	C	**5:43**	C	11 38	5	4 14	9	9½	4:30	D	**3:40**	C	AQU	27
69	10	**F**	7:04	C	**6:45**	C	11 41	6	3 50	10¾	11¼	6:03	D	**5:49**	D	AQU	28
70	11	M.	7:02	C	**6:46**	C	11 44	6	3 27	11¾	—	6:34	D	**6:56**	D	PSC	0
71	12	Tu.	7:00	C	**6:47**	C	11 47	6	3 03	12	12½	7:04	C	**8:02**	E	PSC	1
72	13	W.	6:59	C	**6:48**	C	11 49	7	2 40	12¾	1¼	7:34	C	**9:06**	E	PSC	2
73	14	Th.	6:57	C	**6:49**	C	11 52	7	2 16	1½	2	8:06	C	**10:08**	E	PSC	3
74	15	Fr.	6:55	C	**6:50**	C	11 55	7	1 52	2¼	2½	8:39	B	**11:08**	E	ARI	4
75	16	Sa.	6:54	C	**6:52**	C	11 58	7	1 28	2¾	3¼	9:16	B	—	–	ARI	5
76	17	**F**	6:52	C	**6:53**	C	12 01	8	1 05	3½	4	9:56	B	12:05	E	TAU	6
77	18	M.	6:50	C	**6:54**	C	12 04	8	0 41	4¼	5	10:41	B	12:58	E	TAU	7
78	19	Tu.	6:48	C	**6:55**	C	12 07	8	0 s. 17	5¼	5¾	11:30	B	1:47	E	TAU	8
79	20	W.	6:47	C	**6:56**	C	12 09	9	0 N.05	6¼	6¾	**12:23**	B	2:31	E	GEM	9
80	21	Th.	6:45	C	**6:57**	C	12 12	9	0 29	7	7¾	**1:19**	B	3:11	E	GEM	10
81	22	Fr.	6:43	C	**6:59**	C	12 16	9	0 53	8	8¾	**2:18**	C	3:47	E	CAN	11
82	23	Sa.	6:41	C	**7:00**	C	12 19	9	1 16	9	9½	**3:20**	C	4:20	E	CAN	12
83	24	**F**	6:40	C	**7:01**	C	12 21	10	1 40	9¾	10¼	**4:23**	D	4:51	D	LEO	13
84	25	M.	6:38	C	**7:02**	C	12 24	10	2 04	10½	11	**5:29**	D	5:21	D	SEX	14
85	26	Tu.	6:36	C	**7:03**	C	12 27	10	2 27	11¼	11½	**6:36**	D	5:52	C	LEO	15
86	27	W.	6:34	C	**7:04**	C	12 30	11	2 51	12	—	**7:45**	E	6:23	C	VIR	16
87	28	Th.	6:33	C	**7:05**	C	12 32	11	3 14	12¼	12¾	**8:56**	E	6:57	C	VIR	17
88	29	Fr.	6:31	C	**7:06**	D	12 35	11	3 37	1	1½	**10:07**	E	7:35	B	VIR	18
89	30	Sa.	6:29	C	**7:08**	D	12 39	12	4 01	1¾	2¼	**11:16**	E	8:18	B	LIB	19
90	31	**F**	6:27	C	**7:09**	D	12 42	12	4 N.24	2½	3¼	—	–	9:08	B	LIB	20

MARCH HATH 31 DAYS • 2013

From Moon being [new], till [3 days] past be the prime,
For grafting and cropping is very good time. –Thomas Tusser

Day of Month	Day of Week	Dates, Feasts, Fasts, Aspects, Tide Heights	Weather
1	Fr.	**St. David** • *Upon St. David's Day, Put oats and barley in the clay.* • {10.7 10.3	*Flurries*
2	Sa.	**St. Chad** • ☾ at ☊ • ☌♄☾ • Statesman Sam Houston born, 1793	*plus*
3	**F**	**3rd S. in Lent** • S. Fossett completed 1st nonrefueled, nonstop flight around world, 2005	*sprinkles:*
4	M.	☿ in inf. ☌ • FDR: "... the only thing we have to fear is fear itself," 1933 • {10.6 9.3	*flinkles?*
5	Tu.	**St. Piran** • ☾ runs low • ☾ at perig. • 3" hail, Colorado Springs, Colo., 1990	*Cold*
6	W.	☌☿♀ • ☌♇☾ • Opera *La Traviata* debuted, Venice, 1853	*and*
7	Th.	**St. Perpetua** • Towed by copter, F. Iglesias "water-skied" barefoot, 153 mph, Acapulco, Mex., 2011	*bright*
8	Fr.	1st year free for Nfld. students, Memorial University, Nfld., 1965 • Tides {10.5 9.7	*on*
9	Sa.	*A best friend is like a four-leaf clover: hard to find and lucky to have.* • Tides {10.7 10.1	*white;*
10	**F**	**Daylight Saving Time begins, 2:00 A.M.** • ☌☿☾ • ☌♆☾ • {10.9 10.5	*mushers*
11	M.	**New ●** • ☾ on Eq. • ☌♀☾ • Tides {11.0 —	*turn*
12	Tu.	☌♂☾ • Blizzard struck N.Y.C., 1888 • {10.8 10.9	*slushers*
13	W.	☌♅☾ • E. Muybridge's Zoopraxiscope, an early movie projector, debuted, London, 1882	*as*
14	Th.	Pelican Island, Fla., became first National Wildlife Refuge, 1903	*it*
15	Fr.	Beware the ides of March. • Sister St. Stanislas Hachard became first Catholic nun ordained in America, 1729	*warms.*
16	Sa.	☾ at ☋ • ☿ stat. • First recorded fire in Boston, 1630 • Tides {10.2 9.4	*Storms,*
17	**F**	**5th S. in Lent** • **St. Patrick's Day** • ☌♃☾ • {9.8 8.9	*then*
18	M.	**Pure Monday** • ☾ rides high • ☾ at apo. • Singer Charley Pride born, 1938	*sunny—*
19	Tu.	**St. Joseph** • *If one is not in a hurry, even an egg will start walking.* • Tides {9.1 8.1	*it's*
20	W.	**Vernal Equinox** • USS *Midway* launched, 1945 • Tides {8.9 8.0	*mild*
21	Th.	Alcatraz prison closed, Calif., 1963 • Tides {8.8 8.1	*enough*
22	Fr.	☌♂♅ • Aldabra tortoise Adwaitya died supposedly at age 255, Kolkata, India, 2006	*to*
23	Sa.	Deadly Easter Sunday tornado, Omaha, Neb., 1913 • {9.2 8.9	*walk*
24	**F**	**Palm Sunday** • **Sunday of Orthodoxy** • Chipmunks emerge from hibernation now.	*your*
25	M.	☾ on Eq. • Poll tax declared unconstitutional for all U.S. elections, 1966 • {10.0 9.9	*honey!*
26	Tu.	**First day of Passover** • Composer Ludwig van Beethoven died, 1827 • {10.3 10.5	*All*
27	W.	**Full Worm ○** • Car designer Sir Henry Royce born, 1863 • Tides {10.6 —	*of*
28	Th.	**Maundy Thursday** • ☌♀♅ • ☌♅☉ • ♀ in sup. ☌	*a*
29	Fr.	**Good Friday** • ☌♄☾ • Tides {11.2 10.7	*sudden,*
30	Sa.	☾ at ☊ • ☾ at perig. • Possible UFO, Little Fox Lake, Y.T., 2000	*everything's*
31	**F**	**Easter** • ☿ Gr. Elong. (28° West) • *Puff not against the wind.*	*buddin'.*

Farmer's Calendar

■ The appearance of sap buckets hanging on maple trees is as sure a sign of Spring as spotting the first robin. Tapping season usually begins in late February and lasts well into March, ending as the leaf buds begin to enlarge. But weather dictates when the sap will actually start to flow. It runs best when nighttime temperatures fall into the 20s and daytime highs are well above 32°F.

As a boy, I often helped my neighbor, John, tap the old maple trees that lined our road. First, he would drill a 7/16-inch hole into a tree trunk 3 feet above the ground. Next, he would use a hammer to drive an iron tap (a hollow tube, also called a spile) into the hole, after which I would hang a bucket on it. I still remember the "ping, ping, ping" as the first drops of sap hit the bottom of the metal pail.

We poured the sap that we had collected into a large, shallow pan and heated it over a roaring wood fire in John's sugarhouse. A pleasant maple aroma filled the air as we boiled down 40 gallons of watery sap to make each gallon of syrup. The boiling was complete when John's candy thermometer showed that the thick liquid in the pan had reached 219°F.

Like the first sweet song of America's intrepid robin, the delicious taste of freshly made maple syrup is a sweet reminder that Spring has indeed sprung.

SKY WATCH ☆ *The Moon meets Jupiter in the west on the 14th. This is the final month for easy viewing of the Giant Planet, which has now faded to magnitude −2.0 but is still the brightest "star" in the heavens. The Moon comes extremely close to the blue star Spica on the 24th and then passes to the lower right of Saturn on the 25th. Both rise at around nightfall. Saturn, with its rings now beautifully "open" (meaning not tilted edgewise to us), has its opposition on the 28th, when it can be seen all night. This is Saturn's brightest and best opposition of the past 6 years. Visible through any telescope, Saturn lights up the otherwise dim constellation of Libra.*

◗	**Last Quarter**	3rd day	0 hour	37th minute
●	**New Moon**	10th day	5th hour	35th minute
◐	**First Quarter**	18th day	8th hour	31st minute
○	**Full Moon**	25th day	15th hour	57th minute

All times are given in Eastern Daylight Time.

Purchase these pages with times set to your zip code at MyLocalAlmanac.com.

Day of Year	Day of Month	Day of Week	☼ Rises h. m.	Rise Key	☼ Sets h. m.	Set Key	Length of Day h. m.	Sun Fast m.	Declination of Sun ° '	High Tide Times Boston		☾ Rises h. m.	Rise Key	☾ Sets h. m.	Set Key	Place	Age
91	1	M.	6:26	C	7:10	D	12 44	12	4 N. 47	3½	4	12:20	E	10:05	B	OPH	21
92	2	Tu.	6:24	C	7:11	D	12 47	12	5 10	4¼	5	1:18	E	11:07	B	SAG	22
93	3	W.	6:22	C	7:12	D	12 50	13	5 33	5¼	6	2:09	E	12:14	C	SAG	23
94	4	Th.	6:21	C	7:13	D	12 52	13	5 56	6½	7¼	2:52	E	1:22	C	SAG	24
95	5	Fr.	6:19	C	7:14	D	12 55	13	6 19	7½	8¼	3:30	E	2:30	C	AQU	25
96	6	Sa.	6:17	C	7:15	D	12 58	14	6 41	8¾	9¼	4:04	D	3:37	D	AQU	26
97	7	**F**	6:16	C	7:17	D	13 01	14	7 04	9¾	10¼	4:35	D	4:43	D	AQU	27
98	8	M.	6:14	C	7:18	D	13 04	14	7 26	10½	11	5:05	C	5:48	D	PSC	28
99	9	Tu.	6:12	B	7:19	D	13 07	14	7 49	11½	11¾	5:34	C	6:52	E	PSC	29
100	10	W.	6:11	B	7:20	D	13 09	15	8 11	12¼	—	6:05	C	7:54	E	PSC	0
101	11	Th.	6:09	B	7:21	D	13 12	15	8 33	12¼	12¾	6:37	B	8:55	E	ARI	1
102	12	Fr.	6:07	B	7:22	D	13 15	15	8 55	1	1½	7:13	B	9:53	E	ARI	2
103	13	Sa.	6:06	B	7:23	D	13 17	15	9 16	1¾	2¼	7:52	B	10:48	E	TAU	3
104	14	**F**	6:04	B	7:25	D	13 21	16	9 38	2¼	3	8:35	B	11:39	E	TAU	4
105	15	M.	6:02	B	7:26	D	13 24	16	9 59	3	3½	9:22	B	—	-	TAU	5
106	16	Tu.	6:01	B	7:27	D	13 26	16	10 21	3¾	4½	10:14	B	12:25	E	ORI	6
107	17	W.	5:59	B	7:28	D	13 29	16	10 42	4½	5¼	11:08	B	1:07	E	GEM	7
108	18	Th.	5:58	B	7:29	D	13 31	17	11 03	5½	6¼	12:05	C	1:44	E	GEM	8
109	19	Fr.	5:56	B	7:30	D	13 34	17	11 23	6¼	7	1:05	C	2:18	E	CAN	9
110	20	Sa.	5:55	B	7:31	D	13 36	17	11 44	7¼	8	2:06	C	2:49	D	LEO	10
111	21	**F**	5:53	B	7:32	D	13 39	17	12 04	8¼	8¾	3:10	D	3:19	D	SEX	11
112	22	M.	5:51	B	7:34	D	13 43	17	12 24	9	9½	4:15	D	3:49	D	LEO	12
113	23	Tu.	5:50	B	7:35	D	13 45	17	12 44	10	10¼	5:23	E	4:19	C	VIR	13
114	24	W.	5:48	B	7:36	D	13 48	18	13 04	10¾	11	6:34	E	4:52	C	VIR	14
115	25	Th.	5:47	B	7:37	D	13 50	18	13 24	11½	11¾	7:46	E	5:28	B	VIR	15
116	26	Fr.	5:46	B	7:38	D	13 52	18	13 43	12¼	—	8:58	E	6:10	B	LIB	16
117	27	Sa.	5:44	B	7:39	D	13 55	18	14 02	12½	1¼	10:07	E	6:58	B	LIB	17
118	28	**F**	5:43	B	7:40	D	13 57	18	14 21	1½	2	11:10	E	7:54	B	OPH	18
119	29	M.	5:41	B	7:41	D	14 00	18	14 39	2¼	3	—	-	8:57	B	SAG	19
120	30	Tu.	5:40	B	7:42	E	14 02	19	14 N. 58	3¼	3¾	12:05	E	10:04	B	SAG	20

APRIL HATH 30 DAYS • 2013

By all the stars in His infinite sky,
We are April-fools, my Love and I. –Mortimer Collins

Day of Month	Day of Week	Dates, Feasts, Fasts, Aspects, Tide Heights	Weather
1	M.	**Easter Monday** • **All Fools'** • ☾ runs low • Choreographer Martha Graham died, 1991	*Foolish*
2	Tu.	☌♇☾ • Juan Ponce de León "discovered" Florida, 1513 • Tides {10.9 9.6	*pleasure,*
3	W.	Deadly avalanche during gold rush, Chilkoot Pass, Alaska/Y.T., 1898 • Tides {10.5 9.4	*days*
4	Th.	*Every frog must know its pond.* • Tides {10.3 9.4	*you'll*
5	Fr.	Seedsman Washington Atlee Burpee born, 1858 • {10.1 9.6	*treasure.*
6	Sa.	☌♀♂ • ☌♆☾ • Paramount Pictures and Elvis agreed to 3-movie contract, 1956	*Plant*
7	**F**	**2nd S. of Easter** • ☾ on Eq. • Dungeons & Dragons game cocreator Dave Arneson died, 2009	*the*
8	M.	**Annunciation**[T] • ☌☿☾ • 28°F, Bakersfield, Calif., 1893 • {10.4 10.6	*garden*
9	Tu.	☌♅☾ • Aerial Ferry Bridge opened, Duluth, Minn., 1905 • Tides {10.4 10.7	*at your*
10	W.	**New** ● • ☌♀☾ • ☌♂☾ • Tides {10.3 —	*leisure.*
11	Th.	*The sudden storm lasts not three hours.* • Tides {10.7 10.1	*Feels*
12	Fr.	☾ at ☊ • ♇ stat. • Golfer Fred Couples won Masters tournament, 1992 • {10.6 9.9	*like*
13	Sa.	U.S. president Thomas Jefferson born, 1743 • Navy navigation satellite *Transit 1B* launched, 1960	*summer,*
14	**F**	**3rd S. of Easter** • ☌♃☾ • Tides {10.2 9.2	*complete*
15	M.	☾ rides high • ☾ at apo. • American School for the Deaf founded, Hartford, Conn., 1817	*with*
16	Tu.	Prince Andrew and Sarah, Duchess of York, announced plans to divorce, 1996 • {9.6 8.6	*thunder!*
17	W.	☌♂☉ • "Hail! Hail! The Gang's All Here!" song copyrighted, 1908 • {9.3 8.4	*You'd*
18	Th.	*Mirth is the medicine of life; / It cures its ills, it calms its strife.*	*better*
19	Fr.	☌☿♅ • WIYY DJ Bob Rivers began on-air vigil 'til Orioles won (258 hours), 1988 • {8.9 8.5	*put*
20	Sa.	Marie and Pierre Curie isolated radium chloride from pitchblende, 1902 • Tides {9.0 8.9	*on a*
21	**F**	**4th S. of Easter** • Tornado outbreak, northern Ill., 1967 • {9.2 9.3	*sweater*
22	M.	☾ on Eq. • Lester Pearson inaugurated as Canada's prime minister, 1963 • Tides {9.5 9.9	*and*
23	Tu.	**St. George** • Organic farming pioneer Paul K. Keene died, 2005 • Tides {9.9 10.5	*bring*
24	W.	*Old Farmer's Almanac* founder Robert B. Thomas born, 1766 • Tides {10.2 11.1	*an*
25	Th.	**St. Mark** • **Full Pink** ○ • **Eclipse** ☾ • ☌♄☾ • {10.5 11.5	*umbrella,*
26	Fr.	☾ at ☋ • Seismologist Charles Richter born, 1900 • Tides {10.7 —	*fella!*
27	Sa.	☾ at perig. • Poplars leaf out about now. • Tides {11.8 10.8	*Bright,*
28	**F**	**5th S. of Easter** • ☾ runs low • ♄ at ☍ • {12.0 10.7	*brisky—*
29	M.	Jacob Hummel received patent for varnish of elastic gum, 1813 • Publisher William R. Hearst born, 1863	*feeling*
30	Tu.	☌♇☾ • *A little neglect may breed great mischief.* • Tides {11.5 10.2	*frisky?*

Some people walk in the rain, others just get wet. –Roger Miller

Farmer's Calendar

■ If you were asked to name the most important appliance in your home, what would your answer be? The television? The computer? The microwave? With as many household conveniences as we have, it might take a bit of thought. But, if the same question were posed to someone a couple of centuries ago, the answer would undoubtedly have been the woodstove.

Before woodstoves became mass-produced in the mid-1700s, the fireplace was the center of the home. It provided warmth, a place to cook, and an area for family and friends to socialize. In early America, your house was often referred to as the "hearthside."

Woodstoves proved a huge advantage over the fireplace. They used less wood and didn't blacken walls, and their flat top provided a convenient cooking surface. Because they projected out into the room, they provided a much more even, radiant heat.

Over the years, wood fuel gave way to other sources of home heat, such as oil, natural gas, and electricity, but the energy crisis of the 1970s sparked a revival that continues today. Wood is a renewable resource, and modern woodstoves burn it more efficiently than early styles and release fewer emissions. With today's high fuel costs, the woodstove may again be the most important appliance for many people in cold climates.

SKY WATCH ☆ *Saturn remains splendid throughout this month and is out all night long. Jupiter is now getting low in the evening twilight. Mercury hovers to the right of returning Venus, only 7 degrees above the western horizon 40 minutes after sunset on the 23rd. Venus closely meets Jupiter, a potentially spectacular sight even though both are near their minimum brightness, on the 27th and 28th. Mercury hovers just above them. However, the planetary trio sits just 6 degrees above the western horizon 40 minutes after sunset and thus requires an unobstructed skyline for viewing. They are easier to see from southern states.*

◑	**Last Quarter**	2nd day	7th hour	14th minute
●	**New Moon**	9th day	20th hour	28th minute
◐	**First Quarter**	18th day	0 hour	35th minute
○	**Full Moon**	25th day	0 hour	25th minute
◑	**Last Quarter**	31st day	14th hour	58th minute

All times are given in Eastern Daylight Time.

Purchase these pages with times set to your zip code at MyLocalAlmanac.com.

Day of Year	Day of Month	Day of Week	☀ Rises h. m.	Rise Key	☀ Sets h. m.	Set Key	Length of Day h. m.	Sun Fast m.	Declination of Sun ° ′	High Tide Times Boston		☾ Rises h. m.	Rise Key	☾ Sets h. m.	Set Key	☾ Place	☾ Age
121	1	W.	5:39	B	7:44	E	14 05	19	15 N.16	4	4¾	12:51	E	11:14	C	SAG	21
122	2	Th.	5:37	B	7:45	E	14 08	19	15 34	5¼	6	1:31	E	12:23	C	AQU	22
123	3	Fr.	5:36	B	7:46	E	14 10	19	15 51	6¼	7	2:06	D	1:30	D	CAP	23
124	4	Sa.	5:35	B	7:47	E	14 12	19	16 09	7¼	8	2:38	D	2:36	D	AQU	24
125	5	F	5:33	B	7:48	E	14 15	19	16 26	8½	9	3:08	D	3:40	D	PSC	25
126	6	M.	5:32	B	7:49	E	14 17	19	16 42	9¼	9¾	3:37	C	4:43	E	PSC	26
127	7	Tu.	5:31	B	7:50	E	14 19	19	16 59	10¼	10½	4:06	C	5:45	E	PSC	27
128	8	W.	5:30	B	7:51	E	14 21	19	17 15	11	11¼	4:38	C	6:46	E	PSC	28
129	9	Th.	5:29	B	7:52	E	14 23	19	17 31	11¾	12	5:12	B	7:45	E	ARI	0
130	10	Fr.	5:27	B	7:53	E	14 26	19	17 47	12½	—	5:49	B	8:41	E	ARI	1
131	11	Sa.	5:26	B	7:55	E	14 29	19	18 02	12½	1¼	6:31	B	9:33	E	TAU	2
132	12	F	5:25	B	7:56	E	14 31	19	18 17	1¼	1¾	7:17	B	10:21	E	TAU	3
133	13	M.	5:24	A	7:57	E	14 33	19	18 32	1¾	2½	8:07	B	11:04	E	ORI	4
134	14	Tu.	5:23	A	7:58	E	14 35	19	18 46	2½	3¼	9:00	B	11:43	E	GEM	5
135	15	W.	5:22	A	7:59	E	14 37	19	19 01	3¼	4	9:56	C	—	–	GEM	6
136	16	Th.	5:21	A	8:00	E	14 39	19	19 14	4	4¾	10:54	C	12:17	E	CAN	7
137	17	Fr.	5:20	A	8:01	E	14 41	19	19 28	4¾	5½	11:53	C	12:49	E	CAN	8
138	18	Sa.	5:19	A	8:02	E	14 43	19	19 41	5¾	6¼	12:54	D	1:19	D	LEO	9
139	19	F	5:18	A	8:03	E	14 45	19	19 54	6½	7¼	1:57	D	1:48	D	SEX	10
140	20	M.	5:17	A	8:04	E	14 47	19	20 06	7½	8	3:02	D	2:17	C	LEO	11
141	21	Tu.	5:16	A	8:05	E	14 49	19	20 18	8½	8¾	4:10	E	2:47	C	VIR	12
142	22	W.	5:16	A	8:06	E	14 50	19	20 30	9¼	9¾	5:21	E	3:21	C	VIR	13
143	23	Th.	5:15	A	8:07	E	14 52	19	20 42	10¼	10½	6:33	E	3:59	B	VIR	14
144	24	Fr.	5:14	A	8:07	E	14 53	19	20 53	11	11¼	7:45	E	4:45	B	LIB	15
145	25	Sa.	5:13	A	8:08	E	14 55	19	21 03	12	—	8:53	E	5:38	B	SCO	16
146	26	F	5:13	A	8:09	E	14 56	19	21 14	12¼	12¾	9:53	E	6:39	B	OPH	17
147	27	M.	5:12	A	8:10	E	14 58	18	21 24	1	1¾	10:45	E	7:47	B	SAG	18
148	28	Tu.	5:11	A	8:11	E	15 00	18	21 33	2	2¾	11:30	E	8:58	C	SAG	19
149	29	W.	5:11	A	8:12	E	15 01	18	21 42	3	3½	—	–	10:10	C	CAP	20
150	30	Th.	5:10	A	8:13	E	15 03	18	21 51	3¾	4½	12:07	E	11:20	D	AQU	21
151	31	Fr.	5:10	A	8:13	E	15 03	18	22 N.00	4¾	5½	12:41	D	12:28	D	AQU	22

May hath 31 days • 2013

All things that have root in the ground
Are alive and abloom in the sun. –Emily Pfeiffer

Day of Month	Day of Week	Dates, Feasts, Fasts, Aspects, Tide Heights	Weather
1	W.	Sts. Philip & James • May Day • Electric streetlights now in Ottawa, Ont., 1885	*Buttercups*
2	Th.	St. Athanasius • 1st provisional government in Pacific NW approved, Champoeg, Oreg., 1843	*and*
3	Fr.	Baseball-size hail west of Mooresville, N.C., 1988 • {10.2 / 9.8	*daffodils*
4	Sa.	☌♆☾ • First on-the-road Spacemobile lecture, 1961 • Tides {10.0 / 10.0	*dot*
5	**F**	**Rogation S.** • **Orthodox Easter** • **Cinco de Mayo** • ☾ ON EQ. • {9.8 / 10.2	*the*
6	M.	☌♅☾ • Barbaro won 132nd Kentucky Derby, Louisville, Ky., 2006 • {9.8 / 10.4	*lush,*
7	Tu.	☌☿♂ • *If the robin sings in the bush, Then the weather will be coarse.*	*sun-dappled*
8	W.	St. Julian of Norwich • Naturalist Sir David Attenborough born, 1926	*hills.*
9	Th.	**Ascension** • **New ●** • **Eclipse ☉** • ☾ AT ☋	*Cloudbursts*
10	Fr.	☌♀☾ • Confederate general Thomas "Stonewall" Jackson died, 1863 • {9.6 / —	*dampen*
11	Sa.	☿ IN SUP. ☌ • Composer Irving Berlin born, 1888 • **Three** • {10.5 / 9.5	*campin'—*
12	**F**	1st S. af. Asc. • **Mother's Day** • ☾ RIDES HIGH • ☌♃☾ • **Chilly**	*more*
13	M.	☾ AT APO. • Cranberries in bud now. • Velcro trademark registered in U.S., 1958 • **Saints**	*chills*
14	Tu.	*You may sometimes be much in the wrong in owning your being in the right.* • Tides {10.0 / 9.0	*than*
15	W.	Shavuot • First live TV pictures from U.S. spacecraft (*Faith 7*), 1963 • {9.7 / 8.9	*thrills.*
16	Th.	Marie Antoinette married future French king Louis XVI, 1770 • Tides {9.5 / 8.8	*Still*
17	Fr.	"Birth of Venus" artist Sandro Botticelli died, 1510	*showering,*
18	Sa.	Montreal, Quebec, founded, 1642 • Tides {9.1 / 9.1	*but*
19	**F**	**Whit S.** • **Pentecost** • ☾ ON EQ. • Tides {9.1 / 9.4	*the*
20	M.	**Victoria Day (Canada)** • First Council of Nicaea (which standardized Easter dates) likely convened, A.D. 325	*scent*
21	Tu.	Poet Alexander Pope born, 1688 • Tides {9.5 / 10.4	*of*
22	W.	Ember Day • American Cancer Society established, 1913 • Tides {9.8 / 11.0	*lilacs*
23	Th.	☾ AT ☊ • ☌♄☾ • South Carolina became 8th U.S. state, 1788	*is*
24	Fr.	Ember Day • ☌☿♀ • Crop circle discovered, Haysville, Kans., 2003	*overpowering.*
25	Sa.	**St. Bede** • **Vesak** • Ember Day • **Full Flower** ○ • **Eclipse** ☾ • ☾ AT PERIG.	*It's*
26	**F**	**Trinity** • ☾ RUNS LOW • *It's the old pot that makes good soup.* • {12.2 / 10.8	*hot.*
27	M.	**Memorial Day (observed)** • ☌☿♃ • ☌♇☾ • Tides {12.3 / 10.8	*Clear*
28	Tu.	☌♀♃ • Three tornadoes tore through Cincinnati, 1809 • Tides {12.1 / 10.7	*the*
29	W.	Comedian Bob Hope born, 1903 • Tides {11.7 / 10.6	*hero's*
30	Th.	First national celebration of Memorial (Decoration) Day, Arlington National Cemetery, Va., 1868	*cemetery*
31	Fr.	Visit. of Mary • ☌♆☾ • *Distance lends enchantment.*	*plot.*

Farmer's Calendar

■ Centuries ago, gardeners learned to time horticultural activities, such as planting, pest control, and harvesting, not by a set date on a calendar, but by signs that Nature provided. In fact, phenology, the study of the timing of animal and plant cycles in relation to climate and seasonal changes, is still used today.

The signaling events and their times may vary by location. Gardeners in certain regions might plant cool-season flowers when aspens and chokecherries leaf out; fertilize the lawn when forsythias and crocuses start to bloom; watch for Mexican bean beetles when foxglove flowers open; sow seeds of beets, lettuce, and carrots when dandelions appear; or set out tomatoes and pepper plants when lilies-of-the-valley blossom.

To use this technique, keep a journal. Note when plants bud, flower, and fruit. Keep track of animal and insect life cycles and activities, such as the emergence of Japanese beetles. Jot down daily weather conditions (temperature, sunlight, precipitation, wind, etc.). Examine each plant's site: Record the exposure to the elements, soil conditions, and any possible stress factors.

Review your notes periodically. You'll begin to notice patterns that will help you to schedule tasks, and you'll become as savvy as those gardeners of long ago.

THE SIXTH MONTH • 2013

SKY WATCH ☆ *A striking vertical line of bright planets forms near the sunset point some 40 minutes after sunset on the 1st. Jupiter, at magnitude –1.9, is closest to the horizon; Venus, at –3.8, is in the middle; and Mercury, at –0.4, stands highest. Mercury is just a scant 10 degrees above the horizon, so the spectacle requires an unobstructed skyline for viewing. The thin 2-day-old crescent Moon hovers to the lower left of Mercury and Venus on the 10th. Look for the Moon, due south at nightfall, next to blue Spica on the 18th and below Saturn on the 19th. Jupiter disappears behind the Sun in a conjunction on the 19th. Summer arrives with the solstice at 1:04 A.M. on the 21st.*

●	**New Moon**	8th day	11th hour	56th minute
◐	**First Quarter**	16th day	13th hour	24th minute
○	**Full Moon**	23rd day	7th hour	32nd minute
◑	**Last Quarter**	30th day	0 hour	54th minute

All times are given in Eastern Daylight Time.

Purchase these pages with times set to your zip code at MyLocalAlmanac.com.

Day of Year	Day of Month	Day of Week	☼ Rises h. m.	Rise Key	☼ Sets h. m.	Set Key	Length of Day h.	m.	Sun Fast m.	Declination of Sun °	'	High Tide Times Boston		☾ Rises h. m.	Rise Key	☾ Sets h. m.	Set Key	☾ Place	☾ Age
152	1	Sa.	5:09	A	**8:14**	E	15	05	18	22	N.08	6	**6½**	1:11	D	**1:33**	D	PSC	23
153	2	**F**	5:09	A	**8:15**	E	15	06	18	22	15	7	**7½**	1:41	C	**2:37**	E	PSC	24
154	3	M.	5:08	A	**8:16**	E	15	08	17	22	23	8	**8½**	2:10	C	**3:39**	E	PSC	25
155	4	Tu.	5:08	A	**8:16**	E	15	08	17	22	30	9	**9¼**	2:41	C	**4:39**	E	PSC	26
156	5	W.	5:08	A	**8:17**	E	15	09	17	22	36	9¾	**10**	3:13	B	**5:38**	E	ARI	27
157	6	Th.	5:07	A	**8:18**	E	15	11	17	22	42	10¾	**10¾**	3:49	B	**6:35**	E	ARI	28
158	7	Fr.	5:07	A	**8:18**	E	15	11	17	22	48	11½	**11½**	4:29	B	**7:28**	E	TAU	29
159	8	Sa.	5:07	A	**8:19**	E	15	12	17	22	53	**12**	—	5:13	B	**8:18**	E	TAU	0
160	9	**F**	5:07	A	**8:20**	E	15	13	16	22	58	12¼	**12¾**	6:02	B	**9:03**	E	TAU	1
161	10	M.	5:07	A	**8:20**	E	15	13	16	23	03	12¾	**1½**	6:54	B	**9:43**	E	GEM	2
162	11	Tu.	5:06	A	**8:21**	E	15	15	16	23	07	1½	**2**	7:49	B	**10:19**	E	GEM	3
163	12	W.	5:06	A	**8:21**	E	15	15	16	23	11	2¼	**2¾**	8:46	C	**10:51**	E	CAN	4
164	13	Th.	5:06	A	**8:22**	E	15	16	16	23	14	2¾	**3½**	9:45	C	**11:21**	D	CAN	5
165	14	Fr.	5:06	A	**8:22**	E	15	16	15	23	17	3½	**4**	10:44	C	**11:50**	D	LEO	6
166	15	Sa.	5:06	A	**8:22**	E	15	16	15	23	19	4¼	**4¾**	11:45	D	—	–	SEX	7
167	16	**F**	5:06	A	**8:23**	E	15	17	15	23	21	5	**5¾**	**12:47**	D	12:18	D	LEO	8
168	17	M.	5:06	A	**8:23**	E	15	17	15	23	23	6	**6½**	**1:52**	E	12:47	C	VIR	9
169	18	Tu.	5:06	A	**8:23**	E	15	17	14	23	24	7	**7¼**	**2:59**	E	1:18	C	VIR	10
170	19	W.	5:07	A	**8:24**	E	15	17	14	23	25	7¾	**8¼**	**4:09**	E	1:53	C	VIR	11
171	20	Th.	5:07	A	**8:24**	E	15	17	14	23	26	8¾	**9¼**	**5:20**	E	2:33	B	LIB	12
172	21	Fr.	5:07	A	**8:24**	E	15	17	14	23	26	9¾	**10**	**6:29**	E	3:21	B	LIB	13
173	22	Sa.	5:07	A	**8:24**	E	15	17	14	23	25	10¾	**11**	**7:34**	E	4:17	B	OPH	14
174	23	**F**	5:07	A	**8:24**	E	15	17	13	23	24	11¾	12	**8:32**	E	5:22	B	SAG	15
175	24	M.	5:08	A	**8:25**	E	15	17	13	23	23	**12½**	—	**9:22**	E	6:34	C	SAG	16
176	25	Tu.	5:08	A	**8:25**	E	15	17	13	23	21	12¾	**1½**	**10:04**	E	7:48	C	SAG	17
177	26	W.	5:08	A	**8:25**	E	15	17	13	23	19	1¾	**2½**	**10:40**	D	9:01	C	AQU	18
178	27	Th.	5:09	A	**8:25**	E	15	16	13	23	17	2¾	**3¼**	**11:13**	D	10:13	D	AQU	19
179	28	Fr.	5:09	A	**8:25**	E	15	16	12	23	14	3½	**4¼**	**11:44**	C	11:21	D	AQU	20
180	29	Sa.	5:10	A	**8:25**	E	15	15	12	23	11	4½	**5**	—	–	**12:27**	D	PSC	21
181	30	**F**	5:10	A	**8:24**	E	15	14	12	23	N.07	5½	**6**	12:14	C	**1:31**	E	PSC	22

 To use this page, see p. 100; for Key letters, see p. 234. ☞ **Bold = P.M.** ☞ Light = A.M.

JUNE HATH 30 DAYS • 2013

The Strawberry, blushing, hides its modest face
Beneath the mantling leaves. –Rev. Dr. John Bidlake

Day of Month	Day of Week	Dates, Feasts, Fasts, Aspects, Tide Heights	Weather
1	Sa.	☾ ON EQ. • Capt. James Lawrence ordered crew, "Don't give up the ship!," 1813 • {10.1 / 10.2	*Squall*
2	**F**	**Corpus Christi** • U.S. First Lady Martha Washington born, 1731 • Tides {9.7 / 10.2	*line,*
3	M.	☌♅☾ • Baseball player Lou Gehrig hit 4 home runs in 1 game, 1932 • Tides {9.4 / 10.2	*then*
4	Tu.	*To be beloved is above all bargains.* • Tides {9.3 / 10.2	*it's*
5	W.	**St. Boniface** • ☾ AT ☋ • 34 tornadoes wound through Ark., 1916 • {9.2 / 10.3	*fine.*
6	Th.	D-Day, 1944 • "Tiny Town" mini city last exhibited, Springfield, Mo., 1925 • {9.2 / 10.3	*Flashes*
7	Fr.	☌♂☾ • ♆ STAT. • Patent for chain saw cleaning brush granted to 11-yr.-old, 1988	*and*
8	Sa.	**New ●** • ☾ RIDES HIGH • U.S. president Andrew Jackson died, 1845 • {9.2 / —	*crashes!*
9	**F**	**3rd S. af. P.** • ☾ AT APO. • ☌♃☾ • Actor Johnny Depp born, 1963	*First*
10	M.	☌☿☾ • ☌♀☾ • Bridget Bishop first to be hanged at Salem Witch trials, 1692 • {10.3 / 9.2	*it*
11	Tu.	**St. Barnabas** • *On St. Barnabas, Put a scythe to the grass.* • Tides {10.2 / 9.1	*rains,*
12	W.	☿ GR. ELONG. (24° EAST) • Amy Singley wed Steven Smith (born same day, same hospital), Pa., 2010 • {10.1 / 9.1	*then*
13	Th.	**Orthodox Ascension** • 2°F, Tamarack, Calif., 1907 • {9.9 / 9.2	*it*
14	Fr.	**St. Basil** • Cows gathered around just-fallen meteorite fragment, St. Robert, Quebec, 1994	*pours;*
15	Sa.	14" rain, Lake Creek Basin, Tex., 1938 • {9.5 / 9.3	*graduations*
16	**F**	**4th S. af. P.** • **Father's Day** • ☾ ON EQ. • {9.3 / 9.6	*have*
17	M.	*The night rinses what the day has soaped.* • Tides {9.3 / 9.9	*to*
18	Tu.	Economist Sylvia Porter born, 1913 • Tides {9.3 / 10.3	*move*
19	W.	☌♃☉ • ☌♄☾ • Hurricane struck fishing fleet from Escuminac, N.B., 1959	*indoors.*
20	Th.	☾ AT ☊ • ☌☿♀ • W.Va. became 35th U.S. state, 1863 • Tides {9.6 / 11.2	*Brides*
21	Fr.	**Summer Solstice** • Sesquicentennial U.S. postage stamp "The Old Man of the Mountains" debuted, 1955	*and*
22	Sa.	**St. Alban** • ☾ RUNS LOW • James Christy discovered Pluto's moon Charon, 1978	*grooms*
23	**F**	**Orthodox Pentecost** • **Full Strawberry** ○ • ☾ AT PERIG. • ☌♇☾	*exchange*
24	M.	**Nativ. John the Baptist** • Midsummer Day • Tides {10.8 / —	*their*
25	Tu.	☿ STAT. • 4-day dedication ceremony for Mackinac Bridge began, Mich., 1958 • {12.3 / 10.9	*vows;*
26	W.	*A summer's sun is worth the having.* • Tides {12.1 / 10.9	*lightning*
27	Th.	☌♆☾ • "Happy Birthday to You" composer Mildred J. Hill born, 1859 • {11.7 / 10.8	*glows*
28	Fr.	**St. Irenaeus** • ☾ ON EQ. • First Corvette car assembled, 1953 • {11.2 / 10.7	*inside*
29	Sa.	**Sts. Peter & Paul** • Twin red panda cubs born, Denver Zoo, Colo., 2008 • {10.5 / 10.5	*each*
30	**F**	**6th S. af. P.** • **Orthodox All Saints'** • ☌♅☾ • {9.9 / 10.2	*cloud.*

The most dangerous food is wedding cake. –James Thurber

Farmer's Calendar

■ Rather than rely on supermarket fare, many folks prefer to raise their own chickens for eggs or meat. The number of people who own chickens in urban areas has been growing steadily in recent years. In response, several towns and cities, including Los Angeles and New York, have changed their ordinances to allow small-scale chicken farming in residential areas.

Farming chickens means that you have control over the quality of your produce and the happiness of your hens. You can give your flock fodder that is free from chemicals and additives and provide lots of room for them to run about. Chickens that are allowed to forage in the yard will add slugs, bugs, grass, and weeds to their menu, resulting in highly nutritious, great-tasting eggs with bright-orange yolks and thick, firm whites. The poultry also create high-nitrogen droppings, which, when aged, are an ideal organic plant food.

As a bonus, these feathered friends are fun pets that entertain for hours with their whimsical antics.

If you would like to raise a few chickens, talk shop with backyard farmers—they are sure to have tales and tips to tell. Also, check local regulations before turning your dream into reality: You don't want to run "a-fowl" of the law.

C
A
L
E
N
D
A
R

SKY WATCH ☆ *Use binoculars to see Venus, still just 10 degrees above the horizon in front of the Beehive star cluster in Cancer, as twilight fades just before fireworks begin on the 4th. Earth reaches aphelion, its annual farthest point from the Sun, on the 5th. The quarter Moon sits next to Virgo's blue star Spica on the 15th and dangles just below brilliant Saturn in the southwestern sky on the 16th. Returning Jupiter is now in its new home of Gemini in the eastern sky during the start of morning twilight, as it passes to the right of dim orange Mars from the 20th to the 22nd. Venus slides closely above Leo's brightest star, blue Regulus, from the 21st to the 23rd.*

● **New Moon**	8th day	3rd hour	14th minute
◐ **First Quarter**	15th day	23rd hour	18th minute
○ **Full Moon**	22nd day	14th hour	16th minute
◑ **Last Quarter**	29th day	13th hour	43rd minute

All times are given in Eastern Daylight Time.

Purchase these pages with times set to your zip code at MyLocalAlmanac.com.

Day of Year	Day of Month	Day of Week	Rises h. m.	Rise Key	Sets h. m.	Set Key	Length of Day h. m.	Sun Fast m.	Declination of Sun ° ′	High Tide Times Boston		Rises h. m.	Rise Key	Sets h. m.	Set Key	Place	Age
182	1	M.	5:11	A	**8:24**	E	15 13	12	23 N. 03	6½	7	12:44	C	**2:32**	E	PSC	23
183	2	Tu.	5:11	A	**8:24**	E	15 13	12	22 58	7½	8	1:16	C	**3:32**	E	ARI	24
184	3	W.	5:12	A	**8:24**	E	15 12	11	22 54	8½	8¾	1:51	B	**4:30**	E	ARI	25
185	4	Th.	5:12	A.	**8:24**	E	15 12	11	22 48	9½	9½	2:29	B	**5:24**	E	TAU	26
186	5	Fr.	5:13	A	**8:23**	E	15 10	11	22 43	10¼	10¼	3:11	B	**6:15**	E	TAU	27
187	6	Sa.	5:14	A	**8:23**	E	15 09	11	22 36	11	11	3:58	B	**7:01**	E	TAU	28
188	7	**F**	5:14	A	**8:23**	E	15 09	11	22 30	11¾	11¾	4:49	B	**7:43**	E	ORI	29
189	8	M.	5:15	A	**8:22**	E	15 07	11	22 23	12¼	—	5:43	B	**8:21**	E	GEM	0
190	9	Tu.	5:16	A	**8:22**	E	15 06	10	22 16	12½	1	6:40	C	**8:55**	E	GEM	1
191	10	W.	5:16	A	**8:21**	E	15 05	10	22 08	1	1½	7:38	C	**9:26**	D	CAN	2
192	11	Th.	5:17	A	**8:21**	E	15 04	10	22 00	1¾	2¼	8:37	C	**9:54**	D	LEO	3
193	12	Fr.	5:18	A	**8:20**	E	15 02	10	21 52	2½	3	9:38	D	**10:22**	D	SEX	4
194	13	Sa.	5:19	A	**8:20**	E	15 01	10	21 43	3	3½	10:39	D	**10:51**	C	LEO	5
195	14	**F**	5:20	A	**8:19**	E	14 59	10	21 34	3¾	4¼	11:41	E	**11:20**	C	VIR	6
196	15	M.	5:20	A	**8:19**	E	14 59	10	21 24	4½	5	**12:46**	E	**11:52**	C	VIR	7
197	16	Tu.	5:21	A	**8:18**	E	14 57	10	21 14	5½	6	1:52	E	—	-	VIR	8
198	17	W.	5:22	A	**8:17**	E	14 55	10	21 04	6½	6¾	3:01	E	12:29	B	LIB	9
199	18	Th.	5:23	A	**8:16**	E	14 53	9	20 54	7½	7¾	4:09	E	1:11	B	LIB	10
200	19	Fr.	5:24	A	**8:16**	E	14 52	9	20 43	8½	8¾	5:14	E	2:02	B	SCO	11
201	20	Sa.	5:25	A	**8:15**	E	14 50	9	20 31	9½	9¾	6:15	E	3:01	B	OPH	12
202	21	**F**	5:26	A	**8:14**	E	14 48	9	20 20	10½	10¾	7:08	E	4:08	B	SAG	13
203	22	M.	5:27	A	**8:13**	E	14 46	9	20 08	11¼	11½	7:55	E	5:21	C	SAG	14
204	23	Tu.	5:28	A	**8:12**	E	14 44	9	19 55	12¼	—	8:35	E	6:35	C	CAP	15
205	24	W.	5:28	A	**8:11**	E	14 43	9	19 43	12½	1¼	9:11	D	7:49	D	CAP	16
206	25	Th.	5:29	A	**8:10**	E	14 41	9	19 30	1½	2	9:43	D	9:01	D	AQU	17
207	26	Fr.	5:30	A	**8:09**	E	14 39	9	19 17	2¼	2¾	10:14	C	10:11	D	PSC	18
208	27	Sa.	5:31	B	**8:08**	E	14 37	9	19 03	3¼	3¾	10:45	C	11:17	E	PSC	19
209	28	**F**	5:32	B	**8:07**	E	14 35	9	18 49	4	4½	11:18	C	**12:21**	E	PSC	20
210	29	M.	5:33	B	**8:06**	E	14 33	9	18 35	5	5½	11:52	B	**1:23**	E	ARI	21
211	30	Tu.	5:34	B	**8:05**	E	14 31	9	18 20	6	6¼	—	-	**2:22**	E	ARI	22
212	31	W.	5:35	B	**8:04**	E	14 29	9	18 N. 05	7	7¼	12:29	B	**3:18**	E	TAU	23

To use this page, see p. 100; for Key letters, see p. 234. ☞ **Bold** = P.M. ☞ Light = A.M.   **2013**

JULY HATH 31 DAYS • 2013

The sky is changed! and such a change! O night,
And storm, and darkness, ye are wondrous strong. –Lord Byron

Day of Month	Day of Week	Dates, Feasts, Fasts, Aspects, Tide Heights	Weather
1	M.	Canada Day • ♇ at ☍ • P.E.I. joined the Canadian Confederation, 1873 • {9.4 10.1	Stick
2	Tu.	*If the gulls are out, / Good luck's about.* • Tides {9.0 9.9	to
3	W.	Dog Days begin. • ☾ at ☋ • Black dust fell in Canada, 1814 • {8.8 9.9	patriotic
4	Th.	**Independence Day** • Construction of Erie Canal began, Rome, N.Y., 1817 • {8.7 9.9	topics;
5	Fr.	☾ rides high • ⊕ at aphelion • Lightning struck oil refinery, Bayonne, N.J., 1900	dress
6	Sa.	☾ at apo. • ☌♂☾ • ☌♃☾ • Tides {8.8 10.1	for
7	**F**	**7th S. af. P.** • Actress Vivien Leigh died, 1967 • Tides {8.9 10.2	the
8	M.	New ● • ☌☿☾ • Declaration of Independence proclaimed, Philadelphia, 1776	tropics!
9	Tu.	**First day of Ramadan** • ☿ in inf. ☌ • ♄ stat. • Tides {10.2 9.2	Beamy,
10	W.	☌♀☾ • Armadillos mate now. • 134°F, Death Valley, Calif., 1913 • {10.2 9.3	dreamy,
11	Th.	U.S. VP Aaron Burr fatally shot Alexander Hamilton in duel, 1804 • Writer E. B. White born, 1899	often
12	Fr.	Rain in Salem, Oreg., broke 113-year "Dry Day" record, 2006 • Tides {10.0 9.5	steamy.
13	Sa.	☾ on eq. • Cornscateous air is everywhere. • {9.9 9.6	So
14	**F**	**8th S. af. P.** • Bastille Day • *Nature goes her own way.* • {9.7 9.8	much
15	M.	St. Swithin • Guam Micronesian kingfisher hatched, National Zoo, Front Royal, Va., 2004	thunder,
16	Tu.	☌♄☾ • 3.4 earthquake, near Germantown, Md., 2010 • Tides {9.3 10.2	nights
17	W.	☾ at ☊ • ♅ stat. • Businessman John Jacob Astor born, 1763 • {9.2 10.5	feel
18	Th.	6-day, 7-night fire started in Rome, A.D. 64 • Tides {9.3 10.8	strange,
19	Fr.	☾ runs low • Morris Nourse earned Carnegie Medal by saving drowning boy, Des Moines, Iowa, 1905	like
20	Sa.	☿ stat. • Black-eyed Susans in bloom now. • {9.7 11.6	living
21	**F**	**9th S. af. P.** • ☾ at perig. • ☌♇☾ • {10.1 11.9	on
22	M.	St. Mary Magdalene • Full Buck ○ • ☌♂♃ • {10.5 12.1	an
23	Tu.	*Provide in leisure to use in haste.* • Tides {10.8 —	artillery
24	W.	Basketball player Karl Malone born, 1963 • {12.1 11.0	range!
25	Th.	St. James • ☌♆☾ • Adult gypsy moths emerge. • {11.9 11.1	We
26	Fr.	St. Anne • ☾ on eq. • First Moon rock samples analyzed, 1969 • Tides {11.5 11.0	ought
27	Sa.	☌♅☾ • Korean War Veterans Memorial dedicated, D.C., 1995 • Tides {10.9 10.8	to
28	**F**	**10th S. af. P.** • *The rain falls on every roof.*	mention
29	M.	St. Martha • National Aeronautics and Space Act signed into law, 1958 • {9.6 10.1	an
30	Tu.	☾ at ☋ • ☿ gr. elong. (20° west) • Puppeteer "Buffalo Bob" Smith died, 1998	occasional
31	W.	St. Ignatius of Loyola • Tornado struck Edmonton, Alta., 1987 • {8.7 9.6	drenchin'.

Farmer's Calendar

■ Most of us anticipate the coming of summer with its long hours of daylight and comfortable warmth. But when temperatures rise into the high double digits, it's time to find ways to stay as cool as a cucumber.

Farmers, landscapers, and others who make their living working outdoors use several methods to make their jobs comfortable in warm weather. Some escape the worst of the heat by starting at first light and stopping early. Others may find relief by working in shady areas during the hottest time of day.

If you need to work outside in hot weather, pace yourself and take frequent breaks out of the sun. Wear loose-fitting clothes and don't forget a wide-brimmed hat and sunscreen to protect your skin from the Sun's rays. Sweating helps to cool your body but causes you to lose much-needed water, so drink plenty of fluids to keep hydrated. And, as much as you might be otherwise inclined on these bright, sunny days, stay away from caffeine and alcohol, as well as protein-rich foods.

While battling the heat, let your thoughts drift to a refreshing swim or a leisurely mountain hike. These contemplations may help you to feel less like a piping-hot, baked potato.

If this fails, slices of cooling cukes on your skin will help you to chill out.

THE EIGHTH MONTH • 2013

SKY WATCH ☆ *Bright Jupiter sits to the left of the waning crescent Moon, with orange Mercury just below at a respectable magnitude –0.3, 40 minutes before sunrise on the 3rd. Jupiter, Mars, and Mercury stand in a row, low in the east in growing morning twilight, with the crescent Moon to their right on the 4th. Venus, still quite low in the west soon after sunset, hovers above the Moon on the 9th. Much higher on the 12th, the Moon is to the lower right of Saturn at nightfall. The Moon will set before midnight on the 11th and 12th and will not spoil the great Perseid meteor shower. Weather permitting, these will be the year's best "shooting stars." Neptune, in Aquarius at magnitude 7.8, requires a small telescope to be seen at its opposition, on the 26th.*

●	**New Moon**	6th day	17th hour	51st minute
◐	**First Quarter**	14th day	6th hour	56th minute
○	**Full Moon**	20th day	21st hour	45th minute
◑	**Last Quarter**	28th day	5th hour	35th minute

All times are given in Eastern Daylight Time.

Purchase these pages with times set to your zip code at MyLocalAlmanac.com.

Day of Year	Day of Month	Day of Week	☼ Rises h. m.	Rise Key	☼ Sets h. m.	Set Key	Length of Day h.	m.	Sun Fast m.	Declination of Sun °	'	High Tide Times Boston		☾ Rises h. m.	Rise Key	☾ Sets h. m.	Set Key	☾ Place	☾ Age
213	1	Th.	5:36	B	**8:03**	E	14	27	9	17 N.	50	8	**8¼**	1:10	B	**4:10**	E	TAU	24
214	2	Fr.	5:37	B	**8:02**	E	14	25	10	17	35	8¾	**9**	1:55	B	**4:58**	E	TAU	25
215	3	Sa.	5:38	B	**8:01**	E	14	23	10	17	19	9¾	**9¾**	2:45	B	**5:42**	E	ORI	26
216	4	**F**	5:39	B	**7:59**	E	14	20	10	17	03	10½	**10½**	3:38	B	**6:21**	E	GEM	27
217	5	M.	5:40	B	**7:58**	E	14	18	10	16	47	11¼	**11¼**	4:34	C	**6:56**	E	GEM	28
218	6	Tu.	5:42	B	**7:57**	E	14	15	10	16	30	11¾	12	5:32	C	**7:29**	E	CAN	0
219	7	W.	5:43	B	**7:56**	E	14	13	10	16	13	**12½**	—	6:31	C	**7:59**	D	CAN	1
220	8	Th.	5:44	B	**7:54**	E	14	10	10	15	56	12¾	**1**	7:31	D	**8:27**	D	LEO	2
221	9	Fr.	5:45	B	**7:53**	E	14	08	10	15	39	1¼	**1¾**	8:32	D	**8:56**	C	LEO	3
222	10	Sa.	5:46	B	**7:52**	E	14	06	11	15	21	2	**2¼**	9:35	D	**9:25**	C	VIR	4
223	11	**F**	5:47	B	**7:50**	E	14	03	11	15	04	2¾	**3**	10:38	E	**9:56**	C	VIR	5
224	12	M.	5:48	B	**7:49**	E	14	01	11	14	46	3½	**3¾**	11:43	E	**10:30**	B	VIR	6
225	13	Tu.	5:49	B	**7:47**	D	13	58	11	14	27	4¼	**4½**	**12:49**	E	**11:10**	B	VIR	7
226	14	W.	5:50	B	**7:46**	D	13	56	11	14	09	5	**5½**	**1:55**	E	**11:56**	B	LIB	8
227	15	Th.	5:51	B	**7:44**	D	13	53	11	13	50	6	**6½**	**3:00**	E	—	–	SCO	9
228	16	Fr.	5:52	B	**7:43**	D	13	51	12	13	31	7	**7½**	**4:01**	E	12:49	B	OPH	10
229	17	Sa.	5:53	B	**7:41**	D	13	48	12	13	12	8	**8½**	**4:56**	E	1:50	B	SAG	11
230	18	**F**	5:54	B	**7:40**	D	13	46	12	12	52	9¼	**9½**	**5:45**	E	2:58	B	SAG	12
231	19	M.	5:55	B	**7:38**	D	13	43	12	12	33	10¼	**10½**	**6:27**	E	4:10	C	CAP	13
232	20	Tu.	5:56	B	**7:37**	D	13	41	13	12	13	11	**11½**	**7:05**	D	5:24	C	AQU	14
233	21	W.	5:57	B	**7:35**	D	13	38	13	11	53	**12**	—	**7:40**	D	6:37	D	AQU	15
234	22	Th.	5:58	B	**7:34**	D	13	36	13	11	33	12¼	**12¾**	**8:12**	C	7:48	D	PSC	16
235	23	Fr.	6:00	B	**7:32**	D	13	32	13	11	12	1	**1½**	**8:44**	C	8:57	E	PSC	17
236	24	Sa.	6:01	B	**7:31**	D	13	30	14	10	52	2	**2¼**	**9:17**	C	10:04	E	PSC	18
237	25	**F**	6:02	B	**7:29**	D	13	27	14	10	31	2¾	**3¼**	**9:51**	B	11:08	E	PSC	19
238	26	M.	6:03	B	**7:27**	D	13	24	14	10	10	3½	**4**	**10:27**	B	**12:10**	E	ARI	20
239	27	Tu.	6:04	B	**7:26**	D	13	22	14	9	49	4½	**4¾**	**11:08**	B	**1:08**	E	ARI	21
240	28	W.	6:05	B	**7:24**	D	13	19	15	9	28	5¼	**5¾**	**11:51**	B	**2:02**	E	TAU	22
241	29	Th.	6:06	B	**7:22**	D	13	16	15	9	07	6¼	**6½**	—	–	**2:52**	E	TAU	23
242	30	Fr.	6:07	B	**7:21**	D	13	14	15	8	45	7¼	**7½**	12:39	B	**3:38**	E	TAU	24
243	31	Sa.	6:08	B	**7:19**	D	13	11	16	8 N.	24	8¼	**8½**	1:31	B	**4:19**	E	GEM	25

 To use this page, see p. 100; for Key letters, see p. 234. ☞ **Bold = P.M.** ☞ Light = A.M.

AUGUST HATH 31 DAYS • 2013

Have you seen the forest-pool
In the summer? Clear and cool . . . –William Canton

Day of Month	Day of Week	Dates, Feasts, Fasts, Aspects, Tide Heights	Weather
1	Th.	Lammas Day • *After Lammas, corn ripens as much by night as by day.* • Tides {8.4 / 9.5}	*It's*
2	Fr.	☾ RIDES HIGH • Architect Pierre-Charles L'Enfant born, 1754 • Tides {8.4 / 9.6}	*cool*
3	Sa.	☾ AT APO. • ☌♃☾ • Distinguished Flying Cross for William Bishop announced, 1918	*and*
4	**F**	**11th S. af. P.** • ☌♂☾ • Aurora visible in much of U.S., 1882	*mucky;*
5	M.	☌☿☾ • Supreme Lodge of Knights of Pythias incorporated, 1870 • Tides {8.9 / 10.1}	*now*
6	Tu.	**Transfiguration** • **New** ● • Baseball pitcher Cy Young made major league debut, 1890	*it's*
7	W.	Maiden voyage of La Salle's *Le Griffon,* 1679 • {9.4 / —}	*ducky!*
8	Th.	**St. Dominic** • Gray squirrels have second litters now. • Tides {10.2 / 9.6}	*Better*
9	Fr.	☾ ON EQ. • ☌♀☾ • Betty Boop debuted in *Dizzy Dishes,* 1930 • {10.2 / 9.8}	*pack*
10	Sa.	**St. Lawrence** • *Who knows himself, knows others.* • {10.1 / 10.0}	*a*
11	**F**	**12th S. af. P.** • Dog Days end. • Mars moon *Deimos* discovered, 1877	*sweater.*
12	M.	Actor William Shatner married Gloria Rand, 1956 • Patent issued for therapeutic horseshoe, 1986	*Meteor*
13	Tu.	☾ AT ☊ • ☌♄☾ • Writer H. G. Wells died, 1946 • Tides {9.6 / 10.3}	*showers*
14	W.	Satellite *Explorer VI* transmitted first picture of Earth from space, 1959 • Tides {9.4 / 10.4}	*amaze*
15	Th.	**Assumption** • *An ant on the move does more than a dozing ox.* • Tides {9.2 / 10.6}	*us.*
16	Fr.	☾ RUNS LOW • 106°F, Nashville, Tenn., 2007 • Tides {9.2 / 10.7}	*Hot*
17	Sa.	Cat Nights commence. • ☌♇☾ • Tides {9.4 / 11.0}	*as*
18	**F**	**13th S. af. P.** • ☾ AT PERIG. • Mongol leader Genghis Khan died, 1227	*blazes!*
19	M.	*Sesame Street* character Mr. Snuffleupagus born (always 4 yrs. old) • Tides {10.2 / 11.6}	*These*
20	Tu.	**Full Sturgeon** ○ • Ragweed in bloom. • Tides {10.6 / 11.7}	*evenings*
21	W.	☌♆☾ • Deadly tornado hit Wilmington, Del., 1888 • Tides {11.0 / —}	*clear*
22	Th.	☾ ON EQ. • Severe frost, Fort Custer, Mont., 1883 • {11.7 / 11.2}	*and*
23	Fr.	5.8 earthquake near Mineral, Va., 2011 • Tides {11.5 / 11.2}	*cool*
24	Sa.	**St. Bartholomew** • ☌♅☾ • ☿ IN SUP. ☌ • Tides {11.1 / 11.0}	*give*
25	**F**	**14th S. af. P.** • *Pogo* cartoonist Walt Kelly born, 1913 • {10.5 / 10.7}	*warning:*
26	M.	☾ AT ☋ • ♆ AT ☍ • Hummingbirds migrate south. • Tides {9.9 / 10.3}	*Soon*
27	Tu.	First autogiro loop-the-loop performed in public, Cleveland, Ohio, 1932 • Tides {9.3 / 9.9}	*comes*
28	W.	**St. Augustine of Hippo** • MLK delivered "I Have a Dream" speech, 1963 • {8.8 / 9.5}	*school,*
29	Th.	**St. John the Baptist** • ☾ RIDES HIGH • Tides {8.5 / 9.3}	*then*
30	Fr.	☾ AT APO. • *Fame is the perfume of heroic deeds.* • {8.3 / 9.2}	*frosty*
31	Sa.	☌♃☾ • Comet Howard-Koomur-Michels collided with Sun, 1979 • {8.3 / 9.3}	*mornings!*

Farmer's Calendar

■ Imagine coming home with bags of salad greens and mushrooms, sacks of delicious nuts, and baskets of berries and not having to pay a cent for them! Many people do just that by foraging, gathering wild edibles in fields, forests, and lawns.

If you'd like to try this, be certain that you identify each plant before eating it: Many have look-alikes that could prove deadly. Be especially careful with mushrooms and berries. Studying illustrated field guides is a good first step in learning about native plants, both those that are safe to eat and those best avoided. Also, check with garden clubs and your state Forest Service to see if there are groups in your area that go on foraging outings; their expertise could prove to be invaluable.

Collect your bounty in areas that are pesticide- and chemical-free. Gather no more than 10 percent of the plants from a given site and cut greens and mushrooms instead of uprooting them; this way, there'll be a crop there for years to come. If you'd like to explore private property, be sure to talk to the owner first.

Foraging is a great way to learn about plants while getting healthy exercise, and it is also an ecologically sound practice. The foods you gather don't have to be packaged or shipped, which saves fuel and resources. Get ready to go wild!

SKY WATCH ☆ *Venus hovers just above blue Spica on the 6th and 7th. The planet stubbornly remains just 10 degrees above the horizon some 40 minutes after sunset but has brightened to magnitude –4.1. It is close to the Moon, with Spica just below and Saturn to the upper left, on the 8th. Saturn stands to the right of the Moon on the 9th and then hovers above Venus from the 15th to the 19th. Jupiter, brightening to magnitude –2.1 and rising ever earlier, clears the horizon at around 1:00 A.M. and is well up for viewing during the predawn hours. It meets the Moon on the 28th and stands high up at dawn. The autumnal equinox brings fall at 4:44 P.M. on the 22nd.*

●	**New Moon**	5th day	7th hour	36th minute
◑	**First Quarter**	12th day	13th hour	8th minute
○	**Full Moon**	19th day	7th hour	13th minute
◐	**Last Quarter**	26th day	23rd hour	55th minute

All times are given in Eastern Daylight Time.

Purchase these pages with times set to your zip code at MyLocalAlmanac.com.

Day of Year	Day of Month	Day of Week	☼ Rises h. m.	Rise Key	☼ Sets h. m.	Set Key	Length of Day h. m.	Sun Fast m.	Declination of Sun ° '	High Tide Times Boston		☾ Rises h. m.	Rise Key	☾ Sets h. m.	Set Key	Place	Age
244	1	F	6:09	B	7:17	D	13 08	16	8 N.02	9	9¼	2:26	B	4:56	E	GEM	26
245	2	M.	6:10	B	7:16	D	13 06	16	7 40	10	10	3:23	C	5:29	E	CAN	27
246	3	Tu.	6:11	B	7:14	D	13 03	17	7 18	10½	10¾	4:22	C	6:00	D	CAN	28
247	4	W.	6:12	B	7:12	D	13 00	17	6 56	11¼	11½	5:22	D	6:30	D	LEO	29
248	5	Th.	6:13	C	7:11	D	12 58	17	6 33	12	—	6:23	D	6:59	D	SEX	0
249	6	Fr.	6:14	C	7:09	D	12 55	18	6 11	12¼	12½	7:26	D	7:28	C	LEO	1
250	7	Sa.	6:15	C	7:07	D	12 52	18	5 49	12¾	1¼	8:30	E	7:59	C	VIR	2
251	8	F	6:16	C	7:05	D	12 49	18	5 26	1½	1¾	9:35	E	8:33	C	VIR	3
252	9	M.	6:17	C	7:04	D	12 47	19	5 03	2¼	2½	10:42	E	9:11	B	VIR	4
253	10	Tu.	6:19	C	7:02	D	12 43	19	4 41	3	3¼	11:48	E	9:55	B	LIB	5
254	11	W.	6:20	C	7:00	C	12 40	19	4 18	3¾	4¼	12:52	E	10:45	B	LIB	6
255	12	Th.	6:21	C	6:58	C	12 37	20	3 55	4¾	5	1:53	E	11:42	B	OPH	7
256	13	Fr.	6:22	C	6:57	C	12 35	20	3 32	5¾	6	2:49	E	—	-	SAG	8
257	14	Sa.	6:23	C	6:55	C	12 32	20	3 09	6¾	7¼	3:38	E	12:46	B	SAG	9
258	15	F	6:24	C	6:53	C	12 29	21	2 46	8	8¼	4:22	E	1:54	C	SAG	10
259	16	M.	6:25	C	6:51	C	12 26	21	2 23	9	9¼	5:00	E	3:05	C	AQU	11
260	17	Tu.	6:26	C	6:49	C	12 23	21	2 00	10	10¼	5:36	D	4:16	C	CAP	12
261	18	W.	6:27	C	6:48	C	12 21	22	1 36	10¾	11¼	6:09	D	5:27	D	AQU	13
262	19	Th.	6:28	C	6:46	C	12 18	22	1 13	11½	12	6:41	C	6:36	D	PSC	14
263	20	Fr.	6:29	C	6:44	C	12 15	23	0 50	12¼	—	7:14	C	7:44	E	PSC	15
264	21	Sa.	6:30	C	6:42	C	12 12	23	0 26	12¾	1	7:47	C	8:50	E	PSC	16
265	22	F	6:31	C	6:41	C	12 10	23	0 N.03	1½	1¾	8:24	B	9:54	E	ARI	17
266	23	M.	6:32	C	6:39	C	12 07	24	0 S.19	2¼	2½	9:03	B	10:55	E	ARI	18
267	24	Tu.	6:33	C	6:37	C	12 04	24	0 43	3	3¼	9:46	B	11:51	E	TAU	19
268	25	W.	6:34	C	6:35	C	12 01	24	1 06	4	4¼	10:33	B	12:44	E	TAU	20
269	26	Th.	6:36	C	6:34	C	11 58	25	1 29	4¾	5	11:23	B	1:31	E	TAU	21
270	27	Fr.	6:37	C	6:32	C	11 55	25	1 53	5¾	6	—	-	2:14	E	GEM	22
271	28	Sa.	6:38	C	6:30	C	11 52	25	2 16	6½	6¾	12:16	B	2:53	E	GEM	23
272	29	F	6:39	C	6:28	C	11 49	26	2 39	7½	7¾	1:12	C	3:27	D	CAN	24
273	30	M.	6:40	C	6:27	C	11 47	26	3 S.03	8½	8¾	2:10	C	3:59	D	CAN	25

SEPTEMBER HATH 30 DAYS • 2013

We'll gather up the golden grain
With thankfulness once more. –Charles Gamage Eastman

Day of Month	Day of Week	Dates, Feasts, Fasts, Aspects, Tide Heights	Weather
1	**F**	**15th S. af. P.** • Deborah Read Rogers became common-law wife of Ben Franklin, 1730	*Scholars*
2	M.	**Labor Day** • ☌♂☾ • *Today is yesterday's pupil.* • {8.8 / 9.8	*are*
3	Tu.	Abolitionist Frederick Douglass escaped slavery, 1838 • Actor Alan Ladd born, 1913 • {9.2 / 10.0	*hot*
4	W.	Russian decree issued, concerning Northwest America, 1821	*under*
5	Th.	**Rosh Hashanah** • **New** ● • ☾ ON EQ. • Tides {9.8 / —	*their*
6	Fr.	☌☿☾ • Smoke from fires in Mich. and Canada caused Northeast's "Yellow Day," 1881 • {10.3 / 10.1	*collars.*
7	Sa.	Cranberry bog harvest begins, Cape Cod, Mass. • {10.3 / 10.4	*Cool*
8	**F**	**16th S. af. P.** • ☌♀☾ • Michelangelo's *David* statue unveiled, Florence, 1504	*and*
9	M.	**St. Omer** • ☾ AT ☊ • ☌♄☾ • Tides {10.1 / 10.7	*sweet;*
10	Tu.	5.8 earthquake in Gulf of Mexico shook Fla., 2006	*sidewalks*
11	W.	**Patriot Day** • 95' rogue wave struck *QE2* ocean liner, 1995	*will*
12	Th.	☾ RUNS LOW • Astronomer Charles Messier cataloged Crab Nebula, 1758 • Tides {9.4 / 10.6	*sauté*
13	Fr.	☌♇☾ • *After rain comes sunshine.* • Tides {9.3 / 10.5	*bare*
14	Sa.	**Holy Cross** • **Yom Kippur** • Sound-absorbing material patented, 1915	*feet!*
15	**F**	**17th S. af. P.** • ☾ AT PERIG. • Physicist Murray Gell-Mann born, 1929	*Save*
16	M.	Royal Canadian Mounted Police began training women troopers, 1974 • Tides {9.9 / 10.9	*your*
17	Tu.	☌♆☾ • 2.42" rain in 3 hours, Yuma, Ariz., 1963 • Tides {10.4 / 11.1	*soles!*
18	W.	Ember Day • ☾ ON EQ. • Aquarium of the Bay, Calif., reported angel shark born, 2007	*Lightning*
19	Th.	**Sukkoth** • **Full Harvest** ○ • ☌♀♄ • Tides {11.1 / 11.1	*flickers:*
20	Fr.	Ember Day • ☌⛢☾ • ♇ STAT. • Folklorist Jacob Grimm died, 1863 • {11.2 / —	*Get*
21	Sa.	**St. Matthew** • Ember Day • U.S. First Lady Margaret Taylor born, 1788	*down*
22	**F**	**18th S. af. P.** • Harvest Home • **Autumnal Equinox** • ☾ AT ☋	*from those*
23	M.	Time capsule (to open in 6939) buried at N.Y. World's Fair, N.Y.C., 1938 • Tides {10.1 / 10.6	*trees,*
24	Tu.	*The fairest apple hangs on the highest bough.* • {9.6 / 10.1	*apple*
25	W.	☾ RIDES HIGH • 20-foot wide, 3,699-pound pumpkin pie set world record, New Bremen, Ohio, 2010	*pickers!*
26	Th.	Poet T. S. Eliot born, 1888 • N.Y. Giant Ali Haji-Sheikh kicked 56-yard field goal, 1983	*Cooling*
27	Fr.	**St. Vincent de Paul** • ☾ AT APO. • SS *Arctic* and SS *Vesta* collided, N. Atlantic, 1854	*trend*
28	Sa.	☌♃☾ • Woodchucks hibernate now. • Tides {8.3 / 9.0	*at*
29	**F**	**19th S. af. P.** • Space shuttle *Discovery* launched, 1988 • {8.4 / 9.1	*summer's*
30	M.	**St. Michael'** • TV series *The Flintstones* premiered, 1960 • Tides {8.7 / 9.3	*end.*

A book is a garden carried in the pocket. –Arabian proverb

Farmer's Calendar

■ Long before supermarkets and big-box stores, the small-town general store was the lifeblood of the community, supplying the townspeople and those living in the surrounding rural area with just about everything that they didn't grow or make themselves.

The store usually had only one room with a counter, a butcher's table, and shelves from floor to ceiling that were packed with a variety of goods. Customers could buy staples such as coffee, spices, and baking supplies, as well as locally grown fruit and vegetables that were often brought in by farmers who bartered for needed items. The dry goods section kept patrons well stocked with essentials, including bolts of cloth, sewing materials, shoes, clothing, guns and ammunition, lamps and lamp oil, cooking utensils, and farming supplies. Wooden barrels filled with apples and dill pickles tempted patrons, and jars of penny candy delighted children. Often, the store housed the post office and provided a bench and a few chairs where residents gathered to catch up on the local news.

You can still find these old-time general stores, although they aren't as plentiful. Much of the merchandise has changed, but they're still great places for sharing a cup of coffee and a little gossip with friends.

SKY WATCH ☆ *Saturn is getting quite low in the west, joining horizon-hugging Venus, which, though still a mere 10 degrees up in fading twilight, brightens to magnitude –4.5 this month. Green Uranus reaches opposition at magnitude 5.7 in Pisces on the 3rd. It's an easy target in binoculars and faintly visible to the naked eye in dark skies, especially during this moonless period. The thin crescent Moon hovers between Mercury and Saturn on the 6th, a low conjunction visible to southern observers. The Moon is to the right of Venus on the 7th and to the right of Jupiter on the 24th. The Giant Planet now rises by 11:00 P.M. and can be well observed after midnight.*

● New Moon	4th day	20th hour	35th minute
◐ First Quarter	11th day	19th hour	2nd minute
○ Full Moon	18th day	19th hour	38th minute
◑ Last Quarter	26th day	19th hour	40th minute

All times are given in Eastern Daylight Time.

Purchase these pages with times set to your zip code at MyLocalAlmanac.com.

Day of Year	Day of Month	Day of Week	☼ Rises h. m.	Rise Key	☼ Sets h. m.	Set Key	Length of Day h. m.	Sun Fast m.	Declination of Sun ° '	High Tide Times Boston		☽ Rises h. m.	Rise Key	☽ Sets h. m.	Set Key	☽ Place	☽ Age
274	1	Tu.	6:41	C	6:25	C	11 44	26	3 s. 26	9¼	9½	3:09	C	4:30	D	LEO	26
275	2	W.	6:42	C	6:23	C	11 41	27	3 49	10	10¼	4:10	D	4:59	D	SEX	27
276	3	Th.	6:43	C	6:21	C	11 38	27	4 12	10¾	11	5:13	D	5:29	C	LEO	28
277	4	Fr.	6:44	C	6:20	C	11 36	27	4 35	11¼	11¾	6:17	D	5:59	C	VIR	0
278	5	Sa.	6:45	D	6:18	C	11 33	28	4 59	12	—	7:23	E	6:33	C	VIR	1
279	6	F	6:46	D	6:16	C	11 30	28	5 22	12½	12¾	8:30	E	7:10	B	VIR	2
280	7	M.	6:48	D	6:15	C	11 27	28	5 44	1	1¼	9:38	E	7:53	B	LIB	3
281	8	Tu.	6:49	D	6:13	C	11 24	28	6 07	2	2	10:44	E	8:42	B	LIB	4
282	9	W.	6:50	D	6:11	C	11 21	29	6 30	2¾	3	11:47	E	9:38	B	OPH	5
283	10	Th.	6:51	D	6:10	C	11 19	29	6 53	3½	3¾	12:45	E	10:40	B	OPH	6
284	11	Fr.	6:52	D	6:08	C	11 16	29	7 15	4½	4¾	1:36	E	11:46	C	SAG	7
285	12	Sa.	6:53	D	6:06	C	11 13	29	7 38	5½	6	2:20	E	—	–	SAG	8
286	13	F	6:54	D	6:05	C	11 11	30	8 00	6¾	7	2:59	E	12:54	C	CAP	9
287	14	M.	6:56	D	6:03	C	11 07	30	8 23	7¾	8	3:35	D	2:04	C	CAP	10
288	15	Tu.	6:57	D	6:01	B	11 04	30	8 45	8¾	9	4:08	D	3:12	D	AQU	11
289	16	W.	6:58	D	6:00	B	11 02	30	9 07	9½	10	4:40	C	4:21	D	PSC	12
290	17	Th.	6:59	D	5:58	B	10 59	31	9 29	10½	11	5:11	C	5:28	E	PSC	13
291	18	Fr.	7:00	D	5:57	B	10 57	31	9 51	11¼	11¾	5:44	C	6:33	E	PSC	14
292	19	Sa.	7:01	D	5:55	B	10 54	31	10 12	12	—	6:20	B	7:38	E	ARI	15
293	20	F	7:03	D	5:54	B	10 51	31	10 34	12½	12¾	6:58	B	8:40	E	ARI	16
294	21	M.	7:04	D	5:52	B	10 48	31	10 55	1¼	1¼	7:39	B	9:39	E	TAU	17
295	22	Tu.	7:05	D	5:51	B	10 46	31	11 16	2	2	8:25	B	10:34	E	TAU	18
296	23	W.	7:06	D	5:49	B	10 43	32	11 37	2¾	2¾	9:14	B	11:24	E	TAU	19
297	24	Th.	7:07	D	5:48	B	10 41	32	11 58	3½	3½	10:07	B	12:09	E	ORI	20
298	25	Fr.	7:09	D	5:46	B	10 37	32	12 19	4¼	4¼	11:01	B	12:49	E	GEM	21
299	26	Sa.	7:10	D	5:45	B	10 35	32	12 39	5	5¼	11:58	C	1:25	E	GEM	22
300	27	F	7:11	D	5:43	B	10 32	32	12 59	6	6¼	—	–	1:58	E	CAN	23
301	28	M.	7:12	D	5:42	B	10 30	32	13 19	6¾	7	12:56	C	2:28	D	CAN	24
302	29	Tu.	7:14	D	5:41	B	10 27	32	13 39	7¾	8	1:55	C	2:57	D	LEO	25
303	30	W.	7:15	D	5:39	B	10 24	32	13 59	8½	8¾	2:56	D	3:27	D	LEO	26
304	31	Th.	7:16	D	5:38	B	10 22	32	14 s. 18	9¼	9¾	3:59	D	3:57	C	VIR	27

To use this page, see p. 100; for Key letters, see p. 234. ☞ **Bold** = P.M. ☞ Light = A.M. **2013**

OCTOBER HATH 31 DAYS • 2013

Now autumn's fire burns slowly along the woods,
And day by day the dead leaves fall and melt. –William Allingham

Day of Month	Day of Week	Dates, Feasts, Fasts, Aspects, Tide Heights	Weather
1	Tu.	☌♂☾ • Sea Gull Monument unveiled, Salt Lake City, Utah, 1913 • {9.0 / 9.6	*Showers*
2	W.	*Good management is better than good income.* • {9.5 / 9.8	*fade*
3	Th.	☾ ON EQ. • ♅ AT ☍ • U.S. Thanksgiving set as last Thursday in November, 1863 • {9.9 / 10.1	*for*
4	Fr.	**St. Francis of Assisi** • **New** ● • Writer Anne Rice born, 1941	*autumn's*
5	Sa.	Shawnee chief Tecumseh died, 1813 • Tides {10.7 / —	*grand*
6	**F**	**20th S. af. P.** • ☾ AT ☊ • ☌☿☾ • {10.4 / 11.0	*parade.*
7	M.	☌♄☾ • First photos taken of dark side of Moon, by *Luna 3,* 1959 • Tides {10.4 / 11.2	*Leaf*
8	Tu.	☌♀☾ • Statesman John Hay born, 1838 • Tides {10.3 / 11.2	*season*
9	W.	☾ RUNS LOW • ☿ GR. ELONG. (25° EAST) • Collegiate School (later, Yale) founded, Conn., 1701	*comes*
10	Th.	☾ AT PERIG. • ☌☿♄ • Painter Benjamin West born, 1738	*with*
11	Fr.	☌♇☾ • 19-lb. 2-oz. weakfish caught, Jones Beach, Long Island, N.Y., 1984	*lightning's*
12	Sa.	*You will never get ahead trying to get even.* • {9.5 / 10.4	*bugles*
13	**F**	**21st S. af. P.** • Several countries adopted Greenwich longitude as prime meridian, 1884	*and*
14	M.	**Columbus Day (observed)** • **Thanksgiving Day (Canada)** • Tides {9.8 / 10.3	*thunder's*
15	Tu.	☌♆☾ • "Hazel II" storm flooded Toronto, 1954 • Tides {10.2 / 10.4	*drums!*
16	W.	☾ ON EQ. • *Warm October, cold February.* • Tides {10.6 / 10.5	*Sumac*
17	Th.	**St. Ignatius of Antioch** • ☌♅☾ • Tides {10.9 / 10.5	*clothed*
18	Fr.	**St. Luke** • **Full Hunter's** ○ • **Eclipse** ☾ • St. Luke's little summer.	*in*
19	Sa.	☾ AT ☋ • Abe Lincoln wrote to 11-yr.-old girl who requested that he grow a beard, 1860	*bright*
20	**F**	**22nd S. af. P.** • Canadian newspaper *La Presse* debuted, 1884	*vermilion,*
21	M.	☿ STAT. • Trimline phone first placed in service, Mich., 1963 • Tides {10.0 / 10.7	*golden*
22	Tu.	Timber rattlesnakes move to winter dens. • Tides {9.7 / 10.4	*maples*
23	W.	**St. James of Jerusalem** • ☾ RIDES HIGH • Tides {9.3 / 10.1	*by*
24	Th.	*He who is afraid of the leaves must not go into the wood.*	*the*
25	Fr.	☾ AT APO. • ☌♃☾ • Little brown bats hibernate now. • Tides {8.7 / 9.3	*million!*
26	Sa.	Michael Jackson rec'd patent for shoes that allow wearer to lean far forward, 1993 • Tides {8.5 / 9.1	*We're*
27	**F**	**23rd S. af. P.** • 16' Burmese python caught in Everglades, Fla., 2011 • {8.5 / 8.9	*not*
28	M.	**Sts. Simon & Jude** • ☌☿♄ • Boston Red Sox won World Series, 2007	*joking:*
29	Tu.	☌♂☾ • Snow hurricane (Ginny) hit Maine, 1963	*a*
30	W.	☾ ON EQ. • Orson Welles' "War of the Worlds" broadcast panicked listeners, 1938	*Halloween*
31	Th.	**All Hallows' Eve** • **Reformation Day** • {9.8 / 9.6	*soaking!*

Farmer's Calendar

■ Compost, often referred to as "black gold," is a safe, efficient fertilizer that contains all essential plant nutrients. In addition, it conditions the soil for maximum root growth and helps to retain soil moisture.

Creating compost is not a new idea. In fact, Nature has been doing it since long before dinosaurs roamed. When leaves and dead branches fall to the forest floor and decay, they are composting. This natural recycling, brought about through the activities of soil microbes, releases nutrients to feed plant roots, allowing future generations of leaves and shoots to flourish.

Gardeners have devised ways to speed up Nature's metabolic method. They mix lots of "brown" (carbon-rich) materials, such as straw and shredded dry leaves, with a smaller amount of "green" (nitrogen-rich) materials, such as grass clippings and garden waste. When combined properly, the materials heat up and decompose with no bad odor. Turning the pile often will hasten the process.

As landfill space becomes increasingly scarce and expensive, composting yard and kitchen waste is becoming a necessity. Some recycling centers compost and allow folks to take home the finished product for their gardens. Perhaps we are learning what Nature has known all along.

NOVEMBER

THE ELEVENTH MONTH • 2013

SKY WATCH ☆ *The year's only total eclipse, of the Sun, occurs on the 3rd and is visible from the equatorial Atlantic Ocean and west central Africa. Saturn is gone, but Venus starts to show some elevation gain as it noticeably brightens to magnitude –4.8. The Moon, dangling below invisible Pluto, stands above Venus on the 6th. The Moon hovers just above Uranus on the 13th, to the lower right of Jupiter on the 21st, and to the right of faint Mars on the 27th. The Orange World is now rising at 1:00 A.M. Mercury, at magnitude –0.7, appears low in the east at about 40 minutes before sunrise, where it closely meets returning planet Saturn, which shines at a bright magnitude 0.6, on the 25th and 26th.*

●	**New Moon**	3rd day	7th hour	50th minute
◐	**First Quarter**	10th day	0 hour	57th minute
○	**Full Moon**	17th day	10th hour	16th minute
◑	**Last Quarter**	25th day	14th hour	28th minute

After 2:00 A.M. on November 3, Eastern Standard Time is given.

Purchase these pages with times set to your zip code at MyLocalAlmanac.com.

Day of Year	Day of Month	Day of Week	☼ Rises h. m.	Rise Key	☼ Sets h. m.	Set Key	Length of Day h. m.	Sun Fast m.	Declination of Sun ° '	High Tide Times Boston		☾ Rises h. m.	Rise Key	☾ Sets h. m.	Set Key	☾ Place	☾ Age
305	1	Fr.	7:17	D	**5:37**	B	10 20	32	14 s. 38	10	**10½**	5:04	E	**4:29**	C	VIR	28
306	2	Sa.	7:18	D	**5:35**	B	10 17	32	14 56	10¾	**11¼**	6:12	E	**5:05**	B	VIR	29
307	3	**F**	6:20	D	**4:34**	B	10 14	32	15 15	10½	**11**	6:21	E	**4:46**	B	VIR	0
308	4	M.	6:21	D	**4:33**	B	10 12	32	15 34	11¼	**11¾**	7:30	E	**5:34**	B	LIB	1
309	5	Tu.	6:22	D	**4:32**	B	10 10	32	15 52	**12**	—	8:36	E	**6:29**	B	SCO	2
310	6	W.	6:23	E	**4:31**	B	10 08	32	16 10	12½	**12¾**	9:38	E	**7:31**	B	OPH	3
311	7	Th.	6:25	E	**4:30**	B	10 05	32	16 27	1½	**1¾**	10:32	E	**8:37**	B	SAG	4
312	8	Fr.	6:26	E	**4:28**	B	10 02	32	16 45	2¼	**2½**	11:20	E	**9:46**	C	SAG	5
313	9	Sa.	6:27	E	**4:27**	B	10 00	32	17 02	3¼	**3½**	**12:01**	E	**10:56**	C	CAP	6
314	10	**F**	6:29	E	**4:26**	B	9 57	32	17 19	4¼	**4¾**	**12:37**	D	—	–	AQU	7
315	11	M.	6:30	E	**4:25**	B	9 55	32	17 35	5¼	**5¾**	**1:10**	D	12:04	D	AQU	8
316	12	Tu.	6:31	E	**4:24**	B	9 53	32	17 51	6½	**6¾**	**1:42**	D	1:11	D	PSC	9
317	13	W.	6:32	E	**4:23**	B	9 51	31	18 07	7½	**7¾**	**2:13**	C	2:17	D	PSC	10
318	14	Th.	6:33	E	**4:22**	B	9 49	31	18 23	8¼	**8¾**	**2:44**	C	3:22	E	PSC	11
319	15	Fr.	6:35	E	**4:22**	B	9 47	31	18 38	9	**9¾**	**3:18**	B	4:26	E	PSC	12
320	16	Sa.	6:36	E	**4:21**	B	9 45	31	18 53	10	**10½**	**3:54**	B	5:28	E	ARI	13
321	17	**F**	6:37	E	**4:20**	B	9 43	31	19 08	10½	**11¼**	**4:34**	B	6:28	E	ARI	14
322	18	M.	6:38	E	**4:19**	B	9 41	31	19 22	11¼	**11¾**	**5:18**	B	7:25	E	TAU	15
323	19	Tu.	6:40	E	**4:18**	B	9 38	30	19 36	**12**	—	**6:06**	B	8:17	E	TAU	16
324	20	W.	6:41	E	**4:18**	B	9 37	30	19 49	12½	**12½**	**6:58**	B	9:04	E	TAU	17
325	21	Th.	6:42	E	**4:17**	B	9 35	30	20 03	1¼	**1¼**	**7:51**	B	9:46	E	GEM	18
326	22	Fr.	6:43	E	**4:16**	B	9 33	30	20 15	2	**2**	**8:47**	C	10:24	E	GEM	19
327	23	Sa.	6:44	E	**4:16**	B	9 32	29	20 28	2¾	**2¾**	**9:44**	C	10:57	E	CAN	20
328	24	**F**	6:46	E	**4:15**	B	9 29	29	20 40	3½	**3½**	**10:42**	C	11:28	D	CAN	21
329	25	M.	6:47	E	**4:14**	A	9 27	29	20 52	4¼	**4½**	**11:41**	D	11:57	D	LEO	22
330	26	Tu.	6:48	E	**4:14**	A	9 26	28	21 03	5	**5¼**	—	–	**12:26**	D	SEX	23
331	27	W.	6:49	E	**4:14**	A	9 25	28	21 14	6	**6¼**	12:42	D	**12:55**	C	LEO	24
332	28	Th.	6:50	E	**4:13**	A	9 23	28	21 24	6¾	**7¼**	1:44	D	**1:25**	C	VIR	25
333	29	Fr.	6:51	E	**4:13**	A	9 22	27	21 34	7½	**8**	2:49	E	**1:58**	C	VIR	26
334	30	Sa.	6:52	E	**4:12**	A	9 20	27	21 s. 44	8¼	**9**	3:57	E	**2:36**	B	VIR	27

 To use this page, see p. 100; for Key letters, see p. 234. ☞ **Bold = P.M.** ☞ Light = A.M.

NOVEMBER HATH 30 DAYS • 2013

The hoar-frost gathered, o'er each leaf and spray
Weaving its filmy network; thin and bright. –Sarah Helen Whitman

Day of Month	Day of Week	Dates, Feasts, Fasts, Aspects, Tide Heights	Weather
1	Fr.	**All Saints'** • ☿ IN INF. ☌ • ♀ GR. ELONG. (47° EAST) • Tides {10.3 / 9.9	*Falling*
2	Sa.	**All Souls'** • Sadie Hawkins Day • Actor Burt Lancaster born, 1913 • {10.8 / 10.1	*drops*
3	**F**	**Daylight Saving Time ends, 2:00 A.M.** • **New ●** • **Eclipse ☉** • ☾ AT ☊	*turn*
4	M.	**Islamic New Year** • Earthquake shook N.Y., New England, and eastern Canada, 1877	*to flying*
5	Tu.	**Election Day** • *He who is a slave of truth is a free man.* • Tides {11.7 / —	*flakes,*
6	W.	☾ RUNS LOW • ☾ AT PERIG. • ☌♀☾ • ☌♄☉ • Tides {10.4 / 11.7	*burying*
7	Th.	☌♇☾ • ♃ STAT. • Black bears head to winter dens now. • {10.3 / 11.5	*hillsides,*
8	Fr.	Montana became 41st U.S. state, 1889 • Tides {10.1 / 11.2	*fields,*
9	Sa.	Canada's first domestic communications satellite, *Anik A1*, launched, 1972 • Tides {10.0 / 10.7	*and*
10	**F**	**25th S. af. P.** • ☿ STAT. • Lutheran church founder Martin Luther born, 1483	*lakes.*
11	M.	**St. Martin of Tours** • **Veterans Day** • ☌♆☾ • Tides {9.9 / 10.1	*Gray*
12	Tu.	Indian Summer • ☾ ON EQ. • Lobsters move to offshore waters. • Tides {10.1 / 9.9	*skies*
13	W.	☌♅☾ • ♆ STAT. • Bob Pettit first to reach 20,000 career points in NBA, 1964	*surprise*
14	Th.	Lightning struck *Apollo 12*, 1969 • Crab apples are ripe now.	*us*
15	Fr.	☌♀♇ • Astronomer Sir William Herschel born, 1738 • Tides {10.7 / 9.8	*with*
16	Sa.	☾ AT ☋ • Racehorse Northern Dancer died, 1990 • {10.8 / 9.8	*temperatures*
17	**F**	**26th S. af. P.** • **Full Beaver** ○ • ☿ GR. ELONG. (19° WEST)	*icy—*
18	M.	72°F, Youngstown, Ohio, 1958 • Tides {10.7 / 9.5	*driving's*
19	Tu.	☾ RIDES HIGH • Skunks hibernate now. • Talk show host Larry King born, 1933	*dicey.*
20	W.	Tucson Municipal Flying Field became first municipal airport in nation, Ariz., 1919	*This*
21	Th.	*As November 21st, so is the winter.* • {9.2 / 10.0	*Thanksgiving,*
22	Fr.	☾ AT APO. • ☌♃☾ • U.S. president JFK assassinated, 1963 • {9.0 / 9.7	*even*
23	Sa.	**St. Clement** • 14" snow, Yarmouth, Mass., 1989 • {8.8 / 9.4	*the*
24	**F**	**27th S. af. P.** • "Battle Above the Clouds," Lookout Mtn., Chattanooga, Tenn., 1863	*turkey*
25	M.	☌☿♄ • Last log entry for *Mary Celeste* before crew disappeared, 1872 • Tides {8.7 / 8.9	*is*
26	Tu.	Thelma Chalifoux first Métis woman to become Canadian senator (Alta.), 1997 • Tides {8.8 / 8.8	*shivering!*
27	W.	☾ ON EQ. • ☌♂☾ • Shakespeare got license to marry Anne Hathaway, 1582	*Mild*
28	Th.	**First day of Chanukah** • **Thanksgiving Day** • {9.5 / 9.0	*reprieve,*
29	Fr.	*Warm food, warm friendships.* • English first used during U.S. Catholic mass, 1964	*we*
30	Sa.	**St. Andrew** • ☾ AT ☊ • Mason jar (by John Mason) patented, 1858 • {10.5 / 9.6	*believe.*

Humor is mankind's greatest blessing. –Mark Twain

Farmer's Calendar

■ After a treacherous voyage and brutal first winter spent along the shore of Cape Cod Bay, the Pilgrims of Plymouth Colony had a stroke of good fortune. Members of the Wampanoag Nation offered to teach them how to gather food from the wild and cultivate native crops such as corn. The first harvest, in 1621, proved so successful that Governor William Bradford ordered a feast to celebrate. We now call this the Pilgrims' first Thanksgiving, although they considered it simply a harvest festival. The event, however, was a far cry from today's observance.

The thankful colonists, soon joined by their generous Native American friends, took part in a 3-day party that included singing, dancing, musket and bow-and-arrow competitions, and footraces.

Historians can document with certainty only two items on the menu for that day: fowl provided by the Pilgrims and venison brought by the Wampanoag. Seafood such as bass, cod, eels, clams, and mussels may have been on the table, possibly along with game such as harbor seal, waterfowl, rabbit, and gray squirrel. Roots, fruit, and nuts were also common fare of the day. We don't know for sure whether turkey was served, but it has somehow become a tradition—and that's another reason to celebrate.

DECEMBER

THE TWELFTH MONTH • 2013

SKY WATCH ☆ *Venus continues to climb higher in the west after sunset as it brightens to magnitude –4.9, its most dazzling display of the year. An easy 25 degrees high, it dangles beneath the crescent Moon on the 5th. The Moon floats above green Uranus on the 10th and is to the left of Taurus's orange star Aldebaran on the 15th. In its fat gibbous phase, the Moon diminishes the normally reliable Geminid meteors on the 13th and stands to the right of Jupiter on the 18th. Jupiter, in Gemini, conveniently rises by 7:00 P.M. and shines at a brilliant magnitude –2.7. The Giant Planet is now a telescopic showpiece in advance of its imminent opposition on January 5. Winter begins with the solstice at 12:11 P.M. on the 21st.*

● **New Moon**	2nd day	19th hour	22nd minute
◐ **First Quarter**	9th day	10th hour	12th minute
○ **Full Moon**	17th day	4th hour	28th minute
◑ **Last Quarter**	25th day	8th hour	48th minute

All times are given in Eastern Standard Time.

Purchase these pages with times set to your zip code at MyLocalAlmanac.com.

Day of Year	Day of Month	Day of Week	☼ Rises h. m.	Rise Key	☼ Sets h. m.	Set Key	Length of Day h.	m.	Sun Fast m.	Declination of Sun °	'	High Tide Times Boston		☾ Rises h. m.	Rise Key	☾ Sets h. m.	Set Key	☾ Place	☾ Age
335	1	**F**	6:53	E	**4:12**	A	9	19	27	21 s.	53	9¼	**9¾**	5:06	E	**3:21**	B	LIB	28
336	2	M.	6:54	E	**4:12**	A	9	18	26	22	02	10	**10½**	6:15	E	**4:13**	B	LIB	0
337	3	Tu.	6:55	E	**4:12**	A	9	17	26	22	11	10¾	**11½**	7:21	E	**5:13**	B	OPH	1
338	4	W.	6:56	E	**4:11**	A	9	15	25	22	19	11½	—	8:21	E	**6:20**	B	SAG	2
339	5	Th.	6:57	E	**4:11**	A	9	14	25	22	26	12¼	**12½**	9:14	E	**7:31**	C	SAG	3
340	6	Fr.	6:58	E	**4:11**	A	9	13	25	22	33	1¼	**1½**	9:59	E	**8:43**	C	SAG	4
341	7	Sa.	6:59	E	**4:11**	A	9	12	24	22	40	2	**2¼**	10:38	E	**9:54**	D	AQU	5
342	8	**F**	7:00	E	**4:11**	A	9	11	24	22	46	3	**3¼**	11:13	D	**11:03**	D	AQU	6
343	9	M.	7:01	E	**4:11**	A	9	10	23	22	52	4	**4¼**	11:45	D	—	–	AQU	7
344	10	Tu.	7:02	E	**4:11**	A	9	09	23	22	57	5	**5½**	**12:16**	C	12:10	D	PSC	8
345	11	W.	7:03	E	**4:11**	A	9	08	22	23	02	6	**6½**	**12:48**	C	1:15	E	PSC	9
346	12	Th.	7:04	E	**4:11**	A	9	07	22	23	07	7	**7½**	**1:20**	C	2:19	E	PSC	10
347	13	Fr.	7:05	E	**4:12**	A	9	07	21	23	11	8	**8½**	**1:55**	B	3:21	E	ARI	11
348	14	Sa.	7:05	E	**4:12**	A	9	07	21	23	14	8¾	**9¼**	**2:33**	B	4:21	E	ARI	12
349	15	**F**	7:06	E	**4:12**	A	9	06	20	23	17	9½	**10¼**	**3:15**	B	5:18	E	TAU	13
350	16	M.	7:07	E	**4:12**	A	9	05	20	23	20	10¼	**10¾**	**4:01**	B	6:11	E	TAU	14
351	17	Tu.	7:08	E	**4:13**	A	9	05	19	23	22	11	**11½**	**4:51**	B	7:00	E	TAU	15
352	18	W.	7:08	E	**4:13**	A	9	05	19	23	23	11½	—	**5:44**	B	7:44	E	GEM	16
353	19	Th.	7:09	E	**4:13**	A	9	04	19	23	25	12¼	**12¼**	**6:39**	C	8:24	E	GEM	17
354	20	Fr.	7:09	E	**4:13**	A	9	04	18	23	25	12¾	**12¾**	**7:35**	C	8:59	E	CAN	18
355	21	Sa.	7:10	E	**4:14**	A	9	04	18	23	26	1½	**1½**	**8:33**	C	9:31	E	CAN	19
356	22	**F**	7:10	E	**4:15**	A	9	05	17	23	25	2	**2¼**	**9:31**	D	10:00	D	LEO	20
357	23	M.	7:11	E	**4:16**	A	9	05	17	23	25	2¾	**3**	**10:29**	D	10:28	D	SEX	21
358	24	Tu.	7:11	E	**4:16**	A	9	05	16	23	24	3½	**3¾**	**11:29**	D	10:56	C	LEO	22
359	25	W.	7:11	E	**4:17**	A	9	06	16	23	22	4¼	**4½**	—	–	11:25	C	VIR	23
360	26	Th.	7:12	E	**4:18**	A	9	06	15	23	20	5	**5½**	12:31	E	11:55	C	VIR	24
361	27	Fr.	7:12	E	**4:18**	A	9	06	15	23	17	6	**6½**	1:36	E	**12:30**	C	VIR	25
362	28	Sa.	7:12	E	**4:19**	A	9	07	14	23	14	6¾	**7½**	2:42	E	**1:09**	B	LIB	26
363	29	**F**	7:12	E	**4:19**	A	9	07	14	23	11	7¾	**8½**	3:50	E	**1:56**	B	LIB	27
364	30	M.	7:13	E	**4:20**	A	9	07	13	23	07	8¾	**9¼**	4:57	E	**2:51**	B	SCO	28
365	31	Tu.	7:13	E	**4:21**	A	9	08	13	23 s.	02	9½	**10¼**	6:01	E	**3:55**	B	OPH	29

DECEMBER HATH 31 DAYS • 2013

Then came the merry maskers in,
And carols roar'd with blithesome din. –Sir Walter Scott

Day of Month	Day of Week	Dates, Feasts, Fasts, Aspects, Tide Heights	Weather
1	F	**1st S. of Advent** • ☌☿☾ • ☌♄☾ • Tides {11.1 9.9	*Spell*
2	M.	St. Viviana • **New ●** • Major League Baseball began accepting cowhide baseballs, 1974	*it*
3	Tu.	☾ RUNS LOW • Meteorologist Cleveland Abbe born, 1838 • {11.9 10.5	*Decembrrrr!*
4	W.	☾ AT PERIG. • ☌♇☾ • G. Washington bade farewell to officers, Fraunces Tavern, N.Y.C., 1783	*Mild*
5	Th.	☌♀☾ • First six astronauts chosen for Canadian Space Program, 1983 • {10.6 12.0	*plus a*
6	Fr.	St. Nicholas • *A fire hard to kindle indicates bad weather.* • Tides {10.6 11.8	*shower,*
7	Sa.	St. Ambrose • **National Pearl Harbor Remembrance Day**	*then a*
8	F	**2nd S. of Advent** • ☌♆☾ • Tides {10.4 10.8	*power*
9	M.	☾ ON EQ. • Public debut of computer mouse, San Francisco, 1968 • Tides {10.2 10.2	*of*
10	Tu.	St. Eulalia • Winterberry fruit especially showy now. • Tides {10.1 9.7	*powder!*
11	W.	☌♅☾ • Astronomer Annie Jump Cannon born, 1863 • Tides {10.1 9.4	*Mercury*
12	Th.	**Our Lady of Guadalupe** • *Before honor is humility.* • Tides {10.1 9.2	*and*
13	Fr.	St. Lucia • ☾ AT ☋ • First strike of Susan B. Anthony dollar, Philadelphia Mint, 1978	*snow*
14	Sa.	Halcyon Days begin. • Alabama became 22nd U.S. state, 1819	*both*
15	F	**3rd S. of Advent** • Beware the Pogonip. • Tides {10.3 9.1	*falling;*
16	M.	☾ RIDES HIGH • Lillian Disney, who named Mickey Mouse, died, 1997 • {10.4 9.1	*malls*
17	Tu.	**Full Cold ○** • ♅ STAT. • Canadian "Maple leaf flag" approved by Senate, 1964	*a-calling!*
18	W.	Ember Day • Civil rights activist Rosa McCauley married Raymond Parks, 1932 • {10.3 —	*Frozen*
19	Th.	☾ AT APO. • ☌♃☾ • –59°F, Yellowstone National Park, Wyo., 1924	*tundra—*
20	Fr.	Ember Day • ♀ STAT. • France transferred Louisiana territory to U.S., 1803	*no*
21	Sa.	St. Thomas • Ember Day • **Winter Solstice** • Tides {9.1 9.8	*wonder*
22	F	**4th S. of Advent** • Geologist Ferdinand V. Hayden died, 1887 • {9.0 9.6	*we're*
23	M.	Part of Van Gogh's left ear cut off, 1888 • Tides {9.0 9.3	*snowed*
24	Tu.	☾ ON EQ. • "O Holy Night" part of first radio program broadcast, Brant Rock, Mass., 1906	*under!*
25	W.	**Christmas** • ☌♂☾ • *One kind word can warm three winter months.*	*Will*
26	Th.	St. Stephen • **Boxing Day (Canada)** • **First day of Kwanzaa** • Tides {9.3 8.7	*winds*
27	Fr.	St. John • ☾ AT ☊ • 12.5" snow, Dumas, Tex., 2000 • {9.6 8.8	*be*
28	Sa.	Holy Innocents • ☌♄☾ • Endangered Species Act signed into U.S. law, 1973	*this*
29	F	**1st S. af. Ch.** • ☿ IN SUP. ☌ • Deuterium discovery made public, 1931	*keen*
30	M.	☾ RUNS LOW • *Everything has an end—except a sausage, which has two.* • Tides {11.1 9.7	*in*
31	Tu.	St. Sylvester • ☌☿♇ • Iolani Palace cornerstone laid, Honolulu, 1879 • {11.6 10.2	*2014?*

Farmer's Calendar

■ If you are like most gardeners, you probably put your tools away at the end of the growing season and don't think very much about them until they are needed in the spring. But if you take a bit of time during the offseason to maintain and repair your tools, they will be safer and easier to use.

Wooden handles on tools such as shovels and iron rakes may become rough and splintery with weather, use, and age. Often, you can restore them by sanding the surface until it becomes smooth again and then applying linseed oil to protect the wood. Handles with deep cracks are a hazard and should be replaced.

Repair rusted metal tools by cleaning them with steel wool or a wire brush and then wiping on 30-weight motor oil to prevent further rusting.

Chances are, the blades on your pruners, loppers, and hedge shears could use sharpening. Use a fine flat file to touch them up. Be careful to keep the original angle of the blade's cutting edge. While you're at it, sharpen the metal edges of shovels and hoes to make digging easier.

Well-maintained, quality garden tools will last for years and can even be passed down from one generation to the next. Perhaps you can pass down the wisdom of how to take care of them, too.

Holidays and Observances

For Movable Religious Observances, see page 103. Federal holidays listed in bold.

Jan. 1	New Year's Day
Jan. 19	Robert E. Lee Day *(Fla., Ky., La., S.C.)*
Jan. 20	Inauguration Day (traditional)
Jan. 21	**Martin Luther King Jr.'s Birthday** *(observed)*
Feb. 2	Groundhog Day
Feb. 12	Abraham Lincoln's Birthday
	Mardi Gras *(Baldwin & Mobile counties, Ala.; La.)*
Feb. 14	Valentine's Day
Feb. 15	Susan B. Anthony's Birthday *(Fla., Wis.)*
Feb. 18	**Washington's Birthday** *(observed)*
Mar. 2	Texas Independence Day
Mar. 5	Town Meeting Day *(Vt.)*
Mar. 15	Andrew Jackson Day *(Tenn.)*
Mar. 17	St. Patrick's Day
	Evacuation Day, traditional *(Suffolk Co., Mass.)*
Mar. 25	Seward's Day *(Alaska)*
Apr. 2	Pascua Florida Day
Apr. 15	Patriots Day *(Maine, Mass.)*
Apr. 21	San Jacinto Day *(Tex.)*
Apr. 22	Earth Day
Apr. 26	National Arbor Day
May 5	Cinco de Mayo
May 8	Truman Day *(Mo.)*
May 12	Mother's Day
May 18	Armed Forces Day
May 20	Victoria Day *(Canada)*
May 22	National Maritime Day
May 27	**Memorial Day** *(observed)*
June 5	World Environment Day
June 11	King Kamehameha I Day *(Hawaii)*
June 14	Flag Day
June 16	Father's Day
June 17	Bunker Hill Day *(Suffolk Co., Mass.)*
June 19	Emancipation Day *(Tex.)*
June 20	West Virginia Day
July 1	Canada Day
July 4	**Independence Day**
July 24	Pioneer Day *(Utah)*
Aug. 1	Colorado Day
Aug. 5	Civic Holiday *(Canada)*
Aug. 16	Bennington Battle Day *(Vt.)*
Aug. 19	National Aviation Day
Aug. 26	Women's Equality Day
Sept. 2	**Labor Day**
Sept. 8	Grandparents Day
Sept. 9	Admission Day *(Calif.)*
Sept. 11	Patriot Day
Sept. 17	Constitution Day
Sept. 21	International Day of Peace
Oct. 7	Child Health Day
Oct. 9	Leif Eriksson Day
Oct. 14	**Columbus Day** *(observed)* Native Americans' Day *(S.Dak.)* Thanksgiving Day *(Canada)*
Oct. 18	Alaska Day
Oct. 24	United Nations Day
Oct. 25	Nevada Day
Oct. 31	Halloween
Nov. 4	Will Rogers Day *(Okla.)*
Nov. 5	Election Day
Nov. 11	**Veterans Day** Remembrance Day *(Canada)*
Nov. 19	Discovery Day *(Puerto Rico)*
Nov. 28	**Thanksgiving Day**
Nov. 29	Acadian Day *(La.)*
Dec. 7	National Pearl Harbor Remembrance Day
Dec. 15	Bill of Rights Day
Dec. 17	Wright Brothers Day
Dec. 25	**Christmas Day**
Dec. 26	Boxing Day *(Canada)* First day of Kwanzaa

Glossary of Almanac Oddities

■ Many readers have expressed puzzlement over the rather obscure entries that appear on our **Right-Hand Calendar Pages, 105–131.** These "oddities" have long been fixtures in the Almanac, and we are pleased to provide some definitions. (Once explained, they may not seem so odd after all!)

−Beth Krommes

Ember Days: The four periods observed by some Christian denominations for prayer, fasting, and the ordination of clergy are called Ember Days. Specifically, these are the Wednesdays, Fridays, and Saturdays that occur in succession following (1) the First Sunday in Lent; (2) Whitsunday–Pentecost; (3) the Feast of the Holy Cross, September 14; and (4) the Feast of St. Lucia, December 13. The word *ember* is perhaps a corruption of the Latin *quatuor tempora*, "four times."

Folklore has it that the weather on each of the 3 days foretells the weather for the next 3 months; that is, in September, the first Ember Day, Wednesday, forecasts the weather for October; Friday predicts November; and Saturday foretells December.

Distaff Day (January 7): This was the first day after Epiphany (January 6), when women were expected to return to their spinning following the Christmas holiday. A distaff is the staff that women used for holding the flax or wool in spinning.

(Hence the term "distaff" refers to women's work or the maternal side of the family.)

Plough Monday (January): Traditionally, the first Monday after Epiphany was called Plough Monday because it was the day when men returned to their plough, or daily work, following the Christmas holiday. (Every few years, Plough Monday and Distaff Day fall on the same day.) It was customary at this time for farm laborers to draw a plough through the village, soliciting money for a "plough light," which was kept burning in the parish church all year. This traditional verse captures the spirit of it:

"Yule is come and Yule is gone,
and we have feasted well;
so Jack must to his flail again
and Jenny to her wheel."

Three Chilly Saints (May): Mamertus, Pancras, and Gervais were three early Christian saints. Because their feast days, on May 11, 12, and 13, respectively, are traditionally cold, they have come to be known as the Three Chilly Saints. An old French saying translates to: "St. Mamertus, St. Pancras, and St. Gervais do not pass without a frost."

Midsummer Day (June 24): To the farmer, this day is the midpoint of the growing season, halfway between planting and harvest. (Midsummer Eve is an occasion for festivity and celebrates fertility.) The Anglican church considered it a "Quarter Day," one of the four major divisions of the liturgical year. It also marks the feast day of St. John the Baptist.

Cornscateous Air (July): First used by early almanac makers, this term signifies warm, damp air. Though it signals ideal climatic conditions for growing corn, it poses a danger to those affected by asthma and other respiratory problems.

Dog Days (July 3–August 11): These 40 days are traditionally the year's hottest and unhealthiest. They once coincided with the year's heliacal (at sunrise) rising of the Dog Star, Sirius. Ancient folks thought that the "combined heat" of Sirius and the Sun caused summer's swelter.

Lammas Day (August 1): Derived from the Old English *hlaf maesse,* meaning "loaf mass," Lammas Day marked the beginning of the harvest. Traditionally, loaves of bread were baked from the first-ripened grain and brought to the churches to be consecrated. Eventually, "loaf mass" became "Lammas." In Scotland, Lammastide fairs became famous as the time when trial marriages could be made. These marriages could end after a year with no strings attached.

Cat Nights Begin (August 17): This term harks back to the days when people believed in witches. An Irish legend says that a witch could turn into a cat and regain herself eight times, but on the ninth time (August 17), she couldn't change back, hence the saying: "A cat has nine lives." Because August is a "yowly" time for cats, this may have initially prompted the speculation about witches on the prowl.

Harvest Home (September): In Europe and Britain, the conclusion of the harvest each autumn was marked by festivals of fun, feasting, and thanksgiving known as "Harvest Home." It was also a time to hold elections, pay workers, and collect rents. These festivals usually took place around the autumnal equinox.

Certain groups in the United States, particularly the Pennsylvania Dutch, have kept the tradition alive.

St. Luke's Little Summer (October): This is a spell of warm weather that occurs on or near St. Luke's feast day (October 18) and is sometimes called Indian summer.

Indian Summer (November): A period of warm weather following a cold spell or a hard frost, Indian summer can occur between St. Martin's Day (November 11) and November 20. Although there are differing dates for its occurrence, for more than 200 years the Almanac has adhered to the saying "If All Saints' (November 1) brings out winter, St. Martin's brings out Indian summer." The term may have come from early Native Americans, some of whom believed that the condition was caused by a warm wind sent from the court of their southwestern god, Cautantowwit.

Halcyon Days (December): This refers to about 2 weeks of calm weather that often follow the blustery winds of autumn's end. Ancient Greeks and Romans experienced this weather around the time of the winter solstice, when the halcyon, or kingfisher, was brooding. In a nest floating on the sea, the bird was said to have charmed the wind and waves so that the waters were especially calm during this period.

Beware the Pogonip (December): The word *pogonip* refers to an uncommon occurrence—frozen fog. The word was coined by Native Americans to describe the frozen fogs of fine ice needles that occur in the mountain valleys of the western United States and Canada. According to their tradition, breathing the fog is injurious to the lungs. □□

TIME AND TIME AGAIN

5509 B.C. 3

THE NEXT TIME SOMEONE SAYS, "SINCE TIME BEGAN . . .," ASK, "WHICH TIME?"

We often measure time in relation to a personal event, such as a birth, graduation, or marriage. A *long* time ago, people came up with year-numbering systems correlated to cycles or to the dates of major events, dubbed "epochs," such as the start of a king's reign, a battle victory, or even the beginning of the world. Each such span is called an "era."

THE CHRISTIAN ERA

The Gregorian calendar (which we use) numbers its years by the Christian era, which was invented by 6th-century Scythian monk Dionysius Exiguus. Dionysius sought to create a year-numbering system based on the Incarnation of Christ (the epoch) rather than employ the then-traditional Diocletian era (see page 139).

Dionysius determined that Christ was born on December 25, 753 A.U.C. (Roman era; see page 138), so he used January 1, 754 A.U.C. as the beginning of the Christian era and dated the year A.D. 1. (Many scholars put the birth date earlier, such as in 4 B.C.) The prefix A.D. stands for *anno Domini,* Latin for "in the year of the Lord."

The idea of "before Christ" (B.C.) did not appear until at least the 8th century, when the English monk Venerable Bede expanded Dionysius's system, designating the period before

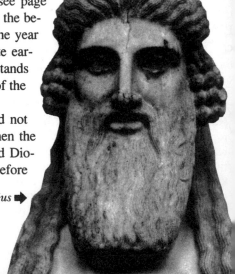

Dionysius ➡

BY HEIDI STONEHILL

01 B.C. 753 B.C. 312 B.C

AS EASY AS A, B, C, D, E—BUT NOT IN THAT ORDER

Although the Christian era uses the suffix B.C. and prefix A.D., some modified systems use religiously neutral abbreviations. One example is B.C.E./C.E.; note that both are used as suffixes:

■ B.C.E. ("Before the Common Era") is a substitute for B.C. (1 B.C.E. is the same as 1 B.C.).

■ C.E. ("Common Era") is a substitute for A.D. (1 C.E. is the same as A.D. 1).

An all-suffix system facilitates computer calculations.

the epoch as *ante uero incarnationis Dominicae tempus,* Latin for "before the time of the true Incarnation of the Lord." Centuries after Bede's system caught on, the Latin was translated to the English "before Christ" and abbreviated as B.C.

ZERO ENTHUSIASM FROM ASTRONOMERS

The Christian era year-numbering system does not include a year "zero." To make calculations easier, astronomers developed their own year-numbering system, which does include 0. They designated 1 B.C. as year 0 C.E. All previous years are negative and all years after 0 are positive. For example, 2 B.C. and A.D. 2 in the Christian era are –1 C.E. and 2 C.E., respectively, in the astronomical system.

MATTERS OF TIME

Here's how the years of other eras listed in this Almanac on page 103 are reckoned:

BYZANTINE ERA
Began: 5509 B.C.

Epoch: creation of the world
Background: Based on the Septuagint version of the Bible. Dates are designated as *anno mundi* (A.M.), Latin for "in the year of the world."

◄ *Venerable Bede*

CONTINUED

137

◀ Allegory of the Creation, *by Jacopo Zucchi (1541–90)*

JEWISH ERA (A.M.)

Began: 3761 B.C.

Epoch: creation of the world

Background: Used for the Hebrew lunisolar calendar. Calculations are largely based on the Tanakh, the Hebrew Bible, as well as on *Seder Olam Rabbah,* a biblical chronology written in the 2nd century.

CHINESE ERA (LUNAR)

Begins: 60-year rotating cycle

Epoch: no true epoch*

Background: Used for the traditional lunisolar Chinese calendar, which is consulted for special events, astrology, and Moon phases. (China adopted the Gregorian calendar for civil purposes.) Years are counted by a 60-year rotating name system called the stem-branch, or sexagenary, cycle. Each year's name contains a celestial stem, taken from a rotating list of 10 terms concerning the yin/yang forms of five elements, and a terrestrial branch, taken from a rotating

*Occasionally, an event is assigned. The accession of the legendary Yellow Emperor, Huangdi, is linked variously to 2698 B.C. (used by this Almanac) and 2697 B.C. An alternate epoch, when Huangdi is said to have invented the Chinese calendar in 2637 B.C., is sometimes used.

list of the 12 animal names of the Chinese zodiac; e.g., the first year in the cycle is *jia-zi* (Year of the Rat).

ROMAN ERA (A.U.C.)

Began: 753 B.C.

Epoch: founding of Rome

Background: Year is approximate. The abbreviation A.U.C. stands for *ab urbe condita,* Latin for "from the founding of the city"; used mainly by Roman historians.

NABONASSAR ERA

Began: 749 B.C.

Epoch: accession of Babylonian king Nabonassar

Background: Created by Greek astronomer Claudius Ptolemy in the 2nd century, while forming a timeline of astronomical events that corresponded with the reigns of ancient rulers (listed in his "Canon of Kings"; Nabonassar is first). Ptolemy calculated that Nabonassar came to power in 747 B.C. Historians later changed this to 749 B.C.

JAPANESE ERA

Began: 660 B.C.

Epoch: accession of the legendary first emperor of Japan, Jimmu

Background: Called the "Imperial year" or "national era," this system has seldom been used since World War II. For civil purposes, Japan uses a modified Gregorian calendar but also counts the years by the "Japanese era name," which begins when an emperor ascends the throne and ends upon his death.

GRECIAN ERA (SELEUCIDAE)

Began: 312 B.C.

Epoch: recapture of Babylonia by Macedonian Seleucus Nicator

Background: Seleucus Nicator was a general under Alexander the Great (356–323 B.C.). In 316 B.C., then-governor Seleucus fled from Babylonia to Egypt to escape his rival, Antigonus. In 312 B.C., he returned to reconquer the area, marking the start of the Seleucid Empire. The Seleucid era starts either in 312 B.C. (Macedonian calendar) or 311 B.C. (Babylonian calendar). Jews named it the "Era of Contracts" because they had to use dates based on this calendar in their written agreements.

INDIAN ERA (SAKA)

Began: A.D. 78

Epoch: various

Background: Used for the Indian national calendar. (The Gregorian calendar is also used by India.) The Saka era began in A.D. 78, but historians disagree about the epoch, which may be linked to the accession of King Salivahana in southern India or his defeat of the Saka, a Central Asian tribe that overran northern India in the 1st century A.D. Alternatively, the epoch may correspond to the defeat of Saka king Vikramaditya by Satavahana king Gautamiputra Satakarni (who was possibly the same as Salivahana) or the accession of Kushan king Kanishka or other rulers.

DIOCLETIAN ERA

Began: A.D. 284

Epoch: accession of Roman emperor Diocletian

Background: Because of Diocletian's substantial reforms during a failing empire, his reign was treated as a separate era from the one based on the foundation of Rome. However, the emperor was also known for his severe persecution of Christians, which led to their naming it the "Era of Martyrs."

ISLAMIC ERA (HEGIRA)

Began: A.D. 622

Epoch: emigration of Muslim prophet Muhammad from Mecca to Medina

Background: Used for the lunar Islamic calendar. In A.D. 622, to escape an assassination plot, Muslim prophet Muhammad left his hometown of Mecca to live in Medina (then called Yathrib). This Hegira, or Hijrah (emigration or departure), was a turning point for the Muslim faith, in part because, due to Muhammad's leadership, Medina became the first Islamic state. Years in the Islamic era are often designated as A.H., for *anno Hegirae,* Latin for "in the year of the Hegira." □□

Heidi Stonehill has been a calendar editor at *The Old Farmer's Almanac* since 2754 A.U.C. of the Roman era.

The Ins and Outs of Vitamins

■ Getting enough vitamins and minerals isn't hard. All you really need to do is eat a healthy diet. Build it around fruits and vegetables (eight to ten servings a day), whole-grain breads and cereals, beans, low-fat poultry and meat, nonfried fish, milk, cheese, and yogurt.

Here's what vitamins do and where they hide in your food:

VITAMIN	WHAT IT DOES	WHERE IT IS
Vitamin A	• good for your eyesight • helps you see in the dark • helps fight infections • helps bone growth	milk, cheese, eggs, liver, fish oil, yellow fruits, dark-green and yellow veggies
B Vitamins	• help make red blood cells • help make energy and release it	whole grains (wheat and oats), fish and seafood, meat, poultry, eggs, dairy products, leafy green veggies, beans and peas, citrus fruits
Vitamin C	• keeps gums and muscles healthy • helps heal cuts • helps body resist infection	citrus fruits and juices, berries, tomatoes, peppers, broccoli, potatoes, cauliflower, cantaloupe
Vitamin D	• makes strong bones and teeth	milk, egg yolks, fish
Vitamin E	• helps make red blood cells • keeps tissues in eyes, skin, and liver healthy • protects lungs from pollution	whole grains (wheat and oats), wheat germ, leafy green veggies, sardines, nuts, egg yolks
Vitamin K	• enables blood to clot	leafy green veggies, pork, liver, dairy products

Hay Fever Foods

If you experience seasonal allergies to pollen, these food compounds may help:

■ **Probiotics** (beneficial bacteria), found in dietary supplements or in yogurt containing live cultures

■ **Omega-3 fatty acids,** found in salmon, halibut, tuna, cod, sardines, fish oil, flaxseed oil, canola oil, shrimp, clams, spinach, and walnuts

■ **Quercetin,** found in citrus, apples, cranberries, grapes, olive oil, blueberries, blackberries, onions, parsley, spinach, broccoli, kale, black and green teas, and red wine. You can also buy quercetin supplements. Research has found that quercetin is more effective when combined with bromelain, an enzyme in pineapple.

■ **Vitamin C,** found in citrus, papaya, cantaloupe, kiwi, strawberries, parsley, bell peppers, broccoli, brussels sprouts, kale, cauliflower, and sweet potatoes

Caution: Some people allergic to pollen may also be allergic to certain fresh fruit, vegetables, nuts, and grains.

Are you tired of feeling "foggy"... absent-minded... or confused?

Reverse up to 4 Years of Memory Loss?

Find out how some people stay sharp and mentally focused - even at age 90! Here's their secret...

By Steven Wuzubia, Health Correspondent;

Clearwater, Florida: Nothing's more frustrating than when you forget names... misplace your keys... or just feel "a little confused". And even though your foggy memory gets laughed off as just another "senior moment", it's not very funny when it keeps happening to you.

Like gray hair and reading glasses… some people accept their memory loss as just a part of getting older. But it doesn't have to be that way.

Today, people in their 70's, 80's even their 90's... are staying mentally fit, focused and "fog-free". So what do they know that you don't? Well, the secret may be as easy as taking a tiny pill called *Lipogen PS Plus*.

Unblock Your Brain

Made exclusively in Israel, this incredible supplement feeds your brain the nutrients it needs to stay healthy. It was developed by Dr. Meir Shinitzky, Ph.D., former visiting professor at Duke University, and recipient of the prestigious J.F. Kennedy Prize.

Dr. Shinitzky explains; "Science has shown, when your brain nutrient levels drop, you can start to experience memory problems. Your ability to concentrate and stay focused becomes compromised. And gradually, a "mental fog" sets in. It can damage every aspect of your life".

In recent years, researchers identified the importance of a remarkable compound called phosphatidylserine (PS). It's the key ingredient in *Lipogen PS Plus*. And crucial to your ability to learn and remember things as you age.

Earth-shaking Science

Published, clinical reports show replenishing your body's natural supply of Phosphatidylserine, not only helps sharpen your memory and concentration— but also helps "perk you up" and put you in a better mood.

Your Memory Unleashed!

Lipogen PS Plus is an impressive fusion of the most powerful, natural memory compounds on Earth. This drug-free brain-boosting formula enters your bloodstream fast (in as little as thirty minutes).

Officially Reviewed by the U.S. Food and Drug Administration:
Lipogen PS safety has been reviewed by the FDA (FDA GRAS Notice No. GRN 000186) PS is the ONLY health supplement with a FDA "qualified health claim" for BOTH, COGNITIVE DYSFUNCTION AND Dementia.

Brain Boosting Compound Reverses Memory Loss up to Four Full Years!

It produces amazing results. Especially for people who have tried everything to improve their memory before, but failed. *Lipogen PS Plus* gives your brain the vital boost it needs to jump-start your focus and mental clarity. "It truly is a godsend!" says Shinitzky.

Significant Improvements

In 1992, doctors tested phosphatidylserine on a select group of people aged 60-80 years old. Their test scores showed impressive memory improvement. Test subjects could remember more and were more mentally alert. But doctors noticed something else.

"My memory was starting to fail me. I would forget all kinds of things. Something I just said would completely slip my mind. I was worried. I read about Lipogen and wanted to try it. I was taking it on a daily basis for 3 months when it hit me, 'I haven't forgotten anything recently'. **I will definitely recommend it to all my friends.** It's given me a lot more self confidence. **Thanks Lipogen for giving me my memory back."** - Donna V., Ocala, FL

The group taking phosphatidylserine, not only enjoyed sharper memory, but were also more upbeat and remarkably happy. In contrast, the moods of the individuals who took the placebo (sugar pill), remained unaffected.

But in order to truly appreciate how well *Lipogen PS Plus* works for your memory— you really have to try it. And now you can...

Special "See For Yourself" Risk-Free Supply

We've made arrangements with the distributor of *Lipogen PS Plus* to offer you a special "Readers Only Discount". This trial is 100% risk-free.

It's a terrific deal. If *Lipogen PS Plus* doesn't help you think better, remember more... and improve your mind, clarity and mood – you won't pay a penny! (except s&h).

But you must act fast. Your order can only be guaranteed if it comes in within the next 7-days. After that, supplies could run out. And your order may not be fulfilled until they are replenished.

So don't wait. Now you can join the thousands of people who think better, remember more—and enjoy clear, "fog-free" memory. Think of it as making a "wake-up call" to your brain.

Call Now, Toll Free! Simply dial...
1-800-609-3558

FOUR SEASONS OF HOMEMADE FIRST AID

WINTER

Cold and flu season got you down?

Add fresh garlic cloves to chicken soup and other foods or swallow small chunks of raw garlic as you would pills. Garlic is a natural antibiotic and helps to support your immune system.

Cold sores causing chaos?

Dab the area twice daily with a warm, wet, black tea bag for 5 minutes. Black tea's tannins have an anti-inflammatory effect on cold sores.

In the course of a year, you could spend hundreds of dollars on products and services to relieve a variety of common seasonal ailments. Instead, why not use these inexpensive and authentic fixes that are probably already in your cupboards? (Not there? Go get them— and be prepared for whatever Mother Nature sends your way.)

compiled by
Sarah Perreault

Is your home's heat drying out your skin?

Immerse yourself in a warm (not hot) oatmeal bath for at least 10 minutes. Oats act as an anti-inflammatory and soothe the itch. Add about 1 cup of finely ground oatmeal to your bath.

Chapped lips pestering your pucker?

Go to bed with honey on your lips or dab some coconut oil on the dry area. Honey's antibacterial properties can help to prevent infection as well as moisturize cracked lips. Coconut oil is loaded with beneficial minerals for moisturizing skin.

SPRING

Allergies leaving you in a congested daze?

Drink hot or iced peppermint tea. The menthol in peppermint helps to thin mucus and acts as an expectorant.

Insect bites bugging you?

Cover the bite with a slice of onion for at least 30 minutes. Onions contain sulfur, which breaks down the venom and leeches out the toxin. Onions also contain flavonoids, which promote healing.

Warm weather causing embarrassing body odor?

Dust areas of excessive sweating with cornstarch and start drinking sage tea, hot or iced, daily. Cornstarch absorbs moisture, and sage has natural antiperspirant properties.

Plagued by pesky poison ivy?

Relieve the itch with a pantry paste: Combine 3 teaspoons of baking soda with 1 teaspoon of water. Apply to the rash. Allow the paste to dry completely. The baking soda will dry out the area.

SUMMER

Stung by a bee or wasp?

Remove the stinger, then generously cover the area with toothpaste. Its alkalinity helps to neutralize the acidic venom.

Humid air causing heat rash (aka prickly heat)?

Rub a slice of raw potato over the affected area. The potato's juices reduce irritation and skin inflammation.

Too much pool time causing swimmer's ear?

Carefully place a few drops of white vinegar inside the aching ear. Vinegar has antibacterial and antifungal properties.

continued . . . ➡

Skin sizzling from overexposure to the sun?

Lather your skin with plain whole milk yogurt. Once dry, rinse with cool water and repeat. Yogurt contains enzymes, acids, and minerals that help to soothe sunburn.

Burn yourself while manning the grill?

Soften cabbage leaves in a bowl of hot water, then tear into small pieces. Place the leaves on the burn, cover with gauze, and apply pressure. Cabbage is loaded with glutamine, which aids new cell growth and provides protection against infection.

Sarah Perreault, senior associate editor of *The Old Farmer's Almanac,* was inspired to write this article after a particularly painful sunburn sent her looking for homemade relief. She now buys yogurt in bulk.

AUTUMN

Crop harvesting causing backache?

Fill an old sock with uncooked plain (not quick-cooking) rice and tie it off. Warm the sock in the microwave for 1 to 2 minutes, then apply to your sore back while lying down. The application of heat allows the back muscles to loosen and relax.

Indigestion after your Thanksgiving feast?

Eat papaya or kiwi, both of which contain protein-dissolving enzymes that help to ease stomach discomfort.

Toothache from too much Halloween candy?

Position two cloves in your mouth between the offending tooth and your cheek so that they stay in place. Cloves contain eugenol, which is both an anesthetic and an antiseptic.

Decrease in sunlight making you feel drowsy?

Eat apricots, apples, grapes, pears, and oranges to stay alert. These fruit boost serotonin levels that increase your energy.

Note: If any of these conditions persist, consult your doctor.

MOTHER NATURE'S JANITOR

Few animals are as unappreciated as North America's only marsupial.

Imagine that you're driving home late one evening and you see an opossum eating the remains of another animal on the road. What do you do?

If you answer, "Let it be," good for you! Carrion is the opossum's diet staple, and this scavenger is simply doing what comes naturally.

For centuries, myths and folklore have fueled undeserved prejudice against the opossum, but facts about this mammal may surprise you.

(continued)

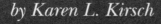
by Karen L. Kirsch

A female Virginia opossum with her babies. The joeys will ride on Mom's back for
several weeks, until they learn the basic skills for survival.

ABOUT THE "O"

The spelling and pronunciation of *Didelphis virginiana*'s common name has varied for centuries, but all refer to the Virginia opossum:

- Native American Algonquians used the word *apasum* ("white animal"), pronounced "possum."

- The spelling "opossum" was first recorded in 1613.

- Promotional literature created by 17th-century colonists in Jamestown, Virginia, used "Apossouns."

Fossil remains indicate that opossums have existed essentially unchanged for 70 million years. The staying power of this primitive animal is due to its remarkable fecundity.

Females mate twice a year, birthing (just 13 days after breeding) sometimes as many as 20 bean-size babies. These joeys (named like their kangaroo cousins) follow the mother's belly hair into a fur-lined pouch called the marsupium, where there are 13 teats. Those that successfully make the journey to the pouch remain there attached to a nipple for about 2 months. (Male opossums do not stick around to help raise the family.)

When the joeys are about the size of a mouse, they emerge to ride on the mother's back (not her tail), where they cling to her hair for several weeks. Should a joey become separated from the mother, it makes a sneezing sound. She responds with a clicking noise, and eventually they reunite.

Within a few months, after the joeys have mastered basic survival skills, they set off on their own.

PERTINENT POSSUM POINTS

- Its intelligence is on a par with that of a pig.

- It is similar to many cats in size, weighing 12 to 15 pounds at maturity.

- It is as fastidious as most cats.

- It has black eyes that may appear "beady" because they do not have an iris.

—Gary Meszaros/Getty Images

Tiny opossum babies in the fur-lined pouch of their mother

This transient seldom stays in one place for more than a few days. Its delicate paws are unsuitable for digging, so it uses dens and burrows that have been vacated by other animals, even taking over unoccupied doghouses. Although opossums don't hibernate and are generally nocturnal, in snowy weather they may hole up for days until hunger drives them out to search for a meal during warmer daylight hours.

Opossums cause little to no harm. They won't dig up your garden or chew wood or wires. They are not aggressive; they do not attack humans or other animals (however, like any wildlife, they may bite if handled).

In controlled environments, such as zoos and laboratories, an opossum can live up to 10 years. In the wild, its life span is 1 year, on average, and it is often a life on the run. Predators abound, with man at the top of the list. Hunters kill opossums for food, for fur (of negligible market value), for sport, and out of fear and ignorance—with little resistance.

(continued)

Opossums cause little to no harm. They won't dig up your garden or chew wood or wires. They are not aggressive.

This animal is essentially defenseless. A prehensile tail and rear feet with opposable halluces (thumbs; singular: hallux) help the opossum to climb away from danger, and its 50 razor-sharp teeth suggest ferocity. When frightened, an opossum will hiss, growl, urinate, and/ or defecate.

If it feels hopelessly cornered, its survival tactic is to lapse into a coma-like state that can last up to several hours. Although the animal may appear and smell dead, studies indicate that its brain is alert while in this state (hence the idiom for feigning death: to play possum).

In a last-ditch effort to discourage a predator, the opossum might secrete from its anal glands a substance that smells like a rotten carcass.

Senselessly killing or running off opossums will only create a vacancy that will quickly be filled by skunks, raccoons, or—worse—rats, to which, by the way, the opossum is *not* related. This omnivore catches and *eats* mice and rats. It devours insects, especially cockroaches; snails; slugs; and snakes. (A natural resistance to some snake venoms allows the opossum to consume rattlesnakes, copperheads, and other poisonous reptiles safely.)

Opossums also eat grasses, overripe fruit and berries, bird eggs, and human garbage and pet foods. (They don't mind sharing a bowl with Kitty.) However, their *favorite* meal is carrion, and this bold appetite helps to keep our environment clean. Ironically, when the feast is roadkill on the pavement, the opossum often meets its own demise.

All of this is why, if you see an opossum, you should let it be. Just consider yourself lucky and thank nature's little janitor for doing its job.

LOVE 'EM AND LEAVE 'EM

Opossums present the least health risk of any wild animal. Rabies and other viral diseases are rare in opossums, possibly due to their low (94° to 97°F) body temperature. Still, they are not candidates for pets. (Confiscation of and death to the animals—and fines for you—can result; laws vary.) Like all warm-blooded mammals, they can host fleas and ticks, and hay or grain that is tainted with their feces has been linked to Equine Protozoal Myloencephalitis, a health threat to horses.

If an opossum temporarily takes up residence in a garage or attic, turn on lights and a radio to hasten its departure. Secure potential entry points and clean up whatever attracted the animal in the first place. (Hint: Feed outside pets during the day and secure garbage can lids.)

To repel opossums in specific areas, soak a rag in ammonia and stuff it inside a coffee can with a perforated lid. Or, spray a mixture of strained cooked onions and peppers or fox or coyote (predator) urine around your property's perimeter. However, such measures are extreme and usually unnecessary.

Karen L. Kirsch lives in Louisville, Ohio, with three dogs, eight cats, two donkeys, a flock of geriatric free-range chickens, and the occasional opossum. She writes about animal and environmental issues for numerous publications and in her blog, http://mysmallcountrylife.com.

OPOSSUM CULTURE

IN THE KITCHEN

■ In the 19th century, opossum was a diet staple for many poor families in the southeastern United States, which may explain many recipes' southern origins. Recipes for cooking opossum are abundant in wild game cookbooks and on Web sites.

■ In the mid-1800s, women applied opossum fat to chapped skin.

■ At a dinner in Georgia at which barbecued opossum was served, William Howard Taft declared that the southern specialty was delicious. Soon after, postcards and buttons championed Taft as "Billy Possum" during his presidential campaign in 1908. After his election to succeed President Teddy Roosevelt, a stuffed toy possum was created with the slogan "Good-bye, Teddy Bear. Hello, Billy Possum."

IN MUSIC

■ "Possum Rag" by Geraldine Dobyns was a hit in 1907.

■ Early 20th-century fiddle tunes such as "Possum Up a Gum Tree" and "Rattler Treed a Possum" are still popular.

■ In 2001, John Craton composed "The 'Possum," a classical piece for piano, as part of his collection of animal compositions.

■ In 2008, the Berlin Philharmonic commissioned Nathan Currier's "Possum Wakes From Playing Dead" for cello and harp.

■ In 2011, Gary Bachlund composed "Possum Lullaby" for tuba and piano.

IN ART

■ Early itinerant artists often depicted joeys hanging by their tails from the mother's tail or with an elongated ratlike body, neither of which is accurate.

■ Walt Kelly (1913–73) popularized the wise, kind, and philosophical Pogo possum character in cartoons from 1941 to 1973.

Pogo in 1943 and the late '50s.

–Okefenokee Glee & Perloo, Inc.

Best Fishing Days and Times

The best times to fish are when the fish are naturally most active. The Sun, Moon, tides, and weather all influence fish activity. For example, fish tend to feed more at sunrise and sunset, and also during a full Moon (when tides are higher than average). However, most of us go fishing when we can get the time off, not because it is the best time. But there *are* best times, according to fishing lore:

The Best Fishing Days for 2013, when the Moon is between new and full:

January 11–26

February 10–25

March 11–27

April 10–25

May 9–25

June 8–23

July 8–22

August 6–20

September 5–19

October 4–18

November 3–17

December 2–17

- One hour before and one hour after high tides, and one hour before and one hour after low tides. (The times of high tides for Boston are given on pages 104–130; also see pages 232–233. Inland, the times for high tides correspond with the times when the Moon is due south. Low tides are halfway between high tides.)

- During the "morning rise" (after sunup for a spell) and the "evening rise" (just before sundown and the hour or so after).

- During the rise and set of the Moon.

- When the barometer is steady or on the rise. (But even during stormy periods, the fish aren't going to give up feeding. The smart fisherman will find just the right bait.)

- When there is a hatch of flies—caddis flies or mayflies, commonly.

- When the breeze is from a westerly quarter, rather than from the north or east.

- When the water is still or rippled, rather than during a wind.

How to Estimate the Weight of a Fish

Measure the fish from the tip of its nose to the tip of its tail. Then measure its girth at the thickest portion of its midsection.

The weight of a fat-bodied fish (bass, salmon) = (length x girth x girth)/800

The weight of a slender fish (trout, northern pike) = (length x girth x girth)/900

Example: If a fish is 20 inches long and has a 12-inch girth, its estimated weight is (20 x 12 x 12)/900 = 2,880/900 = 3.2 pounds

salmon

trout

catfish

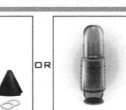

WINNERS
in the 2012 Essay Contest

How *The Old Farmer's Almanac* Has Influenced My Life

Thank you to everyone who submitted an essay. We were overwhelmed with words of appreciation and shared memories from across the United States and Canada, both from families who have read and used the Almanac for generations and from folks who have only recently come to know it. In addition to the stories here, folks wrote of making and keeping a wood fire, marketing grain crops by the Moon, digging clams or going crabbing, fund-raising, weaning a child from the bottle, giving speeches, researching woodcut art, and writing a novel. Most writers offered praise for our advice on farming and gardening (especially by the Moon), husbandry, fishing and nature, astronomical sightings and Moon names, recipes, accurate weather forecasts, and the ability to lift spirits in good times and sad. From all of your kind words, we are humbled, heartened, and inspired.

FIRST PRIZE

Two years ago, I became an ordained minister in the United Church of Canada and was sent from Toronto to serve three tiny farming towns in rural Saskatchewan. I think that my congregants were as nervous as I was about how a city minister was going to fit in with a community of farmers and ranchers. At Coffee House after my first church service, I mentioned a fact about seeding wheat. There was a stunned silence. Then someone asked how a city person would know that.

"Oh, I read *The Old Farmer's Almanac*," I answered.

You could almost hear the sigh of relief go up. From that moment on, I was one of them!

–Anne Hines, Lucky Lake, Saskatchewan

SECOND PRIZE

In 1982, I was a city girl in my early 30s when John, a farm boy, was hired and assigned to share an office with me. Other than age, we had little in common. One day, he was reading *The Old Farmer's Almanac,* a book I had never seen before. His obvious enjoyment piqued my interest. We began talking about left- vs. right-hand calendar pages and astronomy vs. astrology, as well as guessing the weather, finding reasons to celebrate obscure holidays, and perusing the home and health tidbits, which he already knew. This eventually led to a special tradition that has continued to connect us. We each buy Almanacs every fall and use them to plan our get-togethers. Even though our lives have taken us in different directions, our tradition with the Almanac has helped us to stay in touch.

–Ellen Waxberg, Skokie, Illinois

THIRD PRIZE

A few years ago, *The Old Farmer's Almanac* explained why the Sun usually does come out at noon. As a roofer, I soon turned this information to my advantage. Whenever we had one of those gray, damp days, someone would invariably say at coffee break, "Well, it looks like we won't see the Sun today."

I'd say, "I bet you it comes out at noon."

"How much you wanna bet?" he'd ask.

"Five bucks."

"You're on!"

Every few months, I'd reel in another one until no one would make a wager except the rookies, who eventually were forewarned, so even they wouldn't bet me.

One day, a buddy cornered me and

asked me how I could be so accurate. "Give me five bucks and I'll tell you," I said. With the cash in hand, I told him: *"The Old Farmer's Almanac."*

–Peter R. Anderson, Bozrah, Connecticut

HONORABLE MENTION

My older brother has always teased me about my knowledge, or lack of it, pertaining to the stars. He and I would go out into a local field to challenge each other's knowledge of the night sky, whenever the weather permitted. He had won all of our weekly contests every year. He did, after all, have an 8-year leg up on me when it came to life and stargazing. But his winning streak had left me downtrodden.

Then, one day, I picked up a copy of *The Old Farmer's Almanac,* which claimed to contain "everything under the Sun, including the Moon." Every week since, I've given him a good run for his money, mostly swamping him with my spot-on predictions!

–Andrew Pearson, Coweta, Oklahoma

ANNOUNCING THE 2013 ESSAY CONTEST TOPIC: MY FUNNIEST FAMILY MOMENT

In 200 words or less, please tell us about the single funniest incident that your family has experienced. See below for details.

ESSAY AND RECIPE CONTEST RULES

Cash prizes (first, $250; second, $150; third, $100) will be awarded for the best essay on the subject "My Funniest Family Moment" and the best recipe using beets and/or beet greens (see page 210). All entries become the property of Yankee Publishing, which reserves all rights to the material. The deadline for entries is Friday, January 25, 2013. Label "Essay Contest" or "Recipe Contest" and mail to The Old Farmer's Almanac, P.O. Box 520, Dublin, NH 03444. You can also enter at Almanac.com/EssayContest or Almanac.com/RecipeContest. Include your name, mailing address, and email address. Winners will appear in *The 2014 Old Farmer's Almanac* and on our Web site, Almanac.com.

We asked researcher Stacey Kusterbeck to paint a statistical picture of the person for whom this Almanac was named 221 years ago.

Just Who Is
the AMERICAN

Overall, the future looks bright for American farmers. "Individual farms face specific challenges, but overall, agriculture looks a lot better than the general economy," says Dr. Bob Young, chief economist of the American Farm Bureau Federation.

The Face of Farming

Farmers are frugal financial managers who are cautious about increasing their debt, according to data collected by the U.S. Department of Agriculture. They are an aging group, with the number over age

65 increasing quickly. Although farmers are still overwhelmingly white and male, there is growing diversity, with many more female farm operators in recent years.

For the first time since before World War II, the number of U.S. farms counted by the census has increased, with an overall trend toward two extremes—small and large farms. (In 2007, the U.S. Census Bureau sought out underrepresented populations, including female, minority, and small-scale farmers.)

Some young farmers are taking over family farms as part of generational transfers, while beginning farmers of all ages, particularly women, are starting up small farms (those with gross cash farm income of less than $250,000).

The Place of Farming

An overwhelming 97 percent of farms and ranches were still family-owned as of 2009, but this figure doesn't include the smallest-scale growers who produce food in their own backyards and/or in community plots to save money and improve their health.

According to the National Gardening

ARMER?

Dinner for Threshers (two details digitally joined) by Grant Wood, 1934

–The Granger Collection, NYC

Association, some 19 million of us planned to grow vegetables in 2009, with 7 million doing so for the first time. Even now, seed companies continue to see sales surge. "There is a feeling that [food] will be a safer product if people can control [the growing process] themselves," says Timothy A. Woods, an agricultural economics professor at the University of Kentucky.

An estimated 18,000 to 20,000 community gardens are planted each year in the United States and Canada. Many cities have waiting lists for participation.

"The sense of community is absolutely huge for people," says Beth Urban, executive director of the American Community Gardening Association in Columbus, Ohio.

The Pace of Farming

To increase profits, farmers are using GPS for precision planting and the targeted application of fertilizer and chemicals that combat weeds and crop diseases.

Consumers are more interested than ever in where their food comes from. In response, farmers have launched Web sites and are using social media platforms (Twitter, Facebook, blogs, and YouTube) to connect with the 99 percent of us who do not farm and to answer our questions about food production.

The number of farmers' markets surged from just 1,755 in 1994 to 7,175 in 2011, with direct-to-consumer sales

of farm products totaling about $1.2 billion in 2011.

While urban shoppers tend to pay premium prices and consume the purchased veggies immediately, rural residents pay lower prices and often buy in bulk, preserving the food for future use by pickling, canning, drying, or freezing.

Some backyard growers sell their excess vegetables at local markets, seeking to make a profit from their own gardens. "It's a great part-time, cash-intensive opportunity that fits in well with retired, unemployed, partially retired, or partially employed folks," says Woods.

BY THE NUMBERS

■ Percentage of the population that farms:
2007: 1
1940: 23.2
1890: 39.3

■ Of that, the percentage that farms part-time:
2007: 65
2002: 55

■ Number of people in the U.S. workforce employed in agriculture (producing, processing, and selling food), 2010:
21 million (15 percent of the total)

(continued)

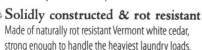

Farming

- Average age of farmers:
  2007: 57
  1987: 52
  1940: 48

- Number of farmers under 25, 2007:
  54,197 (down 30 percent from 2002)

- Number of farmers 75 or older, 2007:
  289,999 (up 20 percent from 2002)

- Percentage of women farmers:
  2007: 10
  1987: 6.3

- Ethnicity of farm population, 2007:
  93.2 percent white
  2.5 percent Hispanic
  2.4 percent Native American
  1.3 percent African-American (46 percent are on beef cattle farms and ranches)
  0.6 percent Asian-American (63 percent are in specialty crop operations)

- Farmers' education:
  In 2007 . . .
  90.3 percent: high school graduates
  48.7 percent: 1 or more years of college
  In 1990 . . .
  81.8 percent: high school graduates
  36.9 percent: 1 or more years of college

- Number of farms:
  2007: 2.2 million
  1940: 6.1 million

- Number of "new" farms that began operation between U.S. Census of Agriculture years 2002 and 2007:
  291,329

- Average size of farms:
  2007: 418 acres
  1940: 174 acres
  1890: 137 acres

- Average gross farm income, including commodity sales, government payments, and other farm-related sources, 2007:
  $137,222

- Average net farm income, 2007:
  $35,126

- Portion of farms reporting positive net income, 2007:
  63 percent

- States with the most farms, 2010:
  Texas: 247,500
  Missouri: 108,000
  Iowa: 92,400
  Oklahoma: 86,500
  Kentucky: 85,700

- States with the highest percentage of beginning farmers, 2007:
  Hawaii: 40 percent
  Florida: 38 percent
  California: 37 percent
  Texas: 35 percent

- Total land in the U.S. devoted to farms (including crop- and pastureland, woodland, etc.):
  2010: 919.9 million acres
  1980: 1.04 billion acres

- Annual production (in billions of pounds), 2009–2010:
  Grain: 874.3
  Hay and silage: 512.6
  Oilseeds: 222.3
  Dairy products: 192.7
  Horticulture: 139.6
  Cotton, tobacco, sugar beets, sugar cane: 132.8
  Poultry: 42.5
  Beef and veal: 26.4
  Pork: 22.4
  Eggs: 11.4

- Percentage of crops produced for export:
  2010: 23 (a combined one-third of which goes to Canada and China)
  1940: 3
  1890: 19

- Number of people fed by each farm worker:
  2009: 154
  1989: 98
  1940: 10.7
  1890: 5.8

- Farmers' portion of every retail dollar spent on food:
  2010: 16 cents (84 cents goes to off-farm costs such as marketing and distribution)
  1980: 31 cents

NOTE: The 2007 numbers in this article were obtained from the U.S. Census of Agriculture, which is taken by the Department of Agriculture every 5 years. Figures from the 2012 census will be available in 2014. □□

Gestation and Mating Tables

	Proper Age or Weight for First Mating	Period of Fertility (yrs.)	Number of Females for One Male	Period of Gestation (days) AVERAGE	RANGE
Ewe	1 yr. or 90 lbs.	6		147 / 151[1]	142–154
Ram	12–14 mos., well matured	7	50–75[2] / 35–40[3]		
Mare	3 yrs.	10–12		336	310–370
Stallion	3 yrs.	12–15	40–45[4] / record 252[5]		
Cow	15–18 mos.[6]	10–14		283	279–290[7] 262–300[8]
Bull	1 yr., well matured	10–12	50[4] / thousands[5]		
Sow	5–6 mos. or 250 lbs.	6		115	110–120
Boar	250–300 lbs.	6	50[2] / 35–40[3]		
Doe goat	10 mos. or 85–90 lbs.	6		150	145–155
Buck goat	well matured	5	30		
Bitch	16–18 mos.	8		63	58–67
Male dog	12–16 mos.	8	8–10		
Queen cat	12 mos.	6		63	60–68
Tom cat	12 mos.	6	6–8		
Doe rabbit	6 mos.	5–6		31	30–32
Buck rabbit	6 mos.	5–6	30		

[1]For fine wool breeds. [2]Hand-mated. [3]Pasture. [4]Natural. [5]Artificial. [6]Holstein and beef: 750 lbs.; Jersey: 500 lbs. [7]Beef; 8–10 days shorter for Angus. [8]Dairy.

Incubation Period of Poultry (days)
Chicken 21
Duck 26–32
Goose. 30–34
Guinea 26–28

Average Life Span of Animals in Captivity (years)
Cat (domestic) 14
Chicken (domestic) 8
Dog (domestic) 13
Duck (domestic) 10

Goat (domestic) 14
Goose (domestic) 20
Horse 22
Rabbit (domestic) 6

	Estral/Estrous Cycle (including heat period) AVERAGE	RANGE	Length of Estrus (heat) AVERAGE	RANGE	Usual Time of Ovulation	When Cycle Recurs If Not Bred
Mare	21 days	10–37 days	5–6 days	2–11 days	24–48 hours before end of estrus	21 days
Sow	21 days	18–24 days	2–3 days	1–5 days	30–36 hours after start of estrus	21 days
Ewe	16½ days	14–19 days	30 hours	24–32 hours	12–24 hours before end of estrus	16½ days
Doe goat	21 days	18–24 days	2–3 days	1–4 days	Near end of estrus	21 days
Cow	21 days	18–24 days	18 hours	10–24 hours	10–12 hours after end of estrus	21 days
Bitch	24 days	16–30 days	7 days	5–9 days	1–3 days after first acceptance	Pseudo-pregnancy
Queen cat		15–21 days	3–4 days, if mated	9–10 days, in absence of male	24–56 hours after coitus	Pseudo-pregnancy

Hey, EWE!

There's a flock of good reasons to keep sheep.

by Elizabeth Creith

If you have a small farm and are looking for one good breed of animal to keep, you should choose sheep. They're small, readily stay in groups, and will follow a tamed lead ewe. Sheep provide four crops; in order of monetary value, these are meat and hides (from lambs), manure (for the garden), wool, and milk. A good milk ewe provides 1 to 2 quarts per day for 200 to 300 days a year.

You can't get just one or two. Sheep are flock animals and feel safe only in groups of five or more. A good starter flock is one ram and four ewes. A ram can breed up to 25 ewes. If you have more ewes, you'll need another ram.

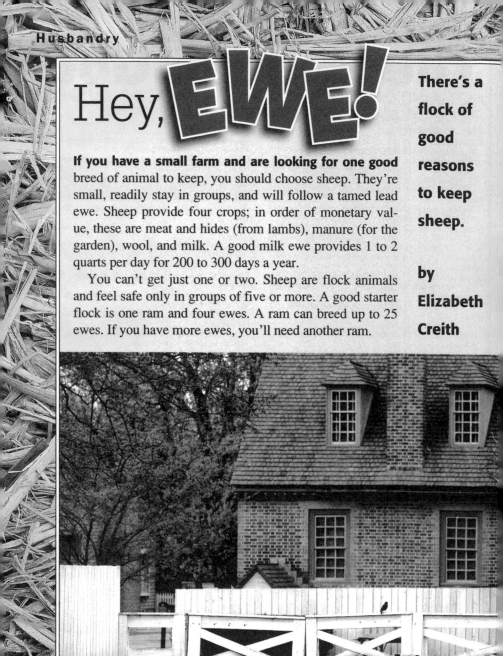

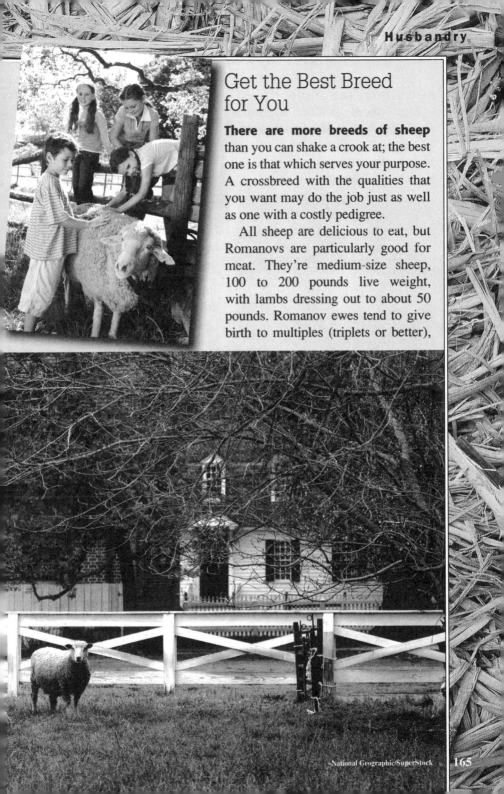

Get the Best Breed for You

There are more breeds of sheep than you can shake a crook at; the best one is that which serves your purpose. A crossbreed with the qualities that you want may do the job just as well as one with a costly pedigree.

All sheep are delicious to eat, but Romanovs are particularly good for meat. They're medium-size sheep, 100 to 200 pounds live weight, with lambs dressing out to about 50 pounds. Romanov ewes tend to give birth to multiples (triplets or better), which means about 150 pounds of meat from one ewe's lambs in 1 year.

Most sheep produce spinnable wool, but some produce finer, softer, or longer fleeces than others. Good wool breeds are Romney, Corriedale, Finnsheep, Shetland, or Icelandic.

–Photoshot/SuperStock

–SuperStock

Above: a Shetland ewe and lamb
Left: a Dorset ram

Although any sheep can be milked, East Friesians are excellent producers and the most common in North America. Many of the northern European short-tailed breeds also are used for milk.

A good dual-purpose sheep is the Dorset, a big, square breed that produces a lot of meat. The wool is not as fine and soft as that of some other breeds, but it is perfectly serviceable for sweaters and socks.

If you want a lawn-ornament sheep, something that looks picturesque, go for the multihorn, multicolor Jacob. A bonus is two or three colors of wool from a single fleece.

Stake Out Some Staying Power

Fencing is the shepherd's biggest job and the key to keeping sheep, which are renowned barnyard escape artists.

■ Sheep's wool and tiny hard hooves insulate them from the effects of a

SHEPHERD SPEAK

Ewe or dam: female sheep
Ram or tup: male sheep
Lamb: newborn sheep, up to a year old
Hogget or hogg: yearling sheep
Wether: castrated male
Polled: without horns

Fleece: woolly coat, sheared each spring
Staple: length of a lock of wool
Dags: pieces of manure caked onto fleece
Moorit: brown wool; a sheep with brown wool

weak electric fence. Invest in electric fencing that runs 8,000-volt pulses through the wires once every second. Alternating three electrified and two or three ground, or nonelectrified, wires will increase the likelihood that your sheep will stay on the right side of the fence.

■ Fallen branches or long grass can reduce the electrical charge and allow sheep to escape, so check your fence regularly.

■ On average, a sheep weighs 80 to 150 pounds and stands small enough to push under a wire, so mind the bottom of your fencing. If one gets out, they'll all be out.

–Nordic Photos/SuperStock

Give Them Shelter

Housing needs vary by breed and climate. Sheep need protection from the hot sun in summer and windchill and wet weather in winter. A shelter can be as simple as a one-sided, roofed structure.

Sheep require fresh water and eat grass, but they'll strip the leaves from any small trees they can reach. (Mine loved aspen.) They'll eat your vegetables and flowers, too, if they get the chance. In winter, they require

BAA-BAA, BLACK SHEEP

In most breeds, the dominant color is white, and it will hide any other color that the animal carries. Black is the next most dominant color, and brown, the most recessive. Spotting, except in multicolor sheep such as the Jacob, is rare.

–Minden Picture/SuperStock

It is lucky to meet a flock of sheep while on a journey.

–proverb

hay—a 100-pound ewe needs about 4 pounds per day.

Grain is necessary only prior to mating, in late pregnancy, and when nursing, but sheep will attempt to convince you that it is a daily necessity year-round. Don't be fooled. (If you want to get their attention, rattle a grain bucket. They'll come running.)

Do the Math

Choose ewes that are healthy and not too small and that have good teeth and udders. If possible, choose from twins or triplets. Multiple lambs help your bottom line, and although genetics is a very small factor in determining whether a ewe has twins or triplets, you want it on your side.

Unless your sheep are only pets, you'll want to breed them. One lamb pays for the ewe's keep, so twins are necessary to pay for the ram's keep or make any money. See the "Gestation and Mating Tables" on page 162 for help in the timing. To increase the likelihood of twins or triplets, 4 weeks before breeding, start giving each ewe a handful of grain every day and increase it gradually to a pound. This is called "raising the nutritional plateau." Keep adding grain to the diet while the ewes are nursing (1 pound of grain per lamb being nursed).

NOT STUPID, JUST SHEEPISH

While sheep have a reputation for stupidity, they're actually quite intelligent. Some of mine responded to their names, and researchers have found evidence that they will remember a human face for up to 2 years.

They are nervous, however, and react to almost any unfamiliar noise by bolting. When keeping sheep, remember Bob Dylan's lyric: "Don't stand in the doorway. Don't block up the hall." If, while visiting the barn, a child squeals in delight, your flock will charge out through the barn door—if you're in the way, too bad for your knees.

Expect Ram-bunctiousness

The ram is half of your breeding stock, so get the best one—or better, two—that you can afford. Ideally, you should have a lead ram and a "cleanup" ram. The lead ram gets the first shot at breeding, while the cleanup ram gets to mate with the ewes that the lead ram missed.

My shepherding mentor advises, "Never marry a ram." Use the cleanup ram for 2 years, then move him up to lead ram. Two years later, replace him. Four years of food, shelter, and a harem before heading for the meat packer makes for a short life, but it's a merry one.

A good ram tends to be aggressive. The flock will run from a predator, but the lead ram will stand up to it or even attack. He'll go after the shepherd, too, if he's feeling protective. Never turn your back on the ram in breeding season.

Don't Stew Over Lambing

If you observe a pregnant ewe pawing at the ground, lying down, and getting up again or staying aside from the flock, she's in labor. Put her in a small pen and sit quietly with her.

Usually, a ewe lambs without help. The front hooves come first, and then the lamb's nose emerges with its knees. As soon as the lamb is born, wipe any fluid from its muzzle, dip the umbilical cord in iodine solution, and squeeze the ewe's teats to make sure that they're open and full of milk. You can leave the rest to the ewe most of the time.

Allow mother and baby to bond in the pen for a day or two, then let them join the rest of the flock.

Enjoy Shear Pleasures

Most sheep must be shorn every year. A professional shearer can shear a sheep in less than 5 minutes. Shearing doesn't hurt the animal, and once a sheep has been set up on its butt by the shearer, it seems to calm down and almost fall asleep. It's the perfect time to give any shots and to trim hooves.

–Photononstop/SuperStock

Take the shorn fleece to a table and "skirt" it, removing the dirty, stained bits and/or anything too full of hay and chaff. Roll the fleece, cut side out, and bag it for shipping or later use.

Take Stock of the Flock

Most problems that sheep have are with the shepherd. Good hygiene in

When sheep turn their backs to the wind, it is a sign of rain.

–proverb

the barn, good feed management and predator control, and vaccinations as necessary will keep them healthy. Look at your flock every day; know your sheep and how they behave. You'll catch problems like foot rot, diarrhea, and small injuries early.

With study and understanding and that all-important good fencing, keeping sheep can be pleasant and rewarding not only in "crops," but also in an inexhaustible fund of stories.

PULLING THE WOOL OVER . . . ?

■ In England, girls who wanted to know if they would marry would go out to the sheepfold at night and grab a sheep at random. A girl who grabbed a ram would marry; a girl who grabbed a ewe would not.

■ To predict the sex of an unborn child, pierce a hole in a charred lamb shoulder bone. Suspend the bone over the back door. The baby will be the same sex as the first visitor to walk through the door.

Classic Yarns

■ In the *Aeneid,* Virgil speaks of priestesses who sleep on sheepskins in order to have visions.

■ The Greek myth of the Golden Fleece was probably based on an old gold-gathering method. Alluvial gold (in rivers) can be panned out by letting the water run over a ridged surface, such as a sheepskin laid fleece-up in the water. The gold dust collects in the fleece and can be shaken out later.

■ For centuries, shepherds in England were buried with a tuft of wool in hand to show St. Peter that their frequent absence from church was due to caring for their sheep.

□□

Elizabeth Creith of Wharncliffe, Ontario, kept Icelandic and Icelandic-Romanov sheep for 10 years. Her work has appeared in numerous publications, including *Canadian Living,* and her CBC Radio series "Shepherd in Residence" on "Richardson's Roundup" served as the basis for a memoir of the same name.

A KISS IS Just

... OR IS IT?

Throughout history, the kiss has been used to express a range of emotions. What makes a pucker so powerful?

by Martie Majoros

–illustrated by Eldon Doty

How This Lip-Smacking Behavior Began

Anthropologists differ in their opinions about who (or what) planted the first kiss, and why:

● Many cite the behavior of an ancient human ancestor from 125 million years ago. The ratlike animal *Eomaia scansoria* sniffed and rubbed its nose on other creatures to identify them as kin, friend, or foe. (*Eomaia,* a Greek word, means "ancient mother," and *scansoria,* a Latin word, means "climber"—a hint at its behavior.)

● Others believe that kissing may have evolved from prehistoric times as a way for mothers to feed prechewed food to their children.

● In humans, kissing may have evolved from sniffing: The area around the mouth and nose contains scent glands that produce pheromones, our personal perfumes. Kissing is a way to sample a person's unique aroma, detect his or her sexual chemistry, determine his or her health, and discern whether he or she is a potential mate.

The Science of the Smooch

Philematology is the study of kissing. Osculation is the act of kissing.

The orbicularis oris is the circular muscle of the lips, or the kissing muscle. It is responsible for closing the lips and making them protrude into a pucker. A quick peck on the lips uses just two parts of one muscle: the upper and lower orbicularis oris. A passionate liplock uses a total of 34 facial muscles.

The act of kissing produces powerful hormones, including adrenaline, serotonin, dopamine, and oxytocin. When combined, these increase our sense of well-being, reduce stress, leave us feeling weak in the knees, and encourage us to establish intimacy and bonding relationships.

Kissing produces extra saliva, which contains immunoglobulins, antibodies that wash the teeth of bacteria that could lead to tooth decay.

Deep kissing exercises underlying face muscles, which can help you to look younger.

Birds Do It . . . and So Do Fish

Birds tap beaks, turtles touch noses, elephants slip their trunks into each other's mouths, prairie dogs rub noses, and chimps slip their tongues into other chimps' mouths. Male "kissing" gourami fish occasionally fight by locking lips: They press their mouths together, sometimes for up to 25 minutes.

Itching From a Kiss?

Kissing bugs *(Triatoma protracta)*, common in the southern United States, are attracted to light in houses at night. Once inside, they hone in on their prey—sleeping humans—by detecting exhaled carbon dioxide and body heat. The bugs often bite, or "kiss," people around the mouth while they sleep. Usually, the bites cause only a minor irritation and itching that soon disappears. Occasionally, the bites produce an extreme allergic reaction leading to anaphylactic shock.

LIP LORE

● In some areas of England, it is believed that a newborn will be influenced later in life by the character of the person (other than its mother) who gives it its first kiss.

● If a girl stands under mistletoe, she can not refuse anyone who wishes to kiss her.

● To protect yourself from lightning, make three crosses in front of yourself and kiss the ground three times.

● For good luck in gambling, kiss the cards before the game begins.

● To cure a toothache, kiss a donkey on his chops.

● If you drop a piece of bread on the floor, kiss it when you pick it up to avoid bad luck.

● Danish custom says that it's a bad omen when the first person you see in the morning is an old woman. Should that happen, you must kiss her to avoid bad luck.

Kiss Good-Bye for Good Luck

According to a study by German psychologist Dr. Arthur Sazbo, people who kissed their spouse good-bye in the morning:

● missed less work due to illness

● had fewer auto accidents on the way to work

● earned 20 to 30 percent more money monthly

● lived approximately 5 years longer than those who did not.

Apparently, There Is a "Right" Way

In 2003, Onur Güntürkün, a German psychologist, reported the results of a survey of 124 couples kissing in public places in the United States, Germany, and Turkey. He found that when they kissed, they

tilted their heads to the right twice as often as to the left. More than a century earlier, sculptor Auguste Rodin captured a similar pose in *The Kiss* (c. 1881–82). Both lovers in this marble sculpture have their heads turned to the right.

Say It Like You Mean It (When You Know What It Means)

Kiss-me-quick refers to a woman's hat, popular in the 1850s, that had no brim and was worn on the back of the head, which made it easy for a suitor to plant a kiss on the wearer.

A **kiss-me-if-you-can** was a hat with a wide brim that made it difficult for a suitor to dip under it to plant a kiss.

If It's Worth Doing, It's Worth Overdoing

Annual kissing contests, often conducted to celebrate Valentine's Day, are a test of endurance rather than romance.

On February 14, 2009, in Mexico City, 39,897 friends, couples, and family members kissed for 10 seconds, establishing a world record for the most simultaneous kisses.

Give Peace a Chance

The kiss of peace originated in the Christian mass and, yes, people kissed each other. In the 13th century, during the time of the bubonic plague, parishioners in England instead kissed an osculatorium, a metal disc with a holy picture in the center.

Eventually, the kiss of peace became secularized and signified a truce between warring parties—or at least that was the idea.

In 1792, during the French Revolution, Bishop Antoine Lamourette urged arguing factions of the Legislative Assembly to set aside their differences and swear everlasting fraternity. Inspired, assembly members embraced, kissed, and vowed to conduct quarrel-free sessions.

The next day, however, arguments resumed. Two years later, Lamourette was guillotined. In French, the expression *baiser de Lamourette* ("Lamourette's kiss") refers to a short-lived truce.

Friends, Romans, Businessmen, Lend Me Your ...

Ancient Romans greeted each other with kisses on the hand, cheek, or mouth. Roman statesman Cato encouraged soldiers returning home to kiss their wives to see if they had been drinking.

Today, kissing greetings are becoming more common in business relationships and often take the place of a handshake. However, Peggy Post, a spokeswoman for the Emily Post Institute, encourages the use of a handshake (not a kiss) in business situations, especially between members of the opposite sex when first meeting.

□□

Martie Majoros, a frequent contributor to Almanac publications, writes from the shores of Lake Champlain in Burlington, Vermont.

What Are You Afraid Of?

pho·bi·a \ 'fō-bē-ə \ *noun*

1. A phobia is a persistent, abnormal, or irrational fear of a specific thing or situation that compels one to avoid the feared stimulus.

2. A phobia is also strong fear, dislike, or aversion.

PHOBIA SUBJECT	PHOBIA TERM
Animals	Zoophobia
Ants	Myrmecophobia
Beards	Pogonophobia
Bees	Apiphobia
Being near an object of great height	Batophobia
Birds	Ornithophobia
Blood	Hematophobia
Choking	Pnigophobia
Crossing bridges	Gephyrophobia
Crowds	Ochlophobia
Dirt	Rupophobia
Dreams	Oneirophobia
Flowers	Anthophobia
Flying	Aerophobia
Frogs	Ranidaphobia
Garlic	Alliumphobia
Germs	Mysophobia
Haircuts	Tonsurphobia
Height	Acrophobia
Hospitals	Nosocomephobia
Illness	Nosemaphobia
Insects	Entomophobia
Lakes	Limnophobia
Lightning and thunder	Astraphobia
Long words	Sesquipedalopphobia
Men	Androphobia
Money	Chrometophobia

PHOBIA SUBJECT	PHOBIA TERM
Moths	Mottephobia
Night, darkness	Nyctophobia
Open or public places	Agoraphobia
Plants	Batonophobia
Shadows	Sciophobia
Snakes	Ophidiophobia
Spiders	Arachnophobia
Sun	Heliophobia
Toads	Bufonophobia
Touch	Haptophobia
Train travel	Siderodromophobia
Trees	Dendrophobia
Vegetables	Lachanophobia
Wasps	Spheksophobia
Water	Hydrophobia
Women	Gynophobia
Worms	Scoleciphobia

Fear is only as deep as the mind allows.

–Japanese proverb

The
PERILS of
PARENTING

Through the Ages

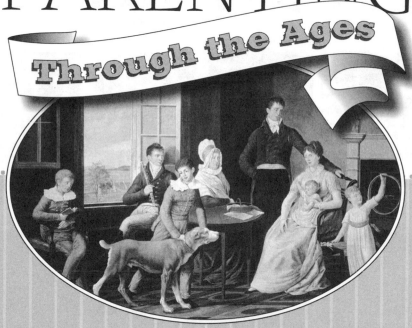

Before I GOT MARRIED, I had SIX THEORIES

about bringing up children; now I have

SIX CHILDREN, and NO THEORIES.

–John Wilmot, earl of Rochester (1647–80)

BY ANDREA CURRY

The child-rearing theories of experts sometimes baffle parents and occasionally defy common sense. Yet, over the centuries, this fact has stopped neither so-called specialists from giving advice nor parents from following (or, at least, considering) it. In fact, with each generation, the pattern repeats as experts expound on parenting and parents strive for perfection. See if any of this sounds familiar . . .

How Many Make a Family?

❧ 18th-century American parents raised seven to nine children, on average. Canadians in the same period attained one of the highest birth rates ever observed—10.8 children per mother, on average.

❧ In the 1800s, the average family size fell steadily until it reached between three and four children. Huge economic changes were behind this trend, as a farming society became industrial. According to historian Steven Mintz, children were "no longer economic assets who could be put productively to work," but instead "required expensive investments in the form of education."

❧ Today, the American fertility rate is 2.1 children per mother, and the Canadian rate is 1.68.

FEEDING TIME

Trust yourself. You know more than you think you do.

–Benjamin Spock, M.D. (1903–98), author of The Common Sense Book of Baby and Child Care *(1946)*

❧ Breast-feeding mothers were once advised to kick back and drink a pint of beer a day. By the mid–19th century, baby care manuals offered nursing mothers strict, often contradictory, advice. Some recommended taking a cold saltwater bath every morning and getting lots of exercise, while others advised avoiding excessive exercise or strong emotions and not reading too many novels!

It was standard for 18th- and 19th-century women to breast-feed their babies for 1 to 2 years, partly to protect their youngsters from contagious diseases and likely contamination in cow's

–Bridgeman Art Library, London/SuperStock

milk or other foods. Extending nursing also helped mothers to have a little extra time between their pregnancies, since nursing delays the return of fertility.

Nearly all mothers breast-fed their babies until the mid–20th century, but there were still times in the 19th and early 20th centuries when women complained about breast-feeding and some wealthy mothers hired wet nurses. In 1896, the author of one child care manual wrote: "I myself know of no greater misery than nursing a child, the physical collapse caused by which is often at the bottom of the drinking habits of which we hear so much."

American and Canadian babies born toward the end of the Baby Boom (1946–64) were the least likely ever in history to be breast-fed. By the 1960s, only 3 percent of American mothers nursed for at least 7 months and only 27 percent nursed their babies at all—a dramatic break with the past. Today, public health campaigns have helped to bring the percentage of mothers who breast-feed their infants up to 75 percent in the United States and 85 percent in Canada.

EAT IT!
IT'S GOOD FOR YOU

Tell me what you eat, and I will tell you who you are.

*–Jean Anthelme Brillat-Savarin,
French lawyer (1755–1826)*

❖ Before the 19th century, U.S. parents fed their children meat two or three times a day. Gradually, as more vegetables were added to the menu, this dropped to once a day. The English and most other Europeans would have none of it: They thought that fruits and vegetables were "acid and indigestible" by children.

As a result of a varied diet, North American children grew taller than their European peers and had better digestion. Because the recommended diet for English children lacked fiber, English

In the 17th and 18th centuries, babies weren't expected to sleep through the night until they were weaned (usually as toddlers), as they would need to wake up to nurse. Babies slept close to their parents, or at least their mothers, to make this easier for the mother. Rocking played a prominent role in getting babies to sleep and keeping them that way; even the barest pioneer cabin usually contained a cradle.

By the turn of the 20th century, baby experts were recommending detailed new schedules and procedures. Famed expert L. Emmett Holt condemned the cradle on the grounds that it was habit-forming.

Various baby care manuals of the

child-rearing manuals of the day included long sections on homemade laxative treatments.

However, food didn't necessarily taste better. Nineteenth-century advisers considered bland, unseasoned food to be "a means, indirectly, of forming human character" in children and believed that anything else led to self-indulgence.

One alternative view left the child's diet to the parents' discretion: Feed dairy, eggs, and bland vegetables to a hyperactive, excitable child to tone him down and give the "dull and lymphatic" child stimulants such as coffee, tea, and even wine.

'NIGHT, 'NIGHT

I am so happy when the children get away to bed that I feel like prolonging the hour of quiet to a great length.

—a 19th-century mother

❀ Today, 76 percent of American parents of children 10 years old and younger say that they are dissatisfied with their child's sleep habits. In the distant past, mothers with small children accepted "night waking" as a fact of life.

day told parents that newborns should sleep 20 to 22 hours a day for the first several months of life. (Modern studies suggest that newborns actually sleep 15 hours a day, on average.) The difference between hours of expected and actual sleep brought maternal anxiety to a fever pitch. Hundreds of mothers' study groups across the United States met to probe the subject. (continued)

TOUGH LOVE

One of the great mysteries of the universe is that there are parents who seem to do everything right and their children grow up with insecurities, anxieties, and self-doubt.

–Nathaniel Branden (b. 1930), Canadian psychotherapist, in Vitality Magazine: Toronto's Monthly Wellness Journal *(September 1991)*

❁ Until the mid–18th century, children bowed or curtsied to their parents and boys took off their hats in their parents' presence. Children also asked their parents' blessing each morning.

Early 20th-century parenting experts

-Christie's Images Ltd./SuperStock

took a hard line against cuddling and playing with babies and children. In *The Care and Feeding of Children*, L. Emmett Holt advised parents never to kiss their babies; he thought that this would spread germs. He also believed that babies were extremely delicate and would become "nervous and irritable . . . and suffer from indigestion" if their parents played with them before they were at least 6 months old. Government pamphlets and other experts echoed this advice for decades.

John B. Watson took this hands-off

parenting style a step further. "Never hug and kiss [your children]," he wrote in 1928. "Never let them sit in your lap. If you must, kiss them once on the forehead when they say goodnight. Shake hands with them in the morning."

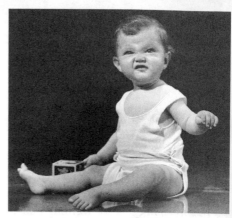

DIAPERS AND DUDS

A baby is an inestimable blessing and a bother.

–Mark Twain (1835–1920), American humorist, in a letter to Annie Webster, September 1, 1876

❁ In the early 20th century, a variety of child care manuals gave detailed instructions on how to toilet train infants, even at as early an age as 3 months, through strict scheduling, holding the child on a chamber pot many times a day and night, and the frequent use of enemas.

Today, the average age for giving up daytime diapers is between 2.5 and 3 years.

Boys and girls alike once wore simple muslin dresses until age 4 or 5. Then little boys were officially "breeched." A new jacket and pants, along with his first "real" haircut, "made a little man" out of the child.

A few stylish babies began to sport pastel shades in the mid-1800s, but white remained the most popular baby clothing color for mothers who wanted to be able to bleach out stains. Colorful clothing gained popularity over the decades, and by the 1940s, cultural consensus had chosen blue for boys and pink for girls.

Mothers also put their baby boys into pants earlier and earlier throughout the 20th century. Finally, by the 1970s, both boy and girl babies frequently wore pants from birth.

PLAYTIME!

I have found that the best way to give advice to children is to find out what they want and then advise them to do it.

–Harry S. Truman (1884–1972), 33rd U.S. president, May 27, 1955

✿ Puritan children played with dolls, dollhouses, cradles, slates, toy boats, swings, and hobbyhorses—all things that their parents could easily make for them. Favorite activities were cutting out paper dolls, pretend play, and collecting rocks, bird eggs, and other curiosities.

Early American parenting advice focused on raising independent children who would relish hard work. Child-rearing manuals told parents that children would be more content and less greedy for more playthings if taught to make their own toys. Many 9-year-old boys, for example, could make a sled, marbles from clay, a bow and arrow, a leather ball stuffed with feathers, or a top to spin. Girls often made dolls from scraps of material or corn husks.

Advice manuals up through the 20th century took for granted that kids needed (and spent) a minimum of 3 hours per day playing outside. Compare that with today's 6- to 8-year-old, who spends a mere hour and 24 minutes per week, on average, of unstructured time outside, and another 2½ hours per week playing organized sports either indoors or outside.

(continued)

Survival of More Than Just the Fittest

Antibiotics and immunization, as well as other medical advances (tetanus treatments, insulin, and fluoride), have done more to change the experience of parenting than any other factor.

❀ In many areas of North America in the 19th century, one in four babies died before the age of 1 year.

❀ Today, only one in 165 American babies and one in 203 Canadian babies dies in the first year of life.

● ●

CHORES AND MORE

No matter how you bring up your children, you turn out badly.

–Richard Needham (1912–96), Canadian newspaper columnist, in You and All the Rest: The Wit and Wisdom of Richard Needham *(1982)*

❀ Early North American families, living off the land, expected and needed their children to perform farm and household chores. A 6-year-old boy was capable of going out and bringing the cows home or helping his father to plow. By age 9, he could be trusted with a truly big job, such as tending a brush fire or cutting all of the limbs off trees his father felled to clear new land.

In those days, girls and younger boys worked in the house or kitchen garden with their mothers. An 8-year-old girl learned to spin yarn and thread on the spinning wheel, and, by age 14, she was an adept weaver of all kinds of cloth, if her family had the equipment. This work was not only essential to the household's survival; preparing children to make their own way in the grown-up world was an essential part of parenting.

Today, 6- to 12-year-old children spend 24 minutes a day, on average, doing chores, usually light tasks like making their beds, cleaning their rooms, feeding a pet, and/or unloading the dishwasher.

However, children today spend far more time in school—180 days a year in the United States and 190 in Canada, compared to fewer than 100 days in 1900. ▯▯

Andrea Curry, a frequent contributor to Old Farmer's Almanac publications, used to have six theories about raising children. Now she has three children and three theories. But they're not the same theories with which she started.

SCIATICA BACK PAIN?

If you suffer from Sciatica symptoms, such as intense pain in the buttocks and lower back, or pain and numbness in your legs and feet, you are not alone. Over 170 million people suffer from the burning, tingling, numbing, and shooting pains because they are not aware of this proven treatment.

MagniLife® Sciatica Relief is a special combination of tested ingredients that was developed to help ease the severe discomfort of Sciatica. It can be taken along with other medications with no side effects. The tablets dissolve under the tongue and contain Colocynthis, which has shown to relieve the shooting pains and tingling sensations. *"The Sciatica Relief tablets are a miracle solution to the pain of Sciatica." - Lillie, CA.*

MagniLife® Sciatica Relief is **available at CVS/pharmacy and Rite Aid Pharmacies**. It can also be ordered risk free for $19.99 (plus $5.95 S&H) for 125 tablets per bottle. Get a **FREE** bottle when you order two for $39.98 (plus $9.95 S&H). Send your name and address with payment to: MagniLife, Dept. S-FA, P.O. Box 6789, McKinney, TX 75071 or call 1-800-628-5430. Satisfaction guaranteed or return the bottles within 90 days for a full refund. Order now at **www.MagniLife.com**.

RINGING IN THE EARS?

If you suffer from Tinnitus and experience ringing in the ears, buzzing, hissing, whistling, or other sounds, you should know that help is available. Many people are putting up with irritating noises because they are not aware of this proven treatment.

MagniLife® Tinnitus Relief has already helped thousands find relief when nothing else has worked. It can be taken along with other medications with no side effects. *"This tablet seems to be the only thing I've found that brings relief." - Bert M., Mt. Pleasant, IA.* The tablets dissolve under the tongue and contain Lycopodium, which reduces noises in the ears. *"I would definitely recommend this product to anyone." - C. Robinson, OH.*

MagniLife® Tinnitus Relief is **available at CVS/pharmacy,** in the pain relievers aisle, **and Rite Aid Pharmacies**. It can also be ordered for $19.99 (plus $5.95 S&H) for 125 tablets per bottle. Get a **FREE** bottle when you order two for $39.98 (plus $9.95 S&H). Send your name and address with payment to: MagniLife, Dept. T-FA, P.O. Box 6789, McKinney, TX 75071 or call 1-800-628-5430. Satisfaction guaranteed or return the bottles within 90 days for a full refund. Order now at **www.MagniLife.com**.

LEG CRAMPS AT NIGHT?

If you experience painful and annoying muscle cramps in your legs, calves, feet, or toes, especially at night, you should know relief is available. Over 100 million people suffer from nocturnal leg cramps and are putting up with the pain and loss of sleep because they are not aware of this proven treatment.

MagniLife® Leg Cramp Relief is now helping people that have been living with painful cramps for years. It can be taken along with other medications with no side effects. *"I highly recommend Leg Cramp Relief. A couple tablets before bed, and no more waking up to painful cramps in my calves." - Joyce, Denver, CO.* Tablets dissolve under the tongue and contain eight active ingredients, such as magnesia phosphorica, which reduces cramps and radiating pains that are worse at night.

MagniLife® Leg Cramp Relief is **available at CVS/pharmacy and Rite Aid Pharmacies**. It can also be ordered risk free for $19.99 (plus $5.95 S&H) for 125 tablets per bottle. Get a **FREE** bottle when you order two for $39.98 (plus $9.95 S&H). Send your name and address with payment to: MagniLife, Dept. L-FA, P.O. Box 6789, McKinney, TX 75071 or call 1-800-628-5430. Satisfaction guaranteed or return the bottles within 90 days for a full refund. Order now at **www.MagniLife.com**.

GOT A FAT CAT

Help your pet's health with these weighty tips.

BY AMY NIESKENS

The obesity epidemic is not limited to humans anymore: Our pets are battling the bulge, too. According to the Association for Pet Obesity Prevention (APOP), 53 percent of American dogs and 55 percent of cats are overweight or obese, and this number is growing each year. (In fact, the number of obese cats in the United States is more than triple that of dogs.)

Experts claim that animal owners are responsible for their plump pets. Allowing pets to consume more calories than they burn inevitably results in weight gain and, over extended periods of time, obesity. Many pet owners are in denial about the problem, says award-winning New Hampshire pet writer Wendy Christensen. "Try to be objective, realistic, and honest about your pet's weight," she advises.

Pets vs. People:

BY THE POUND

Just a couple of extra pounds can pose a significant health risk for cats and dogs.

For example, a healthy domestic shorthair cat should weigh about 12 pounds. One that weighs 19 pounds is analogous to . . .

- a 5-foot 4-inch woman weighing 276 pounds

- a 5-foot 9-inch man weighing 321 pounds

As another example, a 42-pound beagle, whose ideal weight is 18 to 30 pounds, is analogous to . . .

- a 5-foot 4-inch woman weighing 203 pounds

- a 5-foot 9-inch man weighing 237 pounds

Because ideal sizes vary among different cat and dog breeds, ask your veterinarian about the optimum weight for your pet.

OR A PORTLY PUP?

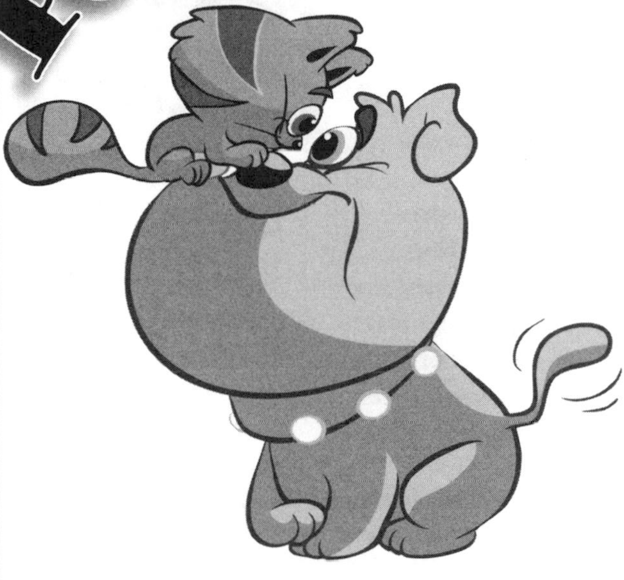

Pet health problems associated with excess weight are similar to those of people: heightened risk of disease or injury, joint problems, depression, and shortened life span. As with humans, diet and exercise for pets should be introduced gradually, and the pet should be given a clean bill of health from a veterinarian before beginning a program.

Each pet has unique energy requirements, depending on age, activity level, and breed. Here are the basics (consult a veterinarian for more details):

- **A healthy 10- to 12-pound cat needs 200 to 300 calories per day.**

- **A healthy 50-pound dog needs 700 to 900 calories per day.**

A major cause of the pet obesity problem is the overuse of treats and table scraps. Devoted owners often "misinterpret requests for attention and play as begging for

food," says Christensen. These sporadic snacks can send a pet's daily caloric intake skyrocketing. It is important to give your pet only what it needs, to pay attention to serving sizes and the frequency of meals, and to stick to a schedule. According to APOP founder and president Dr. Ernie Ward, "The single most valuable tool that a pet owner has in the fight against

obesity is a measuring cup."

Depending on your pet's weight, your veterinarian may prescribe a special diet food; you can also make healthful pet food at home. Try the treats on page 188. Check your pet's dietary and nutritional requirements with a veterinarian before using any homemade recipes.

CONTINUED

CAT NIPS

1 egg, beaten
¼ cup grated cheddar
cheese
1½ cups whole wheat
bread, crumbled
¼ cup finely chopped raw
broccoli, string beans,
or grated carrots
1 teaspoon brewer's yeast
pinch of catnip (optional)

Mix all of the ingredients
well, mashing with a fork
or your fingers. Drop by
teaspoonfuls onto a
lightly greased baking
sheet. Bake at 350°F for
8 minutes. Cool. Break the
treats in half before
serving. Store in an airtight
container for up to 10 days
or freeze. **Makes about
36 treats.**

Dirty Rice
FOR DOGS

1 pound chicken livers
1 can (14.5 ounces)
chicken broth or water
and chicken bouillon
2 tablespoons butter,
bacon drippings, or
olive oil (great for
the coat)
2 cups cooked brown rice

Boil the chicken livers
in the chicken broth and

butter for 10 minutes.
Remove from the broth
and chop most of the
meat, mashing a small
portion. Return all of
meat to the broth along
with the cooked rice.
Add water, if needed, to
make it moist. Stir well.
**Make sure that
your serving size is
appropriate.**

• • • • • • • • • • • •

**Find more recipes
and additional pet
care advice at
Almanac.com/Pets.**

• • • • • • • • • • • •

Fit or FAT?

To determine if your pet
is overweight, perform an
informal Body Condition Scor
evaluation. This technique,
used by veterinarians, classi-
fies animals as being in one o
five categories: (1) emaciated;
(2) thin; (3) moderate;
(4) stout; or (5) obese. (The
ideal BCS classification can
vary by species; e.g., that
for pigs differs from that for

Go Out and Play

Studies show that both you and your pet can benefit from regular exercise. To make it easy, make it fun.

ACTIVITIES FOR
DOGS

A dog's exercise needs depend on its age and breed, but 30 minutes to 2 hours of activity daily

is average. One of the best forms of exercise for dogs is swimming. It moves all muscles without putting strain on joints. On dry land, daily brisk walks are recommended, along with an occasional vigorous game of catch (for able dogs).

FITNESS FOR
FELINES

As cat owners know, cats tend to be indepen-

dent and seldom take to being put on a leash; however, they will climb a tower and play with a wand toy or even an old ball of yarn, if you provide it. Cats also have a natural instinct to chase and tussle with one another. This form of aerobic activity is their way of socializing, so help your cat find friends.   □□

Amy Nieskens, former associate editor of *The Old Farmer's Almanac,* grew up with a black Lab whose daily walks deterred canine corpulence.

dogs.) The ideal body condition (3) for dogs and cats is manifested as follows:

- Ribs should be palpable, with no noticeable fat deposits over the back, chest, and tail.

- The waist should be observed behind ribs when viewed from above.

- The abdomen should be tucked up (not be convex or swollen) when viewed from the side.

If this does not describe your pet, he or she is probably tipping the scales too much and needs to lose weight.

How We Predict the Weather

We derive our weather forecasts from a secret formula that was devised by the founder of this Almanac, Robert B. Thomas, in 1792. Thomas believed that weather on Earth was influenced by sunspots, which are magnetic storms on the surface of the Sun.

Over the years, we have refined and enhanced that formula with state-of-the-art technology and modern scientific calculations. We employ three scientific disciplines to make our long-range predictions: solar science, the study of sunspots and other solar activity; climatology, the study of prevailing weather patterns; and meteorology, the study of the atmosphere. We predict weather trends and events by comparing solar patterns and historical weather conditions with current solar activity.

Our forecasts emphasize temperature and precipitation deviations from averages, or normals. These are based on 30-year statistical averages prepared by government meteorological agencies and updated every 10 years. The most-recent tabulations span the period 1981 through 2010.

We believe that nothing in the universe happens haphazardly, that there is a cause-and-effect pattern to all phenomena. However, although neither we nor any other forecasters have as yet gained sufficient insight into the mysteries of the universe to predict the weather with total accuracy, our results are almost always very close to our traditional claim of 80 percent.

How Accurate Was Our Forecast for Winter 2011–12?

■ Last year, we correctly predicted that "temperatures across most of the nation will be above normal, on average, over the November to March winter season." Although we may have been the only source to predict relatively warm winter temperatures, we failed to recognize just how far above normal temperatures would be in what for many was "the year without a winter." The accuracy of our winter season temperature forecasts is shown in the table below, using a city selected from each region. We were correct in the direction of departure from normal in 12 of the 16 regions, although most regions were warmer than we forecast, and our forecasts differed from actual conditions by 3.1 degrees F, on average.

We were also correct in our forecast that "[w]hile most of the area from Texas and western Louisiana northward to Nebraska and Iowa will have relatively mild temperatures, on average, below-normal precipitation will increase drought concerns," as drought began or intensified in much of this area. We also forecast below-normal precipitation in Florida, the Southeast, the Desert Southwest, the southern Intermountain region, and most other areas that experienced drought this past winter.

We correctly forecast the direction of change in temperature from the previous winter season (November through March) in 75 percent of the regions and in precipitation in 69 percent of the regions. For the heart of winter (December through February), we correctly forecast the direction of change of precipitation in 88 percent of the regions.

Region/ City	Dec.–Feb. Temp. Variations From Normal (degrees F) PREDICTED	ACTUAL	Region/ City	Dec.–Feb. Temp. Variations From Normal (degrees F) PREDICTED	ACTUAL
1/Augusta	−1.0	+4.6	9/Marquette	−2.2	+7.2
2/Philadelphia	−0.4	+5.6	10/Kansas City	+2.7	+6.2
3/Roanoke	+0.5	+5.4	11/Oklahoma City	+2.2	+2.8
4/Savannah	+0.4	+3.9	12/Denver	+2.0	+1.5
5/Orlando	+0.1	+2.3	13/Boise	+1.3	+1.7
6/Cleveland	+1.2	+6.2	14/Tucson	−1.1	−0.8
7/Charleston	+0.9	+5.2	15/Eugene	+1.3	−1.0
8/Mobile	+1.3	+4.4	16/Los Angeles	−0.6	−0.4

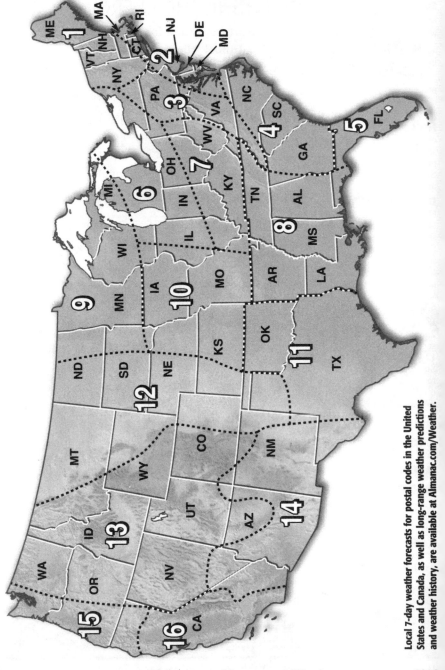

Northeast

SUMMARY: Winter will be colder and drier than normal, with below-normal snowfall. The coldest periods will be from Christmas through early January and in mid-January and early, mid-, and late February. The snowiest periods will be in mid-November, mid- to late December, mid- to late February, and early March.

April and May will be slightly warmer than normal. Rainfall will be below normal in the north and above normal in the south.

Summer will be drier than normal, with near-normal temperatures. The hottest periods will occur in early July and mid-August.

September and October will be warmer and drier than normal.

NOV. 2012: Temp. 35° (4° below avg.); precip. 3" (0.5" below avg.). 1–4 Rain and snow showers, chilly. 5–6 Rainy, mild. 7–15 Snowy periods, cold. 16–17 Rainy, mild. 18–25 Snow, then flurries, very cold. 26–30 Rain and snow, then sunny, cold.

DEC. 2012: Temp. 26.5° (1.5° below avg.); precip. 4" (1" above avg.). 1–3 Rain and snow, then rain. 4–6 Snow to rain. 7–11 Flurries, seasonable. 12–15 Snow, then rain showers, mild. 16–20 Snow showers, cold. 21–24 Heavy snow, then sunny, cold. 25–31 Snowy periods, very cold.

JAN. 2013: Temp. 22° (1° below avg.); precip. 2.5" (0.5" below avg.). 1–6 Snow showers, then sunny, bitter cold. 7–11 Snow, then flurries, cold. 12–15 Snow north, showers south; mild. 16–18 Snow, then sunny, cold. 19–22 Snow, then rainy, mild. 23–24 Snow north, rain south. 25–28 Rainy, mild. 29–31 Snow showers, seasonable.

FEB. 2013: Temp. 15° (8° below avg.); precip. 1.5" (1" below avg.). 1–7 Snowy periods, very cold. 8–10 Snow showers, milder. 11–16 Snow showers, very cold. 17–21 Sunny, turning milder. 22–28 Snowstorm, then sunny, cold.

MAR. 2013: Temp. 37° (3° above avg.); precip. 3.5" (0.5" above avg.). 1–4 Flurries and sprinkles, turning milder. 5–8 Snow, then sunny, cold. 9–14 Rainy periods, warmer. 15–19 Snow to rainstorm, then sunny. 20–25 Showers, warm. 26–31 Scattered showers; cool north, warm south.

APR. 2013: Temp. 49° (3° above avg.); precip. 3" (avg.). 1–7 Sunny, turning quite warm. 8–11 Showers, then sunny, nice. 12–16 Rain north; sunny, warm south. 17–22 T-storms, then sunny, cool. 23–30 Scattered showers, then sunny, cool.

MAY 2013: Temp. 55° (1° below avg.); precip. 3.5" (1" below avg. north, 1" above south). 1–8 Showers, then sunny, warm. 9–14 Rainy periods, cool. 15–21 Showers, then sunny, cool. 22–28 Scattered showers, seasonable. 29–31 Sunny, hot.

JUNE 2013: Temp. 65° (avg.); precip. 3.5" (avg.). 1–4 T-storms, then sunny, cool. 5–9 T-storms, warm. 10–21 Showers, cool. 22–25 Sunny, hot. 26–30 Scattered t-storms, cool.

JULY 2013: Temp. 71° (1° above avg.); precip. 3" (1" below avg.). 1–2 Sunny, hot. 3–7 T-storms, then sunny, warm. 8–12 Scattered t-storms, hot and humid. 13–16 Sunny, warm. 17–23 Scattered t-storms, turning cool. 24–31 A couple of t-storms, warm.

AUG. 2013: Temp. 65° (1° below avg.); precip. 2" (2" below avg.). 1–5 Showers, cool. 6–8 Sunny, hot. 9–12 T-storms, cool. 13–18 Scattered t-storms, hot. 19–25 Sunny, cool. 26–31 A couple of showers, warm.

SEPT. 2013: Temp. 63° (4° above avg.); precip. 3" (1" below avg.). 1–3 Sunny, very warm. 4–8 T-storms, then sunny, cool. 9–17 Sunny, hot. 18–23 T-storms, then sunny, cool. 24–25 Sunny, very warm. 26–30 Showers, then sunny, cool.

OCT. 2013: Temp. 51° (3° above avg.); precip. 3.5" (avg.). 1–5 A few showers. 6–11 Sunny, warm. 12–18 Scattered t-storms, mild. 19–24 Rain, then sunny, cool. 25–29 Sunny, warm. 30–31 Showers.

Caribou · Augusta · Burlington · Concord · Albany

W E A T H E R

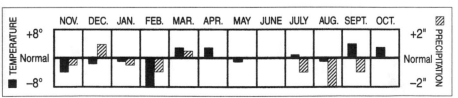

Atlantic Corridor

SUMMARY: Winter will be colder and drier than normal, with snowfall below normal in the north and near normal in the south. The coldest periods will be from Christmas through early January and in early and mid-February. The snowiest periods will be in mid-December, just before Christmas, and in mid- to late February.

April and May will be slightly warmer and drier than normal.

Summer will be slightly warmer and drier than normal, with the hottest periods in mid- to late June, mid- and late July, and mid-August. The strongest threat of a tropical storm will be in early June.

September and October will be warmer and drier than normal.

NOV. 2012: Temp. 42° (5° below avg.); precip. 3" (0.5" below avg.). 1–5 Showers and flurries, then sunny, warmer. 6–14 Rain to snow, then sunny, cold. 15–22 Rain, then sunny, cold. 23–25 Wet snow, cold. 26–30 Rain, then sunny, cool.

DEC. 2012: Temp. 38° (1° below avg.); precip. 4.5" (1.5" above avg.). 1–5 Rainy periods, mild. 6–10 Sunny, cool. 11–14 Showers, then sunny, mild. 15–20 Rain and snow, then sunny, cold. 21–25 Periods of rain and snow, turning cold. 26–29 Snow showers, cold. 30–31 Ice and snow, cold.

JAN. 2013: Temp. 35° (avg.); precip. 2.5" (1" below avg.). 1–5 Snow showers, then sunny, very cold. 6–10 Snow to rain, then sunny, cold. 11–15 Sunny, mild. 16–20 Rain to snow, then sunny, seasonable. 21–27 Rainy periods, mild. 28–31 Sunny, seasonable.

FEB. 2013: Temp. 29° (5° below avg.); precip. 1" (2" below avg.). 1–6 Snow showers, then sunny, very cold. 7–12 A few flurries, cold. 13–15 Snow showers, then sunny, very cold. 16–21 Sunny, cold. 22–28 Rain and snow, then sunny, cold.

MAR. 2013: Temp. 47.5° (3.5° above avg.); precip. 5" (1" above avg.). 1–4 Rain arriving, turning warm. 5–8 Rain and snow, then sunny, cool. 9–15 Heavy rain, then sunny and very warm south; drizzly north. 16–19 Showers, then sunny, pleasant. 20–28 A few showers, warm. 29–31 Sunny, cool.

APR. 2013: Temp. 54° (2° above avg.); precip. 2" (1.5" below avg.). 1–7 Sunny, pleasant. 8–12 T-storms, then sunny, pleasant. 13–16 Showers, cool north; sunny, warm south. 17–19 T-storms, then

sunny. 20–25 Rainy periods, cool. 26–30 Scattered t-storms, warm.

MAY 2013: Temp. 61° (1° below avg.); precip. 4" (1" above avg.). 1–3 Sunny, warm. 4–7 Rain, then sunny, cool. 8–17 Rainy periods, cool north; a couple of showers, warm south. 18–23 Sunny, then heavy rain, cool. 24–28 Scattered t-storms, seasonable. 29–31 Sunny, hot.

JUNE 2013: Temp. 70° (1° below avg.); precip. 5.5" (2" above avg.). 1–5 A few t-storms, warm. 6–8 Tropical storm threat. 9–15 Occasional t-storms, turning cooler. 16–17 Sunny, warm. 18–22 Heavy rain north, t-storms south; turning cool. 23–25 Sunny, hot. 26–30 Scattered t-storms, seasonable.

JULY 2013: Temp. 78° (2° above avg.); precip. 3" (1" below avg.). 1–7 T-storms, then sunny, seasonable. 8–12 Scattered t-storms, hot. 13–24 T-storms, then sunny, cooler. 25–31 Scattered t-storms, hot and humid.

AUG. 2013: Temp. 74° (avg.); precip. 2.5" (1.5" below avg.). 1–6 Showers, then sunny, pleasant. 7–12 Scattered t-storms; cool north, hot south. 13–18 T-storms, then sunny, hot. 19–24 Sunny, cool. 25–29 Showers, then sunny, cooler. 30–31 T-storms.

SEPT. 2013: Temp. 68° (1° above avg.); precip. 2" (1.5" below avg.). 1–8 T-storms, then sunny, cool. 9–16 Sunny, warm. 17–25 T-storms, then sunny, warm. 26–29 T-storms, then sunny, cool. 30 Heavy rain.

OCT. 2013: Temp. 59° (3° above avg.): precip. 2.5" (1" below avg.). 1–5 Sunny, turning warm. 6–11 Showers, then sunny, very warm. 12–16 Rain, then sunny, warm. 17–25 Showers, then sunny, cool. 26–30 Rain, then sunny, cool. 31 Rain.

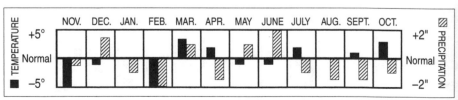

Appalachians

SUMMARY: Winter will be colder and drier than normal. The coldest periods will be from late December through early January and in early and mid-February. Snowfall will be below normal in the north and above normal in the south, with the snowiest periods in mid- to late December and early January.

April and May will be slightly warmer and drier than normal, with a hot Memorial Day weekend.

Summer will be drier and a bit warmer than normal, with the hottest periods in mid- to late June, early to mid-July, late July, and mid-August.

September and October will be warmer and drier than normal in most of the region.

NOV. 2012: Temp. 40° (4° below avg.); precip. 2.5" (1" below avg.). 1–5 Sunny; cool, then warm. 6–14 Rain and snow showers, then sunny, cold. 15–22 Rain and snow, then sunny, cool. 23–25 Snow north, rain south. 26–29 Rain, then sunny, seasonable. 30 Showers, mild.

DEC. 2012: Temp. 35.5° (0.5° below avg.); precip. 3" (1" below avg. north, 1" above south). 1–7 Showers, then sunny, mild. 8–9 Flurries, seasonable. 10–14 Rain, then sunny, warm. 15–20 Rain, then flurries, cold. 21–23 Snowstorm, then sunny, cold. 24–31 Snow showers, very cold.

JAN. 2013: Temp. 30° (avg.); precip. 3" (avg.). 1–5 Snow showers, very cold. 6–15 Snowstorm, then sunny, turning mild. 16–20 Snow, then sunny, cold. 21–27 A few showers, mild. 28–31 Sunny, seasonable.

FEB. 2013: Temp. 24° (6° below avg.); precip. 0.5" (2" below avg.). 1–6 Snow showers, very cold. 7–10 Sunny, seasonable. 11–20 Snow showers, then flurries, cold. 21–28 Snow, then flurries, cold.

MAR. 2013: Temp. 45° (5° above avg.); precip. 4" (1" above avg.). 1–2 Sunny, warm. 3–7 Rain, then flurries, chilly. 8–13 Rain, then sunny, warm. 14–21 Rain to snow, then sunny, turning warm. 22–28 Rainy periods, mild. 29–31 Sunny, cool.

APR. 2013: Temp. 52° (2° above avg.); precip. 2.5" (1" below avg.). 1–7 Showers, then sunny, warm. 8–10 Showers, seasonable. 11–13 Sunny, very warm. 14–19 T-storms, then sunny, cool. 20–30 A few showers, cool.

MAY 2013: Temp. 59° (1° below avg.); precip. 4" (avg.). 1–7 Showers, seasonable. 8–12 Scattered t-storms, warm. 13–19 Showers, then sunny, cool. 20–27 A few t-storms, cool. 28–31 Sunny, turning hot.

JUNE 2013: Temp. 68° (avg.); precip. 3" (1" below avg.). 1–3 Sunny, hot. 4–8 T-storms, then sunny, cool. 9–16 T-storms, then sunny, cool. 17–21 T-storms, cool. 22–25 Sunny, hot. 26–30 T-storms, then sunny, cool.

JULY 2013: Temp. 74° (1° above avg.); precip. 3.5" (avg.). 1–4 T-storms, then sunny, cool. 5–10 Sunny, hot. 11–14 T-storms, then sunny, cool. 15–23 T-storms, then sunny, cool. 24–31 A few t-storms, hot and humid.

AUG. 2013: Temp. 70.5° (0.5° below avg.); precip. 2.5" (1" below avg.). 1–2 Sunny, hot. 3–7 T-storms, then sunny, cool. 8–18 Scattered t-storms, hot. 19–25 Sunny, cool. 26–31 Scattered t-storms, seasonable.

SEPT. 2013: Temp. 64° (avg.); precip. 2" (1.5" below avg.). 1–8 Rain, then sunny, cool. 9–18 Sunny, then t-storms, warm. 19–24 Sunny, pleasant. 25–30 Rainy periods, turning cool.

OCT. 2013: Temp. 55° (2° above avg.); precip. 3.5" (1" below avg. north, 2" above south). 1–6 Sunny, turning warm. 7–12 Scattered t-storms, warm. 13–17 Sunny, pleasant. 18–24 Showers, then sunny, cool. 25–31 Sunny, then showers, mild.

Map labels: Elmira, Scranton, Harrisburg, Frederick, Roanoke, Asheville

WEATHER

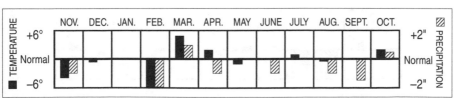

2013

Southeast

SUMMARY: Winter temperatures will be below normal, with below-normal rainfall and near- or above-normal snowfall. The coldest periods will be in early January and early and mid-February. The greatest snow and ice threats will be in late December, early and mid-January, and early and mid-February.

April and May will be rainier than normal, with near-normal temperatures.

Summer will be drier and slightly hotter than normal, with the hottest periods in late July and mid-August. Expect hurricane threats in the first week of June and in mid-October.

September and October will be slightly warmer than normal, with near-normal rainfall.

W E A T H E R

NOV. 2012: Temp. 53° (2° below avg.); precip. 2.5" (0.5" below avg.). 1–4 Sunny, cool. 5–13 Sunny; mild, then cold. 14–20 Rainy periods, milder. 21–26 Showers, cool. 27–30 Sunny, nice.

DEC. 2012: Temp. 49° (2° above avg.); precip. 5.5" (2" above avg.). 1–8 Rainy periods, mild. 9–14 Showers, then sunny, warm. 15–20 Rain, then sunny, cool. 21–24 Rain, then sunny, cool. 25–28 Rainy, mild. 29–31 Sunny, then rain, freezing rain, and sleet.

JAN. 2013: Temp. 43° (2° below avg.); precip. 2.5" (2" below avg.). 1–6 Rainy periods, snow at times, cold. 7–15 Sunny; cold, then mild. 16–18 Rain to snow. 19–22 Sunny, turning mild. 23–26 Showers, mild. 27–31 Sunny, cold.

FEB. 2013: Temp. 40° (6° below avg.); precip. 2" (2" below avg.). 1–7 Snow, then sunny, cold. 8–13 Showers, then sunny, cold. 14–20 Rain and wet snow, then sunny, cold. 21–28 Snow, then sunny, cold.

MAR. 2013: Temp. 56° (1° above avg.); precip. 3.5" (1" below avg.). 1–5 Rainy periods, mild. 6–8 Sunny, chilly. 9–15 Rain, then sunny, warm. 16–19 Rain, then sunny, cool. 20–24 Sunny, warm. 25–31 Rainy periods, turning cool.

APR. 2013: Temp. 64° (1° above avg.); precip. 2.5" (0.5" below avg.). 1–3 T-storms, warm. 4–7 Sunny, cool. 8–14 Showers, then sunny, warm. 15–22 Scattered t-storms, cooler. 23–26 Sunny,

warm. 27–30 T-storms, then sunny, cool.

MAY 2013: Temp. 70° (1° below avg.); precip. 5.5" (2" above avg.). 1–3 Sunny, cool. 4–11 Scattered t-storms, warm. 12–22 Sunny, then scattered t-storms, cool. 23–29 Sunny, cool. 30–31 Heavy rain.

JUNE 2013: Temp. 77.5° (0.5° below avg.); precip. 4.5" (avg.). 1–5 Scattered t-storms west, hurricane threat east. 6–8 Sunny, cool. 9–20 Isolated t-storms, warm. 21–25 Sunny, hot. 26–30 T-storms, cooler.

JULY 2013: Temp. 82.5° (0.5° above avg.); precip. 4" (0.5" below avg.). 1–8 Scattered t-storms, cool. 9–16 T-storms, then sunny, cool. 17–31 Scattered PM t-storms, hot.

AUG. 2013: Temp. 81° (1° above avg.); precip. 3" (2" below avg.). 1–6 Scattered t-storms, turning cool. 7–12 Isolated t-storms, hot. 13–18 Sunny, hot. 19–23 Sunny, cool. 24–31 A few t-storms; cool, then warm.

SEPT. 2013: Temp. 73° (1° below avg.); precip. 2.5" (2" below avg.). 1–9 Scattered t-storms, then sunny, cool. 10–18 T-storms, then sunny, warm. 19–25 Scattered t-storms, warm. 26–30 Sunny, cool.

OCT. 2013: Temp. 65.5° (1.5° above avg.); precip. 6" (2" above avg.). 1–5 Showers, then sunny, warm. 6–11 T-storms, warm. 12–15 Hurricane threat. 16–24 Sunny, cool. 25–31 Showers; warm, then cool.

Raleigh
Columbia
Atlanta
Savannah

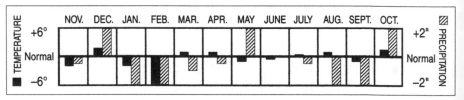

Florida

SUMMARY: Winter will be colder and drier than normal, with the best chance for snow in the north in mid-February. The coldest temperatures will occur in mid-December, early and mid-January, and early February.

April will be warm and dry; May will be cooler and much rainier than normal.

Summer will be rainier than normal, with near-normal temperatures. The hottest periods will be in mid- and late August. Expect several hurricane threats: in early and mid-June, early to mid-August, and early to mid-October.

September and October will be warmer and rainier than normal.

NOV. 2012: Temp. 68° (1° below avg.); precip. 0.5" (2" below avg.). 1–2 Sunny, cool. 3–11 Sunny north, a few t-storms south; cool. 12–20 Sunny, turning warm. 21–26 Showers, turning cool. 27–30 Sunny, warm.

DEC. 2012: Temp. 66° (3° above avg.); precip. 3.5" (2" above avg. north, 0.5" below south). 1–9 A few t-storms, warm. 10–13 Sunny, warm. 14–20 Showers, then sunny, cool. 21–24 T-storms, then sunny, cool. 25–31 Scattered showers, warm.

JAN. 2013: Temp. 59° (1° below avg.); precip. 2" (2" below avg. north, 1" above south). 1–10 T-storms, then sunny, cool. 11–15 Sunny north, showers south; seasonable. 16–20 Showers, then sunny, warm. 21–25 Sunny, warm. 26–31 T-storms, then sunny, cool.

FEB. 2013: Temp. 56° (5° below avg.); precip. 2" (0.5" below avg.). 1–3 Sunny, cool. 4–9 Showers, then sunny, cool. 10–17 Rainy periods, cool. 18–21 Sunny, cool. 22–28 Showers, then sunny, cool.

MAR. 2013: Temp. 66° (1° below avg.); precip. 1" (2" below avg.). 1–2 T-storms, then sunny, cool. 3–7 T-storms, then sunny, cool. 8–14 Showers, then sunny, nice. 15–19 Scattered showers, chilly. 20–31 Sunny, turning warm.

APR. 2013: Temp. 73° (2° above avg.); precip. 1.5" (1" below avg.). 1–8 Scattered t-storms, warm. 9–16 Sunny; very warm north, seasonable south. 17–23 A few t-storms. 24–30 Sunny, then t-storms, cool.

MAY 2013: Temp. 76° (1° below avg.); precip. 10" (4" above avg. north, 8" above south). 1–7 Scattered t-storms; hot north, cool south. 8–11 Sunny, warm. 12–21 A couple of t-storms north, daily t-storms south; seasonable. 22–27 Sunny, warm north; t-storms south. 28–31 Heavy t-storms, windy and cool.

JUNE 2013: Temp. 81° (1° below avg.); precip. 10.5" (2" above avg. north, 6" above south). 1–5 Hurricane threat. 6–10 Sunny, warm north; t-storms, cool south. 11–14 Hurricane threat. 15–16 Sunny, nice. 17–21 T-storms; hot north, cool south. 22–30 Scattered t-storms north, daily t-storms south; cool.

JULY 2013: Temp. 83° (1° above avg. north, 1° below south); precip. 6.5" (avg.). 1–5 Daily t-storms, cool. 6–14 Scattered t-storms, seasonable. 15–17 Sunny, nice. 18–24 Isolated t-storms; hot north, seasonable south. 25–31 Daily t-storms, warm and humid.

AUG. 2013: Temp. 83° (1° above avg.); precip. 7" (2" above avg. north, 3" below south). 1–4 Scattered t-storms, warm. 5–7 Hurricane threat. 8–13 T-storms north, sunny south; hot. 14–20 Sunny north, scattered t-storms south; hot. 21–24 Heavy rain, cool north; a couple of t-storms south. 25–31 Scattered t-storms, hot and humid.

SEPT. 2013: Temp. 82° (2° above avg.); precip. 6.5" (1" below avg. north, 3" above south). 1–4 Scattered t-storms, warm. 5–10 T-storms, then sunny, nice. 11–17 Daily t-storms, seasonable. 18–26 Sunny north, daily t-storms south; warm. 27–30 Scattered t-storms, warm.

OCT. 2013: Temp. 75.5° (2° above avg. north, 1° below south); precip. 6" (2" above avg.). 1–9 Showers and t-storms; warm north, seasonable south. 10–12 Hurricane threat. 13–16 Sunny, warm. 17–24 T-storms, then sunny, cool. 25–31 Showers, then sunny, warm.

W E A T H E R

Jacksonville

Tampa

Orlando

Miami

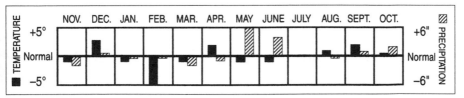

Lower Lakes

SUMMARY: Winter will be colder than normal in the east, with above-normal temperatures in the west. The coldest periods will be from late December through early January and in mid-January and early and mid-February. Precipitation and snowfall will generally be below normal, with the snowiest periods in early to mid-November, early January, and early March.

April and May will be warmer and drier than normal, with an especially warm first half of April.

Summer temperatures and rainfall will be near normal, on average, despite a tropical rainstorm threat in mid-June. The hottest periods will be in early to mid-July, late July, and mid-August.

September and October will be warmer and drier than normal.

NOV. 2012: Temp. 40° (3° below avg. east, 1° above west); precip. 1.5" (1" below avg.). 1–5 Sunny, then showers, mild. 6–8 Lake snows, cold. 9–16 Periods of rain and snow, chilly. 17–19 Sunny, mild. 20–24 Snow showers, cold. 25–30 Heavy rain, then showers, mild.

DEC. 2012: Temp. 31° (1° below avg.); precip. 3" (1" below avg. east, 0.5" above west). 1–5 Rainy periods, mild. 6–9 Sunny, cooler. 10–15 Showers, then t-storms, turning warm. 16–31 Flurries and lake snows, cold.

JAN. 2013: Temp. 30° (0.5° below avg. east, 6° above west); precip. 2.5" (0.5" below avg. east, 1" above west). 1–5 Snow showers, cold. 6–9 Snowstorm, then flurries, cold. 10–15 A shower, mild. 16–19 Snow showers, cold. 20–26 Showers, mild. 27–31 Sunny, then snow showers, mild.

FEB. 2013: Temp. 20° (7° below avg.); precip. 0.5" (1.5" below avg.). 1–6 Lake snows, cold. 7–16 Snow showers, cold. 17–19 Sunny, cold. 20–22 Snow, then snow showers, cold. 23–28 Snow, then sunny, cold.

MAR. 2013: Temp. 43° (5° above avg.); precip. 3.5" (0.5" above avg.). 1–3 Showers, mild. 4–7 Snow, then sunny, cold. 8–13 Showers, mild. 14–17 Rain and snow, then flurries, cold. 18–23 Showers, then sunny, warm. 24–27 Rain, then sunny, warm. 28–31 T-storms, then sunny, cool.

APR. 2013: Temp. 51° (3° above avg.); precip. 2" (1.5" below avg.). 1–6 Sunny, warm. 7–12 Showers, then sunny, warm. 13–20 Scattered t-storms; warm, then cool. 21–30 A few showers, cool.

MAY 2013: Temp. 56.5° (1.5° below avg.); precip. 4.5" (1" above avg.). 1–6 Rain, then sunny, cool. 7–10 T-storms, then sunny, cool. 11–14 Rainy periods, cool. 15–20 Sunny east, t-storms west; cool. 21–26 Scattered t-storms, cool. 27–31 Sunny, hot.

JUNE 2013: Temp. 64.5° (1.5° below avg.); precip. 3.5" (avg.). 1–2 Sunny, hot. 3–7 T-storms, then sunny, cool. 8–16 Scattered t-storms; cool, then warm. 17–21 Tropical rains, chilly. 22–23 Sunny, warm. 24–30 Scattered t-storms, cool.

JULY 2013: Temp. 72° (1° above avg.); precip. 3.5" (avg.). 1–8 Showers, then sunny, hot. 9–14 T-storms, then sunny, cool. 15–23 T-storms, then sunny, cool. 24–31 Scattered t-storms, hot.

AUG. 2013: Temp. 69° (avg.); precip. 4.5" (0.5" above avg.). 1–7 T-storms, then sunny, cool. 8–11 Scattered t-storms, warm. 12–17 T-storms east, sunny west; hot. 18–23 Sunny, cool. 24–31 A few t-storms, cool.

SEPT. 2013: Temp. 64° (2° above avg.); precip. 3" (0.5" below avg.). 1–8 T-storms, then sunny, warm. 9–14 Sunny east, t-storms west; warm. 15–22 T-storms, then sunny, cool. 23–25 Sunny, warm. 26–30 Showers, cool.

OCT. 2013: Temp. 55° (3° above avg.); precip. 2" (0.5" below avg.). 1–9 T-storms, then sunny, turning very warm. 10–14 Rain, then sunny, mild. 15–22 Scattered showers, cool. 23–29 Sunny, mild. 30–31 Heavy rain.

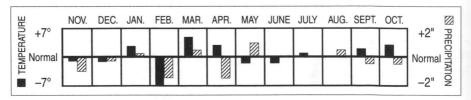

Ohio Valley

SUMMARY: Winter will be colder and drier than normal, with above-normal snowfall. The coldest periods will be from late December through early January and in early and mid-February. The snowiest periods will occur in mid- to late November, mid- to late December, and early to mid-January.

April and May will be warmer and rainier than normal.

Summer will be slightly warmer and rainier than normal, with the hottest periods in late July and mid-August.

September and October will be warmer and drier than normal.

NOV. 2012: Temp. 43° (3° below avg.); precip. 3.5" (avg.). 1–2 Sunny, cool. 3–5 Rainy, mild. 6–9 Snow showers, cold. 10–17 Rainy periods, cool. 18–22 Sunny, cold. 23–30 Snowstorm, then rainy periods, mild.

DEC. 2012: Temp. 35° (2° below avg.); precip. 3" (avg.). 1–7 Rainy periods, mild. 8–9 Sunny, cold. 10–14 Showers, quite mild. 15–20 Rain to snow, then snow showers, cold. 21–23 Snowstorm, then flurries, cold. 24–31 Snow, then snow showers, very cold.

JAN. 2013: Temp. 34° (1° below avg. east, 3° above west); precip. 2" (1" below avg.). 1–5 Snow showers, cold. 6–9 Snowstorm, then flurries, cold. 10–15 Sunny, mild. 16–19 Snow, then sunny, cold. 20–26 Rainy periods, mild. 27–31 Sunny, seasonable.

FEB. 2013: Temp. 26° (8° below avg.); precip. 1" (2" below avg.). 1–7 Snow showers, very cold. 8–12 Sunny, cold. 13–19 Snow showers, then sunny, cold. 20–25 Snow showers, cold. 26–28 Showers, milder.

MAR. 2013: Temp. 48° (3° above avg.); precip. 5.5" (1.5" above avg.). 1–3 Showers, warm. 4–7 Rain to snow, then sunny, cold. 8–12 Showers, then sunny, warm. 13–18 Rain to snow, then sunny, cool. 19–24 Scattered t-storms, warm. 25–31 Sunny, then t-storms, cool.

APR. 2013: Temp. 57° (2° above avg.); precip. 2.5" (1" below avg.). 1–4 T-storms, then sunny, cool. 5–6 Sunny, warm. 7–10 T-storms, then sunny, cool. 11–15 Sunny, warm. 16–18

T-storms, then sunny, cool. 19–26 Scattered t-storms, seasonable. 27–30 Sunny, cool.

MAY 2013: Temp. 62° (1° below avg.); precip. 7.5" (3" above avg.). 1–5 Rainy periods, seasonable. 6–13 A few t-storms; warm, then cool. 14–15 Sunny, cool. 16–27 T-storms, cool. 28–31 Sunny, warm.

JUNE 2013: Temp. 70° (1° below avg.); precip. 3" (1" below avg.). 1–4 Sunny, hot. 5–8 T-storms, then sunny, cool. 9–19 Scattered t-storms, turning warm. 20–24 Sunny, hot. 25–30 T-storms, then sunny, cool.

JULY 2013: Temp. 77° (2° above avg.); precip. 6" (2" above avg.). 1–5 Sunny, warm. 6–20 Scattered t-storms, warm. 21–23 Sunny, cool. 24–31 Scattered t-storms, turning hot.

AUG. 2013: Temp. 73° (avg.); precip. 4" (avg.). 1–5 T-storms, then sunny, cool. 6–12 A few t-storms, warm. 13–18 Sunny, hot. 19–24 T-storms, then sunny, cool. 25–31 Scattered t-storms, seasonable.

SEPT. 2013: Temp. 66.5° (0.5° below avg.); precip. 2.5" (0.5" below avg.). 1–7 T-storms, then sunny, cool. 8–17 T-storms, then sunny, warm. 18–23 T-storms, then sunny, cool. 24–30 T-storms, then sunny, cool.

OCT. 2013: Temp. 59.5° (2.5° above avg.); precip. 1.5" (1" below avg.). 1–9 Showers, then sunny, warm. 10–14 Rain, then sunny, cool. 15–24 A few showers, cool. 25–31 Showers, mild.

WEATHER

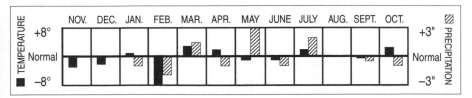

Deep South

SUMMARY: Winter will be much colder and drier than normal, with the coldest periods in mid- to late December, early January, and early February. Snowfall will be near to above normal, with the snowiest periods in the north in mid- to late December, early January, and mid-March, and the best chance for snow in the south in mid-February.

April and May will be slightly warmer than normal, with precipitation above normal in the north and below normal in the south.

Summer will be cooler and drier than normal, with the hottest periods in mid-July and early and mid-August. September and October will be near normal in the north, but cooler and drier than normal in the south.

NOV. 2012: Temp. 55.5° (1° below avg. north, 2° above south); precip. 3" (2" below avg.). 1–2 Sunny, cool. 3–13 T-storms, warm, then sunny, cool. 14–21 T-storms, warm, then sunny, cool. 22–30 T-storms, then sunny, nice.

DEC. 2012: Temp. 48.5° (1° below avg. north, 2° above south); precip. 7" (2" above avg.). 1–5 Heavy rain, then sunny, cool. 6–14 A few t-storms, warm. 15–19 Sunny, cold. 20–25 Periods of snow north, rain south; cold. 26–31 Rainy periods, cool.

JAN. 2013: Temp. 45° (1° above avg. north, 1° below south); precip. 3" (2" below avg.). 1–4 Rainy, cool. 5–10 Rain and snow, then sunny, cold. 11–14 Sunny, turning warm. 15–18 T-storms, then sunny, cold. 19–26 Sunny, then t-storms, warm. 27–31 Sunny, cool.

FEB. 2013: Temp. 39° (8° below avg.); precip. 3" (2" below avg.). 1–6 Snow showers, then sunny, cold. 7–13 Snow north, rain south, then sunny, cool. 14–20 Rain and snow, then sunny, cool. 21–22 Snow showers north, t-storms south. 23–28 Sunny north, rainy periods south; cool.

MAR. 2013: Temp. 55° (1° below avg.); precip. 6" (1" above avg. north, 1" below south). 1–7 Rain, then sunny, cold. 8–12 T-storms, then sunny, warm. 13–18 Heavy snow north, t-storms south, then sunny, cold. 19–22 Sunny, warm. 23–28 T-storms, warm. 29–31 Sunny, cool.

APR. 2013: Temp. 63° (avg.); precip. 2.5" (2" below avg.). 1–5 T-storms, then sunny, cool.

Little Rock

Nashville

Tupelo

Shreveport

Montgomery

Jackson

Mobile

New Orleans

6–10 T-storms, then sunny, nice. 11–16 Scattered t-storms north, sunny south; warm. 17–26 Scattered t-storms; cool, then warm. 27–30 Sunny, cool.

MAY 2013: Temp. 71.5° (0.5° above avg.); precip. 5.5" (3" above avg. north, 2" below south). 1–11 Scattered t-storms, warm. 12–15 Sunny, cool. 16–26 A few t-storms; warm, then cool. 27–31 Sunny, turning warm.

JUNE 2013: Temp. 78° (avg.); precip. 4" (1" below avg.). 1–3 Sunny, hot. 4–8 T-storms, then sunny, cool. 9–16 Scattered t-storms, seasonable. 17–19 Hurricane threat. 20–23 Sunny, hot. 24–30 T-storms, then sunny, cool.

JULY 2013: Temp. 80° (1° below avg.); precip. 6.5" (2" above avg.). 1–7 A few t-storms, cool. 8–17 Scattered t-storms north, daily t-storms south; warm. 18–25 T-storms; cool north, hot south. 26–31 Sunny, hot north; t-storms south.

AUG. 2013: Temp. 80° (avg.); precip. 2.5" (2" below avg.). 1–7 Scattered t-storms; hot, then cool. 8–17 Sunny, hot north; t-storms south. 18–26 Sunny, cool. 27–31 T-storms, then sunny.

SEPT. 2013: Temp. 74° (2° below avg.); precip. 4.5" (2" above avg. north, 2" below south). 1–7 T-storms, then sunny, cool. 8–16 T-storms sunny, nice. 17–24 T-storms, then sunny, warm. 25–30 Scattered t-storms, cool.

OCT. 2013: Temp. 65° (2° above avg. north, 2° below south); precip. 1" (2" below avg.). 1–11 A few t-storms, warm. 12–16 Sunny, cool. 17–23 T-storms, then sunny, chilly. 24–26 Sunny, warm. 27–31 Scattered t-storms, cool.

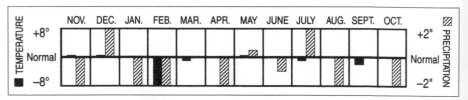

Upper Midwest

SUMMARY: Winter temperatures will be above normal on average, with below-normal precipitation and snowfall in most of the region. The coldest periods will be in late December and in early and mid-February. The snowiest periods will occur in mid-December, early January, and late March.

April and May will be a bit wetter than normal, with near-normal temperatures.

Summer will be slightly cooler than normal with near-normal rainfall. The hottest periods will occur in late June, mid- and late July, and mid-August.

September and October will be warmer and wetter than normal.

NOV. 2012: Temp. 32.5° (1° above avg. east, 6° above west); precip. 1" (1" below avg.). 1–4 Sunny, turning warm. 5–8 Snow showers, cold. 9–18 Flurries, mild. 19–22 Snow showers, cold. 23–30 Sunny, then snow showers, mild.

DEC. 2012: Temp. 12° (4° below avg.); precip. 1" (1" below avg. east, 1" above avg.). 1–5 Snowy periods, mild. 6–8 Flurries, cold. 9–13 Rain east, snow west; mild. 14–24 Flurries, turning very cold. 25–31 Snow showers, very cold.

JAN. 2013: Temp. 20° (7° above avg.); precip. 0.5" (0.5" below avg.). 1–3 Snow showers, cold. 4–14 Snow, then sunny, quite mild. 15–16 Snow showers, colder. 17–31 Snow showers, mild.

FEB. 2013: Temp. 10° (3° below avg.); precip. 0.5" (0.5" below avg.). 1–9 Snow showers, cold. 10–15 Sunny, very cold. 16–28 Snow showers, turning mild.

MAR. 2013: Temp. 33° (5° above avg.); precip. 1.5" (1" below avg. east, 1" above avg.). 1–6 Rain to snow, then sunny, cold. 7–10 Snow, then sunny, warm. 11–16 Rain to snow, then sunny, cold. 17–23 A couple of showers, warm. 24–26 Sunny, mild. 27–29 Rain to snow, then sunny, cool. 30–31 Showers.

APR. 2013: Temp. 44° (2° above avg.); precip. 2" (0.5" below avg. east, 1" above avg.). 1–5 Showers, then sunny, warm. 6–11 Rain to snow, then sunny, cool. 12–14 Rainy, mild. 15–18 Snow, then sunny, cool. 19–25 Showers, then sunny, warm. 26–30 Showers, cool.

MAY 2013: Temp. 53° (2° below avg.); precip. 4" (1" above avg.). 1–6 Showers, then sunny, cool. 7–12 Rain, then snow showers, chilly. 13–21 Sunny, then rainy periods, cool. 22–28 Sunny, turning hot. 29–31 T-storms, warm.

JUNE 2013: Temp. 60° (3° below avg.); precip. 4.5" (2" above avg. east, 1" below west). 1–3 T-storms, warm. 4–11 Showery, cool. 12–16 Scattered t-storms, seasonable. 17–24 Rainy periods, cool. 25–30 A couple of showers, turning warm.

JULY 2013: Temp. 68° (avg.); precip. 3.5" (avg.). 1–3 Sunny, cool. 4–10 Scattered t-storms, hot. 11–24 A few showers, cool. 25–31 Sunny, then t-storms, hot.

AUG. 2013: Temp. 64° (2° below avg.); precip. 3.5" (avg.). 1–4 Sunny, cool. 5–11 Scattered t-storms, cool. 12–14 Sunny, hot. 15–20 T-storms, then sunny, cool. 21–26 T-storms, then sunny, cool. 27–31 T-storms, cool.

SEPT. 2013: Temp. 60° (2° above avg.); precip. 5" (2" above avg.). 1–2 Rainy, cool. 3–7 Sunny, warm. 8–13 T-storms, then sunny, cool. 14–16 Rainy, warm. 17–24 Sunny; cool, then warm. 25–30 Showers, cool.

OCT. 2013: Temp. 50° (3° above avg.); precip. 2.5" (avg.). 1–7 Rain, then sunny, warm. 8–12 Rainy, cool. 13–15 Sunny, mild. 16–21 Showers, cool. 22–28 Sunny, mild. 29–31 Snow showers, cold.

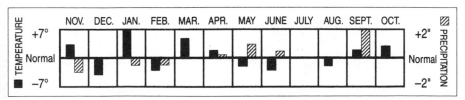

Heartland

SUMMARY: Winter temperatures will be higher than normal, on average, with precipitation and snowfall near normal in the east and below normal in the west. The coldest periods will be in late December, early January, and early and mid-February. The snowiest periods will be in mid- to late November, mid- to late December, early January, and early March.

April and May will have near-normal temperatures and rainfall, on average, with hot temperatures in late May.

Summer will be drier and slightly cooler than normal, on average, despite hot spells in late June, mid- and late July, and mid-August.

September and October will be slightly drier than normal, with near-normal temperatures.

NOV. 2012: Temp. 45° (2° above avg.); precip. 1.5" (1" below avg.). 1–5 Showers, mild. 6–11 Sunny; cool, then mild. 12–16 Showers, cool. 17–21 Sunny; mild, then cold. 22–26 Rain to snow, then sunny, cold. 27–30 Rainy periods, mild.

DEC. 2012: Temp. 30° (2° below avg.); precip. 2" (2" above avg. east, 1" below west). 1–8 Rain, then flurries, cold. 9–13 Showers, mild. 14–16 T-storms, then flurries, cold. 17–24 Snowy periods, cold. 25–31 Snow showers, turning very cold.

JAN. 2013: Temp. 35° (6° above avg.); precip. 2" (1" above avg.). 1–3 Flurries, cold. 4–9 Snow, then sunny, cold. 10–15 Sunny, mild. 16–20 Flurries, then sunny, mild. 21–29 Rainy periods, then sunny, mild. 30–31 Showers, colder.

FEB. 2013: Temp. 27° (4° below avg.); precip. 0.5" (1" below avg.). 1–7 Flurries, turning very cold. 8–13 Snow showers, cold. 14–22 Sunny, then snow showers, cold. 23–28 Sunny, turning mild.

MAR. 2013: Temp. 46° (2° above avg.); precip. 1.5" (1" below avg.). 1–2 Rainy, mild. 3–6 Snowy, cold. 7–12 Rainy periods, warm. 13–16 Snow, then flurries, cold. 17–23 Sunny, warm. 24–31 Scattered t-storms, then sunny, cool.

APR. 2013: Temp. 56° (2° above avg.); precip. 2.5" (1" below avg.). 1–5 Sunny, turning warm. 6–15 A few t-storms, warm. 16–24 Sunny; cool, then very warm. 25–30 Showers, turning cool.

MAY 2013: Temp. 62° (2° below avg.); precip. 5" (1" below avg. north, 2" above south). 1–5 Sunny north, t-storms south; cool. 6–9 T-storms, warm. 10–14 Sunny, cool. 15–24 Rainy periods, cool. 25–31 Sunny, turning hot.

JUNE 2013: Temp. 71° (1° below avg.); precip. 3.5" (1" below avg.). 1–3 Sunny, hot. 4–10 T-storms, then sunny, cool. 11–15 T-storms, then sunny, hot. 16–27 T-storms, then sunny, cool. 28–30 T-storms, warm.

JULY 2013: Temp. 77° (avg.); precip. 4" (avg.). 1–4 Sunny, cool. 5–15 Scattered t-storms, then sunny, warm. 16–27 Several t-storms; hot, then cool. 28–31 Sunny, hot.

AUG. 2013: Temp. 74° (1° below avg.); precip. 3.5" (avg.). 1–6 T-storms, then sunny, cool. 7–16 T-storms, then sunny, hot. 17–22 T-storms, then sunny, cool. 23–31 Scattered t-storms, cool.

SEPT. 2013: Temp. 66° (1° below avg.); precip. 2.5" (1" below avg.). 1–7 Showers, then sunny, cool. 8–16 A few t-storms, turning warm. 17–20 Sunny, nice. 21–27 T-storms, then sunny, chilly. 28–30 Rain, then sunny, cool.

OCT. 2013: Temp. 57° (1° above avg.); precip. 3.5" (0.5" above avg.). 1–4 Showers, cool. 5–9 Scattered t-storms, warm. 10–13 Sunny, cool. 14–22 Showers, then sunny, cool. 23–25 Sunny, warm. 26–31 Rainy periods, turning cool.

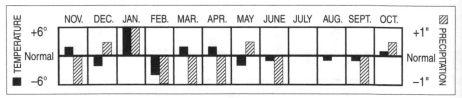

Texas–Oklahoma

SUMMARY: Winter temperatures will be slightly colder than normal, on average, with precipitation and snowfall near or a bit above normal. The coldest periods will occur in late December and early January and through much of February. The snowiest periods will be in early to mid-February and early March.

April and May will be wetter than normal, with temperatures below normal in the north and above normal in the south.

Summer will be cooler and a bit rainier than normal, with the hottest periods in mid-July and in early and mid-August. Watch for a hurricane in mid-June.

September and October will be drier and a bit warmer than normal.

NOV. 2012: Temp. 61° (4° above avg.); precip. 2" (1" below avg.). 1–5 A couple of t-storms, warm. 6–19 Sunny, warm. 20–27 Scattered showers, cool. 28–30 Sunny, warm.

DEC. 2012: Temp. 49° (3° below avg. north, 1° above south); precip. 2.5" (avg.). 1–10 Rainy periods, mixed with snow north; turning cold. 11–13 Sunny, warm. 14–21 Sunny, cold. 22–31 Snow showers north, rainy periods south; cold.

JAN. 2013: Temp. 50° (4° above avg. north, 2° below south); precip. 4" (2" above avg.). 1–9 Rain and wet snow, then sunny, cold. 10–15 Rain and t-storms, mild. 16–19 Sunny, turning warm. 20–25 Occasional rain, warm. 26–31 Sunny, turning cold.

FEB. 2013: Temp. 45° (5° below avg.); precip. 1.5" (0.5" below avg.). 1–4 Sunny, cold north; rain south. 5–10 Snowstorm, then sunny north; rainy periods south; cold. 11–16 Rain and snow north; showers south; cold. 17–22 Sunny, cool. 23–28 A couple of showers north, rainy south; cool.

MAR. 2013: Temp. 58° (1° below avg.); precip. 2.5" (avg.). 1–7 Rain to snow north, showers south; warm, then cold. 8–10 Sunny, nice. 11–17 Rain and snow north, showers south, then sunny, cool. 18–23 Sunny, turning warm. 24–31 T-storms, then sunny, cool.

APR. 2013: Temp. 67° (1° above avg.); precip. 3.5" (0.5" above avg.). 1–3 Sunny north, rain south; cool. 4–10 T-storms, then sunny, warm. 11–20 T-storms, then sunny, cool. 21–25 Sunny, turning warm. 26–30 T-storms, seasonable.

MAY 2013: Temp. 72.5° (3° below avg. north, 2° above south); precip. 6" (1" above avg.). 1–6

A few t-storms; cool north, warm south. 7–13 T-storms, then sunny, cool. 14–18 T-storms north; sunny, warm south. 19–28 Scattered t-storms; cool north, warm south. 29–31 Sunny, warm.

JUNE 2013: Temp. 77° (2° below avg.); precip. 5" (1" above avg.). 1–7 Sunny, hot. 8–13 T-storms, then sunny, cool north; t-storms, cool south. 14–19 Hurricane threat. 20–23 Sunny, warm. 24–30 T-storms, then sunny, cool north; scattered t-storms south.

JULY 2013: Temp. 80° (1° below avg.); precip. 2" (1" below avg.). 1–6 Sunny, cool north; a couple of t-storms, seasonable south and central. 7–14 Scattered t-storms, warm. 15–23 Sunny, hot north; scattered t-storms, warm south. 24–31 T-storms, then sunny, hot north; scattered t-storms, seasonable south.

AUG. 2013: Temp. 80° (1° below avg.); precip. 3.5" (1" above avg.). 1–3 Sunny, hot. 4–8 T-storms, cool north; sunny, hot south. 9–16 Sunny north, scattered t-storms south; hot. 17–22 T-storms, then sunny cool north; t-storms south. 23–31 T-storms, then sunny, cool.

SEPT. 2013: Temp. 75° (1° below avg.); precip. 2.5" (1" below avg.). 1–6 Sunny north, a few t-storms south; cool. 7–10 T-storms; cool north, warm south. 11–16 Scattered t-storms north, sunny south; warm. 17–25 Showers, then sunny, warm. 26–30 T-storms, then sunny, cool north; a few t-storms, warm south.

OCT. 2013: Temp. 69° (2° above avg.); precip. 3" (1" below avg.). 1–8 T-storms, then sunny, warm. 9–13 T-storms, then sunny, cool. 14–21 T-storms, then sunny, cool. 22–25 Sunny, warm. 26–31 T-storms, then sunny, cool.

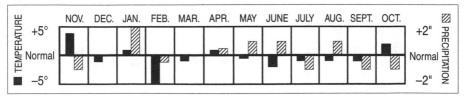

High Plains

SUMMARY: Winter temperatures will be 1 to 3 degrees above normal, on average, with slightly above-normal rainfall and below-normal snowfall. The coldest periods will occur in early to mid-December, late December, and early and mid-February. The snowiest periods will be in mid-December, early February, and early March.

April and May will be cooler than normal, with precipitation slightly above normal in the east and below normal in the west.

Summer temperatures will be 1 to 2 degrees cooler than normal, on average, with rainfall above normal in the north and a bit below normal in the south. The hottest periods will be in mid-June and late July.

September and October will be warmer and slightly drier than normal.

W E A T H E R

NOV. 2012: Temp. 43° (6° above avg.); precip. 0.5" (0.5" below avg.). 1–10 Sunny, mild. 11–19 Rain and snow, then sunny, cold. 20–24 Snow showers, cold. 25–30 Sunny, quite mild.

DEC. 2012: Temp. 23° (5° below avg.); precip. 1" (0.5" above avg.). 1–4 Sunny, mild. 5–10 Snowy periods, cold. 11–15 Snow showers, very cold. 16–17 Rain and snow showers, mild. 18–22 Snowy periods, seasonable. 23–31 Snow showers, very cold.

JAN. 2013: Temp. 34° (6° above avg.); precip. 1" (avg. north, 1" above south). 1–5 Snow showers, cold. 6–13 Sunny, quite mild. 14–18 Rain, then sunny, mild. 19–22 Snow, cold north; sunny, mild south. 23–31 Rain and snow showers, then sunny, mild.

FEB. 2013: Temp. 28.5° (3° below avg. east, 4° above west); precip. 0.5" (avg.). 1–3 Sunny, mild. 4–11 Snow, then flurries, cold. 12–16 Rain to snow, then sunny, cold. 17–19 Sunny, mild. 20–24 Rain and snow showers; mild north, cold south. 25–28 Sunny, mild.

MAR. 2013: Temp. 41° (2° above avg.); precip. 1" (avg.). 1–9 Snow, then sunny, mild. 10–15 Snowy periods, cold. 16–22 Sunny, warm. 23–31 A few rain and snow showers, cold.

APR. 2013: Temp. 48° (avg.); precip. 1.5" (0.5" below avg.). 1–3 Sunny, nice. 4–8 Snow, cold north; sunny, warm south. 9–15 Rain and snow showers, chilly. 16–18 Sunny, cool. 19–25 Showers, then sunny, warm. 26–30 Showers, cool.

MAY 2013: Temp. 56° (2° below avg.); precip.

Billings ⊙
Bismarck ⊙
Rapid City ⊙
Cheyenne ⊙
Denver ⊙
Amarillo ⊙

2.5" (1" above avg. east, 1" below west). 1–3 Rain and snow north, t-storms south; cool. 4–5 Sunny, warm north; rainy, cool south. 6–14 Showers, then sunny, cool. 15–20 Scattered t-storms, cool. 21–26 T-storms, then sunny, warm. 27–31 T-storms, turning cool.

JUNE 2013: Temp. 65° (2° below avg.); precip. 3.5" (2" above avg. north, 1" below south). 1–4 Rain, then sunny, cool. 5–10 Rainy periods, cool north; t-storms, warm south. 11–16 Showers north, sunny south; very warm. 17–21 T-storms, then sunny, cool. 22–27 Sunny, hot north; t-storms, cool south. 28–30 Sunny, hot north; t-storms, cool south.

JULY 2013: Temp. 72° (avg.); precip. 1" (1" below avg.). 1–3 Sunny, warm. 4–8 T-storms, then sunny, warm. 9–14 T-storms, then sunny, warm. 15–24 Scattered t-storms, cool. 25–31 A couple of t-storms, hot.

AUG. 2013: Temp. 68.5° (4° below avg. north, 1° below south); precip. 3" (1" above avg.). 1–6 T-storms, then sunny, cool. 7–16 Daily t-storms, cool north; t-storms, then sunny, hot south. 17–19 Sunny, warm. 20–28 Scattered t-storms, cool. 29–31 Sunny, warm.

SEPT. 2013: Temp. 61.5° (0.5° above avg.); precip. 1" (0.5° below avg.). 1–7 Sunny, warm. 8–10 Scattered t-storms, cool. 11–16 A couple of t-storms; cool north, warm south. 17–23 Sunny, warm. 24–30 T-storms, then sunny, cool.

OCT. 2013: Temp. 50.5° (1.5° above avg.); precip. 1" (avg.). 1–6 Sunny, turning warm. 7–12 Rain, then sunny, cool. 13–19 Sunny, turning warm. 20–22 Showers, then sunny, warm. 23–27 Showers, mild. 28–31 Rain and snow, cold.

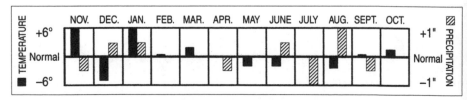

Intermountain

SUMMARY: Winter temperatures will be above normal in the north and slightly below normal in the south, with the coldest periods in early to mid-December, late December, and mid- to late January. Precipitation will be below normal in the north and above normal in the south. Snowfall will be above normal in northern Utah and southwest Wyoming and below normal elsewhere. The snowiest periods will occur in mid- to late November, early to mid-December, mid- to late January, and early and mid-March.

April and May will be cooler and drier than normal.

Summer will be cooler than normal, especially in the south, with the hottest periods in late June, early July, and mid- to late July. Rainfall will be slightly above normal in the north and slightly below in the south.

September and October will be cooler than normal, with rainfall above normal in the north and below in the south.

NOV. 2012: Temp. 42° (2° above avg.); precip. 1" (0.5" below avg.). 1–8 Showers north, sunny south; mild. 9–13 Scattered showers, mild. 14–19 Rain, then sunny, cool. 20–25 Snow, then sunny, cool. 26–30 Periods of rain and snow north, sunny south; cool.

DEC. 2012: Temp. 27° (6° below avg.); precip. 2.5" (0.5" above avg. north, 2" above south). 1–5 Snow, then sunny, cold. 6–12 Snow showers north, heavy snow south; cold. 13–18 Flurries, mild north; sunny, cold south. 19–23 Sunny. 24–31 Snow, then sunny, cold.

JAN. 2013: Temp. 32.5° (3° above avg. north, 2° below south); precip. 1" (0.5" below avg.). 1–17 Rain and snow showers, mild north; sunny, cold south. 18–21 Snow showers, cold north; snowstorm south. 22–27 Snow, then rainy periods, mild north; showers, then sunny, cold south. 28–31 Sunny, mild.

FEB. 2013: Temp. 39° (5° above avg.); precip. 2" (0.5" above avg.). 1–7 Sunny north, periods of rain and snow south; seasonable. 8–16 Rainy periods north, sunny south; mild. 17–28 Sunny, mild.

MAR. 2013: Temp. 43° (avg.); precip. 1" (0.5" below avg.). 1–4 Sunny north, snow south; cool. 5–9 Rain, mild north; sunny, cool south. 10–17 Snow showers, then sunny, mild. 18–24 Rain, then sunny, cool north; sunny, mild south. 25–31 Showers north; snow, then sunny south; cool.

APR. 2013: Temp. 46.5° (2.5° below avg.); precip. 0.5" (0.5" below avg.). 1–3 Sunny, turning warm. 4–10 Sunny, cool north; a few showers, warm south. 11–15 Sunny north, heavy snowstorm central and south. 16–22 Sunny, turning

warm. 23–30 Showers, then sunny, cool.

MAY 2013: Temp. 57° (avg.); precip. 1" (avg.). 1–3 Sunny, warm. 4–12 Showers, then sunny, warm. 13–20 Scattered showers, cool north; sunny, warm south. 21–24 Sunny; cool north, warm south. 25–31 Showers north, sunny south; warm.

JUNE 2013: Temp. 66.5° (2° above avg. north, 1° below south); precip. 0.2" (0.3" below avg.). 1–7 Showers, then sunny, cool. 8–11 Sunny, hot. 12–18 Scattered t-storms, warm. 19–30 Sunny; cool, then hot.

JULY 2013: Temp. 74° (1° above avg.); precip. 0.8" (0.5" below avg. north, 1" above south). 1–4 Sunny, hot. 5–12 Isolated t-storms; cool north and south, hot central. 13–22 Sunny, turning hot north; t-storms, cool south. 23–31 T-storms, then sunny, cool north; scattered t-storms, cool south.

AUG. 2013: Temp. 68° (4° below avg.); precip. 1" (1" above avg. north, 1" below south). 1–4 Sunny, warm north; showers, cool south. 5–16 T-storms north, sunny south; cool. 17–27 Isolated t-storms, cool. 28–31 Sunny, warm.

SEPT. 2013: Temp. 60° (2° above avg.); precip. 0.5" (0.5" below avg.). 1–3 Sunny, warm. 4–14 Scattered showers, cool. 15–25 Sunny, nice. 26–30 Scattered t-storms, cool.

OCT. 2013: Temp. 50° (1° below avg.); precip. 1" (1" above avg. north, 1" below south). 1–5 Rainy, cool north; showers, turning warm central; sunny, cool south. 6–8 Showers, cool. 9–21 Showers, then sunny north; sunny south; turning warm. 22–31 Scattered showers, cool.

W
E
A
T
H
E
R

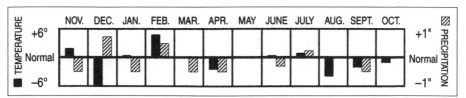

Desert Southwest

SUMMARY: Winter will be cooler and wetter than normal, with near- to above-normal snowfall. The coldest periods will occur in early and mid-December and late February. The snowiest periods will occur in early to mid-December and early to mid-February.

April and May will be much cooler than normal, with near-normal rainfall.

Summer will be 3 degrees cooler than normal, on average, with slightly above-normal rainfall. The hottest periods will be in mid-June and early July.

September and October will be cooler and drier than normal.

NOV. 2012: Temp. 57° (1° above avg.); precip. 1" (avg. east, 1" above west). 1–11 Sunny; cool, then warm. 12–18 T-storms, then sunny; warm east, cool west. 19–27 Scattered t-storms, cool. 28–30 Sunny, cool.

DEC. 2012: Temp. 43° (5° below avg.); precip. 1.5" (1" above avg.). 1–5 Sunny, cold. 6–12 Snow east, rain and wet snow west; cold. 13–21 Sunny; cold, then mild. 22–31 Snow showers, then sunny, cool east; sunny, cold west.

JAN. 2013: Temp. 47° (1° below avg.); precip. 0.2" (0.3" below avg.). 1–11 Snow showers, then sunny east; sunny west; cool. 12–18 Snow showers, then sunny, cool east; sunny, mild west. 19–24 Showers, then sunny, mild. 25–31 Sunny; cool east, mild west.

FEB. 2013: Temp. 54° (3° above avg.); precip. 0.7" (0.6" above avg. east, 0.3" below west). 1–7 Showers, then snow, cold east; showers, then sunny, mild west. 8–13 Sunny, turning warm. 14–19 Showers, then sunny, warm. 20–27 Rain and snow showers, cold east; sunny, mild west. 28 Sunny.

MAR. 2013: Temp. 55° (3° below avg.); precip. 0.8" (0.7" above avg. east, 0.1" below west). 1–4 Rain to snow east, rainy periods west; cool. 5–11 Sunny, cool. 12–23 Showers, then sunny, turning warm. 24–31 Showers, then sunny, cool.

APR. 2013: Temp. 62° (3° below avg.); precip. 0.5" (avg.). 1–5 Scattered showers, cool. 6–12 Sunny, cool. 13–22 Showers, then sunny east; sunny west; cool. 23–25 Sunny, warm. 26–30 Scattered showers, turning cool.

MAY 2013: Temp. 72° (2° below avg.); precip. 0.5" (avg.). 1–5 Scattered t-storms, cool. 6–11 Sunny, cool. 12–30 Sunny, warm. 31 T-storms, cool.

JUNE 2013: Temp. 81° (2° below avg.); precip. 1" (0.5" above avg.). 1–5 T-storms, then sunny, cool. 6–12 Scattered t-storms, cool east; sunny, hot west. 13–22 Sunny, hot. 23–30 A few t-storms, turning cooler.

JULY 2013: Temp. 84° (3° below avg.); precip. 1.5" (avg.). 1–7 Isolated t-storms, hot, then a bit cooler. 8–10 Sunny, seasonable. 11–15 Scattered t-storms, warm east; sunny, hot west. 16–31 Scattered t-storms, cool.

AUG. 2013: Temp. 81° (4° below avg.); precip. 1.1" (0.4" below avg.). 1–6 Scattered t-storms, cool. 7–12 Sunny, warm. 13–19 Scattered t-storms, cool. 20–31 Scattered t-storms, cool east; sunny, hot west.

SEPT. 2013: Temp. 77° (2° below avg.); precip. 0.5" (0.5" below avg.). 1–7 Isolated t-storms; cool east, hot west. 8–18 Sunny, cool. 19–26 Isolated t-storms, warm. 27–30 Sunny, cool.

OCT. 2013: Temp. 68° (avg.); precip. 0.5" (0.5" below avg.). 1–6 Sunny, turning warm. 7–13 Isolated showers, cool. 14–22 Sunny, turning warm. 23–31 Isolated t-storms, turning cool.

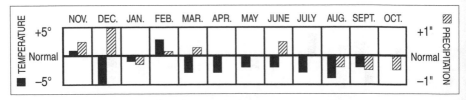

Pacific Northwest

SUMMARY: Winter temperatures will be a couple of degrees above normal, on average, with the coldest periods in early to mid-December, late December, and mid- to late January. Rainfall will be below normal, while snowfall will be near normal. The snowiest periods will occur in early to mid-December and mid- to late January. The stormiest periods will come in early to mid-January, late January, and mid-February.

April and May will be slightly cooler than normal, with near-normal rainfall.

Summer will be rainier and slightly warmer than normal, with the hottest periods in mid-June, late June, mid- to late July, and early August.

September and October will be cooler and rainier than normal.

NOV. 2012: Temp. 49° (2° above avg.); precip. 5" (1.5" below avg.). 1–7 Rainy, mild. 8–14 Showers, then sunny, cool. 15–20 Occasional rain, turning cool. 21–27 Rain, heavy at times, mild. 28–30 Rain, cool.

DEC. 2012: Temp. 43° (avg.); precip. 3.5" (3" below avg.). 1–5 Occasional rain, cool. 6–8 Sunny, cold. 9–14 Periods of rain and snow, cool. 15–25 Occasional rain, mild. 26–31 Periods of rain and snow, cool.

JAN. 2013: Temp. 45° (2° above avg.); precip. 8" (2" above avg.). 1–4 Rain to snow, cool. 5–14 Rain, heavy at times, mild. 15–17 Misty, mild. 18–23 Snowy periods, cold. 24–28 Stormy, mild. 29–31 Sunny, cool, then mild.

FEB. 2013: Temp. 50° (6° above avg.); precip. 4.5" (0.5" above avg. north, 1" below south). 1–8 Sunny; warm, then cool. 9–16 Stormy, turning quite mild. 17–25 A.M. mist, P.M. sunshine and warmth. 26–28 Rainy, mild.

MAR. 2013: Temp. 48° (1° above avg.); precip. 4" (1" above avg. north, 1" below south). 1–3 Sunny, cool. 4–10 Rainy; warm, then cool. 11–14 Sunny, mild. 15–22 Rainy periods, turning cool. 23–24 Sunny, mild. 25–28 Rainy periods, mild. 29–31 Misty, cool.

APR. 2013: Temp. 48° (2° below avg.); precip. 1" (2" below avg.). 1–9 Periods of light rain and drizzle, turning cool. 10–16 A few showers, cool. 17–22 Sunny, turning warm. 23–30 A few showers, cool.

MAY 2013: Temp. 56° (1° above avg.); precip. 4" (2" above avg.). 1–4 Sunny, warm. 5–10 Showers, then sunny, warm. 11–13 Heavy rain, warm. 14–19 Rainy periods, seasonable. 20–23 Misty, cool. 24–31 Heavy rain, then sunny, cool.

JUNE 2013: Temp. 62° (2° above avg.); precip. 1" (0.5 below avg.). 1–6 A few showers, cool. 7–11 Sunny, warm. 12–15 Showers, cool. 16–18 Sunny, hot. 19–22 Rainy, cool. 23–30 Sunny, turning hot.

JULY 2013: Temp. 66° (1° above avg.); precip. 0.5" (avg.). 1–3 Sunny, very warm. 4–12 Rainy periods north, a few sprinkles south; cool. 13–16 Sunny, cool. 17–25 Sunny, turning hot. 26–31 Showers, then sunny, cool.

AUG. 2013: Temp. 64° (2° below avg.); precip. 4" (3" above avg.). 1–4 Sunny, hot. 5–14 Rainy periods, cool. 15–20 Rain, some heavy, cool. 21–25 Scattered showers, cool north; sunny, hot south. 26–31 Sunny, warm.

SEPT. 2013: Temp. 59° (2° below avg.); precip. 2.5" (1" above avg.). 1–3 Sunny, cool. 4–13 Rainy periods, cool. 14–25 Sunny; cool north, warm south. 26–30 Rain, then sunny, cool.

OCT. 2013: Temp. 53° (1° below avg.); precip. 5" (2" above avg.). 1 Sunny, cool. 2–14 Rainy periods, cool. 15–17 Sunny, warm. 18–21 Showers, warm. 22–26 Rainy periods, cool. 27–28 Sunny, cool. 29–31 Rainy, cool.

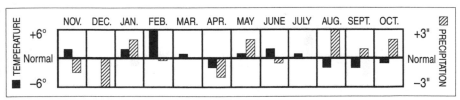

Pacific Southwest

SUMMARY: Winter temperatures will be above normal, on average, with the coldest periods in mid- and late December and mid- to late January. Rainfall will be a bit below normal in the Bay Area and above normal elsewhere. The stormiest periods will be in mid-November, mid- to late January, and early March. Mountain snowfall will be near to below normal, with the heaviest snows in mid- to late January.

April and May will be drier than normal, with near-normal temperatures.

Summer will be warmer than normal on the coast but cooler inland, with near-normal rainfall. The hottest periods will be in early and late July.

September and October will be cooler than normal, with above-normal rainfall inland and slightly below-normal rainfall on the coast. Expect hot weather in mid-September.

W E A T H E R

NOV. 2012: Temp. 60° (2° above avg.); precip. 4" (1" above avg. north, 4" above south). 1–4 Sunny, warm. 5–11 A few showers north, sunny south; warm. 12–15 Sunny, mild north; stormy, heavy rains south. 16–18 Sunny, mild. 19–26 Rainy periods, then sunny, cool. 27–30 Showers.

DEC. 2012: Temp. 52° (2° below avg.); precip. 1.5" (1" below avg. north, avg. south). 1–4 Sunny, cool. 5–9 Scattered showers, chilly. 10–13 Rainy, cool. 14–20 Sunny, turning warm. 21–26 Clouds and fog A.M., sunny P.M.; cool. 27–31 Sunny coast, clouds and drizzle inland; cool.

JAN. 2013: Temp. 55° (1° above avg.); precip. 3" (1" above avg. north, 1.5" below south). 1–5 T-storms, then sunny, mild. 6–9 Rain north; sunny, then showers south; cool. 10–18 Sunny, warm. 19–24 Rain and t-storms, chilly. 25–31 Clouds and drizzle north, sunny south; mild.

FEB. 2013: Temp. 58° (3° above avg.); precip. 2" (1" below avg.). 1–6 Occasional rain and drizzle, cool. 7–14 Rainy periods north, fog and drizzle south; mild. 15–26 Sunny, mild. 27–28 Rainy.

MAR. 2013: Temp. 56.5° (0.5° below avg.); precip. 2" (0.5° below avg.). 1–4 Stormy, then sunny, cool. 5–9 Stormy north, showers south. 10–14 Sunny. 15–19 Showers north, sunny south. 20–24 Sunny, warm. 25–31 Rain, then sunny, cool.

APR. 2013: Temp. 61° (1° above avg.); precip. 0" (1" below avg.). 1–5 Sunny, very warm. 6–14 Sunny north; A.M. clouds, P.M. sun south; cool. 15–20 Sprinkles, then sunny, warm. 21–30 Sunny; cool coast, warm inland.

MAY 2013: Temp. 63° (1° below avg.); precip.

0.5" (avg.). 1–4 Sunny, cool. 5–9 T-storms, then sunny, cool. 10–19 A.M. clouds, P.M. sun. 20–26 Sunny, warm. 27–31 A.M. clouds and sprinkles, P.M. sun coast; sunny, cool inland.

JUNE 2013: Temp. 68° (2° above avg. northwest, 2° below southeast); precip. 0.1" (avg.). 1–6 Drizzle coast; sunny, cool inland. 7–17 Sunny; cool coast, hot inland. 18–23 Sunny, cool north; A.M. sprinkles, P.M. sun, cool south. 24–30 A.M. drizzle, P.M. sun coast; sunny, hot inland.

JULY 2013: Temp. 72° (1° above avg.); precip. 0.05" (avg. north, 0.1" above south). 1–4 Clouds and mist A.M., sun P.M., cool north coast; sunny, hot elsewhere. 5–12 Sunny; cool, then hot. 13–21 A.M. fog and drizzle, P.M. sun coast; sunny inland; seasonable. 22–28 Showers, then sunny, cool. 29–31 Sunny, turning hot.

AUG. 2013: Temp. 70° (1° below avg.); precip. 0.1" (avg.). 1–4 Sunny, warm. 5–14 A.M. clouds, P.M. sun coast; sunny inland; cool. 15–20 Sunny, warm. 21–23 Sunny; hot north, warm south. 24–31 Scattered showers, then sunny, seasonable.

SEPT. 2013: Temp. 69° (1° above avg.); precip. 0.2" (avg.). 1–3 Sunny, warm. 4–8 A.M. clouds, mist coast; sunny inland; cool. 9–11 Sunny; hot north, cool south. 12–15 Sunny, cool. 16–23 Sunny; hot, then cooler. 24–30 A.M. clouds and drizzle, P.M. sun coast; sunny inland; cool.

OCT. 2013: Temp. 64° (1° below avg.); precip. 3" (2" above avg. east, 0.3" below west). 1–4 A.M. clouds and drizzle, P.M. sun coast; sunny inland; cool. 5–9 Rain, then sunny, cool. 10–15 Scattered showers, then sunny, cool. 16–20 Sunny, warm. 21–31 Rainy episodes, cool.

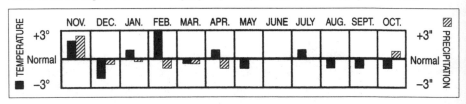

Frosts and Growing Seasons

■ Dates given are normal averages for a light freeze; local weather and topography may cause considerable variations. The possibility of frost occurring after the spring dates and before the fall dates is 50 percent. The classification of freeze temperatures is usually based on their effect on plants. **Light freeze:** 29° to 32°F—tender plants killed. **Moderate freeze:** 25° to 28°F—widely destructive effect on most vegetation. **Severe freeze:** 24°F and colder—heavy damage to most plants. *–courtesy of National Climatic Data Center*

State	City	Growing Season (days)	Last Spring Frost	First Fall Frost	State	City	Growing Season (days)	Last Spring Frost	First Fall Frost
AK	Juneau	148	May 8	Oct. 4	ND	Bismarck	129	May 14	Sept. 21
AL	Mobile	273	Feb. 28	Nov. 29	NE	Blair	167	Apr. 25	Oct. 10
AR	Pine Bluff	240	Mar. 16	Nov. 12	NE	North Platte	137	May 9	Sept. 24
AZ	Phoenix	*	*	*	NH	Concord	123	May 20	Sept. 21
AZ	Tucson	332	Jan. 19	Dec. 18	NJ	Newark	217	Apr. 3	Nov. 7
CA	Eureka	322	Jan. 27	Dec. 16	NM	Carlsbad	215	Mar. 31	Nov. 2
CA	Sacramento	296	Feb. 10	Dec. 4	NM	Los Alamos	149	May 11	Oct. 8
CA	San Francisco	*	*	*	NV	Las Vegas	283	Feb. 16	Nov. 27
CO	Denver	156	Apr. 30	Oct. 4	NY	Albany	153	May 2	Oct. 3
CT	Hartford	165	Apr. 26	Oct. 9	NY	Syracuse	167	Apr. 28	Oct. 13
DE	Wilmington	202	Apr. 10	Oct. 30	OH	Akron	192	Apr. 18	Oct. 28
FL	Miami	*	*	*	OH	Cincinnati	192	Apr. 13	Oct. 23
FL	Tallahassee	239	Mar. 22	Nov. 17	OK	Lawton	222	Mar. 29	Nov. 7
GA	Athens	227	Mar. 24	Nov. 7	OK	Tulsa	224	Mar. 27	Nov. 7
GA	Savannah	268	Mar. 1	Nov. 25	OR	Pendleton	187	Apr. 13	Oct. 18
IA	Atlantic	148	May 2	Sept. 28	OR	Portland	236	Mar. 23	Nov. 15
IA	Cedar Rapids	163	Apr. 25	Oct. 6	PA	Franklin	163	May 6	Oct. 17
ID	Boise	148	May 10	Oct. 6	PA	Williamsport	167	Apr. 30	Oct. 15
IL	Chicago	186	Apr. 20	Oct. 24	RI	Kingston	147	May 8	Oct. 3
IL	Springfield	182	Apr. 13	Oct. 13	SC	Charleston	260	Mar. 9	Nov. 25
IN	Indianapolis	181	Apr. 17	Oct. 16	SC	Columbia	213	Apr. 1	Nov. 1
IN	South Bend	175	Apr. 26	Oct. 19	SD	Rapid City	140	May 9	Sept. 27
KS	Topeka	174	Apr. 19	Oct. 11	TN	Memphis	235	Mar. 22	Nov. 13
KY	Lexington	192	Apr. 15	Oct. 25	TN	Nashville	204	Apr. 6	Oct. 28
LA	Monroe	256	Mar. 3	Nov. 15	TX	Amarillo	184	Apr. 18	Oct. 20
LA	New Orleans	301	Feb. 12	Dec. 11	TX	Denton	242	Mar. 18	Nov. 16
MA	Worcester	170	Apr. 26	Oct. 14	TX	San Antonio	269	Feb. 28	Nov. 25
MD	Baltimore	200	Apr. 11	Oct. 29	UT	Cedar City	132	May 21	Oct. 1
ME	Portland	156	May 2	Oct. 6	UT	Spanish Fork	167	May 1	Oct. 16
MI	Lansing	145	May 10	Oct. 3	VA	Norfolk	247	Mar. 20	Nov. 23
MI	Marquette	154	May 11	Oct. 13	VA	Richmond	206	Apr. 6	Oct. 30
MN	Duluth	124	May 21	Sept. 23	VT	Burlington	147	May 8	Oct. 3
MN	Willmar	153	Apr. 30	Oct. 1	WA	Seattle	251	Mar. 10	Nov. 17
MO	Jefferson City	187	Apr. 13	Oct. 18	WA	Spokane	153	May 2	Oct. 3
MS	Columbia	247	Mar. 13	Nov. 16	WI	Green Bay	150	May 6	Oct. 4
MS	Vicksburg	240	Mar. 20	Nov. 16	WI	Sparta	133	May 13	Sept. 24
MT	Fort Peck	140	May 8	Sept. 26	WV	Parkersburg	183	Apr. 21	Oct. 22
MT	Helena	121	May 19	Sept. 18	WY	Casper	119	May 22	Sept. 19
NC	Fayetteville	221	Mar. 28	Nov. 5					

Frosts do not occur every year.

WINNERS

in the 2012 Bacon Recipe Contest

Results from one of the most delicious tasting sessions ever!

FIRST PRIZE

Spicy Bacon Pizza With Caramelized Onions and Blue Cheese

12 slices bacon, diced
2 tablespoons olive oil, divided
3 cups sliced onions
¼ teaspoon salt
¼ teaspoon crushed red pepper flakes
¼ cup mascarpone cheese
2 tablespoons sour cream
1 tablespoon minced fresh thyme
1 tablespoon cornmeal
1 pound store-bought pizza dough
6 thin slices provolone cheese
1 large beefsteak tomato, sliced into thin
    rounds
½ cup sliced black olives
2 ounces crumbled blue cheese

Preheat the oven to 400°F. Cook the bacon in a 12-inch skillet over medium-high heat until crisp. Remove the bacon with a slotted spoon and set aside on paper towels to drain. Discard all but 1 tablespoon of bacon drippings from the skillet. Add 1 tablespoon of olive oil to the skillet and heat over medium heat. Add the onions and cook until they begin to caramelize, about 15 minutes. Stir in the salt and red pepper flakes. While the onions cook, blend the mascarpone cheese, sour cream, and thyme in a small bowl. Lightly grease a 12-inch pizza pan (if you have a pizza

stone, skip this step and heat it when heating the oven). Sprinkle the pan or stone with cornmeal. Press or roll out the dough to a 12-inch round and place it on the prepared pan or stone. Brush the crust with the remaining 1 tablespoon of olive oil. Arrange the provolone slices over the entire crust in a single layer. Spread the mascarpone mixture over the provolone. Top with the sliced tomatoes in a single layer. Spoon the onions over the tomatoes. Top with the olives and crisp bacon. Sprinkle blue cheese over all. Bake for 15 to 20 minutes, or until the topping is browned and bubbly. Cut into wedges. **Makes 6 to 8 servings.**

–Gilda Lester, Millsboro, Delaware

SECOND PRIZE

Bacon, Italian Sausage, and Bean Soup

4 slices bacon
2 links fresh sweet Italian turkey sausage,
    skinned and crumbled
¼ teaspoon crushed red pepper flakes
½ cup chopped onion
¼ cup chopped carrot
¼ cup chopped celery
2 cloves garlic, minced
1 can (15 ounces) black beans, drained and
    ¼ of them mashed with a fork
1 can (15 ounces) red kidney beans, drained
    and ¼ of them mashed with a fork

1 can (14.5 ounces) reduced sodium chicken
   broth
1 can (14 ounces) diced tomatoes
2 tablespoons chopped fresh cilantro
1 tablespoon tomato paste
1 tablespoon fresh lime juice
1 teaspoon cumin
⅛ teaspoon cayenne pepper
½ cup light sour cream
cilantro leaves, for garnish

Cook the bacon in a Dutch oven over medium heat until crisp, then remove it and set aside on paper towels to drain. Crumble the bacon. Add the sausage to the bacon drippings in the pan and cook until browned. Stir in the red pepper flakes. Remove the sausage from the pan and set aside. Add the onion, carrot, celery, and garlic to the pan and sauté for 3 minutes, or until tender. Remove the vegetables and set aside in a medium bowl. Wipe the pan and return the sausage and sautéed vegetables to it, along with the beans, broth, tomatoes, cilantro, tomato paste, lime juice, cumin, and cayenne pepper. Add the bacon and stir to combine. Bring the ingredients to a boil, reduce the heat to low and simmer uncovered for 10 minutes, or until thickened. Ladle the soup into bowls, then top each with a dollop of sour cream and garnish with cilantro leaves. **Makes 4 to 6 servings.**

–Charlene Chambers, Ormond Beach, Florida

THIRD PRIZE

Creamy Spaghetti Torte With Bacon

1 pound bacon, coarsely chopped
8 ounces sliced fresh mushrooms
salt and coarsely ground pepper, to taste

1 cup heavy cream
2 cups grated Parmesan cheese
12 ounces spaghetti, cooked al dente and
   drained
⅓ cup minced fresh parsley
2 eggs, beaten

Preheat the oven to 375°F. Butter the interior of a 9-inch springform pan. Fry the bacon pieces in a skillet over medium-high heat until crispy. Remove the bacon pieces to paper towels to drain. In the same skillet with the bacon drippings, sauté the mushrooms for 4 minutes, or until tender. Season with salt and pepper, to taste. Whisk in the heavy cream and grated cheese. Reduce the heat to medium-low and cook, stirring, until the cheese melts. Remove the skillet from the heat. Add the spaghetti to the skillet and toss to coat evenly with the cream mixture. Toss in the bacon and parsley, then stir in the eggs until well blended. Press the spaghetti mixture into the prepared springform pan. Bake for 40 minutes. Let stand for 5 minutes. Remove the sides of the pan. Cut in cake-like slices. **Makes 6 to 8 servings.**

–Karen Kuebler, Dallas, Texas

□□

Want more? Sample two honorable mention bacon recipes at **Almanac.com/RecipeContest.**

ENTER THE 2013 RECIPE CONTEST: BEETS

What is your favorite recipe using beets and/or beet greens? Enter it to win! It must be yours, original, and unpublished. Amateur cooks only, please. See contest rules on page 155.

Table of Measures

APOTHECARIES'
1 scruple = 20 grains
1 dram = 3 scruples
1 ounce = 8 drams
1 pound = 12 ounces

AVOIRDUPOIS
1 ounce = 16 drams
1 pound = 16 ounces
1 hundredweight = 100 pounds
1 ton = 2,000 pounds
1 long ton = 2,240 pounds

LIQUID
4 gills = 1 pint
63 gallons = 1 hogshead
2 hogsheads = 1 pipe or butt
2 pipes = 1 tun

DRY
2 pints = 1 quart
4 quarts = 1 gallon
2 gallons = 1 peck
4 pecks = 1 bushel

LINEAR
1 hand = 4 inches
1 link = 7.92 inches

1 span = 9 inches
1 foot = 12 inches
1 yard = 3 feet
1 rod = 5½ yards
1 mile = 320 rods = 1,760 yards = 5,280 feet
1 international nautical mile = 6,076.1155 feet
1 knot = 1 nautical mile per hour
1 fathom = 2 yards = 6 feet
1 furlong = ⅛ mile = 660 feet = 220 yards
1 league = 3 miles = 24 furlongs
1 chain = 100 links = 22 yards

SQUARE
1 square foot = 144 square inches
1 square yard = 9 square feet
1 square rod = 30¼ square yards = 272¼ square feet
1 acre = 160 square rods = 43,560 square feet
1 square mile = 640 acres = 102,400 square rods
1 square rod = 625 square links

1 square chain = 16 square rods
1 acre = 10 square chains

CUBIC
1 cubic foot = 1,728 cubic inches
1 cubic yard = 27 cubic feet
1 cord = 128 cubic feet
1 U.S. liquid gallon = 4 quarts = 231 cubic inches
1 imperial gallon = 1.20 U.S. gallons = 0.16 cubic foot
1 board foot = 144 cubic inches

KITCHEN
3 teaspoons = 1 tablespoon
16 tablespoons = 1 cup
1 cup = 8 ounces
2 cups = 1 pint
2 pints = 1 quart
4 quarts = 1 gallon

TO CONVERT CELSIUS AND FAHRENHEIT :
$°C = (°F − 32)/1.8$
$°F = (°C × 1.8) + 32$

Metric Conversions

LINEAR
1 inch = 2.54 centimeters
1 centimeter = 0.39 inch
1 meter = 39.37 inches
1 yard = 0.914 meter
1 mile = 1.61 kilometers
1 kilometer = 0.62 mile

SQUARE
1 square inch = 6.45 square centimeters
1 square yard = 0.84 square meter

1 square mile = 2.59 square kilometers
1 square kilometer = 0.386 square mile
1 acre = 0.40 hectare
1 hectare = 2.47 acres

CUBIC
1 cubic yard = 0.76 cubic meter
1 cubic meter = 1.31 cubic yards

HOUSEHOLD
½ teaspoon = 2 mL
1 teaspoon = 5 mL
1 tablespoon = 15 mL

¼ cup = 60 mL
⅓ cup = 75 mL
½ cup = 125 mL
⅔ cup = 150 mL
¾ cup = 175 mL
1 cup = 250 mL
1 liter = 1.057 U.S. liquid quarts
1 U.S. liquid quart = 0.946 liter
1 U.S. liquid gallon = 3.78 liters
1 gram = 0.035 ounce
1 ounce = 28.349 grams
1 kilogram = 2.2 pounds
1 pound = 0.45 kilogram

WHY SO MANY PENALTIES in HOCKEY?

Players and coaches are always looking for devious, dirty, and downright strange ways to get advantages over their opponents.

If you've ever watched an NHL hockey game, you know some of the rules and resulting penalties for common infractions, such as tripping and holding, roughing and boarding, offside and icing. But these pertain to only a few of the regulations in the NHL rule book.

When the league began in 1916, hockey was so unregulated that all of the rules and the schedule and the previous season's records were printed in a pamphlet less than a quarter-inch thick.

In time, of course, new regulations were conceived and added. The reasons why may surprise you. Take these 10, numbered as they appeared in the 2011–12 rule book . . .

by Ellen Etchingham

RULE 67.2:
Handling the Puck

In the early 1920s, Fred "Cyclone" Taylor of the Vancouver Millionaires had a habit of picking up the puck and throwing it to the fans when he needed a few seconds of rest during a hectic game. Before long, other players began doing it, too, thus frustrating forwards everywhere. In 1928, the NHL formally prohibited players from closing their hands on the puck.

The Vancouver Millionaires pose in 1915 for a group photo. Fred "Cyclone" Taylor is circled.

RULE 1.7:
The Crease

In the early days, goaltenders could be bodychecked (bumped into hard) anywhere, anytime, just like other skaters. Goalies got no special

In hockey rules, a painted crease eventually became mandatory.

protection and took a lot of punishment. Owners wanted to protect their netminders, so during the 1933–34 season, the NHL requested that all rinks mark lines on the ice in front of the net designating a protected goalies-only zone (a "crease"). Toronto Maple Leafs owner Conn Smythe refused, and the Leafs continued to crash into opposing goalies during home games. Other teams complained, but the league was forced to rule in favor of the Leafs that season. The next edition of the rules made a painted crease mandatory in all rinks.

In 1934, Boston's Eddie Shore *(right),* whose later antics would lead to the 10-minute misconduct, shakes hands with Toronto's Ace Bailey, whose career he had ended with a vicious hit a year earlier.

RULE 22.1:
The 10-Minute Misconduct

In the 1930s, abuse of officials by players was an escalating problem. One of the worst repeat offenders was Boston Bruins defenseman Eddie Shore. In a game against the Maple Leafs in 1936, Shore became so angry with referee Odie Cleghorn that he chased the official around the ice, yelling at him. When Cleghorn ignored him, Shore fired the puck straight into his back. With that, Cleghorn invented the 10-minute game misconduct and sent Shore to the penalty box, where he watched the Leafs score four goals. The NHL added the 10-minute misconduct to the rules the following year.

CONTINUED

RULE 40.1:
Physical Abuse of Officials

In 1937, a game between the Maple Leafs and the New York Rangers descended into a brawl that brought every player onto the ice. In the midst of the chaos, Maple Leafs owner Conn Smythe attempted to tell off referee Ag Smith, who was trying to break up the fighting. Although Smythe managed to keep his anger verbal, his player Red Horner was not so restrained and ended the argument by punching Smith in the face. The next year, the NHL added a game misconduct on top of the 10-minute misconduct, allowing officials to force repeat offenders to leave the game.

RULE 63.2:
Falling on the Puck

Old-school goalies played only one way: standing up in the net. Montreal Canadien Jacques Plante developed a different style. Fearless and physical, Plante would dive out of his crease and throw his body over the puck anywhere on the ice—even in the circles, if he could get there. This made it nearly impossible for opponents to maintain offensive pressure. Other coaches thought that it was unfair, and fans found it boring. In 1959, the League declared that the goaltender could fall on, or cover, the puck only inside the crease or else draw a penalty.

RULE 10.1:
Restrictions on the Curvature of Sticks

With few exceptions, players used flat stick blades prior to the 1960s. That's when Stan Mikita and Bobby Hull of the Chicago Blackhawks began hand-curving their sticks, often by soaking them in water and using a door hinge to bend the wood. They found that the curve made their shots faster and less predictable: They intimidated and confused goalies, but the puck could also fly off the ice and into the crowd. Goalies feared bodily

Until the rule changed in 1959, goalie Jacques Plante would cover the puck not just inside the crease, as shown here, but as far out as the circles.

harm, and the league brass became concerned for the safety of paying customers. In 1968, the NHL began to limit the curve on a stick's blade and instituted a minor penalty for any player found to be using a so-called "banana blade."

–photo above, Graphic Artists/Hockey Hall of Fame

RULE 53.7:
Equipment Blocking the Goal Crease

In a close game, the trailing team will often pull their goalie during the last minute and replace him with a sixth skater. A defenseless net, of course, gives the leading team an easy opportunity to score. This was why Philadelphia Flyers coach Roger Neilson proposed having the goalie drop his stick in front of the net before leaving it. The idea worked—too well. The league ruled that the goalie can not leave equipment behind when he vacates his net.

RULE 63.3:
Players Persisting Offside

In 1979, when one Montreal Canadien scored, the entire roster came onto the ice for a group hug. This annoyed opponents and wasted time, but nobody did anything about it until the Habs met the Bruins in the playoffs. When the Canadiens scored their first goal of the series and the team poured onto the ice, Bruins coach Don Cherry sent his squad out to "console" goalie Gerry Cheevers. Cherry did this every time the Habs scored. Finally, the referee asked both coaches to stop, and they did. The next year, the league put a rule against excessive celebration into the books.

RULE 63.4:
Objects Thrown on the Ice

During the Florida Panthers' 1996 playoff run, a rat was found in the players' dressing room before a game. Forward Scott Mellanby used his stick to kill the animal and later scored two goals with the stick. When the story got out, fans began bringing stuffed or plastic rats to games and throwing them onto the ice after any Panthers goal. It got so that thousands of rats would come raining down every time the home team scored. The next year, the NHL ruled that the home team would receive a 2-minute penalty if fans threw objects onto the ice during a game. (The only exception permitted is for a "hat trick," when fans throw their hats onto the ice to salute a player who scores three goals in a game.)

RULE 75.1:
Unsportsmanlike Conduct

In 2008, in a game against the New Jersey Devils, Rangers forward Sean Avery, trying to screen opposing goalie Martin Brodeur, turned to face Brodeur and began dancing from side to side and waving his stick back and forth in front of

The day after the April 13, 2008, playoff game at Madison Square Garden, the NHL created "The Avery Rule."

Sports

Brodeur's mask. Because Avery never made contact with the goalie, he did not merit a goaltender interference penalty. The next day, however, the NHL declared that, henceforth, any such behavior would draw a 2-minute penalty for unsportsman-like conduct.

OVERTIME

■ In 1926–27, Odie Cleghorn was coaching a then-new expansion team, the Pittsburgh Pirates, and looking for a competitive advantage. He began encouraging his players to change in midshift: to go on or off the ice without waiting for a stoppage. This strategy was technically against the NHL rules, but Cleghorn found that it confused opponents and kept his players from tiring, so he did it anyway. Other teams complained, but the league thought that the idea was a good one and, in 1928, modified the rules to allow changing "on the fly."

■ In the 1940s, NHL rinks had no audio systems, making it difficult for spectators to know what penalty was called on a player. This inspired Bill Chadwick to invent a system of hand gestures, or signals. Although critics called them silly and undignified, the signals became so popular with spectators that the NHL made them obligatory for all referees starting in 1947. □□

Ellen Etchingham, an occasional contributor to *The Old Farmer's Almanac,* is the author of the hockey blog "A Theory of Ice." She lives and works in Toronto.

Relaxation Techniques

Stressed out? Here are some exercises to help you relax.

Deep Breathing

■ Breathe from your abdomen, not your chest. Slowly take in a deep breath through your nose; you should feel your stomach expand. Then exhale slowly through your mouth, getting rid of all of the air in your lungs. Repeat until you feel calmer.

Progressive Muscle Relaxation (PMR)

■ Lie down or sit in a comfortable chair. Close your eyes. Focus on your toes; tense the muscles for a few seconds and then relax them. Move on upward through your body, tensing and then releasing the muscles in each section, until all parts of your body are relaxed.

Visualization

■ Sit or lie down. Close your eyes. Picture yourself in a peaceful place. Think about the sights, sounds, fragrances, textures, temperature, and so forth. Focus on this place until you feel relaxed and then gradually return to the present with those peaceful feelings.

AGE-OLD ADVICE

The young man who is in the habit of early rising, will and must be in the habit of retiring early, and, of course, will put himself out of the way of many temptations and dangers which come under the veil of midnight.

–*Rev. John Todd*, The Student's Manual, *1854*

Tips to Help You Fall Asleep

Can't sleep? Try these tips for a restful night:

■ Sleep and wake on a regular schedule. Don't sleep late to make up for a late night. Avoid napping during the day, unless necessary.

■ Cut out the caffeine, at least after lunch. Avoid coffee, chocolate, and caffeinated sodas or tea.

■ Exercise in the late afternoon. It can help to deepen sleep stages at night.

■ Plan a relaxing routine just before bedtime. Soak in a tub.

■ Listen to soft music or do some light reading.

■ Skip the alcohol at night. Initially, it can act as a sedative, but it can disrupt sleep later on that evening.

■ Don't drink or eat too much before going to bed, and avoid spicy dinners.

Salute to a SOMBER

13 LITTLE-KNOWN FACTS ABOUT TH

Union troops advance from the right during the battle of Gettysburg

SESQUICENTENNIAL

B A T T L E   O F   G E T T Y S B U R G   ✒ *compiled by Jeff Baker*

FROM JULY 1 TO 3, 1863, A FIERCE CONFLICT RAGED in and around the small Pennsylvania town of Gettysburg. When the echoes of the last shots had faded, nearly 8,000 men, Union and Confederate forces combined, lay dead, and tens of thousands more were wounded or missing, amounting to the largest number of casualties from any single battle in the Civil War. Considered by many to be the turning point of the war because it repelled Confederate general Robert E. Lee's invasion of the north, the Battle of Gettysburg is famous. Less well known but deserving of our attention are these anecdotes.

*Confederate general
Robert E. Lee*

---

1. TWO FIRSTS

EVERY BATTLE BEGINS WITH A FIRST SHOT; GETTYSBURG had two, and today the Gettysburg National Military Park has two "first shot" monuments. How could this be? One shot was the opening artillery round that probably started the fighting on July 1; the other was a shot fired earlier that day by Union soldiers at a distance too great to have any effect. Debate about which shot was truly the "first" continues among some impassioned historians. The matter is further complicated by the fact that three Union and two Confederate regiments also claimed to have fired the first shot.

(continued)

2. SCARED TO DEATH

THE FIRST FATALITY OF THE BATTLE WAS A CIVILIAN. EPHRAIM WISLER, A FARMER upon whose land troops were skirmishing, was drawn outside his house to observe the action. After being nearly struck by Confederate artillery fire, he quickly retreated back inside. He was so shaken by the near-miss that he suffered a fatal heart attack later that day.

3. CAUGHT IN THE CROSSFIRE

–U.S. Army

THE ONLY CIVILIAN TO DIE AS A DIRECT RESULT OF THE BATtle was 20-year-old Jennie Wade, who was staying with her sister, baking bread for the Union army. The sister's house was situated in such a way that it received fire from both armies. While in the kitchen, Jenny was struck and killed by a stray bullet.

4. NEVER TOO OLD

–U.S. Army

JOHN BURNS, A 72-YEAR-OLD VETERAN OF THE WAR OF 1812, could not sit by as the battle started. With his outdated but trusty flintlock rifle in hand, he walked from his home in Gettysburg to McPherson Ridge, where he asked a Union officer how he could help. Burns ended up fighting for the Union's "Iron Brigade" and retired from the field only after having been injured three times. He later became a national hero, and Abraham Lincoln asked to meet him when he went to Gettysburg to dedicate the national cemetery.

5. YOU'RE OUT!

ABNER DOUBLEDAY, BEST KNOWN FOR BEING CREDITED WITH inventing baseball, is also famous for firing the first Union cannon at Fort Sumter in 1861, thus officially starting the Civil War. At Gettysburg, Major General Doubleday led fewer than 10,000 Union troops against almost twice as many Confederates. When Doubleday withdrew his troops to another part of the battlefield after realizing that they could not continue to hold back the

Confederates, the movement deteriorated into a chaotic retreat. Major General Oliver O. Howard accused Doubleday of unnecessarily allowing the Union line to break, and Doubleday was relieved of his command the next day.

6. "CHILDREN OF THE BATTLEFIELD"

A UNION SOLDIER KILLED IN BATTLE ON JULY 1 WAS FOUND CLUTCHING A PHOTOGRAPH of three children. No names appeared on the photo, and the man carried no identification.

The photo came into the possession of John Bourns, a Philadelphia doctor, who contacted the *Philadelphia Enquirer,* which published an article offering detailed descriptions of the three "Children of the Battlefield." (Newspapers did not use photographs at the time.) The story was picked up by newspapers across the country.

When Phylinda Humiston of Portville, New York, read the article, she realized that the descriptions fit her own children. After contacting Bourns, who sent her a copy of the photo, she verified that the soldier had been her husband, Amos. Bourns eventually built an orphanage for the children of deceased Union soldiers, and it was run by Phylinda Humiston.

7. A TRUE BEST FRIEND

A DOG NAMED SALLIE FOLLOWED THE 11TH PENNSYLVANIA THROUGHOUT THE WAR, rushing into battle with the regiment, barking at the enemy. When the Union line collapsed on July 1, the men realized that Sallie wasn't among them. Two days later, she was found weak from lack of food and water and lying at the side of her fallen master. The men nursed her back to health and she remained with them. Two years later, Sallie died in battle in Virginia. The men of the 11th Pennsylvania added her likeness to their regiment's monument to commemorate her loyalty.

8. PEACE TIMES

WHILE THERE WERE NO OFFICIAL TRUCES DECLARED ON JULY 1, 2, OR 3, 1863, BOTH sides experienced moments of peace—even friendship.

Both Union and Confederate military surgeons typically treated injured soldiers regardless of their loyalties, and more than a few reports exist of soldiers helping an "enemy" to a field hospital.

(continued)

➤ One Union officer, upon being wounded, yelled out a Masonic code-phrase ("My mother is a widow!") and a number of his fellow Masons, Union and Confederate alike, rushed to his aid.

➤ One battlefield straddled a spring-fed creek, the only nearby fresh water. The Union had control of one bank and the Confederates, the other; the spring itself was a "no-man's-land" that could not be safely accessed by either side. During the night, however, soldiers from both sides would reportedly sneak to the spring to get water, trade food, and share tobacco. The next morning, they became enemies again.

9. TEMPTING FATE

AS UNION MAJOR GENERAL JOHN SEDGWICK POSITIONED HIS troops for battle, Confederate sharpshooters began firing. When their first shots fell short, Sedgwick scoffed, "They couldn't hit an elephant at this distance!" Moments later, a sharpshooter's bullet struck Sedgwick under his left eye, killing him instantly.

–Library of Congress, Prints and Photographs Division, LC-DIG-cwpb-06381

10. UNIFORM BEHAVIOR

WHEN BODIES OF CONFEDERATE SOLDIERS WERE BEING PREPARED FOR BURIAL, IT WAS discovered that one was a woman who had dressed as a man, presumably to fight alongside her husband. (This practice was not unique to Gettysburg. Historians estimate that as many as 400 women donned uniforms during the Civil War, both blue and gray, and fought as "one of the boys.")

11. THE BOUNTY OF WAR

ON JULY 2, FIGHTING RAGED ON ALL SIDES OF REV. JOSEPH SHERFY'S HOME AND IN HIS orchard, the source of a thriving canning business. Many bullets struck the house and troop movements, horses, and artillery fire decimated the orchard. After the battle, Rev. Sherfy salvaged what he could of his farm. Then, in an inspired moment, he began promoting his peaches as having come from trees on the Gettysburg battlefield, a "canny" marketing strategy that lifted sales.

12. FIRST AND LAST BURIED

THE FIRST SOLDIER BURIED IN GETTYSBURG CEMETERY DID NOT DIE IN THE BATTLE OR even fight in it. He fell from a railroad car and died before the battle began.

The last burial took place in 1997. In March of 1996, visitors to the battlefield discovered skeletal remains in the rocks on the infamous "railroad cut," a scene of intense fighting on July 1. After a 5-day archaeological excavation and lengthy period of forensic testing, the National Park Service concluded that the remains most likely belonged to a soldier from the 2nd Mississippi Infantry Regiment. The remains were given a proper military ceremony and interred in the Soldiers' National Cemetery. (This was not the first such discovery. Other remains

Soldiers' National Cemetery at Gettysburg, Pennsylvania

attributed to the battle were found in 1914 and 1939, and some historians estimate that as many as 1,000 bodies may remain undiscovered in the woods or in the many shallow graves that were dug at around the time of the battle.)

13. INFAMOUS FAUX-TOGRAPHY

AMONG THE IMAGES IN *GARDNER'S PHOTOGRAPHIC SKETCH BOOK OF THE CIVIL WAR* by Alexander Gardner, a collection of captioned photographs depicting wartime scenes, are several of the Battle of Gettysburg. Gardner's photographs were considered to be not only of historical importance, but also artful representations; the images defined the war for many Americans for nearly a century.

Then, in 1961, Frederic Ray, art director of the *Civil War Times,* wondered if Gardner had been too artful: Ray began to suspect that one of the scenes had been arranged. In one photo, captioned "A Sharpshooter's Last Sleep" *(left),* a Confederate soldier's body lay in an area known as Devil's Den. However, in an image labeled "The Home of a Rebel Sharpshooter," the same body is shown lying in a rocky niche 40 yards away from the Devil's Den. This convinced Ray and other photography experts that Gardner, hoping for more dramatic impact, had moved the body, turned the soldier's head toward the camera, and even propped the scene: The gun in the photo is not a sharpshooter's rifle. □□

Adapted from So You Think You Know Gettysburg? The Stories Behind the Monuments and the Men Who Fought One of America's Most Epic Battles *(John F. Blair, 2010) by James and Suzanne Gindlesperger; used with permission of the publisher, www.blairpub.com.*

Jeff Baker's work has appeared in *The New York Times Magazine, The Oxford American,* and other publications.

Planting by the Moon's Phase

According to this age-old practice,
cycles of the Moon affect plant growth.

■ Plant flowers and vegetables that bear crops above ground during the light, or waxing, of the Moon: from the day the Moon is new to the day it is full.

■ Plant flowering bulbs and vegetables that bear crops below ground during the dark, or waning, of the Moon: from the day after it is full to the day before it is new again.

The Moon Favorable columns give the best planting days based on the Moon's phases for 2013. (See the **Left-Hand Calendar Pages, 104–130,** for the exact days of the new and full Moons.) The Planting Dates columns give the safe periods for planting in areas that receive frost. See **Frosts and Growing Seasons, page 209,** for first/last frost dates and the average length of the growing season in your area.

Get local seed-sowing dates at Almanac.com/PlantingTable.

■ Aboveground crops are marked *.
■ (E) means early; (L) means late.
■ Map shades correspond to shades of date columns.

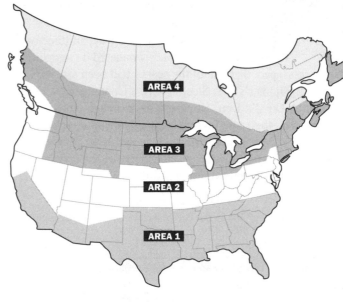

AREA 4
AREA 3
AREA 2
AREA 1

* Barley	
* Beans	(E)
	(L)
Beets	(E)
	(L)
* Broccoli plants	(E)
	(L)
* Brussels sprouts	
* Cabbage plants	
Carrots	(E)
	(L)
* Cauliflower plants	(E)
	(L)
* Celery plants	(E)
	(L)
* Collards	(E)
	(L)
* Corn, sweet	(E)
	(L)
* Cucumbers	
* Eggplant plants	
* Endive	(E)
	(L)
* Kale	(E)
	(L)
Leek plants	
* Lettuce	
* Muskmelons	
* Okra	
Onion sets	
* Parsley	
Parsnips	
* Peas	(E)
	(L)
* Pepper plants	
Potatoes	
* Pumpkins	
Radishes	(E)
	(L)
* Spinach	(E)
	(L)
* Squashes	
Sweet potatoes	
* Swiss chard	
* Tomato plants	
Turnips	(E)
	(L)
* Watermelons	
* Wheat, spring	
* Wheat, winter	

Planting Dates	Moon Favorable	Planting Dates	Moon Favorable	Planting Dates	Moon Favorable	Planting Dates	Moon Favorable
	AREA 1		**AREA 2**		**AREA 3**		**AREA 4**
15–3/7	2/15–25	3/15–4/7	3/15–27	5/15–6/21	5/15–25, 6/8–21	6/1–30	6/8–23
15–4/7	3/15–27	4/15–30	4/15–25	5/7–6/21	5/9–25, 6/8–21	5/30–6/15	6/8–15
7–31	8/7–20	7/1–21	7/8–21	6/15–7/15	6/15–23, 7/8–15	—	—
7–28	2/7–9, 2/26–28	3/15–4/3	3/28–4/3	5/1–15	5/1–8	5/25–6/10	5/26–6/7
4–30	9/1–4, 9/20–30	8/15–31	8/21–31	7/15–8/15	7/23–8/5	6/15–7/8	6/24–7/7
15–3/15	2/15–25, 3/11–15	3/7–31	3/11–27	5/15–31	5/15–25	6/1–25	6/8–23
7–30	9/7–19	8/1–20	8/6–20	6/15–7/7	6/15–23	—	—
11–3/20	2/11–25, 3/11–20	3/7–4/15	3/11–27, 4/10–15	5/15–31	5/15–25	6/1–25	6/8–23
11–3/20	2/11–25, 3/11–20	3/7–4/15	3/11–27, 4/10–15	5/15–31	5/15–25	6/1–25	6/8–23
15–3/7	2/26–3/7	3/7–31	3/7–10, 3/28–31	5/15–31	5/26–31	5/25–6/10	5/26–6/7
4–9/7	8/1–5, 8/21–9/4	7/7–31	7/7, 7/23–31	6/15–7/21	6/24–7/7	6/15–7/8	6/24–7/7
15–3/7	2/15–25	3/15–4/7	3/15–27	5/15–31	5/15–25	6/1–25	6/8–23
7–31	8/7–20	7/1–8/7	7/8–22, 8/6–7	6/15–7/21	6/15–23, 7/8–21	—	—
15–28	2/15–25	3/7–31	3/11–27	5/15–6/30	5/15–25, 6/8–23	6/1–30	6/8–23
15–30	9/15–19	8/15–9/7	8/15–20, 9/5–7	7/15–8/15	7/15–22, 8/6–15	—	—
11–3/20	2/11–25, 3/11–20	3/7–4/7	3/11–27	5/15–31	5/15–25	6/1–25	6/8–23
7–30	9/7–19	8/15–31	8/15–20	7/1–8/7	7/8–22, 8/6–7	—	—
15–31	3/15–27	4/1–17	4/10–17	5/10–6/15	5/10–25, 6/8–15	5/30–6/20	6/8–20
7–31	8/7–20	7/7–21	7/8–21	6/15–30	6/15–23	—	—
7–4/15	3/11–27, 4/10–15	4/7–5/15	4/10–25, 5/9–15	5/7–6/20	5/9–25, 6/8–20	5/30–6/15	6/8–15
7–4/15	3/11–27, 4/10–15	4/7–5/15	4/10–25, 5/9–15	6/1–30	6/8–23	6/15–30	6/15–23
15–3/20	2/15–25, 3/11–20	4/7–5/15	4/10–25, 5/9–15	5/15–31	5/15–25	6/1–25	6/8–23
15–9/7	8/15–20, 9/5–7	7/15–8/15	7/15–22, 8/6–15	6/7–30	6/8–23	—	—
1–3/20	2/11–25, 3/11–20	3/7–4/7	3/11–27	5/15–31	5/15–25	6/1–15	6/8–15
7–30	9/7–19	8/15–31	8/15–20	7/1–8/7	7/8–22, 8/6–7	6/25–7/15	7/8–15
15–4/15	2/26–3/10, 3/28–4/9	3/7–4/7	3/7–10, 3/28–4/7	5/15–31	5/26–31	6/1–25	6/1–7, 6/24–25
15–3/7	2/15–25	3/1–31	3/11–27	5/15–6/30	5/15–25, 6/8–23	6/1–30	6/8–23
15–4/7	3/15–27	4/15–5/7	4/15–25	5/15–6/30	5/15–25, 6/8–23	6/1–30	6/8–23
15–6/1	4/15–25, 5/9–25	5/25–6/15	5/25, 6/8–15	6/15–7/10	6/15–23, 7/8–10	6/25–7/7	—
4–28	2/1–9, 2/26–28	3/1–31	3/1–10, 3/28–31	5/15–6/7	5/26–6/7	6/1–25	6/1–7, 6/24–25
20–3/15	2/20–25, 3/11–15	3/1–31	3/11–27	5/15–31	5/15–25	6/1–15	6/8–15
15–2/4	1/27–2/4	3/7–31	3/7–10, 3/28–31	4/1–30	4/1–9, 4/26–30	5/10–31	5/26–31
15–2/7	1/15–26	3/7–31	3/11–27	4/15–5/7	4/15–25	5/15–31	5/15–25
15–30	9/15–19	8/7–31	8/7–20	7/15–31	7/15–22	7/10–25	7/10–22
20	3/11–20	4/1–30	4/10–25	5/15–6/30	5/15–25, 6/8–23	6/1–30	6/8–23
0–28	2/26–28	4/1–30	4/1–9, 4/26–30	5/1–31	5/1–8, 5/26–31	6/1–25	6/1–7, 6/24–25
20	3/11–20	4/23–5/15	4/23–25, 5/9–15	5/15–31	5/15–25	6/1–30	6/8–23
1–3/1	1/27–2/9, 2/26–3/1	3/7–31	3/7–10, 3/28–31	4/15–30	4/26–30	5/15–6/5	5/26–6/5
1–21	10/1–3, 10/19–21	9/7–30	9/20–30	8/15–31	8/21–31	7/10–31	7/23–31
–3/15	2/10–25, 3/11–15	3/15–4/20	3/15–27, 4/10–20	5/15–31	5/15–25	6/1–25	6/8–23
1–21	10/4–18	8/1–9/15	8/6–20, 9/5–15	7/17–9/4	7/17–22, 8/6–20	7/20–8/5	7/20–22
15–4/15	3/15–27, 4/10–15	4/15–30	4/15–25	5/15–6/15	5/15–25, 6/8–15	6/1–30	6/8–23
3–4/6	3/28–4/6	4/21–5/9	4/26–5/8	5/15–6/15	5/26–6/7	6/1–30	6/1–7, 6/24–30
–3/15	2/10–25, 3/11–15	3/15–4/15	3/15–27, 4/10–15	5/1–31	5/9–25	5/15–31	5/15–25
–20	3/11–20	4/7–30	4/10–25	5/15–31	5/15–25	6/1–15	6/8–15
0–2/15	1/27–2/9	3/15–31	3/28–31	4/7–30	4/7–9, 4/26–30	5/10–31	5/26–31
–10/15	9/1–4, 9/20–10/3	8/1–20	8/1–5	7/1–8/15	7/1–7, 7/23–8/5	—	—
15–4/7	3/15–27	4/15–5/7	4/15–25	5/15–6/30	5/15–25, 6/8–23	6/1–30	6/8–23
15–28	2/15–25	3/1–20	3/11–20	4/7–30	4/10–25	5/15–6/10	5/15–25, 6/8–10
15–12/7	10/15–18, 11/3–17, 12/2–7	9/15–10/20	9/15–19, 10/4–18	8/11–9/15	8/11–20, 9/5–15	8/5–30	8/6–20

Secrets of the Zodiac

Ancient astrologers believed that each astrological sign influenced a specific part of the body. The first sign of the zodiac—Aries—was attributed to the head, with the rest of the signs moving down the body, ending with Pisces at the feet.

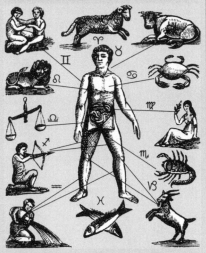

♈	Aries, head	**ARI**	*Mar. 21–Apr. 20*
♉	Taurus, neck	**TAU**	*Apr. 21–May 20*
♊	Gemini, arms . . .	**GEM**	*May 21–June 20*
♋	Cancer, breast	**CAN**	*June 21–July 22*
♌	Leo, heart	**LEO**	*July 23–Aug. 22*
♍	Virgo, belly	**VIR**	*Aug. 23–Sept. 22*
♎	Libra, reins	**LIB**	*Sept. 23–Oct. 22*
♏	Scorpio, secrets . .	**SCO**	*Oct. 23–Nov. 22*
♐	Sagittarius, thighs	**SAG**	*Nov. 23–Dec. 21*
♑	Capricorn, knees	**CAP**	*Dec. 22–Jan. 19*
♒	Aquarius, legs . .	**AQU**	*Jan. 20–Feb. 19*
♓	Pisces, feet	**PSC**	*Feb. 20–Mar. 20*

Astrology vs. Astronomy

■ **Astrology** is a tool we use to plan events according to the placements of the Sun, the Moon, and the planets in the 12 signs of the zodiac. In astrology, the planetary movements do not cause events; rather, they explain the path, or "flow," that events tend to follow. **Astronomy** is the study of the actual placement of the known planets and constellations. *(The placement of the planets in the signs of the zodiac is not the same astrologically and astronomically.)* The Moon's astrological place is given on **page 229**; its astronomical place is given in the **Left-Hand Calendar Pages, 104–130**.

The dates in the **Best Days table, page 230,** are based on the astrological passage of the Moon. However, consider all indicators before making any major decisions.

When Mercury Is Retrograde

■ Sometimes the other planets appear to be traveling backward through the zodiac; this is an illusion. We call this illusion *retrograde motion.*

Mercury's retrograde periods can cause our plans to go awry. However, this is an excellent time to reflect on the past. Intuition is high during these periods, and coincidences can be extraordinary.

When Mercury is retrograde, remain flexible, allow extra time for travel, and avoid signing contracts. Review projects and plans at these times, but wait until Mercury is direct again to make any final decisions.

In 2013, Mercury will be retrograde from February 23–March 17, June 26–July 20, and October 21–November 10.

–Celeste Longacre

Gardening by the Moon's Sign

Use the chart on the next page to find the best dates for the following garden tasks:

■ **Plant, transplant, and graft:** Cancer, Scorpio, or Pisces.

■ **Harvest:** Aries, Leo, Sagittarius, Gemini, or Aquarius.

■ **Build/fix fences or garden beds:** Capricorn.

■ **Control insect pests, plow, and weed:** Aries, Gemini, Leo, Sagittarius, or Aquarius.

■ **Prune:** Aries, Leo, or Sagittarius. During a waxing Moon, pruning encourages growth; during a waning Moon, it discourages growth.

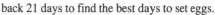

Setting Eggs by the Moon's Sign

■ Chicks take about 21 days to hatch. Those born under a waxing Moon, in the fruitful signs of Cancer, Scorpio, and Pisces, are healthier and mature faster. To ensure that chicks are born during these times, determine the best days to "set eggs" (to place eggs in an incubator or under a hen). To calculate, find the three fruitful birth signs on the chart below. Use the **Left-Hand Calendar Pages, 104–130,** to find the dates of the new and full Moons.

Using only the fruitful dates between the new and full Moons, count back 21 days to find the best days to set eggs.

E X A M P L E :

The Moon is new on June 8 and full on June 23. Between these dates, on June 19 and 20, the Moon is in the sign of Scorpio. To have chicks born on June 19, count back 21 days; set eggs on May 29.

The Moon's Astrological Place, 2012–13

	Nov.	Dec.	Jan.	Feb.	Mar.	Apr.	May	June	July	Aug.	Sept.	Oct.	Nov.	Dec.
1	GEM	CAN	VIR	LIB	LIB	SAG	AQU	PSC	ARI	GEM	CAN	LEO	LIB	SCO
2	GEM	CAN	VIR	SCO	SCO	CAP	AQU	ARI	TAU	GEM	LEO	VIR	LIB	SAG
3	CAN	LEO	VIR	SCO	SCO	CAP	AQU	ARI	TAU	CAN	LEO	VIR	SCO	SAG
4	CAN	LEO	LIB	SAG	SAG	AQU	PSC	TAU	GEM	CAN	VIR	LIB	SCO	CAP
5	CAN	VIR	LIB	SAG	SAG	AQU	PSC	TAU	GEM	LEO	VIR	LIB	SAG	CAP
6	LEO	VIR	SCO	SAG	CAP	PSC	ARI	TAU	GEM	LEO	VIR	SCO	SAG	AQU
7	LEO	VIR	SCO	CAP	CAP	PSC	ARI	GEM	CAN	LEO	LIB	SCO	CAP	AQU
8	VIR	LIB	SAG	CAP	AQU	PSC	TAU	GEM	CAN	VIR	LIB	SAG	CAP	PSC
9	VIR	LIB	SAG	AQU	AQU	ARI	TAU	CAN	LEO	VIR	SCO	SAG	AQU	PSC
10	LIB	SCO	CAP	AQU	PSC	ARI	TAU	CAN	LEO	LIB	SCO	CAP	AQU	ARI
11	LIB	SCO	CAP	PSC	PSC	TAU	GEM	CAN	LEO	LIB	SAG	CAP	PSC	ARI
12	SCO	SAG	AQU	PSC	ARI	TAU	GEM	LEO	VIR	LIB	SAG	CAP	PSC	ARI
13	SCO	SAG	AQU	ARI	ARI	GEM	CAN	LEO	VIR	SCO	CAP	AQU	ARI	TAU
14	SAG	CAP	PSC	ARI	ARI	GEM	CAN	VIR	LIB	SCO	CAP	AQU	ARI	TAU
15	SAG	CAP	PSC	TAU	TAU	GEM	CAN	VIR	LIB	SAG	AQU	PSC	TAU	GEM
16	CAP	AQU	ARI	TAU	TAU	CAN	LEO	VIR	SCO	SAG	AQU	PSC	TAU	GEM
17	CAP	AQU	ARI	TAU	GEM	CAN	LEO	LIB	SCO	CAP	PSC	ARI	TAU	GEM
18	AQU	PSC	ARI	GEM	GEM	LEO	VIR	LIB	SCO	CAP	PSC	ARI	GEM	CAN
19	AQU	PSC	TAU	GEM	GEM	LEO	VIR	SCO	SAG	AQU	ARI	TAU	GEM	CAN
20	PSC	ARI	TAU	CAN	CAN	LEO	LIB	SCO	SAG	AQU	ARI	TAU	CAN	LEO
21	PSC	ARI	GEM	CAN	CAN	VIR	LIB	SAG	CAP	PSC	ARI	GEM	CAN	LEO
22	PSC	ARI	GEM	CAN	LEO	VIR	LIB	SAG	CAP	PSC	TAU	GEM	CAN	LEO
23	ARI	TAU	GEM	LEO	LEO	LIB	SCO	CAP	AQU	ARI	TAU	GEM	LEO	VIR
24	ARI	TAU	CAN	LEO	VIR	LIB	SCO	CAP	AQU	ARI	GEM	CAN	LEO	VIR
25	TAU	GEM	CAN	VIR	VIR	SCO	SAG	AQU	PSC	TAU	GEM	CAN	VIR	LIB
26	TAU	GEM	LEO	VIR	VIR	SCO	SAG	AQU	PSC	TAU	GEM	LEO	VIR	LIB
27	TAU	GEM	LEO	LIB	LIB	SAG	CAP	PSC	ARI	TAU	CAN	LEO	VIR	SCO
28	GEM	CAN	LEO	LIB	LIB	SAG	CAP	PSC	ARI	GEM	CAN	LEO	LIB	SCO
29	GEM	CAN	VIR	—	SCO	CAP	AQU	ARI	TAU	GEM	LEO	VIR	LIB	SCO
30	CAN	LEO	VIR	—	SCO	CAP	AQU	ARI	TAU	CAN	LEO	VIR	SCO	SAG
31	—	LEO	LIB	—	SAG	—	PSC	—	GEM	CAN	—	LIB	—	SAG

Best Days for 2013

This chart is based on the Moon's sign and shows the best days each month for certain activities.

—Celeste Longacre

	JAN.	FEB.	MAR.	APR.	MAY	JUNE	JULY	AUG.	SEPT.	OCT.	NOV.	DEC.
Quit smoking	2, 6, 29	3, 7, 26	2, 10, 30	7, 26	4, 9, 31	5, 28	2, 25, 29	22, 26	22, 27	2, 19, 24	21, 26, 30	18, 23, 29
Begin diet to lose weight	2, 6, 29	3, 7, 26	2, 10, 30	7, 26	4, 9, 31	5, 28	2, 25, 29	22, 26	22, 27	2, 19, 24	21, 26, 30	18, 23, 29
Begin diet to gain weight	15, 19	11, 16	15, 25	12, 17	19, 23	15, 19	12, 17	9, 13	9, 18	6, 15	11, 16	8, 13
Cut hair to encourage growth	14, 15, 19, 20	11, 12, 15, 16	15, 16	11, 12, 23, 24	21, 22	17, 18	14, 15	11, 12	7, 8	15, 16	11, 12	8, 9
Cut hair to discourage growth	4, 5, 31	1, 27, 28	10, 28	6, 7	4, 5, 31	5, 6, 27, 28	2, 3, 29, 30	25, 26, 27	22, 23	4, 22, 23	1, 2, 28, 29	25, 26
Have dental care	1, 2, 3, 29, 30	25, 26	24, 25, 26	21, 22	18, 19	14, 15, 16	12, 13	8, 9	4, 5, 6	2, 3, 29, 30	25, 26, 27	23, 24
Start projects	12, 13	11, 12	12, 13	11, 12	11, 12	9, 10	9, 10	7, 8	6, 7	6, 7	4, 5	4, 5
End projects	9, 10	8, 9	9, 10	8, 9	8, 9	6, 7	6, 7	4, 5	3, 4	3, 4	1, 2	1, 2
Go camping	8, 9	4, 5	4, 5, 31	1, 27, 28	25, 26	21, 22	19, 20	15, 16	11, 12	8, 9	5, 6	2, 3, 30, 31
Plant aboveground crops	14, 15, 24, 25	11, 12, 20, 21	20, 21	16, 17	13, 14, 23, 24	19, 20	16, 17, 18	13, 14	9, 10	6, 7, 15	4, 11, 12	8, 9
Plant belowground crops	6, 7, 29	2, 3, 26	2, 3, 29, 30	6, 7	4, 5, 31	1, 27, 28	7, 25, 26	3, 4, 30, 31	27, 28	24, 25	20, 21, 22	1, 27, 28, 29
Destroy pests and weeds	16, 17, 18	13, 14	12, 13	9, 10	6, 7	2, 3, 29, 30	1, 27, 28	23, 24	19, 20, 21	17, 18	13, 14	11, 12
Graft or pollinate	24, 25	20, 21	20, 21	16, 17	13, 14, 15	9, 10, 11	7, 8	3, 4, 30, 31	1, 27, 28	24, 25	20, 21, 22	18, 19
Prune to encourage growth	17, 18	13, 14	12, 13	19, 20	16, 17	12, 13	9, 10, 11	15, 16	11, 12	8, 9	13, 14	10, 11, 12
Prune to discourage growth	8, 9, 28	4, 5	4, 5, 31	1, 27, 28	6, 7, 26	2, 3, 30	1, 27, 28	23, 24	2, 3, 29, 30	27, 28	23, 24	20, 21
Harvest aboveground crops	19, 20	15, 16	15, 16	11, 12, 21, 22	18, 19	14, 15, 16	12, 13	8, 9	13, 14	10, 11	15, 16	13, 14
Harvest belowground crops	2, 3, 29, 30	7, 8, 26	6, 7	2, 3, 30	8, 9, 27, 28	4, 5, 6	2, 3, 29, 30	25, 26, 27	4, 22, 23	2, 3, 29, 30	25, 26, 27	23, 24
Can, pickle, or make sauerkraut	6, 7	2, 3	2, 3, 29, 30	6, 7, 8, 26	4, 5, 31	1, 27, 28	7, 25, 26	3, 4, 30, 31	1, 27, 28	24, 25	20, 21, 22	1, 27, 28, 29
Cut hay	16, 17, 18	13, 14	4, 5, 31	9, 10	6, 7	2, 3, 29, 30	1, 27, 28	23, 24	19, 20, 21	17, 18	13, 14	11, 12
Begin logging	10, 11	7, 8	6, 7	2, 3, 29, 30	27, 28	23, 24	21, 22	17, 18	13, 14	10, 11, 12	7, 8	4, 5
Set posts or pour concrete	10, 11	7, 8	6, 7	2, 3, 29, 30	27, 28	23, 24	21, 22	17, 18	13, 14	10, 11, 12	7, 8	4, 5
Breed animals	6, 7	2, 3	2, 3, 29, 30	25, 26	23, 24	19, 20	16, 17, 18	13, 14	9, 10	6, 7	3, 4, 30	1, 27, 28, 29
Wean animals or children	2, 6, 29	3, 7, 26	2, 10, 30	7, 26	4, 9, 31	5, 28	2, 25, 29	22, 26	22, 27	2, 19, 24	21, 26, 30	18, 23, 29
Castrate animals	12, 13	9, 10	8, 9	4, 5	29, 30	26, 27	23, 24	19, 20	15, 16	13, 14	9, 10	6, 7
Slaughter livestock	6, 7	2, 3	2, 3, 29, 30	25, 26	23, 24	19, 20	16, 17, 18	13, 14	9, 10	6, 7	3, 4, 30	1, 27, 28, 29

See what to do when at Almanac.com/BestDays. **2013**

Tidal Glossary

Apogean Tide: A monthly tide of decreased range that occurs when the Moon is at apogee (farthest from Earth).

Diurnal Tide: A tide with one high water and one low water in a tidal day of approximately 24 hours.

Mean Lower Low Water: The arithmetic mean of the lesser of a daily pair of low waters, observed over a specific 19-year cycle called the National Tidal Datum Epoch.

Neap Tide: A tide of decreased range that occurs twice a month, when the Moon is in quadrature (during its first and last quarters, when the Sun and the Moon are at right angles to each other relative to Earth).

Perigean Tide: A monthly tide of increased range that occurs when the Moon is at perigee (closest to Earth).

Semidiurnal Tide: A tide with one high water and one low water every half day. East Coast tides, for example, are semidiurnal, with two highs and two lows during a tidal day of approximately 24 hours.

Spring Tide: A tide of increased range that occurs at times of syzygy each month. Named not for the season of spring but from the German *springen* ("to leap up"), a spring tide also brings a lower low water.

Syzygy: The nearly straight-line configuration that occurs twice a month, when the Sun and the Moon are in conjunction (on the same side of Earth, at the new Moon) and when they are in opposition (on opposite sides of Earth, at the full Moon). In both cases, the gravitational effects of the Sun and the Moon reinforce each other, and tidal range is increased.

Vanishing Tide: A mixed tide of considerable inequality in the two highs and two lows, so that the lower high (or higher low) may appear to vanish. □□

Tide Corrections

■ Many factors affect the times and heights of the tides: the shoreline, the time of the Moon's southing (crossing the meridian), and the Moon's phase. The High Tide column on the **Left-Hand Calendar Pages, 104–130,** lists the times of high tide at Commonwealth Pier in Boston Harbor. The heights of some of these tides, reckoned from Mean Lower Low Water, are given on the **Right-Hand Calendar Pages, 105–131.** Use the table below to calculate the approximate times and heights of high tide at the places shown. Apply the time difference to the times of high tide at Boston and the height difference to the heights at Boston. A tide calculator can be found at **Almanac.com/Tides.**

E X A M P L E :

The conversion of the times and heights of the tides at Boston to those at Cape Fear, North Carolina, is given below:

High tide at Boston	11:45 A.M.
Correction for Cape Fear	– 3 55
High tide at Cape Fear	7:50 A.M.
Tide height at Boston	11.6 ft.
Correction for Cape Fear	– 5.0 ft.
Tide height at Cape Fear	6.6 ft.

Estimations derived from this table are *not* meant to be used for navigation. *The Old Farmer's Almanac* accepts no responsibility for errors or any consequences ensuing from the use of this table.

Tidal Site	Difference: Time (h. m.)	Height (ft.)
Canada		
Alberton, PE	*–5 45	–7.5
Charlottetown, PE	*–0 45	–3.5
Halifax, NS.	–3 23	–4.5
North Sydney, NS	–3 15	–6.5
Saint John, NB	+0 30	+15.0
St. John's, NL	–4 00	–6.5
Yarmouth, NS	–0 40	+3.0
Maine		
Bar Harbor	–0 34	+0.9
Belfast	–0 20	+0.4
Boothbay Harbor	–0 18	–0.8
Chebeague Island	–0 16	–0.6
Eastport	–0 28	+8.4
Kennebunkport	+0 04	–1.0
Machias	–0 28	+2.8
Monhegan Island	–0 25	–0.8
Old Orchard	0 00	–0.8
Portland	–0 12	–0.6
Rockland	–0 28	+0.1
Stonington	–0 30	+0.1
York	–0 09	–1.0
New Hampshire		
Hampton	+0 02	–1.3
Portsmouth	+0 11	–1.5
Rye Beach	–0 09	–0.9
Massachusetts		
Annisquam	–0 02	–1.1
Beverly Farms	0 00	–0.5
Boston	0 00	0.0

Tidal Site	Difference: Time (h. m.)	Height (ft.)
Cape Cod Canal		
East Entrance	–0 01	–0.8
West Entrance	–2 16	–5.9
Chatham Outer Coast	+0 30	–2.8
Inside	+1 54	**0.4
Cohasset	+0 02	–0.07
Cotuit Highlands	+1 15	**0.3
Dennis Port	+1 01	**0.4
Duxbury–Gurnet Point	+0 02	–0.3
Fall River	–3 03	–5.0
Gloucester	–0 03	–0.8
Hingham	+0 07	0.0
Hull	+0 03	–0.2
Hyannis Port	+1 01	**0.3
Magnolia–Manchester	–0 02	–0.7
Marblehead	–0 02	–0.4
Marion	–3 22	–5.4
Monument Beach	–3 08	–5.4
Nahant	–0 01	–0.5
Nantasket	+0 04	–0.1
Nantucket	+0 56	**0.3
Nauset Beach	+0 30	**0.6
New Bedford	–3 24	–5.7
Newburyport	+0 19	–1.8
Oak Bluffs	+0 30	**0.2
Onset–R.R. Bridge	–2 16	–5.9
Plymouth	+0 05	0.0
Provincetown	+0 14	–0.4
Revere Beach	–0 01	–0.3
Rockport	–0 08	–1.0
Salem	0 00	–0.5
Scituate	–0 05	–0.7

Tidal Site	Difference: Time (h. m.)	Height (ft.)
Wareham	−3 09	−5.3
Wellfleet	+0 12	+0.5
West Falmouth	−3 10	−5.4
Westport Harbor	−3 22	−6.4
Woods Hole		
Little Harbor	−2 50	**0.2
Oceanographic		
Institute	−3 07	**0.2
Rhode Island		
Bristol	−3 24	−5.3
Narragansett Pier	−3 42	−6.2
Newport	−3 34	−5.9
Point Judith	−3 41	−6.3
Providence	−3 20	−4.8
Sakonnet	−3 44	−5.6
Watch Hill	−2 50	−6.8
Connecticut		
Bridgeport	+0 01	−2.6
Madison	−0 22	−2.3
New Haven	−0 11	−3.2
New London	−1 54	−6.7
Norwalk	+0 01	−2.2
Old Lyme		
Highway Bridge	−0 30	−6.2
Stamford	+0 01	−2.2
Stonington	−2 27	−6.6
New York		
Coney Island	−3 33	−4.9
Fire Island Light	−2 43	**0.1
Long Beach	−3 11	−5.7
Montauk Harbor	−2 19	−7.4
New York City–Battery	−2 43	−5.0
Oyster Bay	+0 04	−1.8
Port Chester	−0 09	−2.2
Port Washington	−0 01	−2.1
Sag Harbor	−0 55	−6.8
Southampton		
Shinnecock Inlet	−4 20	**0.2
Willets Point	0 00	−2.3
New Jersey		
Asbury Park	−4 04	−5.3
Atlantic City	−3 56	−5.5
Bay Head–Sea Girt	−4 04	−5.3
Beach Haven	−1 43	**0.24
Cape May	−3 28	−5.3
Ocean City	−3 06	−5.9
Sandy Hook	−3 30	−5.0
Seaside Park	−4 03	−5.4
Pennsylvania		
Philadelphia	+2 40	−3.5
Delaware		
Cape Henlopen	−2 48	−5.3

Tidal Site	Difference: Time (h. m.)	Height (ft.)
Rehoboth Beach	−3 37	−5.7
Wilmington	+1 56	−3.8
Maryland		
Annapolis	+6 23	−8.5
Baltimore	+7 59	−8.3
Cambridge	+5 05	−7.8
Havre de Grace	+11 21	−7.7
Point No Point	+2 28	−8.1
Prince Frederick		
Plum Point	+4 25	−8.5
Virginia		
Cape Charles	−2 20	−7.0
Hampton Roads	−2 02	−6.9
Norfolk	−2 06	−6.6
Virginia Beach	−4 00	−6.0
Yorktown	−2 13	−7.0
North Carolina		
Cape Fear	−3 55	−5.0
Cape Lookout	−4 28	−5.7
Currituck	−4 10	−5.8
Hatteras		
Inlet	−4 03	−7.4
Kitty Hawk	−4 14	−6.2
Ocean	−4 26	−6.0
South Carolina		
Charleston	−3 22	−4.3
Georgetown	−1 48	**0.36
Hilton Head	−3 22	−2.9
Myrtle Beach	−3 49	−4.4
St. Helena		
Harbor Entrance	−3 15	−3.4
Georgia		
Jekyll Island	−3 46	−2.9
St. Simon's Island	−2 50	−2.9
Savannah Beach		
River Entrance	−3 14	−5.5
Tybee Light	−3 22	−2.7
Florida		
Cape Canaveral	−3 59	−6.0
Daytona Beach	−3 28	−5.3
Fort Lauderdale	−2 50	−7.2
Fort Pierce Inlet	−3 32	−6.9
Jacksonville		
Railroad Bridge	−6 55	**0.1
Miami Harbor Entrance	−3 18	−7.0
St. Augustine	−2 55	−4.9

*Varies widely; accurate only to within 1½ hours. Consult local tide tables for precise times and heights.

**Where the difference in the Height column is so marked, the height at Boston should be multiplied by this ratio.

Time Corrections

■ Astronomical data for Boston is given on **pages 88, 92–93,** and **104–130.** Use the Key Letter shown to the right of each time on those pages with this table to find the number of minutes that you must add to or subtract from Boston time to get the correct time for your city. (Because of complex calculations for different locales, times are approximate.) For more information on the use of Key Letters and this table, **see How to Use This Almanac, page 100.**

Get times simply and specifically: Purchase astronomical times calculated for your zip code and presented like a Left-Hand Calendar Page at **MyLocalAlmanac.com.**

TIME ZONES: Codes represent *standard time.* Atlantic is –1, Eastern is 0, Central is 1, Mountain is 2, Pacific is 3, Alaska is 4, and Hawaii-Aleutian is 5.

State	City	North Latitude °	North Latitude ′	West Longitude °	West Longitude ′	Time Zone Code	A (min.)	B (min.)	C (min.)	D (min.)	E (min.)
AK	Anchorage	61	10	149	59	4	–46	+27	+71	+122	+171
AK	Cordova	60	33	145	45	4	–55	+13	+55	+103	+149
AK	Fairbanks	64	48	147	51	4	–127	+2	+61	+131	+205
AK	Juneau	58	18	134	25	4	–76	–23	+10	+49	+86
AK	Ketchikan	55	21	131	39	4	–62	–25	0	+29	+56
AK	Kodiak	57	47	152	24	4	0	+49	+82	+120	+154
AL	Birmingham	33	31	86	49	1	+30	+15	+3	–10	–20
AL	Decatur	34	36	86	59	1	+27	+14	+4	–7	–17
AL	Mobile	30	42	88	3	1	+42	+23	+8	–8	–22
AL	Montgomery	32	23	86	19	1	+31	+14	+1	–13	–25
AR	Fort Smith	35	23	94	25	1	+55	+43	+33	+22	+14
AR	Little Rock	34	45	92	17	1	+48	+35	+25	+13	+4
AR	Texarkana	33	26	94	3	1	+59	+44	+32	+18	+8
AZ	Flagstaff	35	12	111	39	2	+64	+52	+42	+31	+22
AZ	Phoenix	33	27	112	4	2	+71	+56	+44	+30	+20
AZ	Tucson	32	13	110	58	2	+70	+53	+40	+24	+12
AZ	Yuma	32	43	114	37	2	+83	+67	+54	+40	+28
CA	Bakersfield	35	23	119	1	3	+33	+21	+12	+1	–7
CA	Barstow	34	54	117	1	3	+27	+14	+4	–7	–16
CA	Fresno	36	44	119	47	3	+32	+22	+15	+6	0
CA	Los Angeles–Pasadena–Santa Monica	34	3	118	14	3	+34	+20	+9	–3	–13
CA	Palm Springs	33	49	116	32	3	+28	+13	+1	–12	–22
CA	Redding	40	35	122	24	3	+31	+27	+25	+22	+19
CA	Sacramento	38	35	121	30	3	+34	+27	+21	+15	+10
CA	San Diego	32	43	117	9	3	+33	+17	+4	–9	–21
CA	San Francisco–Oakland–San Jose	37	47	122	25	3	+40	+31	+25	+18	+12
CO	Craig	40	31	107	33	2	+32	+28	+25	+22	+20
CO	Denver–Boulder	39	44	104	59	2	+24	+19	+15	+11	+7
CO	Grand Junction	39	4	108	33	2	+40	+34	+29	+24	+20
CO	Pueblo	38	16	104	37	2	+27	+20	+14	+7	+2
CO	Trinidad	37	10	104	31	2	+30	+21	+13	+5	0
CT	Bridgeport	41	11	73	11	0	+12	+10	+8	+6	+4
CT	Hartford–New Britain	41	46	72	41	0	+8	+7	+6	+5	+4
CT	New Haven	41	18	72	56	0	+11	+8	+7	+5	+4
CT	New London	41	22	72	6	0	+7	+5	+4	+2	+1
CT	Norwalk–Stamford	41	7	73	22	0	+13	+10	+9	+7	+5
CT	Waterbury–Meriden	41	33	73	3	0	+10	+9	+7	+6	+5
DC	Washington	38	54	77	1	0	+35	+28	+23	+18	+13
DE	Wilmington	39	45	75	33	0	+26	+21	+18	+13	+10

Time Corrections

State	City	North Latitude °	North Latitude ′	West Longitude °	West Longitude ′	Time Zone Code	A (min.)	B (min.)	C (min.)	D (min.)	E (min.)
FL	Fort Myers	26	38	81	52	0	+87	+63	+44	+21	+4
FL	Jacksonville	30	20	81	40	0	+77	+58	+43	+25	+11
FL	Miami	25	47	80	12	0	+88	+57	+37	+14	−3
FL	Orlando	28	32	81	22	0	+80	+59	+42	+22	+6
FL	Pensacola	30	25	87	13	1	+39	+20	+5	−12	−26
FL	St. Petersburg	27	46	82	39	0	+87	+65	+47	+26	+10
FL	Tallahassee	30	27	84	17	0	+87	+68	+53	+35	+22
FL	Tampa	27	57	82	27	0	+86	+64	+46	+25	+9
FL	West Palm Beach	26	43	80	3	0	+79	+55	+36	+14	−2
GA	Atlanta	33	45	84	24	0	+79	+65	+53	+40	+30
GA	Augusta	33	28	81	58	0	+70	+55	+44	+30	+19
GA	Macon	32	50	83	38	0	+79	+63	+50	+36	+24
GA	Savannah	32	5	81	6	0	+70	+54	+40	+25	+13
HI	Hilo	19	44	155	5	5	+94	+62	+37	+7	−15
HI	Honolulu	21	18	157	52	5	+102	+72	+48	+19	−1
HI	Lanai City	20	50	156	55	5	+99	+69	+44	+15	−6
HI	Lihue	21	59	159	23	5	+107	+77	+54	+26	+5
IA	Davenport	41	32	90	35	1	+20	+19	+17	+16	+15
IA	Des Moines	41	35	93	37	1	+32	+31	+30	+28	+27
IA	Dubuque	42	30	90	41	1	+17	+18	+18	+18	+18
IA	Waterloo	42	30	92	20	1	+24	+24	+24	+25	+25
ID	Boise	43	37	116	12	2	+55	+58	+60	+62	+64
ID	Lewiston	46	25	117	1	3	−12	−3	+2	+10	+17
ID	Pocatello	42	52	112	27	2	+43	+44	+45	+46	+46
IL	Cairo	37	0	89	11	1	+29	+20	+12	+4	−2
IL	Chicago–Oak Park	41	52	87	38	1	+7	+6	+6	+5	+4
IL	Danville	40	8	87	37	1	+13	+9	+6	+2	0
IL	Decatur	39	51	88	57	1	+19	+15	+11	+7	+4
IL	Peoria	40	42	89	36	1	+19	+16	+14	+11	+9
IL	Springfield	39	48	89	39	1	+22	+18	+14	+10	+6
IN	Fort Wayne	41	4	85	9	0	+60	+58	+56	+54	+52
IN	Gary	41	36	87	20	1	+7	+6	+4	+3	+2
IN	Indianapolis	39	46	86	10	0	+69	+64	+60	+56	+52
IN	Muncie	40	12	85	23	0	+64	+60	+57	+53	+50
IN	South Bend	41	41	86	15	0	+62	+61	+60	+59	+58
IN	Terre Haute	39	28	87	24	0	+74	+69	+65	+60	+56
KS	Fort Scott	37	50	94	42	1	+49	+41	+34	+27	+21
KS	Liberal	37	3	100	55	1	+76	+66	+59	+51	+44
KS	Oakley	39	8	100	51	1	+69	+63	+59	+53	+49
KS	Salina	38	50	97	37	1	+57	+51	+46	+40	+35
KS	Topeka	39	3	95	40	1	+49	+43	+38	+32	+28
KS	Wichita	37	42	97	20	1	+60	+51	+45	+37	+31
KY	Lexington–Frankfort	38	3	84	30	0	+67	+59	+53	+46	+41
KY	Louisville	38	15	85	46	0	+72	+64	+58	+52	+46
LA	Alexandria	31	18	92	27	1	+58	+40	+26	+9	−3
LA	Baton Rouge	30	27	91	11	1	+55	+36	+21	+3	−10
LA	Lake Charles	30	14	93	13	1	+64	+44	+29	+11	−2
LA	Monroe	32	30	92	7	1	+53	+37	+24	+9	−1
LA	New Orleans	29	57	90	4	1	+52	+32	+16	−1	−15
LA	Shreveport	32	31	93	45	1	+60	+44	+31	+16	+4
MA	Brockton	42	5	71	1	0	0	0	0	0	−1
MA	Fall River–New Bedford	41	42	71	9	0	+2	+1	0	0	−1
MA	Lawrence–Lowell	42	42	71	10	0	0	0	0	0	+1
MA	Pittsfield	42	27	73	15	0	+8	+8	+8	+8	+8
MA	Springfield–Holyoke	42	6	72	36	0	+6	+6	+6	+5	+5
MA	Worcester	42	16	71	48	0	+3	+2	+2	+2	+2

(continued)

Time Corrections

State	City	North Latitude °	'	West Longitude °	'	Time Zone Code	Key Letters A (min.)	B (min.)	C (min.)	D (min.)	E (min.)
MD	Baltimore..................	39	17	76	37	0	+32	+26	+22	+17	+13
MD	Hagerstown	39	39	77	43	0	+35	+30	+26	+22	+18
MD	Salisbury	38	22	75	36	0	+31	+23	+18	+11	+6
ME	Augusta	44	19	69	46	0	−12	−8	−5	−1	0
ME	Bangor....................	44	48	68	46	0	−18	−13	−9	−5	−1
ME	Eastport	44	54	67	0	0	−26	−20	−16	−11	−8
ME	Ellsworth	44	33	68	25	0	−18	−14	−10	−6	−3
ME	Portland	43	40	70	15	0	−8	−5	−3	−1	0
ME	Presque Isle	46	41	68	1	0	−29	−19	−12	−4	+2
MI	Cheboygan................	45	39	84	29	0	+40	+47	+53	+59	+64
MI	Detroit–Dearborn..........	42	20	83	3	0	+47	+47	+47	+47	+47
MI	Flint......................	43	1	83	41	0	+47	+49	+50	+51	+52
MI	Ironwood	46	27	90	9	1	0	+9	+15	+23	+29
MI	Jackson	42	15	84	24	0	+53	+53	+53	+52	+52
MI	Kalamazoo.................	42	17	85	35	0	+58	+57	+57	+57	+57
MI	Lansing	42	44	84	33	0	+52	+53	+53	+54	+54
MI	St. Joseph.................	42	5	86	26	0	+61	+61	+60	+60	+59
MI	Traverse City	44	46	85	38	0	+49	+54	+57	+62	+65
MN	Albert Lea	43	39	93	22	1	+24	+26	+28	+31	+33
MN	Bemidji...................	47	28	94	53	1	+14	+26	+34	+44	+52
MN	Duluth....................	46	47	92	6	1	+6	+16	+23	+31	+38
MN	Minneapolis–St. Paul.......	44	59	93	16	1	+18	+24	+28	+33	+37
MN	Ortonville.................	45	19	96	27	1	+30	+36	+40	+46	+51
MO	Jefferson City.............	38	34	92	10	1	+36	+29	+24	+18	+13
MO	Joplin.....................	37	6	94	30	1	+50	+41	+33	+25	+18
MO	Kansas City	39	1	94	20	1	+44	+37	+33	+27	+23
MO	Poplar Bluff...............	36	46	90	24	1	+35	+25	+17	+8	+1
MO	St. Joseph.................	39	46	94	50	1	+43	+38	+35	+30	+27
MO	St. Louis..................	38	37	90	12	1	+28	+21	+16	+10	+5
MO	Springfield................	37	13	93	18	1	+45	+36	+29	+20	+14
MS	Biloxi.....................	30	24	88	53	1	+46	+27	+11	−5	−19
MS	Jackson	32	18	90	11	1	+46	+30	+17	+1	−10
MS	Meridian...................	32	22	88	42	1	+40	+24	+11	−4	−15
MS	Tupelo	34	16	88	34	1	+35	+21	+10	−2	−11
MT	Billings	45	47	108	30	2	+16	+23	+29	+35	+40
MT	Butte	46	1	112	32	2	+31	+39	+45	+52	+57
MT	Glasgow...................	48	12	106	38	2	−1	+11	+21	+32	+42
MT	Great Falls	47	30	111	17	2	+20	+31	+39	+49	+58
MT	Helena....................	46	36	112	2	2	+27	+36	+43	+51	+57
MT	Miles City	46	25	105	51	2	+3	+11	+18	+26	+32
NC	Asheville	35	36	82	33	0	+67	+55	+46	+35	+27
NC	Charlotte	35	14	80	51	0	+61	+49	+39	+28	+19
NC	Durham	36	0	78	55	0	+51	+40	+31	+21	+13
NC	Greensboro................	36	4	79	47	0	+54	+43	+35	+25	+17
NC	Raleigh....................	35	47	78	38	0	+51	+39	+30	+20	+12
NC	Wilmington	34	14	77	55	0	+52	+38	+27	+15	+5
ND	Bismarck	46	48	100	47	1	+41	+50	+58	+66	+73
ND	Fargo	46	53	96	47	1	+24	+34	+42	+50	+57
ND	Grand Forks...............	47	55	97	3	1	+21	+33	+43	+53	+62
ND	Minot.....................	48	14	101	18	1	+36	+50	+59	+71	+81
ND	Williston	48	9	103	37	1	+46	+59	+69	+80	+90
NE	Grand Island..............	40	55	98	21	1	+53	+51	+49	+46	+44
NE	Lincoln....................	40	49	96	41	1	+47	+44	+42	+39	+37
NE	North Platte	41	8	100	46	1	+62	+60	+58	+56	+54
NE	Omaha....................	41	16	95	56	1	+43	+40	+39	+37	+36
NH	Berlin.....................	44	28	71	11	0	−7	−3	0	+3	+7
NH	Keene.....................	42	56	72	17	0	+2	+3	+4	+5	+6

Get local rise, set, and tide times at Almanac.com/Astronomy.

State	City	North Latitude °	'	West Longitude °	'	Time Zone Code	A (min.)	B (min.)	C (min.)	D (min.)	E (min.)
NH	Manchester–Concord	42	59	71	28	0	0	0	+1	+2	+3
NH	Portsmouth	43	5	70	45	0	−4	−2	−1	0	0
NJ	Atlantic City	39	22	74	26	0	+23	+17	+13	+8	+4
NJ	Camden	39	57	75	7	0	+24	+19	+16	+12	+9
NJ	Cape May	38	56	74	56	0	+26	+20	+15	+9	+5
NJ	Newark–East Orange	40	44	74	10	0	+17	+14	+12	+9	+7
NJ	Paterson	40	55	74	10	0	+17	+14	+12	+9	+7
NJ	Trenton	40	13	74	46	0	+21	+17	+14	+11	+8
NM	Albuquerque	35	5	106	39	2	+45	+32	+22	+11	+2
NM	Gallup	35	32	108	45	2	+52	+40	+31	+20	+11
NM	Las Cruces	32	19	106	47	2	+53	+36	+23	+8	−3
NM	Roswell	33	24	104	32	2	+41	+26	+14	0	−10
NM	Santa Fe	35	41	105	56	2	+40	+28	+19	+9	0
NV	Carson City–Reno	39	10	119	46	3	+25	+19	+14	+9	+5
NV	Elko	40	50	115	46	3	+3	0	−1	−3	−5
NV	Las Vegas	36	10	115	9	3	+16	+4	−3	−13	−20
NY	Albany	42	39	73	45	0	+9	+10	+10	+11	+11
NY	Binghamton	42	6	75	55	0	+20	+19	+19	+18	+18
NY	Buffalo	42	53	78	52	0	+29	+30	+30	+31	+32
NY	New York	40	45	74	0	0	+17	+14	+11	+9	+6
NY	Ogdensburg	44	42	75	30	0	+8	+13	+17	+21	+25
NY	Syracuse	43	3	76	9	0	+17	+19	+20	+21	+22
OH	Akron	41	5	81	31	0	+46	+43	+41	+39	+37
OH	Canton	40	48	81	23	0	+46	+43	+41	+38	+36
OH	Cincinnati–Hamilton	39	6	84	31	0	+64	+58	+53	+48	+44
OH	Cleveland–Lakewood	41	30	81	42	0	+45	+43	+42	+40	+39
OH	Columbus	39	57	83	1	0	+55	+51	+47	+43	+40
OH	Dayton	39	45	84	10	0	+61	+56	+52	+48	+44
OH	Toledo	41	39	83	33	0	+52	+50	+49	+48	+47
OH	Youngstown	41	6	80	39	0	+42	+40	+38	+36	+34
OK	Oklahoma City	35	28	97	31	1	+67	+55	+46	+35	+26
OK	Tulsa	36	9	95	60	1	+59	+48	+40	+30	+22
OR	Eugene	44	3	123	6	3	+21	+24	+27	+30	+33
OR	Pendleton	45	40	118	47	3	−1	+4	+10	+16	+21
OR	Portland	45	31	122	41	3	+14	+20	+25	+31	+36
OR	Salem	44	57	123	1	3	+17	+23	+27	+31	+35
PA	Allentown–Bethlehem	40	36	75	28	0	+23	+20	+17	+14	+12
PA	Erie	42	7	80	5	0	+36	+36	+35	+35	+35
PA	Harrisburg	40	16	76	53	0	+30	+26	+23	+19	+16
PA	Lancaster	40	2	76	18	0	+28	+24	+20	+17	+13
PA	Philadelphia–Chester	39	57	75	9	0	+24	+19	+16	+12	+9
PA	Pittsburgh–McKeesport	40	26	80	0	0	+42	+38	+35	+32	+29
PA	Reading	40	20	75	56	0	+26	+22	+19	+16	+13
PA	Scranton–Wilkes-Barre	41	25	75	40	0	+21	+19	+18	+16	+15
PA	York	39	58	76	43	0	+30	+26	+22	+18	+15
RI	Providence	41	50	71	25	0	+3	+2	+1	0	0
SC	Charleston	32	47	79	56	0	+64	+48	+36	+21	+10
SC	Columbia	34	0	81	2	0	+65	+51	+40	+27	+17
SC	Spartanburg	34	56	81	57	0	+66	+53	+43	+32	+23
SD	Aberdeen	45	28	98	29	1	+37	+44	+49	+54	+59
SD	Pierre	44	22	100	21	1	+49	+53	+56	+60	+63
SD	Rapid City	44	5	103	14	2	+2	+5	+8	+11	+13
SD	Sioux Falls	43	33	96	44	1	+38	+40	+42	+44	+46
TN	Chattanooga	35	3	85	19	0	+79	+67	+57	+45	+36
TN	Knoxville	35	58	83	55	0	+71	+60	+51	+41	+33
TN	Memphis	35	9	90	3	1	+38	+26	+16	+5	−3
TN	Nashville	36	10	86	47	1	+22	+11	+3	−6	−14

Time Corrections

State/Province	City	North Latitude °	North Latitude '	West Longitude °	West Longitude '	Time Zone Code	A (min.)	B (min.)	C (min.)	D (min.)	E (min.)
TX	Amarillo	35	12	101	50	1	+85	+73	+63	+52	+43
TX	Austin	30	16	97	45	1	+82	+62	+47	+29	+15
TX	Beaumont	30	5	94	6	1	+67	+48	+32	+14	0
TX	Brownsville	25	54	97	30	1	+91	+66	+46	+23	+5
TX	Corpus Christi	27	48	97	24	1	+86	+64	+46	+25	+9
TX	Dallas–Fort Worth	32	47	96	48	1	+71	+55	+43	+28	+17
TX	El Paso	31	45	106	29	2	+53	+35	+22	+6	−6
TX	Galveston	29	18	94	48	1	+72	+52	+35	+16	+1
TX	Houston	29	45	95	22	1	+73	+53	+37	+19	+5
TX	McAllen	26	12	98	14	1	+93	+69	+49	+26	+9
TX	San Antonio	29	25	98	30	1	+87	+66	+50	+31	+16
UT	Kanab	37	3	112	32	2	+62	+53	+46	+37	+30
UT	Moab	38	35	109	33	2	+46	+39	+33	+27	+22
UT	Ogden	41	13	111	58	2	+47	+45	+43	+41	+40
UT	Salt Lake City	40	45	111	53	2	+48	+45	+43	+40	+38
UT	Vernal	40	27	109	32	2	+40	+36	+33	+30	+28
VA	Charlottesville	38	2	78	30	0	+43	+35	+29	+22	+17
VA	Danville	36	36	79	23	0	+51	+41	+33	+24	+17
VA	Norfolk	36	51	76	17	0	+38	+28	+21	+12	+5
VA	Richmond	37	32	77	26	0	+41	+32	+25	+17	+11
VA	Roanoke	37	16	79	57	0	+51	+42	+35	+27	+21
VA	Winchester	39	11	78	10	0	+38	+33	+28	+23	+19
VT	Brattleboro	42	51	72	34	0	+4	+5	+5	+6	+7
VT	Burlington	44	29	73	13	0	0	+4	+8	+12	+15
VT	Rutland	43	37	72	58	0	+2	+5	+7	+9	+11
VT	St. Johnsbury	44	25	72	1	0	−4	0	+3	+7	+10
WA	Bellingham	48	45	122	29	3	0	+13	+24	+37	+47
WA	Seattle–Tacoma–Olympia	47	37	122	20	3	+3	+15	+24	+34	+42
WA	Spokane	47	40	117	24	3	−16	−4	+4	+14	+23
WA	Walla Walla	46	4	118	20	3	−5	+2	+8	+15	+21
WI	Eau Claire	44	49	91	30	1	+12	+17	+21	+25	+29
WI	Green Bay	44	31	88	0	1	0	+3	+7	+11	+14
WI	La Crosse	43	48	91	15	1	+15	+18	+20	+22	+25
WI	Madison	43	4	89	23	1	+10	+11	+12	+14	+15
WI	Milwaukee	43	2	87	54	1	+4	+6	+7	+8	+9
WI	Oshkosh	44	1	88	33	1	+3	+6	+9	+12	+15
WI	Wausau	44	58	89	38	1	+4	+9	+13	+18	+22
WV	Charleston	38	21	81	38	0	+55	+48	+42	+35	+30
WV	Parkersburg	39	16	81	34	0	+52	+46	+42	+36	+32
WY	Casper	42	51	106	19	2	+19	+19	+20	+21	+22
WY	Cheyenne	41	8	104	49	2	+19	+16	+14	+12	+11
WY	Sheridan	44	48	106	58	2	+14	+19	+23	+27	+31
CANADA											
AB	Calgary	51	5	114	5	2	+13	+35	+50	+68	+84
AB	Edmonton	53	34	113	25	2	−3	+26	+47	+72	+93
BC	Vancouver	49	13	123	6	3	0	+15	+26	+40	+52
MB	Winnipeg	49	53	97	10	1	+12	+30	+43	+58	+71
NB	Saint John	45	16	66	3	−1	+28	+34	+39	+44	+49
NS	Halifax	44	38	63	35	−1	+21	+26	+29	+33	+37
NS	Sydney	46	10	60	10	−1	+1	+9	+15	+23	+28
ON	Ottawa	45	25	75	43	0	+6	+13	+18	+23	+28
ON	Peterborough	44	18	78	19	0	+21	+25	+28	+32	+35
ON	Thunder Bay	48	27	89	12	0	+47	+61	+71	+83	+93
ON	Toronto	43	39	79	23	0	+28	+30	+32	+35	+37
QC	Montreal	45	28	73	39	0	−1	+4	+9	+15	+20
SK	Saskatoon	52	10	106	40	1	+37	+63	+80	+101	+119

Get local rise, set, and tide times at Almanac.com/Astronomy.

General Store Classifieds

For advertising information, contact Bernie Gallagher, 203-263-7171.

ART

BUYING VINTAGE MOVIE POSTERS,
lobby cards, photos, live music posters. All sizes, any condition. Will buy entire collections!
Ralph, 800-392-4050
http://ralphdeluca.com

ASTROLOGY

GIFTED HEALER
Solves all problems, troubles, unusual sickness, bad luck, love, life. Removes evil influences & nature problems; brings back lovers to stay, good luck, money. Uncle Doc Shedrickrack, Hwy. 48, 7905 Bluff Rd., Gadsden SC 29052
803-353-0659

MISS LISA. A gifted astrology reader and advisor with positive results. Will help you with all problems. Waycross, GA. 912-283-3206.

SARAH DAVIS. Helps in all problems. Removes curses, evil, voodoo, bad luck. Returns loved ones. Marriage, business, health, money. Call for lucky numbers: 512-586-3696.

OLIVIA BROOKS
Solves all problems. Reunites lovers, removes bad luck & evil influence.
Restores nature.
Calls enemies by name.
Call **214-646-4865**

WWW.AZUREGREEN.NET Pyramid-charged magical products. Jewelry, incense, bumper stickers, herbs, candles. 7,000 items. 413-623-2155.

SISTER SALLY solves all problems. Love, marriage, money, health. Removes bad luck. Guaranteed results. Call 843-518-1060.

REV. DOCTOR ADAMS
Spiritual Healer
100% guarantee. $39 to cast love spells.
Bring that man or woman back.
Results, no matter the spell you need.
Write 1770 Howell Mill Rd., Atlanta GA 30318, or call **770-622-9191**

GOD-GIFTED PSYCHIC
SARAH KNOWLES
Miracles on demand! Extraordinary powers!
Love specialist. Always accurate.
100% successful! Guaranteed!
Call now: **214-335-0294 or 866-524-6689**

ATTENTION!
Savannah, GA's Own Angel Guide Cathrine
I will help you. One free question!
Guarantee to reunite lovers forever!
There is no problem I cannot solve.
Call Angel Guide Cathrine, 912-713-1110
www.angelguidecathrine.com

ASHLEY LOVE SPELLS. Resolves all problems. Returns lovers. Restores happiness. Immediate results. Call 972-201-5576.

REV. EVETTE. Answers all questions, solves life's problems. Need help desperately? Does what others claim! Call immediately, 100% guaranteed! PO Box 80322, Chattanooga TN 37414. 423-894-6699.

PSYCHIC READINGS BY MARTHA. Helps with love life, health, happiness, job, marriage. Reunites lovers. Immediate results! 214-363-4740.

FREE MAGIC SPELL!
Tell us exactly what you need!
Ekses, POB 9315(B),
San Bernardino CA 92427-9315
909-473-7470
www.Ekses.com

PSYCHIC ADVISOR. Call gifted Georgia! Solves problems. Reunites lovers. Removes bad luck. Relieves stress, anxiety. Answers questions! Results in 24 hours! 951-977-8334.

MRS. RACHEL. Psychic reader, astrology—palm reading—advice on all problems. 832-315-7741.

FREE SPIRITUAL CATALOG
Luck, money, love can be yours.
Over 5,000 items.
Church Goods Co., Dept. OFA, PO Box 718,
Glenview IL 60025
www.LuckShop.com

Classifieds

DO YOU WANT LUCK, LOVE, MONEY? With spiritual cleansing, you can achieve your goals in life. Call for your free Tarot card reading today! 803-371-7711. 811 Saluda St., Rockhill SC 29730.

MRS. RUTH, Southern-born spiritualist. Removes evil, bad luck. Helps all problems. Free sample reading. 3938 Hwy. 431 South, Eufaula AL 36027. Call 334-616-6363.

SISTER ROGERS, psychic reader and advisor. Can help you with problems, love, business, marriage, and health. 912-285-2066 or 903-454-4406.

GOD'S MESSENGER, ALEXIS MORGAN, brings lovers home forever! Never fails! 10-minute free reading! 415-691-5218.

REV. MOTHER BLACK helps all problems. Reunites lovers. Reveals all! Past, present, future. Guaranteed! 956-223-3324.

ANN, SPIRITUALIST RELATIONSHIP SPECIALIST. Reunites lovers. Advice: cheating, marriage, business. Clears negativity. Immediate results. 910-334-5137.

DR. SAMUEL
CHARLESTON, SC
Solves impossible problems.
Love, lost nature, sickness, bad luck,
court cases, evil spells, lucky bags.
Call 866-954-7256

FREE MINI READINGS
Psychic Diana has the ability to solve all
problems. Removes spells and reunites
loved ones. Toronto, Ontario.
416-226-5418

SPELL DOCTOR.
Guarantees to bring you love, luck, money,
protection against enemies. Helps in court cases.
I have a spell for you!
Call 912-713-1110

HOLYLAND CRYSTALS
Can change your life overnight.
Help in love, health, and money, and remove evil.
$25. They really work!
PO Box 111852, Nashville TN 37222.
Toll-free: **800-399-0604**

FREE PSYCHIC READING! Solves problems. Removes evil. Permanent results! 817-298-0316.

SISTER BENNETT. Second-generation intuitive Tarot card reader and healer. Knowledgeable about candle magic. Call 904-486-6381.

NEED HELP FAST?! Spiritualist Leza cures all evil spells. Reunites lovers; potions; luck. Valdosta, GA. 229-630-5386 or 229-244-1306.

CALL BOB NOW! 877-992-2211
Brings back love in 1 day!! Specializes in
love problems, no matter how severe.
Bob gives his clients 100%. Never fails!
Tired of lonely days/nights?
Lost lover/spouse to another?
Physically/emotionally frustrated?
Not communicating? Bob stops
ex-lover/spouse from interfering.
Reunites lover to want only you with
more passion immediately!
Helps in all relationships, family matters.
Removes bad luck/witchcraft.
Call now! **310-553-6711**

BEER & WINE MAKING

FREE ILLUSTRATED CATALOG. Fast service. Since 1967. Write to: Kraus, PO Box 7850-YB, Independence MO 64054. Phone: 800-841-7404. www.eckraus.com/offers/fd.asp

BOOKS/PUBLICATIONS/CATALOGS

FREE BOOKLETS: Life, Immortality, Soul, Pollution Crisis, Judgment Day, Restitution. Sample magazine. Bible Standard (OF), 1156 St. Matthews Rd., Chester Springs PA 19425. www.biblestandard.com

FREE BOOKLET: Pro-and-con assessment of Jehovah's Witnesses teachings. Bible Standard (OFA), 1156 St. Matthews Rd., Chester Springs PA 19425. www.biblestandard.com

---

A SACK OF BLUE MUSSELS
by Cassandra N. Hancock
Introducing a collection of light verse and
prose from around the globe, in language
accessible and compelling.
Visit **www.amazon.com**
Search under book title.

BUILDING

BUILD UNDERGROUND houses/shelters/greenhouses dirt cheap! Live protected. Slash energy costs. "Brilliant breakthrough thinking"–*Countryside Magazine*. Featured on HGTV. 800-328-8790. www.undergroundhousing.com

Classifieds

Classifieds

MADISON, reader and advisor. Call 516-308-4443.

WILMA WHITE. 30 years' experience. Knows all, sees all, tells all. Guaranteed to solve all problems. Reunites lovers. 850-319-3711.

STEAM MODEL TOYS

WORKING STEAM ENGINES! Stationary engines, steam tractors, rollers, trains, and accessories. Great discounts! Catalog: $6.95, refundable. Yesteryear Toys & Books Inc., Box 537, Alexandria Bay NY 13607. 800-481-1353. www.yesteryeartoys.com

The Old Farmer's Almanac consistently reaches a proven, responsive audience and is known for delivering readers who are active buyers. The 2014 edition closes on May 3, 2013. Ad opportunities are available in the *All-Seasons Garden Guide*, which closes on January 11, 2014, and on our Web site, Almanac.com. For ad rates, Web classifieds, or ad information, please contact Bernie Gallagher by email at OFAads@aol.com, by phone at 203-263-7171, by fax at 203-263-7174, or by mail at The Old Farmer's Almanac, PO Box 959, Woodbury CT 06798.

WANTED TO BUY

BUYING VINTAGE RADIOS, vacuum tubes, microphones, Western Electric items, audio amplifiers, turntables, old movie equipment. 203-272-6030. Larry2942@cox.net

CASH FOR 78-RPM RECORDS!
Send $2 (refundable) for illustrated booklet identifying collectible labels, numbers, with actual prices I pay.
Docks, Box 780218(FA),
San Antonio TX 78278-0218

Index to Advertisers

248   *There's more of everything at* Almanac.com.   2013

Index to Advertisers

Animal Groups

ANIMAL	COLLECTIVE NAME
Ant	Colony, nest, army, state, swarm
Antelope	Herd
Bear	Sleuth, sloth
Beaver	Family, colony
Bee	Swarm, grist, cluster, nest, hive, erst
Buffalo	Troop, herd, gang
Camel	Flock, train, caravan
Caribou	Herd
Cat	Clowder, clutter (kindle or kendle of kittens)
Cattle	Drove, herd
Chicken	Flock, run, brood, clutch, peep
Deer	Herd, leash
Dog	Pack (cry or mute of hounds, leash of greyhounds)
Donkey	Pace, drove, herd
Duck	Brace, team, paddling, raft, bed, flock, flight
Elephant	Herd
Fox	Leash, skulk, cloud, troop
Giraffe	Herd, corps, troop
Goat	Tribe, trip, flock, herd
Goose	Flock (on land), skein (in flight), gaggle or plump (on water)
Horse	Haras, stable, remuda, stud, herd, string, field, set, pair, team
Kangaroo	Mob, troop, herd
Leopard	Leap
Lion	Pride, troop, flock, sawt, souse
Moose	Herd
Partridge	Covey
Pig	Drift, sounder, herd, trip (litter of pigs), farrow (litter of pigs)
Quail	Bevy, covey
Reindeer	Herd
Seal	Pod, herd, trip, rookery, harem
Sheep	Flock, drove, hirsel, trip, pack
Swan	Herd, team, bank, wege, bevy
Termite	Colony, nest, swarm, brood
Walrus	Pod, herd
Whale	Gam, pod, school, herd
Zebra	Herd

How Old Is Your Dog?

Multiplying your dog's age by seven is easy, but it isn't very accurate. This more carefully graded system piles the equivalent human years onto a dog's life more quickly during the dog's rapid growth to maturity. One "dog year" equals 4 "human years" from ages 2–14 and 2½ "human years" thereafter.

dog years	human years	dog years	human years
1	15	16	77
2	24	17	79½
3	28	18	82
4	32	19	84½
5	36	20	87
6	40	21	89½
7	44	22	92
8	48	23	94½
9	52	24	97
10	56	25	99½
11	60	26	102
12	64	27	104½
13	68	28	107
14	72	29	109½
15	74½	30	112

Amusement

A sampling from the hundreds of letters, clippings, articles, and emails sent to us by

Almanac readers from all over the United States and Canada during the past year.

10 Great Headlines

Think before you write!

–courtesy of S. P., Manchester, New Hampshire

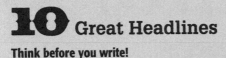

1. Hospitals Sued by 7 Foot Doctors

2. Police Begin Campaign to Run Down Jaywalkers

3. Panda Mating Fails; Veterinarian Takes Over

4. War Dims Hope for Peace

5. Astronaut Takes Blame for Gas in Spacecraft

6. Juvenile Court to Try Shooting Defendant

7. Something Went Wrong in Jet Crash

8. New Study of Obesity Looks for Larger Test Group

9. Cold Wave Linked to Temperatures

10. Typhoon Rips Through Cemetery; Hundreds Dead

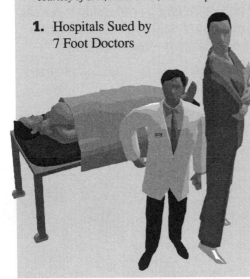

How to Determine the Number and Sex of the Children You'll Have

All you need is a pencil, a needle, and some thread (well, and maybe a small grain of salt!). *–courtesy of K.C.O., Erie, Pennsylvania*

■ I wrote you about this 25 years ago. It worked for my children then; and since then, for my grandchildren. So here's how to do it: First, take an ordinary wooden pencil with an eraser and stick a threaded needle into the center of the top of the eraser. Then lay your left arm on a

252

---

table with the palm of your hand facing upward. Pick up the thread and dangle the pencil above your wrist. You'll note that the pencil will begin to move. If it moves across your wrist, you'll have a boy; up and down your arm, a girl. The pencil will go in circles between each signal for more than one child, although twins will be treated as one. It will come to a stop or wiggle when the count is finished. Please remember that this does not work for women using birth control pills but does work for both men and women.

Something About Chickens That You Might Not Want to Know

It's rare, but it happens.

–courtesy of C.F.N., Toronto, Ontario, who credits Cambridge-news.co.uk

Can you imagine a regular egg-laying hen turning into a crowing rooster? Well, it happened to the chicken of a Cambridge, England, couple, Jim and Jeanette Howard, whose chicken, Gertie, stopped producing eggs and began strutting around their garden and crowing like a rooster.   *(continued)* ➡

A Little Quiz

Seven Famous People With Names You Never Knew

Can you guess their stage names? (Answers below.) ⬇

–courtesy of R. B., San Simon, Arizona

1. Alphonso D'Abruzzo gave us a lot of laughs when he played a Korean War medic.

2. Jacob Cohn often complained about not getting any respect.

3. Laszio Lowenstein often appeared with a portly costar, as he did in *Casablanca*.

4. William Henry Pratt appeared in a lot of scary movies, such as *Bride of Frankenstein*.

5. Jane Peters married a leading man, but her life came to a sudden, sad end at the tender age of 33.

6. Frances Smith and her screen-star husband chased the bad guys.

7. Lucile LeSueur's daughter complained about Mom's parenting skills.

Answers: 1. Alan Alda; 2. Rodney Dangerfield; 3. Peter Lorre; 4. Boris Karloff; 5. Carole Lombard; 6. Dale Evans; 7. Joan Crawford

Over the following weeks, Gertie put on weight, developed masculine wattles beneath her (his?) beak, and grew more plumage. Gertie even grew a scarlet "cockscomb" on her/his head. They decided to rename him Bertie.

Subsequently, they learned from experts at the Poultry Club of Great Britain that one in 10,000 female chickens, or hens, undergoes sex changes to become a male chicken, or rooster.

One more thing: It is reported in the *Chicken Health Handbook* (Storey Communications Inc., 1994) that it can go the other way, too—i.e., from rooster to hen. In 1474, an English rooster named Basel was accused of witchcraft for laying eggs and was actually burned at the stake.

Poor Basel. He/she certainly didn't deserve that.

How Joe Sprinz Lost His Teeth

Never heard of Joe Sprinz? Well, he holds the record for attempting to catch the highest fly ball ever! —*courtesy of V.M.P., Tulsa, Oklahoma*

I suspect that your readers enjoy odd records. Here's one that hardly anyone knows about. Back in the old days (August 1939), there was a baseball catcher named Joe Sprinz. Played for a team called the San Francisco Seals. One day, he participated in a promotional event to catch a baseball dropped from a blimp circling at an altitude of about 1,000 feet. After two tries—the ball kept falling too far away—he actually did do it. Sort of. He made the catch with his glove held just above his face. The ball made contact with his glove all right, but then struck him on the side of the face. It knocked out five of his teeth, broke 12 bones, and caused numerous lacerations.

For all of this, he earned a mention in the *Guinness Book of Records* for the highest catch attempted.

Have You Ever Heard of "Cooler Corn"?

Did you know that you can cook corn on the cob without using a pot—or a stove or a cooker? —*courtesy of J.S.T., Graham, North Carolina*

■ Say that you have a big crowd in for a barbecue and all of your pots are being used on the stove for lobster or whatever and everyone wants two or three ears of corn. Okay, here's what you do: Get out your camping cooler, wipe it clean, fill it with shucked ears of corn, pour about two kettles-full of boiling water over them, and close the lid of the cooler. Thirty minutes later, the corn will be perfectly cooked. Try it!

Can you cook corn in a cooler? Yes. Should you cook corn in a cooler? Probably not.

Oh, How I Wish I'd Said That!

A few "wisdoms" to enjoy . . .

–courtesy of J. C., Seattle, Washington

- *War does not determine who is right— only who is left.*
- *The early bird might get the worm, but the second mouse gets the cheese.*
- *To steal ideas from one person is plagiarism. To steal from many is research.*
- *How is it that one careless match can start a forest fire, but it takes a whole box to start a campfire?*
- *A bank is a place that will lend you money if you can prove that you don't need it.*
- *Why do Americans choose from just two people running for president and 50 for Miss America?*
- *Behind every successful man is a woman. Behind the fall of a successful man is often another woman.*
- *When you're tempted to fight fire with fire, remember that the fire department usually uses water.*
- *A clear conscience is usually the sign of a bad memory.*

Oh, How I Wish I'd NOT Said That!

A few famous boo-boos to remember . . .

–courtesy of I.G.M., Atlanta, Georgia

- "This crash is not going to have much effect on business."

–Arthur Reynolds, chairman of Continental Illinois Bank of Chicago, October 24, 1929

- "For the majority of people, smoking has a beneficial effect."

–Dr. Ian G. Macdonald, 1963

- "There is not doubt that [Adolf Hitler] has become more thoughtful during his imprisonment . . . and does not contemplate acting against existing authority."

–Otto Leybold, warden of Landsberg Prison, in which Hitler served time as a young man, September 1924

- "I am finished."

–Winston Churchill, after being replaced as First Lord of the Admiralty during World War I, 1915

- "The thought of being president frightens me. I do not think I want the job."   *–Ronald Reagan, 1973*

- "The bullet hasn't been made that can kill me."

–Jack "Legs" Diamond, 1929, who was shot dead 2 years later

- "I will never marry again."

Barbara Hutton, after divorcing her second husband in 1941, and prior to her five subsequent marriages

Finally, Another Unanswerable Question:

➡ Why is it that our feet smell and our nose runs?

☐☐

Send your contribution for *The 2014 Old Farmer's Almanac* by January 25, 2013, to "A & P," The Old Farmer's Almanac, P.O. Box 520, Dublin, NH 03444, or email it to almanac@ypi.com (subject: A & P).

Vinegar Can Be Used For WHAT?

CANTON (Special)- Research from the U.S. to Asia reports that VINEGAR-- *Mother Nature's Liquid Gold*-- is one of the most powerful aids for a healthier, longer life.

Each golden drop is a natural storehouse of vitamins and minerals to help fight ailments and extend life. In fact:
* Studies show it helps boost the immune system to help prevent cancer, ease arthritic pain, and fight cholesterol build-up in arteries.

And that's not all!

Want to control Your weight?

Since ancient times a teaspoon of apple cider vinegar in water at meals has been the answer. Try it.

Worried about age spots? Troubled by headaches? Aches and pain?

You'll find a vinegar home remedy for your problem among the 308 researched and available for the first time in the exclusive *"The Vinegar Book,"* by natural health author Emily Thacker.

As *The Wall Street Journal* wrote in a vinegar article: "Have a Problem? Chances are Vinegar can help solve it."

This fascinating book shows you step by step how to mix *inexpensive* vinegar with kitchen staples to help:
* Lower blood pressure
* Speed up your metabolism
* Fight pesky coughs, colds
* Relieve painful leg cramps
* Soothe aching muscles
* Fade away headaches
* Gain soft, radiant skin
* Help lower cholesterol
* Boost immune system in its prevention of cancer
* Fight liver spots
* Natural arthritis reliever
* Use for eye and ear problems
* Destroy bacteria in foods
* Relieve itches, insect bites
* Skin rashes, athlete's foot
* Heart and circulatory care, and so much more

You'll learn it's easy to combine vinegar and herbs to create tenderizers, mild laxatives, tension relievers.

Enjoy bottling your own original and delicious vinegars. And tasty pickles and pickling treats that win raves!

You'll discover vinegar's amazing history through the ages *PLUS easy-to-make cleaning formulas that save you hundreds of dollars every year.*

"The Vinegar Book" is so amazing that you're invited to use and enjoy its wisdom on a **90 day No-Risk Trial basis. If not delighted simply tear off and return *the cover only* for a prompt refund.** To order right from the publisher at the introductory low price of $12.95 plus $3.98 postage & handling (total of $16.93, OH residents please add 6.25% sales tax) do this now:

Write "Vinegar Preview" on a piece of paper and mail it along with your check or money order payable to: James Direct Inc., Dept. V1284, 500 S. Prospect Ave., Box 980, Hartville, Ohio 44632.

You can charge to your VISA, MasterCard, Discover or American Express by mail. Be sure to include your card number, expiration date and signature.

Want to save even more? Do a favor for a relative or friend and order 2 books for only $20 postpaid. It's such a thoughtful gift.

Remember: It's not available in book stores at this time. And you're protected by the publisher's 90-Day Money Back Guarantee.

SPECIAL BONUS - Act promptly and you'll also receive Brain & Health Power Foods booklet absolutely FREE. It's yours to keep just for previewing *"The Vinegar Book."* Supplies are limited. Order today.

©2012 JDI V0122S02

http://www.jamesdirect.com

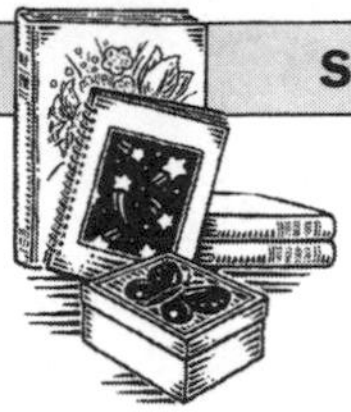

A Reference Compendium

R
E
F
E
R
E
N
C
E

PHASES OF THE MOON

New

WAXING

First Quarter

Full

WANING

Last Quarter

New

The Origin of Full-Moon Names

■ Historically, the Native Americans who lived in the area that is now the northern and eastern United States kept track of the seasons by giving a distinctive name to each recurring full Moon. This name was applied to the entire month in which it occurred. These names, and some variations, were used by the Algonquin tribes from New England to Lake Superior.

Name	Month	Variations
Full Wolf Moon	**January**	Full Old Moon
Full Snow Moon	**February**	Full Hunger Moon
Full Worm Moon	**March**	Full Crow Moon Full Crust Moon Full Sugar Moon Full Sap Moon
Full Pink Moon	**April**	Full Sprouting Grass Moon Full Egg Moon Full Fish Moon
Full Flower Moon	**May**	Full Corn Planting Moon Full Milk Moon
Full Strawberry Moon	**June**	Full Rose Moon Full Hot Moon
Full Buck Moon	**July**	Full Thunder Moon Full Hay Moon
Full Sturgeon Moon	**August**	Full Red Moon Full Green Corn Moon
Full Harvest Moon*	**September**	Full Corn Moon Full Barley Moon
Full Hunter's Moon	**October**	Full Travel Moon Full Dying Grass Moon
Full Beaver Moon	**November**	Full Frost Moon
Full Cold Moon	**December**	Full Long Nights Moon

The Harvest Moon is always the full Moon closest to the autumnal equinox. If the Harvest Moon occurs in October, the September full Moon is usually called the Corn Moon.

R E F E R E N C E

When Will the Moon Rise Today?

■ A lunar puzzle involves the timing of moonrise. If you enjoy the out-of-doors and the wonders of nature, you may wish to commit to memory the following gem:

 The new Moon always rises near sunrise;

 The first quarter near noon;

The full Moon always rises near sunset;

 The last quarter near midnight.

Moonrise occurs about 50 minutes later each day.

Many Moons Ago

January's full Moon was called the **Wolf Moon** because it appeared when wolves howled in hunger outside the villages.

February's full Moon was called the **Snow Moon** because it was a time of heavy snow. It was also called the **Hunger Moon** because hunting was difficult and hunger often resulted.

March's full Moon was called the **Worm Moon** because, as the Sun increasingly warmed the soil, earthworms became active and their castings (excrement) began to appear.

April's full Moon was called the **Pink Moon** because it heralded the appearance of the moss pink, or wild ground phlox—one of the first spring flowers.

May's full Moon was called the **Flower Moon** because blossoms were abundant everywhere at this time.

June's full Moon was called the **Strawberry Moon** because it appeared when the strawberry harvest took place.

July's full Moon was called the **Buck Moon** because it arrived when male deer started growing new antlers.

August's full Moon was called the **Sturgeon Moon** because this large fish, which is found in the Great Lakes and Lake Champlain, was caught easily at this time.

September's full Moon was called the **Corn Moon** because this was the time to harvest corn.

The **Harvest Moon** is the full Moon that occurs closest to the autumnal equinox. It can occur in either **September** or **October.** At this time, crops such as corn, pumpkins, squash, and wild rice are ready for gathering.

October's full Moon was called the **Hunter's Moon** because this was the time to hunt in preparation for winter.

November's full Moon was called the **Beaver Moon** because it was the time to set beaver traps, before the waters froze over.

December's full Moon was called the **Cold Moon.** It was also called the **Long Nights Moon** because nights at this time of year were the longest.

R
E
F
E
R
E
N
C
E

The Origin of Month Names

January. For the Roman god Janus, protector of gates and doorways. Janus is depicted with two faces, one looking into the past, the other into the future.

February. From the Latin *februa,* "to cleanse." The Roman Februalia was a month of purification and atonement.

March. For the Roman god of war, Mars. This was the time of year to resume military campaigns that had been interrupted by winter.

April. From the Latin *aperio,* "to open (bud)," because plants begin to grow now.

May. For the Roman goddess Maia, who oversaw the growth of plants. Also from the Latin *maiores,* "elders," who were celebrated now.

June. For the Roman goddess Juno, patroness of marriage and the well-being of women. Also from the Latin *juvenis,* "young people."

July. To honor Roman dictator Julius Caesar (100 B.C.–44 B.C.). In 46 B.C., with the help of Sosigenes, he developed the Julian calendar, the precursor to the Gregorian calendar we use today.

August. To honor the first Roman emperor (and grandnephew of Julius Caesar), Augustus Caesar (63 B.C.–A.D. 14).

September. From the Latin *septem,* "seven," because this was the seventh month of the early Roman calendar.

October. From the Latin *octo,* "eight," because this was the eighth month of the early Roman calendar.

November. From the Latin *novem,* "nine," because this was the ninth month of the early Roman calendar.

December. From the Latin *decem,* "ten," because this was the tenth month of the early Roman calendar.

Easter Dates (2013–17)

■ Christian churches that follow the Gregorian calendar celebrate Easter on the first Sunday after the paschal full Moon on or just after the vernal equinox.

YEAR	EASTER
2013	March 31
2014	April 20
2015	April 5
2016	March 27
2017	April 16

■ Eastern Orthodox churches follow the Julian calendar.

YEAR	EASTER
2013	May 5
2014	April 20
2015	April 12
2016	May 1
2017	April 16

Friggatriskaidekaphobia Trivia

Here are a few facts about Friday the 13th:

■ In the 14 possible configurations for the annual calendar (see any perpetual calendar), the occurrence of Friday the 13th is this:

6 of 14 years have one Friday the 13th.
6 of 14 years have two Fridays the 13th.
2 of 14 years have three Fridays the 13th.

■ No year is without one Friday the 13th, and no year has more than three.

■ 2013 has two Fridays the 13th, in September and December.

■ Months that have a Friday the 13th begin on a Sunday.

The Origin of Day Names

■ The days of the week were named by ancient Romans with the Latin words for the Sun, the Moon, and the five known planets. These names have survived in European languages, but English names also reflect Anglo-Saxon and Norse influences.

English	Latin	French	Italian	Spanish	Anglo-Saxon and Norse
SUNDAY	dies Solis (Sol's day)	dimanche	domenica	domingo	Sunnandaeg (Sun's day)
		from the Latin for "Lord's day"			
MONDAY	dies Lunae (Luna's day)	lundi	lunedì	lunes	Monandaeg (Moon's day)
TUESDAY	dies Martis (Mars's day)	mardi	martedì	martes	Tiwesdaeg (Tiw's day)
WEDNESDAY	dies Mercurii (Mercury's day)	mercredi	mercoledì	miércoles	Wodnesdaeg (Woden's day)
THURSDAY	dies Jovis (Jupiter's day)	jeudi	giovedì	jueves	Thursdaeg (Thor's day)
FRIDAY	dies Veneris (Venus's day)	vendredi	venerdì	viernes	Frigedaeg (Frigga's day)
SATURDAY	dies Saturni (Saturn's day)	samedi	sabato	sábado	Saeterndaeg (Saturn's day)
		from the Latin for "Sabbath"			

How to Find the Day of the Week for Any Given Date

To compute the day of the week for any given date as far back as the mid–18th century, proceed as follows:

■ Add the last two digits of the year to one-quarter of the last two digits (discard any remainder), the day of the month, and the month key from the key box below. Divide the sum by 7; the remainder is the day of the week (1 is Sunday, 2 is Monday, and so on). If there is no remainder, the day is Saturday. If you're searching for a weekday prior to 1900, add 2 to the sum before dividing; prior to 1800, add 4. The formula doesn't work for days prior to 1753. From 2000 through 2099, subtract 1 from the sum before dividing.

Example:

The Dayton Flood was on March 25, 1913.

Last two digits of year:	13
One-quarter of these two digits:	3
Given day of month:	25
Key number for March:	4
Sum:	45

45 ÷ 7 = 6, with a remainder of 3. The flood took place on Tuesday, the third day of the week.

KEY	
January	1
leap year	0
February	4
leap year	3
March	4
April	0
May	2
June	5
July	0
August	3
September	6
October	1
November	4
December	6

REFERENCE

Animal Signs of the Chinese Zodiac

■ The animal designations of the Chinese zodiac follow a 12-year cycle and are always used in the same sequence. The Chinese year of 354 days begins 3 to 7 weeks into the western 365-day year, so the animal designation changes at that time, rather than on January 1. **See page 103** for the exact date of the start of the Chinese New Year.

Rat
Ambitious and sincere, you can be generous with your money. Compatible with the dragon and the monkey. Your opposite is the horse.

1900	1936	1984
1912	1948	1996
1924	1960	2008
1972		

Dragon
Robust and passionate, your life is filled with complexity. Compatible with the monkey and the rat. Your opposite is the dog.

1904	1940	1988
1916	1952	2000
1928	1964	2012
1976		

Monkey
Persuasive, skillful, and intelligent, you strive to excel. Compatible with the dragon and the rat. Your opposite is the tiger.

1908	1944	1992
1920	1956	2004
1932	1968	2016
1980		

Ox or Buffalo
A leader, you are bright, patient, and cheerful. Compatible with the snake and the rooster. Your opposite is the sheep.

1901	1937	1985
1913	1949	1997
1925	1961	2009
1973		

Snake
Strong-willed and intense, you display great wisdom. Compatible with the rooster and the ox. Your opposite is the pig.

1905	1941	1989
1917	1953	2001
1929	1965	2013
1977		

Rooster or Cock
Seeking wisdom and truth, you have a pioneering spirit. Compatible with the snake and the ox. Your opposite is the rabbit.

1909	1945	1993
1921	1957	2005
1933	1969	2017
1981		

Tiger
Forthright and sensitive, you possess great courage. Compatible with the horse and the dog. Your opposite is the monkey.

1902	1938	1986
1914	1950	1998
1926	1962	2010
1974		

Horse
Physically attractive and popular, you like the company of others. Compatible with the tiger and the dog. Your opposite is the rat.

1906	1942	1990
1918	1954	2002
1930	1966	2014
1978		

Dog
Generous and loyal, you have the ability to work well with others. Compatible with the horse and the tiger. Your opposite is the dragon.

1910	1946	1994
1922	1958	2006
1934	1970	2018
1982		

Rabbit or Hare
Talented and affectionate, you are a seeker of tranquility. Compatible with the sheep and the pig. Your opposite is the rooster.

1903	1939	1987
1915	1951	1999
1927	1963	2011
1975		

Sheep or Goat
Aesthetic and stylish, you enjoy being a private person. Compatible with the pig and the rabbit. Your opposite is the ox.

1907	1943	1991
1919	1955	2003
1931	1967	2015
1979		

Pig or Boar
Gallant and noble, your friends will remain at your side. Compatible with the rabbit and the sheep. Your opposite is the snake.

1911	1947	1995
1923	1959	2007
1935	1971	2019
1983		

REFERENCE

A Table Foretelling the Weather Through All the Lunations of Each Year, or Forever

■ This table is the result of many years of actual observation and shows what sort of weather will probably follow the Moon's entrance into any of its quarters. For example, the table shows that the week following January 4, 2013, will be fair and frosty, because the Moon enters the last quarter that day at 10:58 P.M. EST. (See the **Left-Hand Calendar Pages, 104–130,** for 2013 Moon phases.)

Editor's note: Although the data in this table is taken into consideration in the yearlong process of compiling the annual long-range weather forecasts for *The Old Farmer's Almanac,* **we rely far more on our projections of solar activity.**

Time of Change	Summer	Winter
Midnight to 2 A.M.	Fair	Hard frost, unless wind is south or west
2 A.M. to 4 A.M.	Cold, with frequent showers	Snow and stormy
4 A.M. to 6 A.M.	Rain	Rain
6 A.M. to 8 A.M.	Wind and rain	Stormy
8 A.M. to 10 A.M.	Changeable	Cold rain if wind is west; snow, if east
10 A.M. to noon	Frequent showers	Cold with high winds
Noon to 2 P.M.	Very rainy	Snow or rain
2 P.M. to 4 P.M.	Changeable	Fair and mild
4 P.M. to 6 P.M.	Fair	Fair
6 P.M. to 10 P.M.	Fair if wind is northwest; rain if wind is south or southwest	Fair and frosty if wind is north or northeast; rain or snow if wind is south or southwest
10 P.M. to midnight	Fair	Fair and frosty

This table was created more than 175 years ago by Dr. Herschell for the Boston Courier; *it first appeared in* The Old Farmer's Almanac *in 1834.*

Safe Ice Thickness*

Ice Thickness	Permissible Load	Ice Thickness	Permissible Load
3 inches	Single person on foot	12 inches	Heavy truck (8-ton gross)
4 inches	Group in single file	15 inches	10 tons
7½ inches	Passenger car (2-ton gross)	20 inches	25 tons
8 inches	Light truck (2½-ton gross)	30 inches	70 tons
10 inches	Medium truck (3½-ton gross)	36 inches	110 tons

*Solid, clear, blue/black pond and lake ice

Slush ice has only half the strength of blue ice. The strength value of river ice is 15 percent less.

Heat Index °F (°C)

Temperature °F (°C)	RELATIVE HUMIDITY (%)								
	40	**45**	**50**	**55**	**60**	**65**	**70**	**75**	**80**
100 (38)	109 (43)	114 (46)	118 (48)	124 (51)	129 (54)	136 (58)			
98 (37)	105 (41)	109 (43)	113 (45)	117 (47)	123 (51)	128 (53)	134 (57)		
96 (36)	101 (38)	104 (40)	108 (42)	112 (44)	116 (47)	121 (49)	126 (52)	132 (56)	
94 (34)	97 (36)	100 (38)	103 (39)	106 (41)	110 (43)	114 (46)	119 (48)	124 (51)	129 (54)
92 (33)	94 (34)	96 (36)	99 (37)	101 (38)	105 (41)	108 (42)	112 (44)	116 (47)	121 (49)
90 (32)	91 (33)	93 (34)	95 (35)	97 (36)	100 (38)	103 (39)	106 (41)	109 (43)	113 (45)
88 (31)	88 (31)	89 (32)	91 (33)	93 (34)	95 (35)	98 (37)	100 (38)	103 (39)	106 (41)
86 (30)	85 (29)	87 (31)	88 (31)	89 (32)	91 (33)	93 (34)	95 (35)	97 (36)	100 (38)
84 (29)	83 (28)	84 (29)	85 (29)	86 (30)	88 (31)	89 (32)	90 (32)	92 (33)	94 (34)
82 (28)	81 (27)	82 (28)	83 (28)	84 (29)	84 (29)	85 (29)	86 (30)	88 (31)	89 (32)
80 (27)	80 (27)	80 (27)	81 (27)	81 (27)	82 (28)	82 (28)	83 (28)	84 (29)	84 (29)

EXAMPLE: *When the temperature is 88°F (31°C) and the relative humidity is 60 percent, the heat index,*

The UV Index for Measuring Ultraviolet Radiation Risk

The U.S. National Weather Service's daily forecasts of ultraviolet levels use these numbers for various exposure levels:

UV Index Number	Exposure Level	Time to Burn	Actions to Take
0, 1, 2	Minimal	60 minutes	Apply SPF 15 sunscreen
3, 4	Low	45 minutes	Apply SPF 15 sunscreen; wear a hat
5, 6	Moderate	30 minutes	Apply SPF 15 sunscreen; wear a hat
7, 8, 9	High	15–25 minutes	Apply SPF 15 to 30 sunscreen; wear a hat and sunglasses; limit midday exposure
10 or higher	Very high	10 minutes	Apply SPF 30 sunscreen; wear a hat, sunglasses, and protective clothing; limit midday exposure

"Time to Burn" and "Actions to Take" apply to people with fair skin that sometimes tans but usually burns. People with lighter skin need to be more cautious. People with darker skin may be able to tolerate more exposure.

85	90	95	100
135 (57)			
126 (52)	131 (55)		
117 (47)	122 (50)	127 (53)	132 (56)
110 (43)	113 (45)	117 (47)	121 (49)
102 (39)	105 (41)	108 (42)	112 (44)
96 (36)	98 (37)	100 (38)	103 (39)
90 (32)	91 (33)	93 (34)	95 (35)
85 (29)	86 (30)	86 (30)	87 (31)

or how hot it feels, is 95°F (35°C).

What Are Cooling/Heating Degree Days?

■ Each degree of a day's average temperature above 65°F is considered one cooling degree day, an attempt to measure the need for air-conditioning. If the average of the day's high and low temperatures is 75°, that's ten cooling degree days.

Similarly, each degree of a day's average temperature below 65° is considered one heating degree and is an attempt to measure the need for fuel consumption. For example, a day with temperatures ranging from 60° to 40° results in an average of 50°, or 15 degrees less than 65°. Hence, that day would be credited as 15 heating degree days.

How to Measure Hail

■ The **Torro Hailstorm Intensity Scale** was introduced by Jonathan Webb of Oxford, England, in 1986 as a means of categorizing hailstorms. The name derives from the private and mostly British research body named the TORnado and storm Research Organisation.

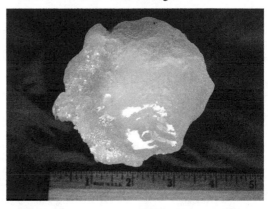

INTENSITY/DESCRIPTION OF HAIL DAMAGE

H0 True hail of pea size causes no damage

H1 Leaves and flower petals are punctured and torn

H2 Leaves are stripped from trees and plants

H3 Panes of glass are broken; auto bodies are dented

H4 Some house windows are broken; small tree branches are broken off; birds are killed

H5 Many windows are smashed; small animals are injured; large tree branches are broken off

H6 Shingle roofs are breached; metal roofs are scored; wooden window frames are broken away

H7 Roofs are shattered to expose rafters; autos are seriously damaged

H8 Shingle and tile roofs are destroyed; small tree trunks are split; people are seriously injured

H9 Concrete roofs are broken; large tree trunks are split and knocked down; people are at risk of fatal injuries

H10 Brick houses are damaged; people are at risk of fatal injuries

R E F E R E N C E

How to Measure Wind Speed

- The **Beaufort Wind Force Scale** is a common way of estimating wind speed. It was developed in 1805 by Admiral Sir Francis Beaufort of the British Navy to measure wind at sea. We can also use it to measure wind on land.

Admiral Beaufort arranged the numbers 0 to 12 to indicate the strength of the wind from calm, force 0, to hurricane, force 12. Here's a scale adapted to land.

"Used Mostly at Sea but of Help to All Who Are Interested in the Weather"

Beaufort Force	Description	When You See or Feel This Effect	Wind Speed (mph)	(km/h)
0	Calm	Smoke goes straight up	less than 1	less than 2
1	Light air	Wind direction is shown by smoke drift but not by wind vane	1–3	2–5
2	Light breeze	Wind is felt on the face; leaves rustle; wind vanes move	4–7	6–11
3	Gentle breeze	Leaves and small twigs move steadily; wind extends small flags straight out	8–12	12–19
4	Moderate breeze	Wind raises dust and loose paper; small branches move	13–18	20–29
5	Fresh breeze	Small trees sway; waves form on lakes	19–24	30–39
6	Strong breeze	Large branches move; wires whistle; umbrellas are difficult to use	25–31	40–50
7	Moderate gale	Whole trees are in motion; walking against the wind is difficult	32–38	51–61
8	Fresh gale	Twigs break from trees; walking against the wind is very difficult	39–46	62–74
9	Strong gale	Buildings suffer minimal damage; roof shingles are removed	47–54	75–87
10	Whole gale	Trees are uprooted	55–63	88–101
11	Violent storm	Widespread damage	64–72	102–116
12	Hurricane	Widespread destruction	73+	117+

Retired Atlantic Hurricane Names

These storms have been some of the most destructive and costly.

NAME	YEAR	NAME	YEAR	NAME	YEAR
Jeanne	2004	Wilma	2005	Ike	2008
Dennis	2005	Dean	2007	Paloma	2008
Katrina	2005	Felix	2007	Igor	2010
Rita	2005	Noel	2007	Tomas	2010
Stan	2005	Gustav	2008	Irene	2011

R E F E R E N C E

Atlantic Tropical (and Subtropical) Storm Names for 2013			Eastern North-Pacific Tropical (and Subtropical) Storm Names for 2013		
Andrea	Ingrid	Rebekah	Alvin	Ivo	Raymond
Barry	Jerry	Sebastien	Barbara	Juliette	Sonia
Chantal	Karen	Tanya	Cosme	Kiko	Tico
Dorian	Lorenzo	Van	Dalila	Lorena	Velma
Erin	Melissa	Wendy	Erick	Manuel	Wallis
Fernand	Nestor		Flossie	Narda	Xina
Gabrielle	Olga		Gil	Octave	York
Humberto	Pablo		Henriette	Priscilla	Zelda

How to Measure Hurricane Strength

■ The **Saffir-Simpson Hurricane Scale** assigns a rating from 1 to 5 based on a hurricane's intensity. It is used to give an estimate of the potential property damage and flooding expected along the coast from a hurricane landfall. Wind speed is the determining factor in the scale, as storm surge values are highly dependent on the slope of the continental shelf in the landfall region. Wind speeds are measured using a 1-minute average.

Category One. Average wind: 74–95 mph. No real damage to building structures. Damage primarily to unanchored mobile homes, shrubbery, and trees. Also, some coastal road flooding and minor pier damage.

Category Two. Average wind: 96–110 mph. Some roofing material, door, and window damage to buildings. Considerable damage to vegetation, mobile homes, and piers. Coastal and low-lying escape routes flood 2 to 4 hours before arrival of center. Small craft in unprotected anchorages break moorings.

Category Three. Average wind: 111–130 mph. Some structural damage to small residences and utility buildings; minor amount of curtainwall failures. Mobile homes destroyed. Flooding near coast destroys smaller structures; larger structures damaged by floating debris.

Category Four. Average wind: 131–155 mph. More extensive curtainwall failures with some complete roof failures on small residences. Major beach erosion. Major damage to lower floors near the shore.

Category Five. Average wind: 156+ mph. Complete roof failures on many residences and industrial buildings. Some complete building failures; small buildings blown over or away. Major damage to lower floors located less than 15 feet above sea level (ASL) and within 500 yards of the shoreline.

R
E
F
E
R
E
N
C
E

How to Measure a Tornado

■ The original **Fujita Scale** (or F Scale) was developed by Dr. Theodore Fujita to classify tornadoes based on wind damage. All tornadoes, and other severe local windstorms, were assigned a number according to the most intense damage caused by the storm. An enhanced F (EF) scale was implemented in the United States on February 1, 2007. The EF scale uses 3-second gust estimates based on a more detailed system for assessing damage, taking into account different building materials.

F SCALE		EF SCALE (U.S.)
F0 • 40–72 mph (64–116 km/h)	light damage	EF0 • 65–85 mph (105–137 km/h)
F1 • 73–112 mph (117–180 km/h)	moderate damage	EF1 • 86–110 mph (138–178 km/h)
F2 • 113–157 mph (181–253 km/h)	considerable damage	EF2 • 111–135 mph (179–218 km/h)
F3 • 158–207 mph (254–332 km/h)	severe damage	EF3 • 136–165 mph (219–266 km/h)
F4 • 208–260 mph (333–419 km/h)	devastating damage	EF4 • 166–200 mph (267–322 km/h)
F5 • 261–318 mph (420–512 km/h)	incredible damage	EF5 • over 200 mph (over 322 km/h)

Wind/Barometer Table

Barometer (Reduced to Sea Level)	Wind Direction	Character of Weather Indicated
30.00 to 30.20, and steady	westerly	Fair, with slight changes in temperature, for one to two days
30.00 to 30.20, and rising rapidly	westerly	Fair, followed within two days by warmer and rain
30.00 to 30.20, and falling rapidly	south to east	Warmer, and rain within 24 hours
30.20 or above, and falling rapidly	south to east	Warmer, and rain within 36 hours
30.20 or above, and falling rapidly	west to north	Cold and clear, quickly followed by warmer and rain
30.20 or above, and steady	variable	No early change
30.00 or below, and falling slowly	south to east	Rain within 18 hours that will continue a day or two
30.00 or below, and falling rapidly	southeast to northeast	Rain, with high wind, followed within two days by clearing, colder
30.00 or below, and rising	south to west	Clearing and colder within 12 hours
29.80 or below, and falling rapidly	south to east	Severe storm of wind and rain imminent; in winter, snow or cold wave within 24 hours
29.80 or below, and falling rapidly	east to north	Severe northeast gales and heavy rain or snow, followed in winter by cold wave
29.80 or below, and rising rapidly	going to west	Clearing and colder

Note: *A barometer should be adjusted to show equivalent sea-level pressure for the altitude at which it is to be used. A change of 100 feet in elevation will cause a decrease of $\frac{1}{10}$ inch in the reading.*

Windchill Table

■ As wind speed increases, your body loses heat more rapidly, making the air feel colder than it really is. The combination of cold temperature and high wind can create a cooling effect so severe that exposed flesh can freeze.

	TEMPERATURE (°F)														
Calm	**35**	**30**	**25**	**20**	**15**	**10**	**5**	**0**	**-5**	**-10**	**-15**	**-20**	**-25**	**-30**	**-35**
5	31	25	19	13	7	1	–5	–11	–16	–22	–28	–34	–40	–46	–52
10	27	21	15	9	3	–4	–10	–16	–22	–28	–35	–41	–47	–53	–59
15	25	19	13	6	0	–7	–13	–19	–26	–32	–39	–45	–51	–58	–64
20	24	17	11	4	–2	–9	–15	–22	–29	–35	–42	–48	–55	–61	–68
25	23	16	9	3	–4	–11	–17	–24	–31	–37	–44	–51	–58	–64	–71
30	22	15	8	1	–5	–12	–19	–26	–33	–39	–46	–53	–60	–67	–73
35	21	14	7	0	–7	–14	–21	–27	–34	–41	–48	–55	–62	–69	–76
40	20	13	6	–1	–8	–15	–22	–29	–36	–43	–50	–57	–64	–71	–78
45	19	12	5	–2	–9	–16	–23	–30	–37	–44	–51	–58	–65	–72	–79
50	19	12	4	–3	–10	–17	–24	–31	–38	–45	–52	–60	–67	–74	–81
55	18	11	4	–3	–11	–18	–25	–32	–39	–46	–54	–61	–68	–75	–82
60	17	10	3	–4	–11	–19	–26	–33	–40	–48	–55	–62	–69	–76	–84

WIND SPEED (mph)

Frostbite occurs in ▮ **30 minutes** ▮ **10 minutes** ▮ **5 minutes**

EXAMPLE: When the temperature is 15°F and the wind speed is 30 miles per hour, the windchill, or how cold it feels, is –5°F. For a Celsius version of this table, visit Almanac.com/WindchillCelsius.

–courtesy National Weather Service

How to Measure Earthquakes

■ In 1979, seismologists developed a measurement of earthquake size called **Moment Magnitude.** It is more accurate than the previously used Richter scale, which is precise only for earthquakes of a certain size and at a certain distance from a seismometer. All earthquakes can now be compared on the same scale.

Magnitude	Effect
Less than 3	Micro
3–3.9	Minor
4–4.9	Light
5–5.9	Moderate
6–6.9	Strong
7–7.9	Major
8 or more	Great

A Gardener's Worst Phobias

Name of Fear	Object Feared
Alliumphobia	Garlic
Anthophobia	Flowers
Apiphobia	Bees
Arachnophobia	Spiders
Batonophobia	Plants
Bufonophobia	Toads
Dendrophobia	Trees
Entomophobia	Insects
Lachanophobia	Vegetables
Melissophobia	Bees
Mottephobia	Moths
Myrmecophobia	Ants
Ornithophobia	Birds
Ranidaphobia	Frogs
Rupophobia	Dirt
Scoleciphobia	Worms
Spheksophobia	Wasps

Herbs to Plant in Lawns

Choose plants that suit your soil and your climate. All these can withstand mowing and considerable foot traffic.

Ajuga or bugleweed *(Ajuga reptans)*
Corsican mint *(Mentha requienii)*
Dwarf cinquefoil *(Potentilla tabernaemontani)*
English pennyroyal *(Mentha pulegium)*
Green Irish moss *(Sagina subulata)*
Pearly everlasting *(Anaphalis margaritacea)*
Roman chamomile *(Chamaemelum nobile)*
Rupturewort *(Herniaria glabra)*
Speedwell *(Veronica officinalis)*
Stonecrop *(Sedum ternatum)*
Sweet violets (*Viola odorata* or *V. tricolor*)
Thyme *(Thymus serpyllum)*
White clover *(Trifolium repens)*
Wild strawberries *(Fragaria virginiana)*
Wintergreen or partridgeberry *(Mitchella repens)*

Lawn-Growing Tips

■ Test your soil: The pH balance should be 7.0 or more; 6.2 to 6.7 puts your lawn at risk for fungal diseases. If the pH is too low, correct it with liming, best done in the fall.

■ The best time to apply fertilizer is just before it rains.

■ If you put lime and fertilizer on your lawn, spread half of it as you walk north to south, the other half as you walk east to west to cut down on missed areas.

■ Any feeding of lawns in the fall should be done with a low-nitrogen, slow-acting fertilizer.

■ In areas of your lawn where tree roots compete with the grass, apply some extra fertilizer to benefit both.

■ Moss and sorrel in lawns usually means poor soil, poor aeration or drainage, or excessive acidity.

■ Control weeds by promoting healthy lawn growth with natural fertilizers in spring and early fall.

■ Raise the level of your lawn-mower blades during the hot summer days. Taller grass resists drought better than short.

■ You can reduce mowing time by redesigning your lawn, reducing sharp corners and adding sweeping curves.

■ During a drought, let the grass grow longer between mowings, and reduce fertilizer.

■ Water your lawn early in the morning or in the evening.

Flowers and Herbs That Attract Butterflies

Allium . . . . *Allium*	Mallow . . . . *Malva*
Aster . . . . *Aster*	Mealycup sage . . . . *Salvia farinacea*
Bee balm . . . . *Monarda*	Milkweed . . . . *Asclepias*
Butterfly bush . . . . *Buddleia*	Mint . . . . *Mentha*
Catmint . . . . *Nepeta*	Oregano . . . . *Origanum vulgare*
Clove pink . . . . *Dianthus*	Pansy . . . . *Viola*
Cornflower . . . . *Centaurea*	Parsley . . . . *Petroselinum*
Creeping thyme . . . . . . *Thymus serpyllum*	*crispum*
Daylily . . . . *Hemerocallis*	Phlox . . . . *Phlox*
Dill . . . . *Anethum graveolens*	Privet . . . . *Ligustrum*
False indigo . . . . *Baptisia*	Purple coneflower . . . *Echinacea purpurea*
Fleabane . . . . *Erigeron*	Rock cress . . . . *Arabis*
Floss flower . . . . *Ageratum*	Sea holly . . . . *Eryngium*
Globe thistle . . . . *Echinops*	Shasta daisy . . . . *Chrysanthemum*
Goldenrod . . . . *Solidago*	Snapdragon . . . . *Antirrhinum*
Helen's flower . . . . *Helenium*	Stonecrop . . . . *Sedum*
Hollyhock . . . . *Alcea*	Sweet alyssum . . . . *Lobularia*
Honeysuckle . . . . *Lonicera*	Sweet marjoram . . . . *Origanum majorana*
Lavender . . . . *Lavandula*	Sweet rocket . . . . *Hesperis*
Lilac . . . . *Syringa*	Tickseed . . . . *Coreopsis*
Lupine . . . . *Lupinus*	Verbena . . . . *Verbena*
Lychnis . . . . *Lychnis*	Zinnia . . . . *Zinnia*

Flowers* That Attract Hummingbirds

Beard tongue . . . . *Penstemon*	Soapwort . . . . *Saponaria*
Bee balm . . . . *Monarda*	Summer phlox . . . . *Phlox paniculata*
Butterfly bush . . . . *Buddleia*	Trumpet honeysuckle . . . . *Lonicera*
Catmint . . . . *Nepeta*	*sempervirens*
Clove pink . . . . *Dianthus*	Verbena . . . . *Verbena*
Columbine . . . . *Aquilegia*	Weigela . . . . *Weigela*
Coral bells . . . . *Heuchera*	
Daylily . . . . *Hemerocallis*	
Desert candle . . . . *Yucca*	
Flag iris . . . . *Iris*	
Flowering tobacco . . . . . . *Nicotiana alata*	
Foxglove . . . . *Digitalis*	
Larkspur . . . . *Delphinium*	
Lily . . . . *Lilium*	
Lupine . . . . *Lupinus*	
Petunia . . . . *Petunia*	
Pincushion flower . . . . *Scabiosa*	
Red-hot poker . . . . *Kniphofia*	
Scarlet sage . . . . *Salvia splendens*	

*Note: Choose varieties in red and orange shades, if available.

pH Preferences of Trees, Shrubs, Vegetables, and Flowers

■ An accurate soil test will indicate your soil pH and will specify the amount of lime or sulfur that is needed to bring it up or down to the appropriate level. A pH of 6.5 is just about right for most home gardens, since most plants thrive in the 6.0 to 7.0 (slightly acidic to neutral) range. Some plants (azaleas, blueberries) prefer more strongly acidic soil in the 4.0 to 6.0 range, while a few (asparagus, plums) do best in soil that is neutral to slightly alkaline. Acidic, or sour, soil (below 7.0) is counteracted by applying finely ground limestone, and alkaline, or sweet, soil (above 7.0) is treated with ground sulfur.

Common Name	Optimum pH Range	Common Name	Optimum pH Range	Common Name	Optimum pH Range
Trees and Shrubs		Walnut, black	6.0–8.0	Carnation	6.0–7.0
Apple	5.0–6.5	Willow	6.0–8.0	Chrysanthemum	6.0–7.5
Ash	6.0–7.5			Clematis	5.5–7.0
Azalea	4.5–6.0	**Vegetables**		Coleus	6.0–7.0
Basswood	6.0–7.5	Asparagus	6.0–8.0	Coneflower, purple	5.0–7.5
Beautybush	6.0–7.5	Bean, pole	6.0–7.5	Cosmos	5.0–8.0
Birch	5.0–6.5	Beet	6.0–7.5	Crocus	6.0–8.0
Blackberry	5.0–6.0	Broccoli	6.0–7.0	Daffodil	6.0–6.5
Blueberry	4.0–5.0	Brussels sprout	6.0–7.5	Dahlia	6.0–7.5
Boxwood	6.0–7.5	Carrot	5.5–7.0	Daisy, Shasta	6.0–8.0
Cherry, sour	6.0–7.0	Cauliflower	5.5–7.5	Daylily	6.0–8.0
Chestnut	5.0–6.5	Celery	5.8–7.0	Delphinium	6.0–7.5
Crab apple	6.0–7.5	Chive	6.0–7.0	Foxglove	6.0–7.5
Dogwood	5.0–7.0	Cucumber	5.5–7.0	Geranium	6.0–8.0
Elder, box	6.0–8.0	Garlic	5.5–8.0	Gladiolus	5.0–7.0
Fir, balsam	5.0–6.0	Kale	6.0–7.5	Hibiscus	6.0–8.0
Fir, Douglas	6.0–7.0	Lettuce	6.0–7.0	Hollyhock	6.0–8.0
Hemlock	5.0–6.0	Pea, sweet	6.0–7.5	Hyacinth	6.5–7.5
Hydrangea, blue-flowered	4.0–5.0	Pepper, sweet	5.5–7.0	Iris, blue flag	5.0–7.5
Hydrangea, pink-flowered	6.0–7.0	Potato	4.8–6.5	Lily-of-the-valley	4.5–6.0
Juniper	5.0–6.0	Pumpkin	5.5–7.5	Lupine	5.0–6.5
Laurel, mountain	4.5–6.0	Radish	6.0–7.0	Marigold	5.5–7.5
Lemon	6.0–7.5	Spinach	6.0–7.5	Morning glory	6.0–7.5
Lilac	6.0–7.5	Squash, crookneck	6.0–7.5	Narcissus, trumpet	5.5–6.5
Maple, sugar	6.0–7.5	Squash, Hubbard	5.5–7.0	Nasturtium	5.5–7.5
Oak, white	5.0–6.5	Tomato	5.5–7.5	Pansy	5.5–6.5
Orange	6.0–7.5			Peony	6.0–7.5
Peach	6.0–7.0	**Flowers**		Petunia	6.0–7.5
Pear	6.0–7.5	Alyssum	6.0–7.5	Phlox, summer	6.0–8.0
Pecan	6.4–8.0	Aster, New England	6.0–8.0	Poppy, oriental	6.0–7.5
Pine, red	5.0–6.0	Baby's breath	6.0–7.0	Rose, hybrid tea	5.5–7.0
Pine, white	4.5–6.0	Bachelor's button	6.0–7.5	Rose, rugosa	6.0–7.0
Plum	6.0–8.0	Bee balm	6.0–7.5	Snapdragon	5.5–7.0
Raspberry, red	5.5–7.0	Begonia	5.5–7.0	Sunflower	6.0–7.5
Rhododendron	4.5–6.0	Black-eyed Susan	5.5–7.0	Tulip	6.0–7.0
Spruce	5.0–6.0	Bleeding heart	6.0–7.5	Zinnia	5.5–7.0
		Canna	6.0–8.0		

R
E
F
E
R
E
N
C
E

Produce Weights and Measures

Vegetables

Asparagus: 1 pound = 3 cups chopped
Beans (string): 1 pound = 4 cups chopped
Beets: 1 pound (5 medium) = 2½ cups chopped
Broccoli: 1 pound = 6 cups chopped
Cabbage: 1 pound = 4½ cups shredded
Carrots: 1 pound = 3½ cups sliced or grated
Celery: 1 pound = 4 cups chopped
Cucumbers: 1 pound (2 medium) = 4 cups sliced
Eggplant: 1 pound = 4 cups chopped = 2 cups cooked
Garlic: 1 clove = 1 teaspoon chopped
Leeks: 1 pound = 4 cups chopped = 2 cups cooked
Mushrooms: 1 pound = 5 to 6 cups sliced = 2 cups cooked
Onions: 1 pound = 4 cups sliced = 2 cups cooked
Parsnips: 1 pound = 1½ cups cooked, puréed
Peas: 1 pound whole = 1 to 1½ cups shelled
Potatoes: 1 pound (3 medium) sliced = 2 cups mashed
Pumpkin: 1 pound = 4 cups chopped = 2 cups cooked and drained
Spinach: 1 pound = ¾ to 1 cup cooked
Squashes (summer): 1 pound = 4 cups grated = 2 cups sliced and cooked
Squashes (winter): 2 pounds = 2½ cups cooked, puréed
Sweet potatoes: 1 pound = 4 cups grated = 1 cup cooked, puréed
Swiss chard: 1 pound = 5 to 6 cups packed leaves = 1 to 1½ cups cooked
Tomatoes: 1 pound (3 or 4 medium) = 1½ cups seeded pulp
Turnips: 1 pound = 4 cups chopped = 2 cups cooked, mashed

Fruit

Apples: 1 pound (3 or 4 medium) = 3 cups sliced
Bananas: 1 pound (3 or 4 medium) = 1¾ cups mashed
Berries: 1 quart = 3½ cups
Dates: 1 pound = 2½ cups pitted
Lemon: 1 whole = 1 to 3 tablespoons juice; 1 to 1½ teaspoons grated rind
Lime: 1 whole = 1½ to 2 tablespoons juice
Orange: 1 medium = 6 to 8 tablespoons juice; 2 to 3 tablespoons grated rind
Peaches: 1 pound (4 medium) = 3 cups sliced
Pears: 1 pound (4 medium) = 2 cups sliced
Rhubarb: 1 pound = 2 cups cooked

R
E
F
E
R
E
N
C
E

Sowing Vegetable Seeds

Sow or plant in cool weather	Beets, broccoli, brussels sprouts, cabbage, lettuce, onions, parsley, peas, radishes, spinach, Swiss chard, turnips
Sow or plant in warm weather	Beans, carrots, corn, cucumbers, eggplant, melons, okra, peppers, squash, tomatoes
Sow or plant for one crop per season	Corn, eggplant, leeks, melons, peppers, potatoes, spinach (New Zealand), squash, tomatoes
Resow for additional crops	Beans, beets, cabbage, carrots, kohlrabi, lettuce, radishes, rutabagas, spinach, turnips

A Beginner's Vegetable Garden

■ A good size for a beginner's vegetable garden is 10x16 feet. It should have crops that are easy to grow. A plot this size, planted as suggested below, can feed a family of four for one summer, with a little extra for canning and freezing (or giving away).

Make 11 rows, 10 feet long, with 6 inches between them. Ideally, the rows should run north and south to take full advantage of the sunlight. Plant the following:

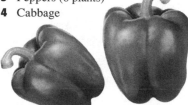

ROW
1 Zucchini (4 plants)
2 Tomatoes (5 plants, staked)
3 Peppers (6 plants)
4 Cabbage

ROW
5 Bush beans
6 Lettuce
7 Beets
8 Carrots
9 Chard
10 Radishes
11 Marigolds (to discourage rabbits!)

Traditional Planting Times

■ Plant **corn** when elm leaves are the size of a squirrel's ear, when oak leaves are the size of a mouse's ear, when apple blossoms begin to fall, or when the dogwoods are in full bloom.

■ Plant **lettuce, spinach, peas,** and other cool-weather vegetables when the lilacs show their first leaves or when daffodils begin to bloom.

■ Plant **tomatoes, early corn,** and **peppers** when dogwoods are in peak bloom or when daylilies start to bloom.

■ Plant **cucumbers** and **squashes** when lilac flowers fade.

■ Plant **perennials** when maple leaves begin to unfurl.

■ Plant **morning glories** when maple trees have full-size leaves.

■ Plant **pansies, snapdragons,** and other hardy annuals after the aspen and chokecherry trees leaf out.

■ Plant **beets** and **carrots** when dandelions are blooming.

REFERENCE

When to . . .

	. . . FERTILIZE	. . . WATER
Beans	After heavy bloom and set of pods	Regularly, from start of pod to set
Beets	At time of planting	Only during drought conditions
Broccoli	3 weeks after transplanting	Only during drought conditions
Brussels sprouts	3 weeks after transplanting	At transplanting
Cabbage	3 weeks after transplanting	2 to 3 weeks before harvest
Carrots	In the fall for the following spring	Only during drought conditions
Cauliflower	3 weeks after transplanting	Once, 3 weeks before harvest
Celery	At time of transplanting	Once a week
Corn	When 8 to 10 inches tall, and when first silk appears	When tassels appear and cobs start to swell
Cucumbers	1 week after bloom, and 3 weeks later	Frequently, especially when fruits form
Lettuce	2 to 3 weeks after transplanting	Once a week
Melons	1 week after bloom, and again 3 weeks later	Once a week
Onion sets	When bulbs begin to swell, and when plants are 1 foot tall	Only during drought conditions
Parsnips	1 year before planting	Only during drought conditions
Peas	After heavy bloom and set of pods	Regularly, from start of pod to set
Peppers	After first fruit-set	Once a week
Potato tubers	At bloom time or time of second hilling	Regularly, when tubers start to form
Pumpkins	Just before vines start to run, when plants are about 1 foot tall	Only during drought conditions
Radishes	Before spring planting	Once a week
Spinach	When plants are one-third grown	Once a week
Squashes, summer	Just before vines start to run, when plants are about 1 foot tall	Only during drought conditions
Squashes, winter	Just before vines start to run, when plants are about 1 foot tall	Only during drought conditions
Tomatoes	2 weeks before, and after first picking	Twice a week

R
E
F
E
R
E
N
C
E

How to Grow Herbs

HERB	START SEEDS INDOORS	START SEEDS OUTDOORS* (weeks before last spring frost)	HEIGHT/SPREAD (inches)	SOIL	LIGHT**
Basil	6–8	Anytime after	12–24/12	Rich, moist	○
Borage	Not recommended	Anytime after	12–36/12	Rich, well-drained, dry	○
Chervil	Not recommended	3–4 before	12–24/8	Rich, moist	◑
Chives	8–10	3–4 before	12–18/18	Rich, moist	○
Cilantro/ coriander	Not recommended	Anytime after	12–36/6	Light	○◑
Dill	Not recommended	4–5 before	36–48/12	Rich	○
Fennel	4–6	Anytime after	48–80/18	Rich	○
Lavender, English	8–12	1–2 before	18–36/24	Moderately fertile, well-drained	○
Lavender, French	Not recommended	Not recommended	18–36/24	Moderately fertile, well-drained	○
Lemon balm	6–10	2–3 before	12–24/18	Rich, well-drained	○◑
Lovage	6–8	2–3 before	36–72/36	Fertile, sandy	○◑
Mint	Not recommended	Not recommended	12–24/18	Rich, moist	◑
Oregano	6–10	Anytime after	12–24/18	Poor	○
Parsley	10–12	3–4 before	18–24/6–8	Medium-rich	◑
Rosemary	8–10	Anytime after	48–72/48	Not too acid	○
Sage	6–10	1–2 before	12–48/30	Well-drained	○
Sorrel	6–10	2–3 after	20–48/12–14	Rich, organic	○
Summer savory	4–6	Anytime after	4–15/6	Medium rich	○
Sweet cicely	6–8	2–3 after	36–72/36	Moderately fertile, well-drained	○◑
Tarragon, French	Not recommended	Not recommended	24–36/12	Well-drained	○◑
Thyme, common	6–10	2–3 before	2–12/7–12	Fertile, well-drained	○◑

*Recommend minimum soil temperature of 70° to germinate

** ○ full sun ◑ partial shade

R
E
F
E
R
E
N
C
E

Growth Type
Annual
Annual, biennial
Annual, biennial
Perennial
Annual
Annual
Annual
Perennial
Tender perennial
Perennial
Perennial
Perennial
Tender perennial
Biennial
Tender perennial
Perennial
Perennial
Annual
Perennial
Perennial
Perennial

Drying Herbs

Before drying, remove any dead or diseased leaves or stems. Wash under cool water, shake off excess water, and put on a towel to dry completely. Air drying preserves an herb's essential oils; use for sturdy herbs. A microwave dries herbs more quickly, so mold is less likely to develop; use for moist, tender herbs.

■ **Hanging Method:** Gather four to six stems of fresh herbs in a bunch and tie with string, leaving a loop for hanging. Or, use a rubber band with a paper clip attached to it. Hang the herbs in a warm, well-ventilated area, out of direct sunlight, until dry. For herbs that have full seed heads, such as dill or coriander, use a paper bag. Punch holes in the bag for ventilation, label it, and put the herb bunch into the bag before you tie a string around the top of the bag. The average drying time is 1 to 3 weeks.

■ **Microwave Method:** This is better for small quantities, such as a cup or two at a time. Arrange a single layer of herbs between two paper towels and put them in the microwave for 1 to 2 minutes on high power. Let the leaves cool. If they are not dry, reheat for 30 seconds and check again. Repeat as needed. Let cool. Do not overcook, or the herbs will lose their flavor.

Storing Herbs and Spices

■ **Fresh herbs:** Dill and parsley will keep for about 2 weeks with stems immersed in a glass of water tented with a plastic bag. Most other fresh herbs (and greens) will keep for short periods unwashed and refrigerated in tightly sealed plastic bags with just enough moisture to prevent wilting. For longer storage, use moisture- and gas-permeable paper and cellophane. Plastic cuts off oxygen to the plants and promotes spoilage.

■ **Spices and dried herbs:** Store in a cool, dry place.

Cooking With Herbs

■ **Bouquet garni** is usually made with bay leaves, thyme, and parsley tied with string or wrapped in cheesecloth. Use to flavor casseroles and soups. Remove after cooking.

■ **Fines herbes** use equal amounts of fresh parsley, tarragon, chives, and chervil chopped fine. Commonly used in French cooking, they make a fine omelet or add zest to soups and sauces. Add to salads and butter sauces, or sprinkle on noodles, soups, and stews.

How to Grow Bulbs

	COMMON NAME	LATIN NAME	HARDINESS ZONE	SOIL	SUN/ SHADE*	SPACING (inches)
SPRING-PLANTED BULBS	Allium	*Allium*	3–10	Well-drained/moist	○	12
	Begonia, tuberous	*Begonia*	10–11	Well-drained/moist	◑●	12–15
	Blazing star/ gayfeather	*Liatris*	7–10	Well-drained	○	6
	Caladium	*Caladium*	10–11	Well-drained/moist	◑●	8–12
	Calla lily	*Zantedeschia*	8–10	Well-drained/moist	○◑	8–24
	Canna	*Canna*	8–11	Well-drained/moist	○	12–24
	Cyclamen	*Cyclamen*	7–9	Well-drained/moist	◑	4
	Dahlia	*Dahlia*	9–11	Well-drained/fertile	○	12–36
	Daylily	*Hemerocallis*	3–10	Adaptable to most soils	○◑	12–24
	Freesia	*Freesia*	9–11	Well-drained/moist/sandy	○◑	2–4
	Garden gloxinia	*Incarvillea*	4–8	Well-drained/moist	○	12
	Gladiolus	*Gladiolus*	4–11	Well-drained/fertile	○◑	4–9
	Iris	*Iris*	3–10	Well-drained/sandy	○	3–6
	Lily, Asiatic/Oriental	*Lilium*	3–8	Well-drained	○◑	8–12
	Peacock flower	*Tigridia*	8–10	Well-drained	○	5–6
	Shamrock/sorrel	*Oxalis*	5–9	Well-drained	○◑	4–6
	Windflower	*Anemone*	3–9	Well-drained/moist	○◑	3–6
FALL-PLANTED BULBS	Bluebell	*Hyacinthoides*	4–9	Well-drained/fertile	○◑	4
	Christmas rose/ hellebore	*Helleborus*	4–8	Neutral–alkaline	○◑	18
	Crocus	*Crocus*	3–8	Well-drained/moist/fertile	○◑	4
	Daffodil	*Narcissus*	3–10	Well-drained/moist/fertile	○◑	6
	Fritillary	*Fritillaria*	3–9	Well-drained/sandy	○◑	3
	Glory of the snow	*Chionodoxa*	3–9	Well-drained/moist	○◑	3
	Grape hyacinth	*Muscari*	4–10	Well-drained/moist/fertile	○◑	3–4
	Iris, bearded	*Iris*	3–9	Well-drained	○◑	4
	Iris, Siberian	*Iris*	4–9	Well-drained	○◑	4
	Ornamental onion	*Allium*	3–10	Well-drained/moist/fertile	○	12
	Snowdrop	*Galanthus*	3–9	Well-drained/moist/fertile	○◑	3
	Snowflake	*Leucojum*	5–9	Well-drained/moist/sandy	○◑	4
	Spring starflower	*Ipheion uniflorum*	6–9	Well-drained loam	○◑	3–6
	Star of Bethlehem	*Ornithogalum*	5–10	Well-drained/moist	○◑	2–5
	Striped squill	*Puschkinia scilloides*	3–9	Well-drained	○◑	6
	Tulip	*Tulipa*	4–8	Well-drained/fertile	○◑	3–6
	Winter aconite	*Eranthis*	4–9	Well-drained/moist/fertile	○◑	3

REFERENCE

	* ○ **full sun**	◑ **partial shade**	● **full shade**

DEPTH (inches)	BLOOMING SEASON	HEIGHT (inches)	NOTES
3–4	Spring to summer	6–60	Usually pest-free; a great cut flower
1–2	Summer to fall	8–18	North of Zone 10, lift in fall
4	Summer to fall	8–20	An excellent flower for drying; north of Zone 7, plant in spring, lift in fall
2	Summer	8–24	North of Zone 10, plant in spring, lift in fall
1–4	Summer	24–36	Fragrant; north of Zone 8, plant in spring, lift in fall
Level	Summer	18–60	North of Zone 8, plant in spring, lift in fall
1–2	Spring to fall	3–12	Naturalizes well in warm areas; north of Zone 7, lift in fall
4–6	Late summer	12–60	North of Zone 9, lift in fall
2	Summer	12–36	Mulch in winter in Zones 3 to 6
2	Summer	12–24	Fragrant; can be grown outdoors in warm climates
3–4	Summer	6–20	Does well in woodland settings
3–6	Early summer to early fall	12–80	North of Zone 10, lift in fall
4	Spring to late summer	3–72	Divide and replant rhizomes every two to five years
4–6	Early summer	36	Fragrant; self-sows; requires excellent drainage
4	Summer	18–24	North of Zone 8, lift in fall
2	Summer	2–12	Plant in confined area to control
2	Early summer	3–18	North of Zone 6, lift in fall
3–4	Spring	8–20	Excellent for borders, rock gardens and naturalizing
1–2	Spring	12	Hardy, but requires shelter from strong, cold winds
3	Early spring	5	Naturalizes well in grass
6	Early spring	14–24	Plant under shrubs or in a border
3	Midspring	6–30	Different species can be planted in rock gardens, woodland gardens, or borders
3	Spring	4–10	Self-sows easily; plant in rock gardens, raised beds, or under shrubs
2–3	Late winter to spring	6–12	Use as a border plant or in wildflower and rock gardens; self-sows easily
4	Early spring to early summer	3–48	Naturalizes well; good cut flower
4	Early spring to midsummer	18–48	An excellent cut flower
3–4	Late spring to early summer	6–60	Usually pest-free; a great cut flower
3	Spring	6–12	Best when clustered and planted in an area that will not dry out in summer
4	Spring	6–18	Naturalizes well
3	Spring	4–6	Fragrant; naturalizes easily
4	Spring to summer	6–24	North of Zone 5, plant in spring, lift in fall
3	Spring	4–6	Naturalizes easily; makes an attractive edging
4–6	Early to late spring	8–30	Excellent for borders, rock gardens, and naturalizing
2–3	Late winter to spring	2–4	Self-sows and naturalizes easily

R E F E R E N C E

Substitutions for Common Ingredients

ITEM	QUANTITY	SUBSTITUTION
Baking powder	1 teaspoon	¼ teaspoon baking soda plus ¼ teaspoon cornstarch plus ½ teaspoon cream of tartar
Buttermilk	1 cup	1 tablespoon lemon juice or vinegar plus milk to equal 1 cup; or 1 cup plain yogurt
Chocolate, unsweetened	1 ounce	3 tablespoons cocoa plus 1 tablespoon butter, shortening, or vegetable oil (dissolve the cocoa in the recipe's liquid)
Cracker crumbs	¾ cup	1 cup dry bread crumbs; or 1 tablespoon quick-cooking oats (for thickening)
Cream, heavy	1 cup	¾ cup milk plus ⅓ cup melted butter (this will not whip)
Cream, light	1 cup	⅞ cup milk plus 3 tablespoons melted, unsalted butter
Cream, sour	1 cup	⅞ cup buttermilk or plain yogurt plus 3 tablespoons melted, unsalted butter
Cream, whipping	1 cup	⅔ cup well-chilled evaporated milk, whipped; or 1 cup nonfat dry milk powder whipped with 1 cup ice water
Egg	1 whole	2 yolks plus 1 tablespoon cold water; or 3 tablespoons vegetable oil plus 1 tablespoon water (for baking); or 2 to 3 tablespoons mayonnaise (for cakes)
Egg white	1 white	2 teaspoons meringue powder plus 3 tablespoons water, combined
Flour, all-purpose	1 cup	1 cup plus 3 tablespoons cake flour (not advised for cookies or quick breads); or 1 cup self-rising flour (omit baking powder and salt from recipe); or 1¼ cups rye or coarsely ground whole grain flour; or 1 cup cornmeal
Flour, cake	1 cup	1 cup minus 3 tablespoons sifted all-purpose flour plus 3 tablespoons cornstarch
Flour, self-rising	1 cup	1 cup all-purpose flour plus 1½ teaspoons baking powder plus ½ teaspoon salt
Herbs, dried	1 teaspoon	1 tablespoon fresh, minced and packed
Honey	1 cup	1¼ cups sugar plus ½ cup liquid called for in recipe (such as water or oil)
Ketchup	1 cup	1 cup tomato sauce plus ¼ cup sugar plus 3 tablespoons apple-cider vinegar plus ½ teaspoon salt plus pinch of ground cloves combined; or 1 cup chili sauce
Lemon juice	1 teaspoon	½ teaspoon vinegar
Mayonnaise	1 cup	1 cup sour cream or plain yogurt; or 1 cup cottage cheese (puréed)
Milk, skim	1 cup	⅓ cup instant nonfat dry milk plus ¾ cup water

R
E
F
E
R
E
N
C
E

ITEM	QUANTITY	SUBSTITUTION
Milk, to sour	1 cup	1 tablespoon vinegar or lemon juice plus milk to equal 1 cup. Stir and let stand 5 minutes.
Milk, whole	1 cup	½ cup evaporated whole milk plus ½ cup water; or ¾ cup 2 percent milk plus ¼ cup half-and-half
Molasses	1 cup	1 cup honey or dark corn syrup
Mustard, dry	1 teaspoon	1 tablespoon prepared mustard less 1 teaspoon liquid from recipe
Oat bran	1 cup	1 cup wheat bran or rice bran or wheat germ
Oats, old-fashioned (rolled)	1 cup	1 cup steel-cut Irish or Scotch oats
Quinoa	1 cup	1 cup millet or couscous (whole wheat cooks faster) or bulgur
Sugar, dark-brown	1 cup	1 cup light-brown sugar, packed; or 1 cup granulated sugar plus 2 to 3 tablespoons molasses
Sugar, granulated	1 cup	1 cup firmly packed brown sugar; or 1¾ cups confectioners' sugar (makes baked goods less crisp); or 1 cup superfine sugar
Sugar, light-brown	1 cup	1 cup granulated sugar plus 1 to 2 tablespoons molasses; or ½ cup dark-brown sugar plus ½ cup granulated sugar
Sweetened condensed milk	1 can (14 oz.)	1 cup evaporated milk plus 1¼ cups granulated sugar. Combine and heat until sugar dissolves.
Vanilla bean	1-inch bean	1 teaspoon vanilla extract
Vinegar, apple-cider	—	malt, white-wine, or rice vinegar
Vinegar, balsamic	1 tablespoon	1 tablespoon red- or white-wine vinegar plus ½ teaspoon sugar
Vinegar, red-wine	—	white-wine, sherry, champagne, or balsamic vinegar
Vinegar, rice	—	apple-cider, champagne, or white-wine vinegar
Vinegar, white-wine	—	champagne, fruit (raspberry), rice, or red-wine vinegar
Yeast	1 cake (⅗ oz.)	1 package or 1 scant tablespoon active dried yeast
Yogurt, plain	1 cup	1 cup sour cream (thicker; less tart) or buttermilk (thinner; use in baking, dressings, sauces)

R
E
F
E
R
E
N
C
E

Types of Fat

■ One way to minimize your total blood cholesterol is to manage the amount and types of fat in your diet. Aim for monounsaturated and polyunsaturated fats; avoid saturated and trans fats.

■ **Monounsaturated fat** lowers LDL (bad cholesterol) and may raise HDL (good cholesterol) or leave it unchanged. Found in almonds, avocados, canola oil, cashews, olive oil, peanut oil, and peanuts.

■ **Polyunsaturated fat** lowers LDL and may lower HDL. Includes omega-3 and omega-6 fatty acids. Found in corn oil, cottonseed oil, fish such as salmon and tuna, safflower oil, sesame seeds, soybeans, and sunflower oil.

■ **Saturated fat** raises both LDL and HDL. Found in chocolate, cocoa butter, coconut oil, dairy products (milk, butter, cheese, ice cream), egg yolks, palm oil, and red meat.

■ **Trans fat** raises LDL and lowers HDL. A type of fat common in many processed foods, such as most margarines (especially stick), vegetable shortening, partially hydrogenated vegetable oil, many commercial fried foods (doughnuts, french fries), and commercial baked goods (cookies, crackers, cakes).

Calorie-Burning Comparisons

■ If you hustle through your chores to get to the fitness center, relax. You're getting a great workout already. The left-hand column lists "chore" exercises, the middle column shows the number of calories burned per minute per pound of body weight, and the right-hand column lists comparable "recreational" exercises. For example, a 150-pound person forking straw bales burns 9.45 calories per minute, the same workout he or she would get playing basketball.

Chore	Calories	Recreational
Chopping with an ax, fast	**0.135**	Skiing, cross country, uphill
Climbing hills, with 44-pound load	**0.066**	Swimming, crawl, fast
Digging trenches	**0.065**	Skiing, cross country, steady walk
Forking straw bales	**0.063**	Basketball
Chopping down trees	**0.060**	Football
Climbing hills, with 9-pound load	**0.058**	Swimming, crawl, slow
Sawing by hand	**0.055**	Skiing, cross country, moderate
Mowing lawns	**0.051**	Horseback riding, trotting
Scrubbing floors	**0.049**	Tennis
Shoveling coal	**0.049**	Aerobic dance, medium
Hoeing	**0.041**	Weight training, circuit training
Stacking firewood	**0.040**	Weight lifting, free weights
Shoveling grain	**0.038**	Golf
Painting houses	**0.035**	Walking, normal pace, asphalt road
Weeding	**0.033**	Table tennis
Shopping for food	**0.028**	Cycling, 5.5 mph
Mopping floors	**0.028**	Fishing
Washing windows	**0.026**	Croquet
Raking	**0.025**	Dancing, ballroom
Driving a tractor	**0.016**	Drawing, standing position

Freezer Storage Time

(freezer temperature 0°F or colder)

Product	Months in Freezer
Fresh meat	
Beef	6 to 12
Lamb	6 to 9
Veal	6 to 9
Pork	4 to 6
Ground beef, veal, lamb, pork	3 to 4
Frankfurters	1 to 2
Sausage, fresh pork	1 to 2
Ready-to-serve luncheon meats	Not recommended
Poultry	
Chicken or turkey (whole)	12
Chicken or turkey (parts), Rock Cornish game hens, game birds	6 to 9
Duck, cooked poultry (in gravy), chicken, turkey	4
Goose, squab	4 to 6
Cooked poultry (breaded, fried)	4
Giblets	3 to 4
Cooked poultry (plain meat)	4
Fresh fruits (prepared for freezing)	
All fruits except those listed below	10 to 12
Avocados, bananas	3
Lemons, limes, plantains	4 to 6
Fresh vegetables (prepared for freezing)	
Beans, beets, bok choy, broccoli, brussels sprouts, cabbage, carrots, cauliflower, celery, corn, greens, kohlrabi, leeks, mushrooms, okra, onions, peas, peppers, soybeans, spinach, summer squashes	10 to 12
Asparagus, rutabagas, turnips	8 to 10
Artichokes, eggplant	6 to 8
Tomatoes (overripe or sliced)	2
Bamboo shoots, cucumbers, endive, lettuce, radishes, watercress	Not recommended
Cheese (except those listed below)	6
Cottage cheese, cream cheese, feta, goat, fresh mozzarella, Neufchâtel, Parmesan, processed cheese (opened)	Not recommended

Product	Months in Freezer
Dairy products	
Margarine (not diet)	12
Butter	6 to 9
Cream, half-and-half	4
Milk	3
Ice cream	1 to 2
Yogurt	1 to 2

Freezing Hints

For meals, remember that a quart container holds four servings, and a pint container holds two servings.

To prevent sticking, spread the food to be frozen (berries, hamburgers, cookies, etc.) on a cookie sheet and freeze until solid. Then place in plastic bags and freeze.

Label foods for easy identification. Write the name of the food, number of servings, and date of freezing on containers or bags.

Freeze foods as quickly as possible by placing them directly against the sides of the freezer.

Arrange freezer into sections for each food category.

If power is interrupted, or if the freezer is not operating normally, do not open the freezer door. Food in a loaded freezer will usually stay frozen for 2 days if the freezer door remains closed during that time period.

R E F E R E N C E

Plastics

■ In your quest to go green, use this guide to use and sort plastic. The number, usually found with a triangle symbol on a container, indicates the type of resin used to produce the plastic. Call **1-800-CLEANUP** for recycling information in your state.

Number 1 • *PETE or PET (polyethylene terephthalate)*

PETE

IS USED IN . . . . microwavable food trays; salad dressing, soft drink, water, and juice bottles
STATUS . . . . hard to clean; absorbs bacteria and flavors; avoid reusing
IS RECYCLED TO MAKE . . carpet, furniture, new containers, Polar fleece

Number 2 • *HDPE (high-density polyethylene)*

HDPE

IS USED IN . . . . household cleaner and shampoo bottles, milk jugs, yogurt tubs
STATUS . . . . transmits no known chemicals into food
IS RECYCLED TO MAKE . . detergent bottles, fencing, floor tiles, pens

Number 3 • *V or PVC (vinyl)*

V

IS USED IN . . . . cooking oil bottles, clear food packaging, mouthwash bottles
STATUS . . . . is believed to contain phalates that interfere with hormonal development; avoid
IS RECYCLED TO MAKE . . cables, mudflaps, paneling, roadway gutters

Number 4 • *LDPE (low-density polyethylene)*

LDPE

IS USED IN . . . . bread and shopping bags, carpet, clothing, furniture
STATUS . . . . transmits no known chemicals into food
IS RECYCLED TO MAKE . . envelopes, floor tiles, lumber, trash-can liners

Number 5 • *PP (polypropylene)*

PP

IS USED IN . . . . ketchup bottles, medicine and syrup bottles, drinking straws
STATUS . . . . transmits no known chemicals into food
IS RECYCLED TO MAKE . . battery cables, brooms, ice scrapers, rakes

Number 6 • *PS (polystyrene)*

PS

IS USED IN . . . . disposable cups and plates, egg cartons, take-out containers
STATUS . . . . is believed to leach styrene, a possible human carcinogen, into food; avoid
IS RECYCLED TO MAKE . . foam packaging, insulation, light switchplates, rulers

Number 7 • *Other (miscellaneous)*

OTHER

IS USED IN . . . . 3- and 5-gallon water jugs, nylon, some food containers
STATUS . . . . contains bisphenol A, which has been linked to heart disease and obesity; avoid
IS RECYCLED TO MAKE . . custom-made products

R E F E R E N C E

Heat Values

Firewood

High Heat Value
1 cord = 200–250 gallons of fuel oil

American beech
Apple
Ironwood
Red oak
Shagbark hickory
Sugar maple
White ash
White oak
Yellow birch

Medium Heat Value
1 cord = 150–200 gallons of fuel oil

American elm
Black cherry
Douglas fir
Red maple
Silver maple
Tamarack
White birch

Low Heat Value
1 cord = 100–150 gallons of fuel oil

Aspen
Cottonwood
Hemlock
Lodgepole pine
Red alder
Redwood
Sitka spruce
Western red cedar
White pine

Fuels

Fuel	BTU (approx.)	Unit of Measure
Oil	141,000	Gallon
Coal	31,000	Pound
Natural gas	1,000	Cubic foot
Steam	1,000	Cubic foot
Electricity	3,413	Kilowatt-hour
Gasoline	124,000	Gallon

How Many Trees in a Cord of Wood?

DIAMETER OF TREE (4½' ABOVE GROUND)	NUMBER OF TREES (PER CORD)
4"	50
6"	20
8"	10
10"	6
12"	4
14"	3

A Few Clues About Cords of Wood

■ A cord of wood is a pile of logs 4 feet wide by 4 feet high by 8 feet long.

■ A cord of wood may contain from 77 to 96 cubic feet of wood.

■ The larger the unsplit logs, the larger the gaps, with fewer cubic feet of wood actually in the cord.

■ A cord of air-dried, dense hardwood weighs about 2 tons (4,000 pounds).

■ From one cord of firewood, you could make 7,500,000 toothpicks, 460,000 personal checks, 30 Boston rockers, or 12 dining room tables with each table seating eight.

Metric Conversion

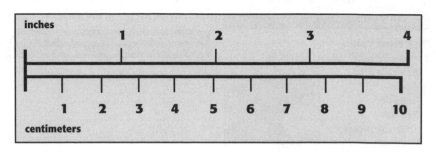

U.S. measure	x this = number	metric equivalent	metric measure	x this = number	U.S. equivalent
inch	2.54	centimeter		0.39	inch
foot	30.48	centimeter		0.033	foot
yard	0.91	meter		1.09	yard
mile	1.61	kilometer		0.62	mile
square inch	6.45	square centimeter		0.15	square inch
square foot	0.09	square meter		10.76	square foot
square yard	0.8	square meter		1.2	square yard
square mile	0.84	square kilometer		0.39	square mile
acre	0.4	hectare		2.47	acre
ounce	28.0	gram		0.035	ounce
pound	0.45	kilogram		2.2	pound
short ton (2,000 pounds)	0.91	metric ton		1.10	short ton
ounce	30.0	milliliter		0.034	ounce
pint	0.47	liter		2.1	pint
quart	0.95	liter		1.06	quart
gallon	3.8	liter		0.26	gallon

■ If you know the U.S. measurement and want to convert it to metric, multiply it by the number in the left shaded column (example: 1 inch equals 2.54 centimeters). If you know the metric measurement, multiply it by the number in the right shaded column (example: 2 meters equals 2.18 yards).

Where Do You Fit in Your Family Tree?

■ Technically it's known as consanguinity; that is, the quality or state of being related by blood or descended from a common ancestor. These relationships are shown below for the genealogy of six generations of one family.

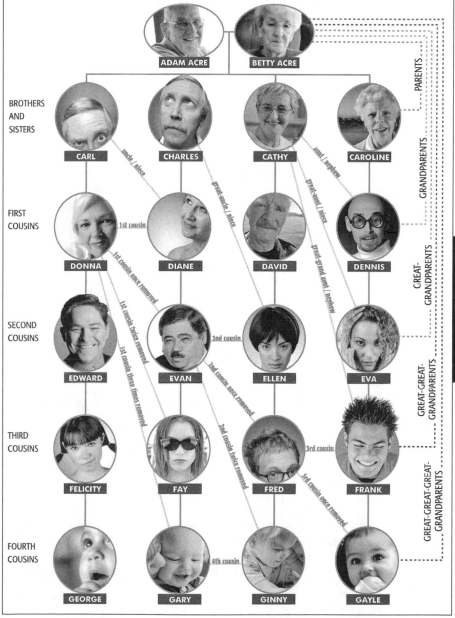

The Golden Rule

(It's true in all faiths.)

Brahmanism:
This is the sum of duty: Do naught unto others which would cause you pain if done to you.
Mahabharata 5:1517

Buddhism:
Hurt not others in ways that you yourself would find hurtful.
Udana-Varga 5:18

Christianity:
All things whatsoever ye would that men should do to you, do ye even so to them; for this is the law and the prophets.
Matthew 7:12

Confucianism:
Surely it is the maxim of loving-kindness: Do not unto others what you would not have them do unto you.
Analects 15:23

Islam:
No one of you is a believer until he desires for his brother that which he desires for himself.
Sunnah

Judaism:
What is hateful to you, do not to your fellowman. That is the entire Law; all the rest is commentary.
Talmud, Shabbat 31a

Taoism:
Regard your neighbor's gain as your own gain and your neighbor's loss as your own loss.
T'ai Shang Kan Ying P'ien

Zoroastrianism:
That nature alone is good which refrains from doing unto another whatsoever is not good for itself.
Dadistan-i-dinik 94:5

–courtesy Elizabeth Pool

Famous Last Words

■ **Waiting, are they? Waiting, are they? Well—let 'em wait.**
(To an attending doctor who attempted to comfort him by saying, "General, I fear the angels are waiting for you.")
–Ethan Allen, American Revolutionary general, d. February 12, 1789

■ **A dying man can do nothing easy.**
–Benjamin Franklin, American statesman, d. April 17, 1790

■ **Now I shall go to sleep. Good night.**
–Lord George Byron, English writer, d. April 19, 1824

■ **Is it the Fourth?**
–Thomas Jefferson, 3rd U.S. president, d. July 4, 1826

■ **Thomas Jefferson—still survives . . .**
(Actually, Jefferson had died earlier that same day.)
–John Adams, 2nd U.S. president, d. July 4, 1826

■ **Friends, applaud. The comedy is finished.**
–Ludwig van Beethoven, German-Austrian composer, d. March 26, 1827

■ **Moose . . . Indian . . .**
–Henry David Thoreau, American writer, d. May 6, 1862

■ **Go on, get out—last words are for fools who haven't said enough.**
(To his housekeeper, who urged him to tell her his last words so she could write them down for posterity.)
–Karl Marx, German political philosopher, d. March 14, 1883

■ **Is it not meningitis?**
–Louisa M. Alcott, American writer, d. March 6, 1888

■ **How were the receipts today at Madison Square Garden?**
–P. T. Barnum, American entrepreneur, d. April 7, 1891

■ **Turn up the lights, I don't want to go home in the dark.**
–O. Henry (William Sidney Porter), American writer, d. June 4, 1910

■ **Get my swan costume ready.**
–Anna Pavlova, Russian ballerina, d. January 23, 1931

■ **Is everybody happy? I want everybody to be happy. I know I'm happy.**
–Ethel Barrymore, American actress, d. June 18, 1959

■ **I'm bored with it all.**
(Before slipping into a coma. He died nine days later.)
–Winston Churchill, English statesman, d. January 24, 1965

■ **You be good. You'll be in tomorrow. I love you.**
–Alex, highly intelligent African Gray parrot, d. September 6, 2007